Romantic writers, perhaps more than any others, revised their works incessantly, in manuscript and in successive published editions. Wordsworth's *Prelude*, for example (which remained in manuscript for fifty-two years), is well known in two editions, but the various drafts and stages of manuscript composition give us many more versions of a poem whose text is rendered increasingly unstable in the process of revision. This collection of essays, the first of its kind, responds to the recent radical overhaul in the editing of romantic texts. Leading American and British editors of William and Dorothy Wordsworth, Coleridge, Byron, Percy and Mary Shelley, Leigh Hunt, Keats, and Clare explain and illustrate the implications of their editorial methods for the ongoing process of revision (in texts and their reception) which they have both reflected and helped to produce. The volume offers insights into the urgent debate over editorial practices and their theoretical bases, while uncovering the complex revisionary processes of creativity at the heart of Romantic writing.

ROMANTIC REVISIONS

ROMANTIC
REVISIONS

EDITED BY

ROBERT BRINKLEY
University of Maine

KEITH HANLEY
University of Lancaster

Published by the Press Syndicate of the University of Cambridge
The Pitt Building, Trumpington Street, Cambridge CB2 1RP
40 West 20th Street, New York NY 10011-4211, USA
10 Stamford Road, Oakleigh, Victoria 3166, Australia

© Cambridge University Press 1992

First published 1992

Printed in Great Britain at the University Press, Cambridge

A cataloguing in publication record for this book is available from the British Library

Library of Congress cataloguing in publication data
Romantic revisions / edited by Robert Brinkley and Keith Hanley.
p.   cm.
Includes index.
ISBN 0-521-38074-X
1. English literature – 19th century – History and criticism.
2. Romanticism – Great Britain.   1. Brinkley, Robert.   11. Hanley, Keith
PR457.R643   1992
821.009'145 – dc20   91–29702   CIP

ISBN 0 521 38074 X hardback

VN

For Ruth Brinkley and John Hanley

CONTENTS

FIGURES

NOTES ON CONTRIBUTORS

JONATHAN BARRON has recently obtained his doctorate from Indiana University, and is now a Lecturer at Marquette University.

JONATHAN BATE is King Alfred Professor of English Literature at the University of Liverpool. His books include *Shakespearean Constitutions: Politics, Theatre, Criticism 1730–1830* (Oxford University Press, 1989) and *Romantic Ecology: Wordsworth and the Environmental Tradition* (Routledge, 1991).

BETTY T. BENNETT is Dean of the College of Arts and Sciences and Professor of Literature at the American University, New York. She is the editor of *The Letters of Mary Wollstonecraft Shelley* (Johns Hopkins University Press, 1984–8), and her other books include *British War Poetry in the Age of Romanticism, 1793–1815* and (as co-editor) *The Evidence of the Imagination* (New York University Press, 1978). She is also book review editor of the *Keats–Shelley Journal*.

ROBERT BRINKLEY is an Associate Professor of English at the University of Maine. He is the author of articles on Milton and Spenser, English Romanticism, critical theory and philosophy, and a member of the Board of Wordsworth Trust (America).

NORMAN FRUMAN is a Professor of English at the University of Minnesota. He is the author of *Coleridge, the Damaged Archangel* (George Braziller, 1971), and his new edition of *Biographia Literaria* is forthcoming from Oxford University Press.

STEPHEN GILL is a Reader in English Literature at the University of Oxford, where he is Fellow and Tutor in English at Lincoln College. His edition of *The Salisbury Plain Poems of William Wordsworth* (1975) inaugurated the Cornell Wordsworth, and he is co-editor, with Jonathan Wordsworth and M.H. Abrams, of the Norton Critical Edition of *The Prelude, 1799, 1805, 1850* (1979). He has also written *William Wordsworth: A Life* (Oxford University Press, 1989).

KEITH HANLEY is a Lecturer in English at the University of Lancaster, where he is the Director of the Wordworth Centre. He has written articles on romantic literature and nineteenth-century poetry, edited selections of Landor (Carcanet, 1981) and Meredith (Carcanet, 1983), and, with Raman Selden, a collection of essays, *Revolution and English Romanticism: Politics and Rhetoric* (Harvester Wheatsheaf, 1990).

KENNETH R. JOHNSTON is a Professor of English at Indiana University. He is the author of *Wordsworth and 'The Recluse'* (Yale University Press, 1984) and co-editor of *The Age of William Wordsworth* (Rutgers University Press, 1987) and *Romantic Revolutions: Theory and Criticism* (Indiana University Press, 1990). He is currently working on a critical biography, *Young Wordsworth: Criticism of the Poet*.

JOHN LUCAS is Professor of English at Loughborough University. Among his books are studies of Dickens, Arnold Bennett, and Elizabeth Gaskell. He has edited selections of poems by Goldsmith, Crabbe, and D.H. Lawrence. His collection of poems, *Studying Grosz on the Bus* (Peterloo Poets, 1989), won the Aldeburgh Poetry Festival award for the best first volume to be published in 1989–90. His most recent book is *England and Englishness: Ideas of Nationhood in English Poetry, 1688–1900* (Hogarth Press, 1991).

JEROME MCGANN is Commonwealth Professor of English at the University of Virginia. He is the editor of *Lord Byron: The Complete Poetical Works* (Clarendon Press, 1980–6, 1991). Among his books are *The Romantic Ideology* (University of Chicago Press, 1982), *A Critique of Modern Textual Criticism* (University of Chicago Press, 1982), *The Beauty of Inflections; Literary Investigations in Historical Method and Theory* (Oxford University Press, 1985), and *Social Values and Poetic Acts* (Harvard University Press, 1987).

PETER J. MANNING is Professor of English at the University of Southern California, and the author of *Byron and His Fictions* (Wayne State University Press, 1978) and *Reading Romantics* (Oxford University Press, 1990).

J.C.C. MAYS is a Reader in English at the University of York after teaching for many years at University College, Dublin. Besides his work for the *Collected Coleridge*, he has written extensively on modern authors and has edited Denis Devlin's poems (Dedalus Press, 1988).

DONALD H. REIMAN has taught English at seven major universities and has written, edited, or compiled over one hundred and fifty volumes on English Romanticism. He is the editor of *Shelley and his Circle 1773–1822*, 8 vols. (Harvard University Press, 1961–86) and *The Bodleian Shelley Manuscripts*, 4 vols. (Garland Publishing, 1986–8).

NICHOLAS ROE is a Lecturer in English at the University of St Andrews. He is author of *Wordsworth and Coleridge: The Radical Years* (Oxford University Press, 1988), and co-editor of *Coleridge's Imagination* (Cambridge University Press, 1985). He has also introduced a new issue of Emile Legouis's *The Early Life of William Wordsworth* (Libris, 1988).

JACK STILLINGER is a Professor of English and permanent member of the Center for Advanced Study at the University of Illinois at Urbana-Champaign. He is the author of *The Texts of Keats's Poems* (Harvard University Press, 1974) and of *Multiple Authorship and the Myth of Solitary Genius* (Oxford University Press, 1991). He is also the editor of *The Poems of John Keats* (Heinemann, 1978).

TIMOTHY WEBB is a Professor of English at the University of Bristol. His books include *The Violet in the Crucible: Shelley and Translation* (Oxford University Press, 1976), *Shelley: A Voice Not Understood* (Manchester University Press, 1977), and *English Romantic Hellenism: 1700–1824* (Manchester University Press, 1982). He has edited annotated selections of the poetry of Shelley and Yeats, and has recently completed an edition of Leigh Hunt's *Autobiography* for Oxford University Press. He is editor of the *Keats–Shelley Review* and general editor of the Penguin *Yeats*.

PAMELA WOOF is a Lecturer at the Centre for Continuing Education, the University of Newcastle upon Tyne. She has written various articles on Dorothy Wordsworth, a monograph, *Dorothy Wordsworth, Writer* (The Wordsworth Trust, 1988), and has recently produced an annotated edition of *The Grasmere Journals* (Clarendon Press, 1991). She is a Trustee of the Wordsworth Trust, Dove Cottage, Grasmere.

JONATHAN WORDSWORTH is the University Lecturer in Romantic Studies at Oxford University, where he is Fellow and Tutor in English at St Catherine's College. He is the author of *The Music of Humanity* (Nelson, 1969), *William Wordsworth: The Borders of Vision* (Oxford University Press, 1982), the co-author of *William Wordsworth and the Age of Revolution* (Rutgers University Press, 1987), and chief editor of the Norton Critical Edition of *The Prelude, 1799, 1805, 1850* (1979) and of the forthcoming Longmans *Wordsworth: An Annotated Selection*. He has chosen and introduced *Revolution and Romanticism, 1789–1834*, a series of facsimile reprints (Woodstock Books, 1989–), and is the Chairman of the Wordsworth Trust, Dove Cottage, Grasmere.

ACKNOWLEDGEMENTS

STEPHEN GILL's essay, here reprinted in a revised form by permission of Oxford University Press, was originally published in *RES* 34 (1983). Jonathan Wordsworth's essay was delivered in an earlier version as a lecture to a conference on 'Romanticism and Revolution' at Bucknell University in 1989.

Various manuscripts held at the Wordsworth Library, Grasmere are quoted by Keith Hanley (DC MSS 38 and 43) and Pamela Woof (DC MS 31), and are reproduced to illustrate the essays of Jonathan Wordsworth (DC MS.19) and Pamela Woof by permission of the Trustees of Dove Cottage. The Bodleian Shelley manuscripts quoted by Robert Brinkley (adds. e. 16), and reproduced to illustrate his and Donald Reiman's essays are used by permission of the Bodleian Library, Oxford. Bodleian MS. Shelley adds. e. 20 is reproduced from Donald H. Reiman (ed.), 'Shelley's Last Notebook', The Bodleian Shelley Manuscripts, VIII (New York and London: Garland Publishing Inc., 1990), p. 320 by the publisher's permission. The Keats draft which illustrates Jack Stillinger's essay is reproduced by permission of the Fitzwilliam Museum, Cambridge. George Dyer's letter to Dr Carey in Nicholas Roe's essay is quoted by permission of the Master and Fellows of Emmanuel College, Cambridge.

In line with their preference for editorial non-interference, the editors have refrained from standardizing the English and American spelling and style either way.

INTRODUCTION

THE essays in this volume offer descriptions of creativity. They tend toward the specific rather than the general and the empirical rather than the theoretical, to engage the particularities and complexities of writing. Many of the essays approach these complexities from the perspective of editors who have worked to make the writing available. Other essays in this volume, whose concerns are not specifically editorial, still reflect the possibilities that editorial practice enables. This need not suggest a reductive thesis in which editors determine readings. What it may indicate are the particular interpretative possibilities that English Romanticism has achieved at the present moment.

EDITORIAL REVISION

Recent editions of English Romantic writings have not fixed but re-opened the idea of a determinate text. The Greg-Bowers principles (the New Bibliography) established the notion of a definitive copy-text which respects final authorial intentions or original demonstrable wishes, but the definitiveness of this notion comes into question as critics respond to the complexity of determinants involved in textual production.[1] What authority should we attribute to the texts that we read? How should this authority be interpreted? As more and more texts become available – manuscript transcriptions, facsimiles, and reading texts edited from the manuscripts (multiple versions of any given poem) – the role of editors becomes increasingly apparent in the history of the texts they present. As Jerome McGann writes on the foundations of literary interpretation, together with bibliography, 'textual criticism . . . [is] conceptually fundamental rather than preliminary to the study of literature'.[2]

We might consider two examples, both of which involve contributors to this volume. In 1965 Donald Reiman published a reading version for the working-draft of Shelley's 'The Triumph of Life'.[3] With minor revisions that

I

reading text has now become the poem that many critics know. It is, for example, the basis of Paul de Man's reading to which Reiman refers in his essay here (p. 238). As Reiman points out, many critics including de Man have confused the reading text with Shelley's draft of the poem. As general editor for *The Bodleian Shelley Manuscripts*,[4] Reiman has now published a facsimile with transcriptions of the draft: readers 'can see for themselves exactly how clear – or how muddled – the textual situation is . . . what went into the difficult decisions that knowledgeable editors have had to make in order to present a coherent poem (a task that may be easier for the critic who remains in blissful ignorance of those intricacies)'.[5] Or, as Reiman suggests in his contribution here: 'those who study Shelley manuscripts . . . must point out . . . the difference between a draft (a private or confidential text, meant for the eyes of the author only or, perhaps, his intimate friends) and a press copy or printed text approved by the author as conveying his or her meaning in the realm of public discourse' (p. 238). It is unlikely that many collections of Romantic poetry would want to include the manuscript transcription, but the reading version can create the illusion that 'The Triumph of Life' is *like* a printed text. While the reading text may well provide the more satisfying poem, it has also led to confused scholarship.

A second example: in 1969 Jonathan Wordsworth published reading texts of 'The Ruined Cottage' and 'The Pedlar' based on MS D, an intermediate manuscript version.[6] The same manuscript now provides the reading text for Stephen Gill in The Oxford Authors *William Wordsworth*.[7] As Gill notes in his essay, 'it is this text, in fact, which seems to have entered the canon', but the text 'is an editorial creation' (p. 56). Similarly with the two-book *Prelude* which is now 'printed as if it were a poem with the same status as . . . "Tintern Abbey"'. What readers ought to be aware of is that . . . an *editorial* act has intervened decisively in the province usually claimed for interpretative criticism, the exposition of "the growth of [Wordsworth's] mind"' (p. 58).

The critical reception of 'The Triumph of Life' exemplifies the problem that even the most carefully edited reading versions of manuscripts can produce. What publication of 'The Ruined Cottage' and the two-book *Prelude* exemplifies as well is the issue of relative authority between different versions of a poem (in the case of 'The Ruined Cottage', Book I of *The Excursion*; in the case of the two-book *Prelude*, the 1805 or 1850 text). Which version should we adopt as copy-text? Which will become the poem that we know? Texts edited from manuscripts can displace the published text; one published version can also displace another (in The Oxford Authors edition, 'Ode: Intimations of Immortality From Recollections of Early Childhood' is simply the 'Ode' Wordsworth published in 1807). Given the Greg-Bowers principle of a definitive copy-text, we may feel the need to prioritize one version over others.

Wordsworth attached 'importance . . . to following strictly the last copy text of an author',[8] but in his case recent editors have tended to disagree. The relative authority of early or late versions has provoked considerable partisanship, a controversy reflected not only in Gill's but also in Jonathan Wordsworth's contribution here. For poems like *The Prelude*, any argument for a definitive copy-text is confronted by the evidence of 'changing authorial intention' (p. 22). Why, given the character of *The Prelude*, a poem '52 years in manuscript' and 'growing through different versions . . . through different phases of reworking' (p. 18), should any set of intentions necessarily be privileged? 'Good and bad texts will always exist (judged either in terms of scholarly consistency, or on aesthetic grounds), but I can't see how there can be such a thing as right and wrong ones. Any text created by a writer at any point in his life is "right", as long as it is scrupulously reproduced' (p. 20).

Together with Gill, Stephen Parish, and the other editors of the Cornell Wordsworth, Jonathan Wordsworth has been largely responsible for a transformation in the Wordsworth texts we read, the choice in recent editions of early versions over later. Given a desire to read the poetry of 1793–1806 in versions from those years, the case for early texts is historical as well as aesthetic; Gill writes in The Oxford Authors edition that 'the growth of the poet's mind' is 'best reveal[ed]' by 'a chronological presentation' in which each 'text . . . comes as close as possible to the state of the poem when it was first completed'.[9] But this, of course, assumes a particular interpretation of the mind that the poetry reveals. If we read the universality of Wordsworth's poetry as specific only to the moment in which 'it was first completed', we may resist editorial revisions – even the poet's own – that obscure the particularity of that moment. What such a choice may in turn erase, however, are the historical and creative moments of which Wordsworth's revisions are the trace.

Gill's choice can be criticized on a number of grounds, based on different editorial experiences. As an editor of Shelley's poetry, Reiman adopts authorial intention as a guideline, partly because he consistently finds Shelley's revisions of aesthetic and intellectual value: 'A poet makes a better personal appearance with his clothes on than he does naked. However interesting it may be to peek into Shelley's private papers, catching him off guard and *au naturel*, his polished writings teach us more' (p. 238). Given this appreciation of Shelley's art, it is not surprising that in other essays on textual criticism, Reiman does not call for any radical questioning of the principles of the New Bibliography.[10] Perhaps what an attentiveness to historical contextualizations can offer is a more 'eclectic and pragmatic approach that can adopt (or *adapt*) the virtues' of the 'textual methodologies developed by the school of Greg, Bowers, and Tanselle', while avoiding the pitfalls of '"scientific" analysis and . . . imaginative reconstructions or idealisations' of texts.[11] On the other hand, given the very different assessment by many readers of the value of Wordsworth's revisions, it may also not be surprising that the New Bibliographical principles have come to seem inadequate. Helen Darbishire 'deplored' the revisions 'which overlay or obscure [the poet's] naive immediate expression'.[12] According to Jonathan Wordsworth, the 'revisions usually took the form of elaboration . . . [E]ven at the height of [Wordsworth's] creative period, they were normally for the worse'.[13] Such an evaluation of Wordsworth's peculiar gift is likely to discover much of his greatest writing obscured by an insistence on final authorial intent. At the same time, what is likely to be privileged is the significance of the 'immediate expression' over the subsequent history of the text. This history goes beyond the poet's biography. As Jack Stillinger suggests, 'the doing away with the later Wordsworth'[14] and 'the inadvertent "*standardizing*" of these earlier texts'[15] is also an 'effacement' of substantial traditions of reception.[16] Stillinger argues that 'we grant the legitimacy and interest . . . of *all* versions . . . of the poem in the canon'. In Jonathan Wordsworth's essay for this volume, he seems to have adopted a similar position.

What constitutes a separate version? Should the copy-text be the author's manuscript, the first edition or the last, perhaps some composite of differing versions? If a manuscript draft is offered, what is the effect of editorial interventions (added punctuation, for example) that give a draft the look of a completed work? It is possible that for some texts, perhaps for some authors as well, even the notion of a copy-text cannot be said to apply. An argument for version rather than copy-text seems essential to Stillinger's criticism of Wordsworth editors and to Jonathan Wordsworth's presentation here. It is also James Mays's conclusion – with respect to Coleridge – in his contribution to this volume. Mays recounts his experience as the editor of the *Poetical Works* for the Bollingen *Collected Coleridge*.[17] In response to the revisionary nature of Coleridge's poetry, the number of variants to be recorded for each work, Mays came to discard the principles of the New Bibliography and adopt in their place the new Germanist emphasis on the version rather than the copy-text. In principle any revision – even a single variant – is productive of a new version.[18] Mays concludes that there is no rule for discriminating in favour of a preferred version. This results in his chosen presentation of the poetic texts: a variorum volume which offers a genetic or synoptic display of the full compositional process for the poems, aiming 'to cluster the variants in the body of the text' (p. 142); a separate volume offering reading texts that have been chosen on the basis of a fresh decision in each case ('each poem separately . . . rests on a decision about the evolution and special features of its more "various" counterpart [in the variorum]' (p. 143)). The variorum makes it possible for different readers to choose (or edit) different texts on the basis of their own decisions, but while many texts are possible, no copy-text has been authorized. From an aesthetic perspective this means that *the* poem has been displaced by its many versions.

Editors of Wordsworth and Coleridge cannot avoid the pervasive quality of their author's revisions. On the other hand, as an editor of Keats, Stillinger finds very largely that he can. As he notes in his essay here, 'Keats's entire poetic career was only four years long . . . Obviously he never had the chance to revise . . . the way that Wordsworth or Coleridge did', but 'from his practice while alive . . . it seems unlikely that Keats, had he lived, would ever have produced radically altered versions' (p. 314). Because he 'was a fundamentally different sort of poet' (p. 315), the issues confronting an editor will also turn out to be different.

At the time Stillinger was editing Keats's poetry, he advocated the ideal of final authorial intentions,[19] but, as he suggests in the preface to his edition of the poems,[20] the application of this ideal could be problematic. Keats's writing was often revised by friends and publishers; in order to hold to the principle of intention in the choice of copy-text, Stillinger adopted an interpretation of the principle that accommodates multiple authorship. In a case such as this, where the transcripts on which the modern editor relies are 'collaborative efforts not just in the printing but at a much earlier stage',[21] collaboration can 'be considered as an essential element in the fulfillment of the poet's intentions'; the 'additional refinements' of 'publishers and printers' fulfill 'these intentions' as well.[22] In the essay for this volume, however, Stillinger's interpretation of Keats's poetry has changed. He wonders whether in a case such as this, intention is still a useful consideration: 'editors of the Greg–Bowers–Tanselle persuasion take single authorship, final or otherwise, as an inviolable standard ("this is what *the author* intended us to read")', but 'scholars are having to adjust to the fact that Woodhouse, Taylor, and others are responsible for small and occasionally larger effects all through some of Keats's best known poetry' (p. 316). How did Keats regard his writing? The problem for the New Bibliography 'goes back to the way [he] drafted his pieces . . . The heart of the problem is whether Keats, characteristically writing even his greatest poems in the manner of extempore effusions, can have had any specific intentions *at all* in the sense in which scholars interpret and edit according to the standard of authorial intention' (p. 316).

As extempore writing that was later revised by friends as well as the author, the texts of Keats's poetry should perhaps be considered social not autonomous productions. The distinction, which is McGann's,[23] reflects his experience as an editor of Byron,[24] but it may also apply very well to concerns Keats's poems raise. Of both writers one can say that they problematize the concept of

5

intention, Keats because his writing is collaborative, Byron because he is one of those authors who demonstrate 'a number of different wishes and intentions about what text . . . [will] be presented to the public'.[25] For both writers it will be inadequate in any case to prioritize an editorial principle that 'emphasise[s] the autonomy of the isolated author'.[26] Nor, as McGann suggests in the essay included here, will 'the text-centered procedures of twentieth century criticism' be adequate: they 'have never been able to read Byron's work' because Byron requires 'a critique of the limits of a theory of autonomous poetry', the 'development of an alternative theory' that can respond to his 'actual practice of installing the poetical experience as a social and historical event' (pp. 194–5).

Nothing in this discussion requires that the principle of a copy-text be abandoned, but if the principle is no longer defined in terms of intentionality, then it has also fundamentally changed. McGann argues that the choice of copy-text should reflect the entire history of production and transmission, 'the complex network of people, materials, and events that have produced and that continue to reproduce the literary works history delivers into our hands'.[27] Textual criticism 'presupposes and reciprocates an understanding of the entire developing process of a literary work's historical transmission'; it 'creates . . . a sense of how many factors enter into the production of a literary work'.[28] Here 'the first obligation' is to 'what has taken place'.[29] If this includes the 'originary textual moment' (author, collaborators, initial production and publication), it also involves 'secondary moments', 'the period of reproduction carried out during the author's lifetime and the periods of production and reproduction that begin with the author's death'. Finally it includes the 'immediate moment' of textual criticism and editing.[30] Given these concerns, relative authority will be determined not by intention but by the principle of 'textual relevance', the relevance of a particular version to the specifics of a given history.[31]

For Byron 'textual relevance' can lead to the choice of printed versions from the poet's lifetime;[32] for Keats the same criterion can explain the choice of a text that friends and publishers revised. Clearly this criterion can also be used to justify the edited transcriptions of manuscripts for Wordsworth, or Mays's variorum for Coleridge. It might lead, as McGann has proposed, to 'an edition of Shelley's *Complete Poetical Works* in which the copy text for the poem would be, in almost all cases, the manuscripts',[33] but it can also justify Reiman's choice of public versions where possible. In each instance what is in question is the history the editor has found and makes legible. It is this then that distinguishes the critical or 'modernized' edition, that it presents a text as historical. From the perspective McGann proposes, the inadequacies of the New Bibliography reflect a restrictive view of history. On the other hand, it can be argued that the concern for history becomes restrictive: it may limit the contexts of poetry to the contextualizations of historical discourse; it may counter a poem's 'timelessness' (the 'image of life', Shelley says, 'expressed in its eternal truth'[34]). Deidealizing notions of authorship and reading may misunderstand the value of idealization and confuse it with illusion. In this regard the notion of authorial intention may again become relevant, particularly for authors who write antithetically that is, against their history.

However these issues are resolved, on the basis of historical concerns the principle of authorial intention may actually achieve a new force. Often, for example, it may only be through a recognition of intention that textual relevance will be determined. This seems particularly the case for less canonical authors, writers who have been consistently treated as less entitled to have their own say. A poet like Clare is exemplary in this respect. As John Lucas shows in his essay for this collection, Clare's poetry has been repeatedly distorted by a disregard for his intentions as an author. Lucas argues that there is still no adequate collected edition and that selections traditionally have perpetuated the censorship imposed by Clare's original editors:[35] 'improvements' in spelling, punctuation, and stanza divisions which have little or nothing to do with Clare's own writing but conformed to the norms for a reading text at the time. That the social text which resulted became the copy-text as well has implications for many of the issues that have been raised in this introduction, the relative authority of different versions, the intervention of editors, the principle of authorial intentions. The implications of Clare's history might well be applied to the editing of other 'uneducated poets' (Southey's phrase) such as Duck, Burns, Bloomfield, perhaps, even Hogg and Crabbe. Here it is more clearly arguable that authorial intentions should be given priority, though later social versions will be historically significant.

REVISIONARY DETERMINANTS

Romanticism celebrates works of the imagination, but what is the relation of the celebration to the particulars of writing? The essays in this volume adopt a variety of approaches, but in relation to absolutes about poetry and the poet, they tend to adopt a 'relative spirit'. The phrase is Walter Pater's and is taken from his portrait of Coleridge: 'The relative spirit . . . dwell[s] on the more fugitive conditions or circumstances of things'; it 'break[s] through a thousand rough and brutal classifications'; it 'give[s] elasticity to inflexible principles'.[36] Among Pater's concerns was the idealization, borrowed by Coleridge from the Germans, of the poet as 'a nature humanised' and of writing as organically formed ('it shapes, as it develops, itself from within, and the fullness of its development is one and the same with the perfection of its outward form'):[37]

7

'That expresses truly the sense of a self-delighting, independent life which the finished work of art gives us: it hardly figures the process by which the work was produced'.[38] By imagining writing in terms of the completed work, Coleridge disallowed the 'many stages of refining', the 'analysis [through which] the artist attains clearness of idea'.[39] What an organic aesthetic also disallows is Coleridge's own uncertainty as a writer, his distrust of what might emerge in the writing. Nor does it allow for other textual determinants: the influence of audience, of other authors living and dead, of friends, associates, publishers – psychological, social, and political constraints. Of the relative spirit, Pater asks, 'Who would gain more than Coleridge by criticism in such a spirit?'[40] Perhaps – without denying the sense of an 'independent life which the finished work' gives – Romanticism has also gained by the circumstantial detail of such a criticism.

Characteristic of many statements by Romantic poets on their writing is an elision of its revisionary art. Thus Byron's and Keats's insistence on the extemporaneous, or Shelley's dismissal of the process of composition: 'when composition begins, inspiration is already on the decline . . . The toil and delay recommended by critics can be justly interpreted to mean no more than a careful observation of the inspired moments . . . a necessity . . . imposed by a limitedness of the poetic faculty.'[41] There is an evasiveness in Wordsworth's discussion of 'successful composition', of the 'state of enjoyment' it entails,[42] which hardly bears witness to the anxieties he actually experienced, the 'uneasiness at [his] stomach and side', and the 'dull pain about [his] heart'.[43] Nor does Shelley adequately account for a poem like 'Mont Blanc', where so much of the inspiration is to be found in the rewriting, in an uncertain relationship between fluency and arrest. Shelley thought that 'Milton conceived the Paradise Lost as a whole before he executed it in portions',[44] but if Milton had executed only what he initially conceived, the first three books of *Paradise Lost* would never have been composed.[45] At various times, Wordsworth conceived, and arguably executed, a two-part, five-book, thirteen-book, and fourteen-book *Prelude*. If Shelley had executed no more than he first conceived, he would not have written 'Mont Blanc'. His description of the poem as an 'undisciplined overflowing of the soul'[46] might better be regarded, not as accurate recollection, but as part of the artist's presentation for the published work. With respect to this presentation, the perspective a more accurate recollection provides need be interpreted not as negation but rather as a historical supplement.

The relation between the published work and the history of its production and transmission may involve a particularly illuminating complementarity. Reiman's essay shows how constant refinements led to the 'aesthetic unities' of Shelley's poetry: 'the drafts show us how much *art* went into what appear to be spontaneous outpourings of sentiment, how well Shelley succeeded in modulating his tone in order to bridge the gap between himself and his readers, and how carefully he contructed through the subtleties of language' (p. 237). In the earliest drafts, Shelley set down 'raw feelings and thoughts', then transformed them 'into almost labyrinthine artifacts' (p. 237). While a great deal can be learned 'about Shelley's creative method by tracing his progress' through the manuscripts, 'in the end, the poet escapes our nets' and 'proves at last what Shelley claimed in *A Defence of Poetry* – the superiority of the creative, synthesizing faculty to the process of analysis' (p. 238).

Reiman celebrates the power of Shelley's finished work, 'the poems that he finished and polished for publication' (p. 238). On the other hand, what Jonathan Wordsworth characterizes as the art of *The Prelude* involves the power of a kind of writing that is revised but remains unfinished: 'If *The Prelude* had merely been an account of Wordsworth's early life, there would have been no need for . . . periodic updatings. But it was also an embodiment of views and values that had to be brought into line as times changed, and as [Wordsworth] responded to change. Revision was a responsibility . . . It is this aspect – the desire to make a prophetic statement, and the urge to get it right – that most clearly links *The Prelude* to the other great English long poems' (p. 21), to a poetry which may not be 'directly autobiographical' but which nonetheless records 'a major portion of the author's life' (p. 24). Because of the length of time over which the writing occurs, 'composition embodies – sometimes indefinably, sometimes by direct allusion – changing personal and political situations, changing views, changing attitudes not least to the material of the poem itself' (pp. 24–5). Against the 'work in process' view of a chronologically evolving composition, Jonathan Wordsworth describes a poetry that necessarily turns out to be composite.

Wordsworth's rewriting of himself can be interpreted as an unusually powerful internalization of pressures that commonly become stronger the more actively social collaboration was involved. The desire for a stable discourse was urgent in the era of Revolution, when private losses and ageing could become images for radical historical anxieties. This, one might say, is the evidence of history, the imprint of the social on the personal, the articulation and silencing of one as the other.

Jonathan Barron and Kenneth Johnston mark particular silences that emerged in 'The Ruined Cottage', the cancelling in MS D of unresolved feeling still apparent in MS B: 'If the various versions of *The Prelude* illustrate Wordsworth's changing conceptions of himself *as* subject, then his revisions of "The Ruined Cottage", which he [also] continued throughout his career, may be said to represent his changing conception of one of his primary subject *matters*, human suffering, and how this subject might best be represented' (p. 64). As Barron and Johnston suggest in their essay, in MS B the gaps are more evident between the Pedlar's apparent wisdom and the evasions it conceals. The move 'from B to D is a shift toward a more distanced, less personally involved and responsible relationship between Margaret and the Pedlar' (p. 72). It also contributes to a tragic aesthetic in the version of 'The Ruined Cottage' which has recently been accorded priority as copy-text.

A case can be made that the stabilities Wordsworth achieves are always evasive, a displacement perhaps of political responsibilities in favour of aesthetic achievement. For many readers, Wordsworth was an apostate, but Nick Roe suggests in the essay included here that Wordsworth's revisions of *The Prelude* do not support this interpretation. *The Prelude* indicates an ideological continuity throughout its different life-stages. Roe recalls Macaulay's opinion of the 1850 text, that the 'poem is to the last degree Jacobinical, indeed Socialist'; he identifies 'passages that might substantiate Macaulay's claim' (p. 88). These passages do not reveal the political and religious reaction with which they have been commonly charged, but an essentially consistent 'radical imagination', an 'introspective Jacobinism' that exists in constant dialogue with the crucial political locations of the 1790s (pp. 92–3). From this perspective *The Prelude* may have been revised in order *not* to evade.

What motivates revision? Norman Fruman's essay portrays Coleridge as a poet of evasions, a writer of 'mysterious details, or passages which elude plausible interpretation, or inexplicable gaps, derive[d] from the wish to conceal something, or from unconscious pressure to express something forbidden' (p. 162). Repressions range from the falsification of borrowings to the denial of sensuality: had he been less 'infected with the romantic cult of originality, [Coleridge] might well have accepted in himself what he dismissed as mere "quickness in imitation"'; 'had he been less driven to present himself to the world as free of those ordinary failings with which most of humanity has always been afflicted', Coleridge's 'career as a poet' would 'certainly [have been] far less problematical' (p. 167). Coleridge revised in conflict with himself, at once knowing and self-deceiving, both misleading and revealing for his friends and his reading public.

The role of audience in Coleridge's writing has become increasingly apparent; in part it may explain the fascination that this poetry had for Byron. As both McGann and Peter Manning suggest in their essays for this volume, Byron tended to write and to revise in relation to specific audiences. McGann engages Byron's practice of 'manipulating his texts before his publics' (p. 195): 'Byron uses different levels of poetic coding to define his audiences . . . As in all such writing, multiplying meanings . . . require some kind of special knowledge to decipher' (p. 194), knowledge available to some readers but not to all. 'It is a procedure which will achieve spectacular display in *Don Juan*', where 'Byron says in a peculiarly important passage that "there is much that could not be appreciated / In any manner by the uninitiated"' (p. 194). Such poetry 'exploits and even encourages' social distinctions (p. 194). By 'manipulating' writing 'so as to draw out and exploit the complicity of readers and audiences', the poetry 'begins to develop a kind of social consciousness: on the one hand, contexts of reading which transcend the immediate are being invoked, and on the other the audience is being made aware of itself as a participant in the construction of those contexts' (pp. 192 and 194).

McGann considers ways in which Byron actively revises his audience. Manning works from a complementary perspective which traces the deliberate self-revisions that responded to audience demands. A dialogue with different publics, critics, publishers, and earlier selves results in a 'play of speakers' in the writing, 'temporary positions in a continuing process' of constructing 'the personality' that readers 'felt as Byron' (p. 213): 'Byron might proclaim a lordly indifference, but he remained uncommonly attuned to the expectations of his readers', and 'questions of revision were inseparable from those of the marketplace' (p. 211). On the one hand, he was particularly susceptible to the opinions of Murray, his publisher, whom he might 'periodically castigate . . . for being a tradesman', but who nonetheless 'shaped [Byron's] career' (p. 211). On the other hand, the interaction with audience makes Byron's writing a kind of oral poetry in print: 'the personality known as "Byron" habitually developed through this give-and-take with his readers' (p. 220); 'Byron's textual self-revision bound his readers to him and illuminates the grounding of the self in dialogue and exchange' (p. 223). As Manning suggests, revision is a public affair because readers make writing a collaborative process.

A history of literary criticism could well be a record of revisionary interpretations. Leigh Hunt's relation to Shelley may be exemplary in this regard. Timothy Webb's essay shows how during revisions of Hunt's *Autobiography* the received portrait of Shelley also came to be revised: Hunt's emerging faith in progress or 'evolutionary melorism' produced not only an altered self-image but a rewriting of Shelley's life, 'a progressive tendency to invest in Shelley a set of values . . . central to [Hunt's own] philosophy' (pp. 286 and 287): 'Hunt's religion of the heart, with its emphasis on generosity and acceptance rather than on exclusiveness and judgment, is in keeping with his efforts . . . to eliminate anger and to cultivate charity and forgiveness' (p. 286), but when it is projected on to Shelley, 'it also deprives the reader of a vital insight into the tensions and complexities of Shelley's character'.

Investments like Hunt's will be familiar to any critic; poetic composition may be shaped by such investments as well. It can be argued that Shelley's 'Mont Blanc' is a re-reading and rewriting of Wordsworth; that Keats's 'Hyperion' fragments re-read and rewrite Milton. Harold Bloom's argument that poetry is 'misinterpretation' conflates the role of poetry and criticism and makes poetry only a 'more drastic' misreading of the kind Hunt's *Autobiography* represents: 'Poets' misinterpretations or poems are more drastic than critics' misinterpretations or criticism, but this is only a difference in degree and not in kind'.[47] The poet or critic 'is not so much a man speaking to men as a man rebelling against being spoken to by a dead man (the precursor) outrageously more alive than himself'.[48]

One can sense the presence of one poem in another and still not agree that the former is the meaning of the latter or that the revision of one poem by another is *a priori* a misreading. While critics may displace poetry with their interpretations, the meaningfulness of a poetic allusion primarily involves a play (often a wrestling or struggle) between difference and similarity, the re-reading and revision that occur when an image or a phrase recurs, when it is rewritten in a different context. What essays in this volume suggest is not that 'the meaning of a poem can only be another poem',[49] but that poetry is written referentially, with other writing among the referents.

Bloom argues that rewriting is evasive; Fruman's essay on Coleridge might be regarded as offering defining examples of evasion. In the case of other authors, however, there is far more explicit revision of the works that they inherit. 'Mont Blanc' by intention is a texture of allusions, a recontextualization of Wordsworth and Wordsworthian images, while *Frankenstein* recontextualizes not only Milton and Wordsworth but Shelley's poem as well. A similar mode of revision is at work in Keats's writing. According to Jonathan Bate, the engagement with Milton in the 'Hyperion' fragments is deliberate, conscious, overt: '"Hyperion" has become a crucial test-case for interpretations of the Romantic attempt to deal with' Milton, but the 'emphasis on Milton's inhibiting effect has led to an over-simplification' (p. 322). 'Contrary to Harold Bloom's kind of revisionism . . . what Keats's rewriting indicates is dependence on memory, not forgetting, a recollection of the precise words and contexts of the precursor text' (p. 323). Furthermore Bloom's misunderstanding of the nature of such revision works to obscure what is at stake in the writing: 'Keats's revisions are bound up . . . with the articulation of a tragic vision in place of a vision of progress for which the most appropriate medium was epic narrative' (p. 322); his sense of tragic art which involves negative capability, 'a refusal to come to conclusions', also requires that his epic remain unfinished (p. 337). But while the fragmentary nature of 'Hyperion' indicates the effect of Keats's vision on Milton's form – Keats makes the form incomplete – it also involves political determinants. Keats's 'progressive politics' were compatible with the epic vision of progress, but his politics 'proved incompatible' with the sympathies tragedy implicates (p. 336). For Keats, aesthetic and political values turned out to have been at odds.

It is illuminating to compare Keats's revision of Milton with Hunt's recreation of Shelley or Coleridge's concealment of sources. Of Keats it cannot be said that he distorts what Milton wrote or that he evades Milton's influence. In part this is because Keats, unlike Coleridge, does not obscure the sources of his poetry. Nor does he adopt the position of a reader who interprets what another author means. Keats refers to what Milton wrote and revises in relation to that reference. He discovers perhaps what allusions to Milton both enable and disallow.

The revisions in Keats's writing that Stillinger details, the collaborative rewriting by friends and editors, also suggests this experimental quality, as does the lack of intentionality in Keats's writing, its openness to what the writing becomes, even in the hands of others: 'The known facts of the revising, editing, and printing of these poems gives us a rather attractive overall picture of Keats, Woodhouse, Taylor, Reynolds, and Brown all pulling together to make Keats's lines presentable to the public; and for the most part, though not always, Keats welcomed his friends' help, indeed regularly depended on it, and was gratefully aware that his poems were the better for it' (p. 316). Among Keats's extempore writings, one can include 'Hyperion' (while some readers have interpreted the holograph draft as a 'fair copy . . . Woodhouse described it as "the original & only copy . . . composed & written down at once as it now stands"', an original draft that only has the appearance of a fair copy).[50] Among the collaborative efforts is the 1820 printing of 'Hyperion'.[51]

In his edition of Keats's poetry, Stillinger notes that during these collaborative efforts, 'Keats was allowed to have his way in things that mattered to him'.[52] Other authors were frequently not so lucky. Keats's publisher John Taylor could be a notoriously high-handed censor. While Keats was Taylor's friend, Clare was never accorded this privilege. According to Lucas's essay, Clare was painfully aware that his poems were *not* better for Taylor's revisions, but Clare had little chance of resisting. As spelling, punctuation, layout and omissions were inflicted on the writing, Clare found himself becoming what he never intended to be, another in a line of 'Peasant Poets'. Here revision has come to mean which poems have been suppressed and how those allowed to appear have been edited and contextualized in order to market the approved image: 'Clare ran up against a number of ultimately insoluble problems in wanting to distinguish between being *a* peasant and *The* poet' (p. 339). 'His publishers wanted him to appear . . . [as the] "quaint" natural genius' who is also 'a harmless curiosity', and 'in order to secure this image they were prepared to interfere decisively in [Clare's] work' (p. 340). By providing an extreme example of editorial revision in the interests of cultural conformity, Taylor clarifies by contrast the obligations of a textual critic.

Conformity exerts its influence on all readers and in any reading version – to produce through omission and arrangement an approved image of the writer. Against these suppressions the textual critic can offer the details of authorship. McGann suggests that 'the best scholarly editions establish their texts according to a catholic set of guidelines and priorities whose relative authority shifts and alters under changing circumstances'.[53] The *relative* authority of theoretical principles clarifies the priority of the writing (the individual and social work, the production and the transmission) over any interpretative conformity, what Wordsworth in *Lyrical Ballads* calls the 'enemy' of readers' 'pleasures', 'our own pre-established codes of decision'.[54] Textual readings can avoid the confusions of a 'thematic criticism [which] sidesteps the concrete, human particulars of the originary works, either to reproduce them within currently acceptable ideological terms, or to translate them into currently unacceptable forms of thought'.[55]

For some Romantic women writers, whose unofficial works are only now receiving substantial critical and editorial attention, new editions will revise ideological codes, not only approved portraits of the authors, but suppositions about genre and style that have worked as much as Clare's publisher to enforce literary conformities. As editor of the first complete edition of Mary Shelley's letters,[56] Betty Bennett suggests in her essay how the textual critic can revise a writer's portrait: 'scholars have generally regarded [Mary Shelley] as a result: William Godwin's and Mary Wollstonecraft's daughter who became Shelley's Pygmalion' (p. 291). An effect of this portrait has been to leave Mary Shelley's writing in 'an intellectual straitjacket', but her letters provide 'another story' (pp. 291–2). It is 'written in her own words, in counterpoint with her own era' (p. 292). 'The letters, in her own voice, reflect an individual in the process of struggling against, revising, and defying' a variety of conventional restraints (p. 305). When her novels and short fiction are taken together with the histories, journals, and letters, when her achievements as Shelley's editor are fully acknowledged as well, the image of 'Shelley's Pygmalion' gives way to an understanding of the complexity of both their collaborative work and her individual authorship.

Bennett's essay reflects her editorial experience. Like so many of the contributions to this volume, Pamela Woof's does so as well. Woof is editor of the new Clarendon edition of Dorothy Wordsworth's *Grasmere Journals*.[57] In Dorothy Wordsworth's case, what is also emerging is a more attentive understanding of collaborative writing and individual authorship. Woof's essay assumes a reader's sense of 'the clear lights and colours of the Journal, their marvellous evocation of place and of the writer' (p. 169). What Woof details are the pressures, 'both the practical ones of time and circumstance, and the more elusive influences of word and memory' (p. 169). The manuscripts show a conscious artistry in which deletion and revision are a patterning of these pressures. On the one hand, Woof suggests that Dorothy Wordsworth intended journal entries to be writing for her brother's poetry ('in describing her encounter with the beggars, in writing an account of the leech-gatherer . . . and in setting down other stories, Dorothy must have had Wordsworth's purpose and poetry in mind' [p. 176]); on the other hand, Woof's essay recreates the space and time in which the Journal's own writing could occur ('it was subject variously to time', to 'everyday activity and Wordsworth's presence', to 'the spaces created by his sleep or his absence' [p. 169]).

Readers may disagree as to the influence of Dorothy Wordsworth's writing on her circle, but like the other contributors to this volume, Woof is attentive not only in theory to the particulars of a specific scene of writing: the host of corrections and insertions the writer made in the act of composition, the shifts and patterns, continuities and discontinuities, the living indeterminacies of mundane constraints, traces of time and circumstance, memory and emotional compulsion. Here a reader's need for Pater's relative spirit – 'to see the parts as parts only'[58] – seems especially insistent; what readers can learn from the Grasmere Journals is an attentiveness to a Romanticism that by nature is not an absolute but that dwells on the 'circumstances of things'. As Pater says of the relative spirit, this Romanticism 'cries out against every formula less living and less flexible than life itself'.[59] It 'begets an intellectual *finesse* of which the ethical result is a delicate and tender justice in the criticism of human life'.[60]

Lancaster and Orono, 1991

NOTES

1 For a useful summary of the principles and practices of the Greg-Bowers school and more recent adaptations, see Donald H. Reiman, 'The Four Ages of Editing and the English Romantics' (1984), reprinted in his *Romantic Texts and Contexts* (Columbia, Missouri, 1987), pp. 85–108.

2 *The Beauty of Inflections: Literary Investigations in Historical Method and Theory* (Oxford, 1985), p. 71.

3 In *Shelley's 'The Triumph of Life': A Critical Study, Based on a Text Newly Edited from the Bodleian Manuscript* (Urbana, Illinois, 1985).

4 Vol. 1, ed. Donald H. Reiman (New York and London: Garland Publishing, 1986). Reiman is also general editor of the companion Garland series, *The Manuscripts of the Younger Romantics*.

5 *Ibid.*, p. 119.

6 In *The Music of Humanity* (New York, 1969). *Cf.* the Cornell Wordsworth Edition, *The Ruined Cottage and The Pedlar*, ed. James Butler (Ithaca and Hassocks, 1979).

7 (Oxford and New York, 1984).

8 *Ibid.*, p. xxx.

9 *Ibid.*, p. xxxi.

10 In addition to 'The Four Ages of Editing and the English Romantics', see Reiman's earlier essay, 'Romantic Bards and Historical Editors' (1982), also reprinted in *Romantic Texts and Contexts*, pp. 109–29.

11 *Ibid.*, p. 85.

12 'Wordsworth's *Prelude*' (1926), reprinted in *Wordsworth: The Prelude*, ed. W. J. Harvey and Richard Gravil, Casebook Series (London and Basingstoke, 1972), p. 84.

13 *The Borders of Vision* (Oxford, 1982), p. 56.

14 'Textual Primitivism and the Editing of Wordsworth', *Studies in Romanticism* 28 (1989), p. 14.

15 *Ibid.*, p. 20.

16 *Ibid.*, p. 21.

17 To be published by Princeton University Press in the United States, and by Routledge in Great Britain, as the final title in the *Collected Coleridge*, Bollingen Series, 16 vols., 1971–, Kathleen Coburn (general editor).

18 For a discussion of the New German emphasis, see Hans Zeller, 'A New Approach to the Critical Constitution of Literary Texts', *Studies in Bibliography* 28 (1975), pp. 231–64. Zeller argues that, as every version is a complete semiotic system, any authorial revision – even a single variant – creates a different system and so a new version.

19 *The Texts of Keats's Poems* (Cambridge, Mass., 1974), p. 284.

20 *The Poems of John Keats* (Cambridge, Mass. and London, 1978), pp. 1–2.

21 *Ibid.*, p. 12.

22 *Ibid.*, p. 13.

23 *A Critique of Modern Textual Criticism* (Chicago and London, 1983), p. 8.

24 Lord Byron, *The Complete Poetical Works*, 5 vols. (Oxford, 1980–6).

25 McGann, *Critique*, p. 32.

26 *Ibid.*, p. 8.

27 'The Monks and the Giants', in *Textual Criticism and Literary Interpretation*, ed. McGann (Chicago and London, 1985), p. 191.

28 *Ibid.*, p. 191.

29 *Ibid.*, pp. 191–2.

30 *Ibid.*, pp. 192–4.

31 From the editorial introduction to the Clarendon Byron, p. xxix.

32 For poems 'printed with Byron's authorization before he left England in 1816', McGann tries 'to take as copy text the latest edition of those works which it can be shown, or reasonably deduced, Byron himself corrected' (*ibid.*, p. xxiv). For poems thereafter and for which Byron 'was much less closely involved in the . . . printing', McGann chooses 'early (normally, the first) editions' (*ibid.*, p. xxxv).

33 McGann, *Critique*, p. 109.

34 *A Defence of Poetry*. As printed in *Shelley's Poetry and Prose*, ed. Donald H. Reiman and Sharon B. Powers (New York, 1977), p. 485.

35 This to some extent includes the Clarendon Editions: ed. Eric Robinson and David Powell, *The Later Poems of John Clare, 1837–1864*, 2 vols. (Oxford, 1984), and *The Early Poems of John Clare*, 2 vols. (Oxford, 1989).

36 *Appreciations* (London and New York, 1895), pp. 104–5.

37 *Coleridge's Shakespearian Criticism*, ed. T. M. Raysor, 2 vols. (London, 1960), Vol. 1, p. 198.

38 Pater, *Appreciations*, pp. 80–1.

39 *Ibid.*, p. 81.

40 *Ibid.*, p. 105.

41 *A Defense of Poetry*, p. 504.

42 Preface to *Lyrical Ballads*, ed. B. L. Brett and A. R. Jones (London and New York, 1965), p. 266.

43 Wordsworth to Coleridge, *The Letters of William and Dorothy Wordsworth: The Early Years, 1787–1805*, ed. Ernest de Selincourt, rev. Chester L. Shaver, 2nd ed. (Oxford, 1967), p. 236.

44 *A Defense of Poetry*, p. 504.

45 *Cf.* Allan Gilbert, *On the Composition of Paradise Lost: A Study of the Ordering and Insertion of Material* (Chapel Hill, North Carolina, 1947).

46 *History of a Six Weeks' Tour* (London, 1817), p. v.

47 *The Anxiety of Influence* (New York, 1973), pp. 94–5.

48 *A Map of Misreading* (New York, 1975), p. 19.

49 Bloom, *Anxiety*, p. 94.

50 Stillinger, *The Poems of John Keats*, p. 639.

51 *Ibid.*, p. 640.

52 *Ibid.*, p. 11.

53 McGann, *Critique*, p. 94.

54 *Lyrical Ballads*, p. 7.

55 McGann, *The Romantic Ideology*, p. 11.

56 *The Letters of Mary Wollstonecraft Shelley*, 3 vols. (Baltimore and London, 1980–8).

57 *Dorothy Wordsworth: The Grasmere Journals* (Oxford, 1991).

58 Pater, *Appreciations*, p. 105.

59 *Ibid.*, p. 105.

60 *Ibid.*, p. 105.

I

REVISION AS MAKING: *THE PRELUDE* AND ITS PEERS

JONATHAN WORDSWORTH

THE PRELUDE is one of strangely few English long poems – at least, strangely few that anyone reads. Time has been more selective in this than in any other genre. From the Middle Ages we have *Piers Plowman, Troilus and Criseyde*, and (if we like to stretch the definition a little) Gower's *Confessio Amantis* and *The Canterbury Tales*. From the Renaissance come *The Faerie Queene* and *Paradise Lost*; from the Romantic period, Blake's *Vala* and *Jerusalem*, together with *The Prelude* and *Don Juan*. The Augustans were, of course, particularly conscious of the epic tradition that lies behind the long poem, and produced their attempts of different kinds, from Pope's *Essay on Man* (and mock-heroic *Dunciad*) to Cowper's *Task*. In retrospect, however, the *Essay* seems to have ruled itself out by adopting a discursive form, rather than narrative; *The Task*, though underrated as a poem, is too modest, too lacking in ambition, to be important in the present context. After the flourish of the Romantic period, the nineteenth and twentieth centuries have little to show. Tennyson (*In Memoriam, Idylls of the King*), Browning (*The Ring and the Book*) and Whitman (*Leaves of Grass*) have produced that variant of the true long poem, the collection. But only Whitman, with his nine expanding editions, has the monolithic quality that attaches to this epic and post-epic tradition. Leaving aside Pound's *Cantos*, which I at least am not qualified to judge, our own impoverished century has achieved only *The Waste Land* and Stevens's *Notes Toward a Supreme Fiction* (examples of the poor relation, the long-poem-in-little, earlier brought to perfection by Pope in *The Rape of the Lock*).

In this context *The Prelude* occupies a special position. Because it remained fifty-two years in manuscript – growing through different versions, changing through different phases of reworking – and because all the various stages are preserved at the Wordsworth Library, Grasmere, we know more about it than any other long poem in the language. There are more than fifty extant manuscripts of *Piers Plowman*, but they are the work of scribes, and only one seems likely to have been copied in Langland's lifetime. Though it now seems clear that the poem survives in four distinct versions, a great deal is guesswork. Only in the broadest terms can we discuss the stages of composition. With *The Prelude*, by contrast, the copyists are members of the family (the one exception being Wordsworth's clerk); all the different lifetime revisions are in some sense authenticated by the poet himself. Nine major fair copies survive, from MSS V and U, containing the text of the two-part *Prelude* as it stood in December 1799, to MS E, printer's copy for the posthumous first edition, transcribed almost exactly forty years later. Alongside these are eight further manuscripts of first-rate importance, beginning with JJ of autumn 1798 and the seminal poem 'Was It For This', from which *The Prelude* in all its many versions is developed.[1] Even this total could be increased by counting Wordsworth notebooks that include *Prelude* material without being part of the main stream of composition.

Since 1926 and the appearance of de Selincourt's parallel-text edition, criticism of *The Prelude* has been a tug-of-war between those who take the 1805 version to represent the poet's original intention (which it doesn't) and those who regard the first edition of July 1850 as being an authorized text (which it isn't). Underlying the discussion is a very narrow definition of revision – regarded simply as tinkering – and a good deal of confusion as to the nature of authority and intention. Insofar as authority consists in obedience to the wishes of the author, the tidiest example would presumably be a published text that the writer himself has seen through the press. The trouble is that *Jerusalem* (where author and printer are one) and *Leaves of Grass* (where the author had been a printer in his time) are the only long poems that certainly conform. Langland and Chaucer lived before the invention of printing (and were unable to keep control of scribal copies); Milton couldn't see the proofs; Byron saw some but not all (and, being in Italy, was too far away to prevent his publisher and friends taking liberties with the text); Wordworth was dead before the type was set up; Spenser just may have supervised publication of the 1596 *Faerie Queene*. Whether we like it or not, we have usually to fall back on printed texts that were unsupervised, and on manuscripts not made by the writer himself.

Regarded in this context, the 1805 *Prelude*, copied in the presence of the poet by his sister and wife, might seem to score over the posthumous first edition (*1850*), for which Wordsworth's executors made a number of unwarranted decisions, and which was anyhow printed from a very inaccurate manuscript. But this is to ignore the two most commonly invoked criteria of authenticity: lastness and excellence. According to the traditional view the writer retains even after publication a certain control over his work, bequeathing it to posterity in the shape that he finally chooses. Texts are willed, revisions have the force of codicils, and the last known document is sacrosanct.[2] Because of this time-honoured way of thinking no one seems to have asked why we all read the twelve-book second edition of *Paradise Lost* (1674), not the ten-book first of 1667. No one has reprinted the three-book *Faerie Queene* of 1590, though it concludes so beautifully in the coming together of Scudamour and Amoret (whereas the six-book version has no sense of an ending). No one has published *Troilus and Criseyde* from one of the manuscripts that retain the greatest love poem in English literature in what is surely its earlier form, without the weighty Boethian insertions.[3]

And yet there have been inconsistencies. Skeat, who did not as editor of Chaucer give to the world the early *Troilus and Criseyde*, did in 1886 publish Langland's *Piers Plowman* in three separate versions, *A* (1362–3), *B* (1377) and *C* (c. 1393). In doing so he made it clear (as de Selincourt was to do years later with *The Prelude*) that he regarded the poet's final revision as a mistake.[4] Following his lead, scholars have tended to cite the *B* text, over-riding in this instance the author's final intention in the name of quality, excellence. The rights of posterity, the readership, have for once been asserted.

Posterity and readership are rather vague terms; it may be worth pausing to ask who in practice decides for us the texts that we use. As perhaps one might expect, it is money that does the talking. The status of a text is decided not by the writer (dead or alive), not by a consensus of expert opinion, but by what the public will buy or the publisher can get most cheaply. Why, one might ask, do Americans tend to prefer (or think they prefer) the 1850 *Prelude* to *1805*, and British readers prefer (or think they prefer) *1805* to *1850*? The answer has little to do with quality and personal choice. Readers, by and large, continue to like best the version they first encounter. *1850* has long been out of copyright, and those who made the anthologies on which American students depend chose it because they did not wish to pay extra for the recently published early text. In Britain, meanwhile, the age of anthologies had not arrived; publication of Wordsworth was dominated by Oxford, and the Oxford editors not unnaturally fostered the sales of their new baby, *1805*.

The criterion of lastness has never been uniformly accepted, and in practice could never be enforced. As well as texts derived from manuscript, those from early printed volumes (reprints of *Lyrical Ballads*, for instance, in the case of Wordsworth) impinge on the principle that the author's final wishes are sacrosanct. People will buy and read what comes to hand. Nor should they do anything else. Good and bad texts will always exist (judged either in terms of scholarly consistency, or on aesthetic grounds), but I cannot see how there can be such a thing as right and wrong ones. Any text created by a writer at any point in his life is 'right', as long as it is scrupulously reproduced. To the best of my belief seventeen distinct versions of *The Prelude* can be detected in the manuscripts. Logically, of course, the alteration of a single word – even of a single comma – must create a new version; those I have in mind, however, appear to be thorough-going revisions, each of which for a time left the poet satisfied with the poem as a whole. The two-part *Prelude* of 1799 which I published in 1970 is now safely a part of the Wordsworth canon.[5] One of these days I shall reconstruct the exciting (and at least nearly completed) five-book version of March 1804.[6] The Cornell editor, meanwhile, is going into print with a text from MS C of 1816–19.[7] Good luck to him! Who knows, if it gets into the right anthologies it may catch on and be the *Prelude* of the future.

If *The Prelude* had been merely an account of Wordsworth's early life, there would have been no need for these periodic updatings. But it was also an embodiment of views and values that had to be brought into line as times changed, and he himself responded to change. Revision was a responsibility. The more so as Wordsworth came to accept that his poem was taking over from the uncompletable *Recluse* as the gift that he would bequeath to posterity. It is this aspect – the desire to make a prophetic statement, and the urge to get it right – that most clearly links *The Prelude* to the other great English long poems. They are of course a heterogeneous group: *Piers Plowman*, *The Faerie Queene*, and Blake's two 'Prophecies' take the form of allegory; *Troilus and Criseyde* is a love poem, and *Paradise Lost* a Christian epic; *The Prelude* and *Leaves of Grass* are variants of autobiography, studies of consciousness; *Don Juan* stands out as being largely comic. With their long periods of composition, however, and the intensity of their writers' commitment, they may have more in common than meets the eye.

Our knowledge of *The Prelude* makes a tempting basis on which to speculate on the nature of the long poem as such. Besides the obvious differences, there are remarkable similarities among the works that have been named. Blake's *Vala* seems to have begun in 1796–7 (as *The Prelude* began in 1798–9) as a relatively short poem. It was probably expanded to its full length in 1802–3[8] (as *The Prelude* was in 1804–5), but Blake was no more able than Wordsworth to leave his work alone. After the completion of *Milton* and *Jerusalem* he returned to it (as Wordsworth would many times return to *The Prelude*) in an attempt to bring his earlier self into line with a new redemptive thinking. Still closer is the parallel between Wordsworth and Langland. Again we have a poet who lived a long time, and could not relinquish his life's work. Printing the *A* text of *Piers Plowman* in 1886, Skeat showed it to be a distinct early version; now it appears that the neglected MS Z represents the poem at a still earlier stage – a stage that contains not merely unique lines and phrases, together with important anticipations of later thematic concerns, but which has (like the 1799 *Prelude*) its own formal integrity.[9]

To put Whitman alongside Langland and Wordsworth is to see this pattern taken to extremes. *Leaves of Grass* appeared in 1855 with twelve untitled and semi-continuous poems. 'To his first readers', Paul Zweig has commented enviably, 'they seemed not like poems at all, but arbitrary lengths of language, defying the impulse to form.'[10] In the second edition, a year later, there were thirty-two poems (now with titles). The great third edition of 1860 (in many ways the high-point of Whitman's inspiration) contained 156. In 1867 there were 236, and in the authorized 'death-bed' text of 1891 the total had risen to 293. Whitman's organic metaphor of the tree – with a 'series of successive growths, yet from one central or seed-purport'[11] – could be justified in that all later developments of his work spring from the 1855 'Song of Myself' (not so-titled till 1891). His 'growths', however, entailed constant reworking, reordering, renaming, pruning, and excision, as well as the accumulation of new poems. Revision, in the sense of changing authorial intention, seems to be inevitable in the making of a long poem. We know nothing of Langland's starting-point, and little enough of Blake's and Whitman's, but there is no possibility that any of these poets set out to create the work that finally emerged.

Certain writers do tell us of their intentions, but their statements serve merely to confirm the pattern of revision as making. Spenser in his 'Letter to Raleigh' of January 1589 offers a persuasive account of his plans for *The Faerie Queene*. There are to be twenty-four books, the first twelve concerning the 'private morall vertues' of Prince Arthur, the second designed to show his 'polliticke vertues . . . after that hee came to be king'.[12] It was a gigantic scheme, comparable to Chaucer's original hopes for the *Tales* (in which every pilgrim was to tell four stories, two on the way to Canterbury, two on the way back) – and no more practicable. In fact the letter to Raleigh was composed after the first three books of *The Faerie Queene*; like other prefaces and manifestos, it is part hopefulness and part rationalization. Comments in the *Amoretti* show that by 1594 Spenser had abandoned the second half of his scheme. Revision at a more basic level is to be seen in the fate of Scudamour and Amoret. At the end of the 1590 text (with three books completed) the lovers are united in the most moving poetry that Spenser ever wrote:

> Lightly he clipt her twixt his armes twaine,
> And streightly did embrace her body bright,
> Her body, late the prison of sad paine,
> Now the sweet lodge of love and deare delight;
> But she faire Lady overcommen quight
> Of huge affection, did in pleasure melt,
> And in sweete ravishment pourd out her spright:
> No word they spake, nor earthly thing they felt,
> But like two senceles stocks in long embracement dwelt.[13]

In 1596 Scudamour and Amoret are put asunder so that their union may form a climax in the narrative at a point never to be reached.

The 'Letter to Raleigh' resembles nothing so much as Wordsworth's retrospective comments on *The Prelude*, published in the 1814 Preface to *The Excursion*:

Several years ago, when the Author retired to his native Mountains, with the hope of being enabled to construct a literary Work that might live [*The Recluse*, of course, not the subsidiary *Prelude*], it was a reasonable thing that he should take a review of his own mind, and examine how far Nature and Education had qualified him for such employment. As a subsidiary to this preparation, he undertook to record, in Verse, the origin and progress of his own powers . . .

'The result of this investigation', Wordsworth continues impressively, 'was a determination to compose a philosophical Poem, containing Views of Man, Nature, and Society; and to be entitled *The Recluse* . . .' There follows the celebrated image of the *The Recluse* as the nave, or 'body', of a Gothic church, and *The Prelude* as 'ante-chapel'.[14]

Though he may at times be seen 'clinging to the palpable' (Coleridge's phrase), Wordsworth was not too much concerned with fact. Chronology is distorted in the *Excursion* Preface as contentedly as it is in the various poems that constitute his autobiography. Past events are reordered in the service of emotional and imaginative truth. *The Recluse*, we know, was planned (in March 1798) before, not after, work was begun on *The Prelude*. So far from being undertaken as the 'reasonable' consequence of the author's retiring to his native mountains, *The Prelude* was completed in its two-part form in early December 1799, just before he and Dorothy set up house in Grasmere. Wordsworth in his retrospect was telling his readers what might have happened, or what should have happened, not what did.

If it weren't for *Paradise Lost*, one might be tempted to conclude that no successful long poem ever turned out as the writer expected. With Milton we have for once the author's earliest thoughts, not a backward-looking preface. The fourth of Milton's drafts in the Trinity MS, written *c.* 1640, offers in surprising detail the plan for a tragic drama, *Adam Unparadised*:

The angel Gabriel . . . describes Paradise. Next the Chorus showing the reason of his coming to keep watch in Paradise after Lucifer's rebellion. [Gabriel] relates what he knew of man as the creation of Eve with their love, and marriage . . . Lucifer appears after his overthrow, bemoans himself, seeks revenge on man . . . the chorus sings of the battle, and victory in heaven against him . . . Man next and Eve having by this time been seduced by the serpent appears confusedly covered with leaves . . . the chorus bewails Adam's fall. Adam then and Eve return accuse one another . . . At last appears Mercy comforts him promises the Messiah . . . [15]

Eighteen years before the writing of *Paradise Lost*, Milton it seems had mapped out a work that was broadly similar. We even know from Edward Phillips that it was to have begun with a version of Satan's address to man in Book IV of the final poem:

> O thou that with surpassing glory crowned
> Look'st from thy sole dominion like the God
> Of this new world; at whose sight all the stars
> Hide their diminished heads; to thee I call,
> But with no friendly voice, and add thy name
> O sun, to tell thee how I hate thy beams
> That bring to my remembrance from what state
> I fell, how glorious once above thy sphere;
> Till pride and worse ambition threw me down
> Warring in heaven against heaven's matchless king . . .[16]

Yet even Milton revised his intentions. *Adam Unparadised* was after all to have been a play, not an epic. As projected in the Trinity MS, it was to have opened with the Archangel Gabriel and the viewpoint of Heaven; Satan's lines, seen by Phillips 'several years before the poem was begun', show Milton rethinking his original intention in order to give Satan the immediate prominence that he receives in *Paradise Lost* Book I. The self-abasement of his references to 'pride and worse ambition', 'heaven's matchless king', suggest an interim stage. Milton was working on a play that had more in common with the morality tradition than with Aeschylus and Sophocles. The signs point to an impersonal drama, where the handling of events was never likely to call into question eternal justice. Milton's sense that God's ways needed to be justified (if one thinks about it, the suggestion is blasphemous) was the result of bitter personal experience. Still more than Wordsworth he was let down by the revolution that ought to have worked. It is a fair bet that if the French in 1789 had achieved liberty, fraternity and equality, *The Prelude* would never have been written; but Wordsworth was let down by man, not God. In 1652 Milton lost his sight. In 1655 he had to resign his post as Secretary for Foreign Tongues (and with it his closeness to the Lord Protector and the centre of political power). In 1658, when the writing of *Paradise Lost* was probably begun, came the death of Cromwell. Two years more, and – despite Milton's pamphlets in defence of republicanism – the monarchy was restored. What had seemed to be the divinely ordained rule of the saints on earth gave place to the remarkably licentious court of Charles II.

Conceived by 1640, written apparently during 1658–63, published in 1667, *Paradise Lost* is a reminder that, whether directly autobiographical or not, the long poem becomes a record of a major portion of the author's life. Its composition embodies – sometimes indefinably, sometimes by direct allusion – changing personal and political situations, changing views, changing attitudes not least to the material of the poem itself. Even translation, predetermined if any literary work can be so, turns very soon into a process of revision. It used to be accepted that the absence of key passages from certain manuscripts of *Troilus and Criseyde* implied the existence of an early version (in which Chaucer stuck close to Boccaccio), followed by a text including his more Boethian second thoughts. The poem's recent editor, B.A. Windeatt, will have none of this. The introduction to his magnificent Longman parallel-text edition of *Troilus* and *Il Filostrato* discredits the manuscript evidence in favour of distinct versions, but seems at times a little categorical:

To say that *Troilus & Criseyde* existed for a while without its philosophical passages is comparable to saying that St Paul's Cathedral existed for a while without its dome: that is, until the plan implied by the rest of the structure was completed.[17]

'The plan implied by the rest of the structure' of *The Rape of the Lock* would certainly include the sylphs, whose attendance on Belinda is so important in the full-length poem of 1717. As, however, Pope chose to publish each of the three successive stages of the *Rape*, we can see that the sylphs were added in 1714 to the original two-canto version of 1712.[18] 'The plan implied' by the printed *Waste Land* would bear little resemblance to the mass of drafts from which Pound constructed Eliot's major work in 1922. Eliot's typescript begins with 'The Burial of the Dead' (section 3 of the first edition), and shows that Pound, with a little help from the author (and some from Vivian Eliot) cut away 254 lines from the drafts that were finally used. Included in the cuts is a feebly Joycean low-life sequence of fifty-four lines that delayed and masked what now seem to be the inspired and inevitable opening words: 'April is the cruellest month.'[19] All this finally imperceptible revision, despite the fact that *The Rape of the Lock* and *Waste Land* are short poems, a fraction of the length of *Troilus and Criseyde*, and taking a fraction of the time to write. 'The plan implied' by the structure of *The Prelude*, as published in fourteen books in 1850, would point to intentions that Wordsworth could not have dreamed of in 1798. Where no working drafts exist, it is dangerous (to say the least) to create the author's intention on the basis of his finished product.

If Chaucer had first planned to leave his cathedral without a dome, how could we hope to detect it? He could have erected and pulled down a succession of architectural features (or indeed complete buildings) without our knowledge. To do Windeatt justice, he does think of the composition of *Troilus* as 'layered'. The layers he perceives, however, are uncommonly orderly. Orderly, that is, until he comes to discuss the matter of transmission. Discrepancies in the manuscript are traced back to scribes (working during the poet's lifetime) who misunderstood their exemplars or had in front of them defective copies. Absent

Boethian passages had, we are asked to believe, been planned from the first, yet were inserted by Chaucer in such a way as to cause this scribal confusion (perhaps on separate pages that became lost).[20] No one has come up with a better explanation. Even so, the accretions, cells and oratories, of Wordsworth's gothic church seem quite as tempting a metaphor for the process of composition as Wren's all-of-a-piece, neo-Classical building.

Wordsworth's own edifice – *The Prelude*, not *The Recluse* – grows from the small Saxon church, represented at Goslar (in Saxony) by the poem 'Was It For This', into the cathedral of 1850. In the process the builder's earlier lofty aspirations are here and there diminished by Victorian restoration. Parts of the original Saxon church survive, but the later buildings are established upon a new foundation: the 'spots of time' doctrine, laid down in January 1799. As drafted in MS JJ, 'Was It For This' had had its own rather different basis. Though conscious that he depended upon an underlying strength, Wordsworth had yet to give it a name. The moment of composition is evocatively described in the Norton *Prelude*:

Starting at the end of a notebook later used by Dorothy for her *Journal* of spring 1802, working backwards and forwards in an irregular progression, and writing across or along the page as the fancy took him, Wordsworth in October–November 1798 made a series of drafts . . .[21]

It now seems to me that in writing this I laid too much stress on eccentricity, too little on the poet's instinctive giving of form. The physical characteristics of these drafts (the backwards and forwards progression, the fact that the opening words, 'was it for this', are a half-line and begin in the lower case) evoke so vividly an original creative moment that it is easy to ignore the form-giving rhetoric that is at work within the poet's urgent questioning: 'was it for this', 'For this didst thou, O Derwent', 'Was it for this that I, a four years child', 'For this in springtime . . . was I a rover then', 'For this . . . did I love / To range through half the night among the cliffs'.[22] Wordsworth wasn't planning, didn't know that he had embarked on what would come to seem his greatest work, yet from the first 'the shaping spirit of imagination' was exercising its control.

Insofar as Wordsworth had an intention in this first *Prelude* draft, it was probably to write himself through the block that was holding up his work on *The Recluse*. Yet very soon he found himself making a different, and quite new, kind of poem. After ninety-four lines he stopped, looked back – the prime act of re-vision – totted up what he had achieved, and set off again with a Miltonic denial that he had ever been at a loss:

Nor while, though doubting yet not lost, I tread
The mazes of this argument, and paint

> How Nature by collateral interest
> And by extrinsic passion peopled first
> My mind with beauteous objects, may I well
> Forget what might demand a loftier song . . .
>
> (98–103)

The mazes of what argument? None has been implied. One has emerged, however, in the backward glance of the reviser.

'What in me is dark, / Illumine', Milton had prayed at the outset of *Paradise Lost*,

> what is low raise and support;
> That to the heighth of *this great argument*
> I may assert eternal providence,
> And justify the ways of God to men.[23]

Wordsworth's concern in 'Was It For This' is no less determinist, no less to do with the shaping of the individual human being by higher forces. His allusion to Milton is twofold, however. Failing to comprehend the 'great argument' of eternal Providence, the fallen angels of *Paradise Lost* Book II find themselves 'in wandering mazes lost' as they reason of fate and free will.[24] By contrast, Wordsworth, like Milton himself (though not in his overtly Christian context), perceives a benevolent Providence at work:

> Ah, not in vain ye beings of the hills,
> And ye that walk the woods and open heaths
> By moon or star-light, thus, from my first day
> Of childhood, did ye love to interweave
> The passions that build up our human soul,
> Not with the mean and vulgar works of man,
> But with high objects, with eternal things,
> With life and Nature, purifying thus
> The elements of feeling and of thought,
> And sanctifying by such discipline
> Both pain and fear, until we recognize
> A grandeur in the beatings of the heart.
>
> (47–58)

We have in 'Was It For This' what nowhere else exists, the germ of one of the great English long poems. Perhaps the closest parallel is with Tennyson – not the poet of *Maud*, though that poem we know was formed, in 1854–5, around the existing (heterosexual) Hallam-lyric,

> O that 'twere possible
> After long grief and pain
> To find the arms of my true love,
> Round me once again![25]

Figure 1.1 *Was It For This*, the beginning of *The Prelude* in MS JJ (DC MS 19).

but the poet of *In Memoriam* who in 1833 began his seventeen-years' labour of love with the lines:

> Fair ship, that from the Italian shore
> Sailest the placid ocean-plains
> With my lost Arthur's loved remains,
> Spread thy full wings, and waft him o'er.
>
> So draw him home to those that mourn
> In vain; a favourable speed
> Ruffle thy mirrored mast, and lead
> Through prosperous floods his holy urn.
>
> All night no ruder air perplex
> Thy sliding keel, till Phosphor, bright
> As our pure love, through early light
> Shall glimmer on the dewy decks.
>
> Sphere all your lights, around, above;
> Sleep, gentle heavens, before thy prow;
> Sleep, gentle winds, as he sleeps now,
> My friend, the brother of my love;
>
> My Arthur, whom I shall not see
> Till all my widowed race be run;
> Dear as the mother to the son,
> More than my brothers are to me.

Christopher Ricks accepts a date of 6 October 1833 for this beautiful lyric (later to be section ix), though news of Hallam's death at Vienna on the 1st could have been known in Lincolnshire only for a matter of hours.[26] With no time to work things out, Tennyson, like the Wordsworth of 'Was It For This', established in his first few lines the form, the tone, the literary context, that would characterize his final yet-undreamt-of poem. It is interesting how both poets reach intuitively into the literary past as a means of placing the private emotion they have to confront. And both, of course, reach for Milton. Tennyson in his need turns to 'Lycidas', greatest of English personal elegies, and by chance also written to lament the death of a Cambridge friend. In a strangely reconciling image, 'the fatal and perfidious bark' cursed by Milton for the drowning of King in 1637 is transformed into a 'fair' and friendly ship, sailing on 'placid ocean-plains'. As the dolphins of 'Lycidas' were to 'waft' the 'hapless' body of King ('hurled', in Milton's fancy, 'beyond the stormy Herbrides'), so the benign ship will 'waft' 'lost Arthur's loved remains' back to his country for burial.

In drafting his opening lines –

> was it for this
> That one, the fairest of all rivers, loved
> To blend his murmurs with my nurse's song . . .
> For this didst thou,
> O Derwent . . .
> Give ceaseless music to the night and day . . .
> (1–9)

– Wordsworth had almost certainly been conscious of an allusion to Manoa in *Samson Agonistes*:

> For this did the angel twice descend, for this
> Ordain thy nurture holy, as of a plant
> Select and sacred?[27]

Failure to proceed with *The Recluse* ranges Wordsworth alongside the fallen Samson as one who has betrayed a God-given trust. Like Tennyson, however, he draws strength from giving form to his emotion, hallowing it with a place in literary tradition. With its reiteration of 'Was it for this?' the poetry insists on self-reproach, but the poet's confidence is no less impressive. As he goes back into memories of a favoured (though not conventionally happy) Cumbrian childhood, Wordsworth is asking at first what went wrong: why, given his sense of being the 'chosen son', was he unable to go ahead and write the great redemptive work that he and Coleridge had planned in the spring? But very soon 'Was It For This' becomes a quest for origins, an exploration that takes for granted the existence of internal sources of power.

At the centre of 'Was It For This' is a Platonist sequence of great importance, little of which remains in later *Prelude* versions. Here for the first time is a Wordsworthian myth of origins. The 'Eternal Spirit' to whom the poet addresses himself in autumn 1798 is

> he that has
> His life in unimaginable things,
> And he who, painting what he is in all
> The visible imagery of all the worlds,
> Is yet apparent chiefly as the soul
> Of our first sympathies . . .

'Oh bounteous power', Wordsworth continues,

> In childhood, in rememberable days,
> How often did thy love renew for me
> Those naked feelings which, when thou wouldst form
> A living thing thou sendest like a breeze
> Into its infant being. (104–14)

'Tintern Abbey' three months before had spoken of 'a motion and a spirit', capable of rousing in the poet 'the joy of elevated thoughts', yet wholly impersonal – 'deeply interfused', but indeterminate, a 'something'. Not so this 'soul of our first sympathies'. It is as an act of love that he inspires and sustains the child, guaranteeing him the imaginative renewal that is to Wordsworth above all precious.

Wordsworth had never written in this way before, and would never do so again. Platonism plays no part in the 'spots of time' sequence, inserted in his expanding poem in January 1799. The poet's thoughts are still on renewal and the role of memory, but his terms are secular now. His tones have the confidence of one who has discovered a formulation that works, a self-reliance that permits him to disengage his intuitions from transcendental ways of thinking:

> There are in our existence spots of time
> Which with distinct preeminence retain
> A fructifying virtue, whence, depressed
> By trivial occupations and the round
> Of ordinary intercourse, our minds
> (Especially the imaginative power)
> Are nourished and invisibly repaired.
>
> (*1799* I, 288–94)

It had taken a good deal of revision – backward-looking into the poem and into the past – to arrive at this formulation, but from the first it had been Wordsworth's hope to bring childhood and its imaginative powers to the aid of adult creativity.

From now on, as *Prelude* version succeeds version, the 'spots of time' will always be central. But the Eternal Spirit does not entirely disappear. He becomes transmuted, returning as the mother whose creative love enables the poet in *1799* Part II to 'trace the progress of our being':

> blest the babe
> Nursed in his mother's arms, the babe who sleeps
> Upon his mother's breast, who, when his soul
> Claims manifest kindred with an earthly soul,
> Doth gather passion from his mother's eye.
>
> (*1799* II, 269–73)

'Such feelings pass into his torpid life', Wordsworth adds, 'Like an awakening breeze'. The 'bounteous' Platonic 'power', so tender in his ministrations –

> In childhood, in rememberable days,
> How often did thy love renew for me
> *Those naked feelings*, which, when thou wouldst form

31

> A living thing thou sendest *like a breeze*
> Into it infant being . . .
>
> (111–14)

– has become the credible human mother, source of love, and source therefore of strength.

It should be said that Wordsworth's assumptions were probably unaltered. He was always broadly a religious thinker, but never a dogmatic one. Rather than suddenly becoming a Platonist, suddenly taking up a humanist position, he finds different ways to understand unchanging intuitions – and different ways to give them form. By recreating his myth of origins in human terms, however, he brought the poetry closer to 'the world of eye and ear', the world in which he had himself 'held mute dialogues with [his] mother's heart' (*1799* II, 313). Part I of *1799* had been concerned with childhood and the sublime, and concluded in the death of the poet's father; Part II has as its overall theme adolescence and the growing awareness of Nature. (The presence of the Infant Babe at its centre is perhaps to be explained by an association of the maternal and the beautiful.) *1799* was completed in early December, just before the move to Dove Cottage, with a touching and appropriate farewell to Coleridge, whose 'Frost at Midnight' had first caused the poet's thoughts to stray to his 'sweet [Cumbrian] birthplace' beside the Derwent.[28] It is a great poem in its own right, and though Wordsworth left open the option of continuing it, he got his helpers to tidy it away into duplicate fair copies (as he did with the thirteen-book version in 1805–6) and turned his mind to other things.

In the context of *The Prelude* as a whole the two-part poem may be seen, like the *Z* text of *Piers Plowman*, as establishing the writer's idiom, setting up within a brief work that has its own integrity the themes and preoccupations that will sustain longer and later versions. Because of what appeared to be its inconsistency, *Z* was thought of until 1983 as a corrupt late manuscript pieced together by a scribe from different sources. The brilliant analysis of George Rigg and Charlotte Brewer, however, leaves no doubt (at least for anyone used to comparing manuscripts and dating stages of composition) that it precedes the text of *A*. Rigg and Brewer argue that *Z* is a corrected fair copy of Langland's earliest version of *Piers Plowman*, transcribed in Oxford *c.* 1376–88 by a certain John Wells of Gloucester College.[29] It offers the dreamer's first two visions (the 'fair field of folk' and the ploughing of Piers's half-acre), just as *1799* offers what come to be the first two books of *The Prelude*. In neither case does the author have any apparent intention to produce a longer work.

Interestingly this early Langland version ends with acceptance of the pardon, which Piers in the *A* and *B* texts tears up 'for pure tene' (vowing as he does so, 'I schal sese of my sowynge and swynke not so harde').[30] The tearing, it seems, is a revision, made when Langland decides to extend his poem into a third vision, introducing the allegory of Dowel, Dobet, and Dobest.[31] It is a fair assumption that this moment of backward-looking and reassessment as a prelude to expansion is typical of the writers of long poems. The poet, who has been composing strongly under the initial impulse, brings his work to a conclusion (or stopping-point), then takes it up again with a new sense of the need to plan.

Byron's case is especially interesting. The first mention of *Don Juan* is as a 'ludicrous' story, 'à la Beppo' (10 July 1818). It is 'in no hurry' to be finished, but no more than Wordsworth (or Tennyson, or Langland) does Byron know that he has embarked on his greatest work. After publication of the first two Cantos, he writes to Murray: 'You ask me for the plan of Donny Johnny – I *have* no plan – I *had* no plan – but I have or had materials . . .' (12 August 1819). Allowance has to be made for bravura, but there seems to be truth in his comment. The said 'materials' carried him through the Julia and Haidée episodes of Cantos I–IV, with no evidence of planning. After sending the fifth canto off to Kinnaird, however, in December 1820, Byron is suddenly in a position to map out for Murray an elaborate and credible plan. Like Giovanni, his Italian counterpart, Juan will be sent to perdition, but via a satirical tour of Europe and a hero's death on the guillotine. Murray, who had been alarmed by the reception of Cantos I–II, and was dragging his feet over publication of III–V, would not have been too sorry if Donny Johnny had been curtailed at once. The fifth canto, Byron tells him with evident mischief on 16 February 1821, 'is so far from being the last of D.J., that it is hardly the beginning'. 'I meant', he continues (apparently using the past tense to describe his position during the writing of Canto V),

to take him the tour of Europe – with a proper mixture of siege – battle – and adventure – and to make him finish as *Anarcharsis Cloots* [guillotined 1794] – in the French revolution. – To how many cantos this may extend – I know not – nor whether (even if I live) I shall complete it – but this way was my notion. – I meant to have made him a Cavalier Servente in Italy and a cause for divorce in England – and a Sentimental 'Werther-faced man' in Germany – so as to show the different ridicules of the society in each of those countries – and to have displayed him gradually gaté and blasé as he grew older – as is natural. – But I had not quite fixed whether to make him end in Hell – or an unhappy marriage, – not knowing which would be the severest. – The Spanish tradition says Hell – but it is probably only an Allegory of the other state. – You are now in possession of my notions on the subject.[32]

As is well known, Wordsworth, who had written the opening of a third part for the 1799 *Prelude* in December 1801 (bringing his story down to the Cambridge period), decided early in 1804 to make a longer version for Coleridge to take with him to the Mediterranean. On 4 January there was an open-air reading 'in the highest and outermost of Grasmere' (chilly, one might think, for a man believed to be dying) of what Coleridge termed 'the second Part of [Wordsworth's] divine Self-biography'.[33] To make his longer poem Wordsworth had only to continue the narrative from the point he had reached. He didn't, however; he embarked on a revision of Part I that led to a complete restructuring. His decision to move the 'spots of time' from Part (or Book) I of *1799* to the end of the new version can be seen in different ways. Reworking the sequence as it stood in MS V, Wordsworth was no doubt impressed by its power, and aware that a longer poem would need a strong conclusion. More important, the 'spots' would have brought home the extent to which he himself had changed in the five summers, and five long winters, since January 1799. The sequence had been written in Germany to authenticate the link he sensed between 'primordial feeling' and adult creativity. Now, in the less confident period of 'Intimations' and 'Ode to Duty', the Goslar thinking would have to bear a heavier weight. The poet's sense of loss had become more acute. He needed more urgently to believe that

> feeling comes in aid
> Of feeling, and diversity of strength
> Attends us if but once we have been strong.
> (*1805* XI, 325–7)

The five-book *Prelude* of January–March 1804 is the first structured version of the poem. Like the Langland who makes Piers tear his pardon, and moves on into the allegory of Dowel, Dobet, and Dobest (and like the Byron who can see in his mind's eye Donny Johnny's tour of Europe and final mounting of the scaffold), Wordsworth has made a fresh start, seen his task in new and larger terms. Perhaps inevitably, this means Miltonic terms. The five-book *Prelude* brings together in a single structure the loss and regaining of paradise. A version of the 'paradise within' (promised to Adam by the Archangel Michael in spite of the Fall)[34] is to be attained in adulthood through the power of imagination, and is offered as a Wordsworthian recompense for loss of the Eden of childhood. To put it in Blakean terms, innocence is followed by experience (as Wordsworth travels south into the lazy sophistication of Cambridge), and finally by the higher innocence of imaginative vision. The first three books of this intermediate *Prelude* are preserved as *1805* I–III; Book IV was a shorter version of *1805* IV and V; Book V opened with the Climbing of Snowdon and ended with the 'spots of time'. In the unique arrangement of this final book we mount to the high places of adult imagination, then descend to learn in the 'spots' how it is that vision has been preserved.[35]

Impressive as it was, the five-book *Prelude* didn't last long. It may or may not have been complete (we are talking about a few lines of transition, lacking in the fair copy of MS W) when in early March 1804 Wordsworth decided to work towards a still longer poem. Book IV was split in two (as the original Canto III of *Don Juan* was split in two), and Coleridge received in London, before he sailed, a version of the first five books of *1805*. There is no likelihood that Wordsworth knew the eventual shape of his poem, but at this stage he set on one side both the 'spots of time' and the Climbing of Snowdon, moving on – this time in a chronological progression – into the Continental Tour of 1790. Following the great work of Steffan's *Variorum Don Juan*, the composition of *The Prelude* ought some day to be tabulated. Perhaps the tables could be plotted as graphs. It should be possible to show not just what passages were written for which versions, and how they were later moved, but what is the relation of composition to the onward narrative of the poem. Dealing in terms of books, it is sufficiently odd that the sequence for March–December 1804 was VI, IX, VIII, VII, X. But this is too crude a measurement. Of the thirteen books of *1805*, only IX and X (for which we have no working drafts) may possibly have been written straight through in the order of the final text. All the others contain earlier material; IV, V, XI, XII and XIII, a great deal of it.

It is an intriguing thought that Blake may, at the very moment when Wordsworth was reconstructing *The Prelude*, have been engaged in the remaking of his own epic psychological poem. *Vala* is surely the most beautiful and most enigmatic of all holograph manuscripts. Described on the title-page as 'A Dream of Nine Nights by William Blake 1797', the poem opens with forty-one pages (almost three 'Nights') on large quarto sheets in Blake's most elegant copper-plate hand.[36] In the margins are designs for illustrations, mostly in pencil; the title and nine other pages are (in varying degrees) touched with watercolour. So far, so good. Blake is making his poem ready for engraving. The paper is Whatman 1794 (surplus sheets, bought for the engraving of Young's *Night Thoughts*); the title is dated 1797. Handsome as the manuscript is, however, it does not in its present state offer us a dependable text, either of 1797, or of a later stage. Blake completes his poem on proof-sheets of the *Night Thoughts* illustrations. The paper is identical, yet he now crams twice as many lines to the page and has abandoned his copperplate. The presence of his engravings (some of them apparently chosen for their relevance to *Vala*) ensures that the manuscript remains extraordinarily elegant; it is, however, downgraded before our eyes from prepared copy, to less careful transcription, to heavily corrected pages, with erasures in the text and insertions in the margins. No part of the manuscript is sacred.

De Quincey's famous image of the palimpsest supposes not merely that 'no such thing as forgetting is possible to the human mind', but that the different layers of text within a manuscript can all be retrieved.[37] Maybe they can if they are classical texts on carefully scraped vellum, but no such thing is possible for *Vala*. It is as though our evidence for the four stages of *Piers Plowman* were concentrated into a single volume. The existence of *Z* (a brief ur-*Vala*, following closely on the *Book of Urizen*) would have to be inferred; *A* (the first extensive *Vala*, presumably of 1797) is clearly represented by the original stage, or layer, of the fair copy, but cannot be recovered as a whole because pages have been reordered, sections inserted, corrections made over erasure; *B* (a full-length *Vala*, written presumably at Felpham, shortly before *Milton* and *Jerusalem*) is there all right, but no text can ever be agreed as the sequence of Blake's reworkings is too hard to determine (there are, for instance, two versions of Night the Seventh); finally, *C* (a late revision, in which *Vala* is to be called *The Four Zoas* and brought into line with the redemptive thinking of *Jerusalem*) complicates our attempts to retrieve the earlier texts, but was never completed.

G. E. Bentley has remarked that if Blake was indeed taking down *Vala* from divine dictation, he received some pretty contradictory instructions. Less whimsically he points to Blake's 'lamentable' failure to take his own advice: 'Let a man who has made a drawing go on & on, & he will produce a Picture or Painting, but if he chooses to leave it before he has spoil'd it, he will do a Better Thing.'[38] Multiple reworkings have given us in *Vala* a perfect case of revision as making. The poem conforms to none of the artificial criteria beloved of scholars and editors. We have no statement of the author's intention, no published text, no single completed text, just an example of work in progress. We may think that Blake should have stopped at a certain stage, as de Selincourt thought that Wordsworth should have stopped at *1805*, but there is no point at which we can say that composition ceased, and revision began.

Can there indeed be a logical distinction between the two activities? 'As there are now several editions of L. of G.', Whitman wrote in his Prefatory Letter of 1889, 'I wish to say that I prefer and recommend the present one, complete . . . the text of these 422 pages.'[39] Like Wordsworth, Whitman had created an inspired early version of his life's work ('I do not suppose I shall ever again have the *afflatus* I had in writing the first *Leaves of Grass*'), then gone on to make and remake his work in a nearly continuous process. Where the many *Preludes* remained in manuscript, *Leaves of Grass* was reissued at each successive stage. Those who imagine that revision may be distinguished from creation have nine published texts on which to ground their case. Each is authorized, and for the time final; each, except the first, is created on the basis of its predecessor. The history of the long poem serves to emphasize that composition is in its nature backward-looking. Every time a poet seeks for the right word, he revises an earlier expression, on paper or within the mind. Every time he seeks to clarify an idea, he revises an earlier conscious thought, an earlier pre-verbal hunch. The organization, not just of poetry, but of language, and thought itself, is comparative – a moving forward by an endless process of substitution, rejection of that which exists in favour of that which is brought into being.

On a small scale the process is enacted for us in every draft of *The Prelude*, and every revised fair copy. On a larger one, revision creates each successive version of the poem, from the ninety-four lines totted up as Wordsworth first looks backward in 'Was It For This', through to the thirteen-book text of 1805. Except, of course, that there isn't a thirteen-book text of 1805. Wordsworth announces his completion of *The Prelude* in a letter to Beaumont on 3 June: 'I have pleasure to say that I finished my Poem about a fortnight ago.' Dorothy on 29 November is more circumspect:

I am now engaged on making a fair and final transcript of the Poem on his own Life. I mean *final*, till it is prepared for the press, which will not be for many years. No doubt before that time he will, either from the suggestions of his Friends or his own or both have some alterations to make, but it appears to us at present to be finished.

Dorothy had been her brother's amanuensis now for eleven years. She knew that 'finished' was not a word to be used of manuscript poems. Friends of the poet (notably Coleridge, to whom *The Prelude* was addressed), the poet himself, or both, would make their changes whatever she might do. In the event Wordsworth reworked the text extensively as she and Mary made their twin, but not identical, fair copies. Dorothy's is normally (not quite always) the master copy; it would seem logical that if we can't retrieve the 1805 *Prelude* that Wordsworth thought of as finished in May, we should take the one that she completed under his direction ten months later (February 1806).

Wordsworth didn't stop making changes, however, and at the end of the year there was Coleridge's long-awaited return from Malta. 1807 opened with the Coleorton reading of *The Prelude*, Coleridge's writing of 'To William Wordsworth', and (as Dorothy had foreseen) more alterations. These might, of course, be excluded from a text of *1805*, except that Dorothy (like Blake in the early revisions of *Vala*) attempted to keep MS A looking nice by making corrections over erasure. No two editors will come up with the same text of the thirteen-book *Prelude* (or of any *Prelude*, for that matter), but the earliest year by which the poem might correctly be identified is 1807. Whether Wordsworth really put the work out of his thoughts at that moment there is no means of telling. Letters from members of the family tell us of the periodic major updatings, but it may be that we should imagine a more or less continuous process. Non-publication of *The Prelude* denied Wordsworth fame, denied his age what would surely have been the most influential work since *Paradise Lost* – imagine if Shelley and Keats had been able to read it (or the Byron of *Childe Harold* Canto III) – but it permitted the poet to hug his earlier self to himself. He didn't work on it all the time, but nor did he have to think of it as gone, detached, grown up. This was a child that he could keep at home.

The *Prelude* is about creativity, about the sustaining of early power, about drawing nourishment from it for the adult's diminishing vision. But it is a young man's poem. By 1804 the Goslar work of 1798 had acquired for the backward-looking poet a special intensity; soon the entire poem would come to be associated not with the adult who needed to draw strength, but with the powers of youth itself. Revision was a going back into the glow of earlier creativity, a sharing in 'youth's golden gleam'. Wordsworth had always been a storer-up (the second visit to Tintern Abbey was expected to bring 'life and food for future years'); by maintaining *The Prelude* as a work in-progress he was able to partake of 'the spirit of the past', so carefully 'enshrine[d] . . . for future restoration' (*1805* XI, 341–2). Had he been able to lay the poem aside it would have become 'Exposed and lifeless as a written book' (*1805* VIII, 727); instead it remained for him a living thing, a work with which he was actively, creatively, in relationship.[40] Changes and reworkings – insertion, for instance, in 1832, of the section 'Genius of Burke' (*1850* VII, 512–43) – reflect, as at earlier stages, changes in and around the poet. But they were made, as they would have been made by almost all these long-poem poets, from a sense of duty, the respect that is owing to truth. 'My Book and I', Whitman wrote in 1888, 'what a period we have presumed to span! those thirty years from 1850 to '80 – and America in them! Proud, proud indeed may we be.'[41]

Revision is not to be dismissed as tinkering and it is not in itself the cause of the weakening of *The Prelude*. It is a truism that Wordsworth lived too long, but Stevens lived a long time too, and gets better and better; Chaucer went on from *Troilus and Criseyde* to write *The Canterbury Tales*. Like Langland, whose *C* text greatly resembles the neatened *Prelude* of 1850, Wordsworth remains true to himself, remains creative, but becomes a less interesting person. Unlike Langland (and Whitman), he also lives into less interesting times. When he changes *1805* XI, 233–4, 'I worshipped then among the depth of things / As my soul bade me', into *1850* XII, 184–5, 'among the depth of things / As piety ordained', or tells us that man is 'born / Of dust, and kindred to the worm' (*1850* VIII, 487–8), it is the voice of Victorian Anglicanism that is speaking. In a poem that depends from the first on the interaction of selves, the changing of viewpoints, Wordsworth could not be wrong to reflect new ways of thinking and changes in himself.

Probably he didn't think of either himself or his poem as changing greatly. In making *The Excursion* of 1814 he had seen no incongruity in using pantheist lines written for *The Recluse* in 1798. Many things are retained in the final *Prelude* that one might have expected to go at an early stage – comments about the French Revolution, for instance, and the poet's astonishing claims, about the 'glory' of his youth, the 'divinity' of his mind:

> Of genius, power,
> Creation and divinity itself
> I have been speaking, for my theme has been
> What passed within me.
>
> (*1805* III, 171–4)

The Climbing of Snowdon, though, has to be muted. The new poetry, with 'Its voices issuing forth to silent light / In one continuous stream' (*1850* XIV, 73–4), is not all bad, but nothing can mask the loss of the 'mighty mind'

> that feeds upon infinity,
> That is exalted by an under-presence,
> The sense of God, or whatso'er is dim
> Or vast in its own being.
>
> (*1805* XIII, 69–73)

This is what *The Prelude* has been about. Perhaps the ageing Wordsworth knew this, and wished to obscure it (as the ageing Langland removed Piers's too assertive tearing of the pardon); but I rather think he no longer knew.[42]

Saddest of all the revisions that make the final *Prelude* – and truest to the new diminished self – must be the 1850 conclusion to the 'spots of time'. 'I do not doubt', Wordsworth had written categorically in 1799,

> That in this later time, when storm and rain
> Beat on my roof at midnight, or by day
> When I am in the woods, unknown to me
> The workings of my spirit thence are brought.
>
> (*1799* I, 370–4)

As in the revisions of Snowdon, there is about the 1850 text a 'shameful garrulity' (*Samson Agonistes*), but that is not the major point. Listen for the final lines. The 'spots of time', which have supported each successive version of *The Prelude* with their theory of the imagination nourished and inspired by early experience, have dwindled to the memories of an old-age pensioner – a way to 'animate an hour of vacant ease':

> on winter nights,
> Down to this very time, when storm and rain
> Beat on my roof, or, haply, at noon-day,
> While in a grove I walk, whose lofty trees,

Laden with summer's thickest foliage, rock
In a strong wind, some workings of my spirit,
Some inward agitations thence are brought,
Whate'er their office, whether to beguile
Thoughts over busy in the course they took,
Or animate an hour of vacant ease.

(*1850* XII, 326–35; my italics)

Within weeks of the poet's death on St George's Day 1850, his son-in-law, Edward Quillinan, his nephew, Christopher Wordsworth, and his clerk, John Carter, were carrying out *their* quite unwarranted revisions (I like to think that my great-grandfather was the villain of the piece). In July *The Prelude* was published. As far as I can see, we can read whatever text we please – as long as we don't think it's the right one. There could be no such thing.

NOTES

1 A text of 'Was It For This' will be presented in the forthcoming Longman Annotated Selection of Wordsworth, ed. Jonathan Wordsworth, Nicola Trott and Duncan Wu; meanwhile, references are given for convenience to the Norton Critical Edition of *The Prelude*, ed. Jonathan Wordsworth, M. H. Abrams and Stephen Gill (New York, 1979), pp. 487–90.

2 Whitman speaks of his 'Backward Glance O'er Travel'd Roads' (1888) as a 'testament – my hurried epilogue of intentions-bequest' (*Leaves of Grass*, Reader's Edition, ed. Harold W. Blodgett and Sculley Bradley (New York, 1973), p. 559). For his bequeathing to posterity of the 'death-bed' text, see below, p. 36.

3 It should be said that B. A. Windeatt, editor of the superb Longman edition of *Troilus and Criseyde* (London and New York, 1984), has argued that the Boethian sequences were intended from the first; see below, pp. 25–6.

4 'On the whole it is inferior to the B-text in general vigour and compactness', *Piers the Plowman*, ed. W. W. Skeat, 2 vols. (Oxford, 1886), Vol. 2, p. xiv. De Selincourt's very just views are quoted at length, Norton *Prelude*, p. 524.

5 As are *The Ruined Cottage* and *The Pedlar*, both of which appeared first in *The Music of Humanity* (London, 1969). First publication of the two-part *Prelude* (*1799* in future references) was in *The Poems of William Wordsworth*, selected and ed. Jonathan Wordsworth, Limited Editions Club (Cambridge, 1973).

6 See Jonathan Wordsworth, 'The Five-Book *Prelude* of Early Spring 1804', *Journal of English and Germanic Philology* 76, no. 1 (1977), pp. 1–25.

7 Mark Reed, forthcoming Cornell Wordsworth Series edition of the thirteen-book *Prelude*.

8 Erdman's terminal date of 1807 (*Complete Poetry and Prose of William Blake* (Berkeley, 1982), p. 817) seems to be playing unnecessarily safe.

9 See *Piers Plowman: The Z Version*, ed. A. G. Rigg and Charlotte Brewer, Pontifical Institute of Mediaeval Studies (Toronto, 1983).

10 *Walt Whitman, The Making of the Poet* (New York, 1984), p. 241.

11 1876 Preface, Blodgett and Bradley, p. 749.

12 *The Faerie Queene* (1590), p. 592; ed. A. C. Hamilton, Longman Annotated Poets (London, 1977), p. 737.

13 1590, pp. 588–9; Hamilton edition, p. 421.

14 1814 *Excursion*, pp. viii–ix.

15 *Poems of John Milton*, ed. John Carey and Alistair Fowler, Longman Annotated Poets (London and Harlow, 1968), pp. 420–1.

16 *Paradise Lost* IV, 32–41.

17 Windeatt edition, p. 51.

18 A plan deduced from the four-book *Dunciad* would of course fail to detect Pope's change of hero from Theobald (1728) to Cibber (1743).

19 See *The Waste Land: A Facsimile*, ed. Valerie Eliot (London, 1971).

20 Windeatt edition, p. 39.

21 Norton *Prelude*, p. 485.

22 The last two of these questions (forming introductions to the woodcock-snaring and birds'-nesting episodes) are cut in *1799*, reducing the sequence from five to three.

23 *Paradise Lost* I, 22–6.

24 *Paradise Lost* II, 558–61.

25 *Maud* Part II, section iv, 1–4.

26 *Poems of Tennyson*, ed. Christopher Ricks, 2nd ed., 2 vols., Longman Annotated Poets (Harlow, 1987), Vol. 2, pp. 304–5.

27 *Samson Agonistes* 361–3.

28 At line 8 of 'Was It For This' Wordsworth quotes 'Frost at Midnight' 32–3 (1798 text, Woodstock Books), 'already had I dreamt / Of my sweet birthplace'. In *Fears in Solitude*, a Woodstock Facsimile (Oxford, 1989), p. 20.

29 Rigg and Brewer *Piers Plowman: The Z Version*, 3–5; it should be noted that evidence for the early date of Z does not depend upon Wells having been the transcriber.

30 A-text, passus viii, 102 (B, passus vii, 117).

31 For a convincing new discussion of the growth of Langland's poem, that takes Z into account, see Malcolm Godden, *The Making of Piers Plowman* (London, 1990), pp. 3–5.

32 *Byron's Letters and Journals*, ed. Leslie A. Marchand, 12 vols. (London, 1973–82), Vol. 8, p. 78.

33 *Notebooks of Samuel Taylor Coleridge*, ed. Kathleen Coburn, 3 vols. (Princeton, 1973), Vol. 1, entry 1801.

34   then wilt thou not be loath
        To leave this Paradise, but shalt possess
        A paradise within thee, happier far.
                (Paradise Lost XII, 585–7)

35 See Jonathan Wordsworth, *William Wordsworth: The Borders of Vision* (Oxford, 1982), pp. 325–46.

36 See G. E. Bentley Jr's huge and magnificent facsimile of *Vala*; also David Erdman, *Complete Blake*, pp. 816–18.

37 *Collected Writings of Thomas De Quincey*, ed. David Masson, 15 vols. (London, 1862–78), Vol. 8, pp. 346–7.

38 Bentley, *Vala*, p. 157.
39 Blodgett and Bradley edition, p. xxvii.
40 Southey makes the point in a less friendly way, commenting to Crabb Robinson in July 1811:

[Wordsworth] has by him poems that would be universally admired, but he has a miserly feeling concerning them, as if by being published they would cease to be his own.

In the same entry Robinson adds, 'Southey . . . blamed his not publishing his great poem on his own life' (*Henry Crabb Robinson on Books and their Writers*, ed. Edith J. Morley, 3 vols. (London, 1983), Vol. 1, p. 41).
41 Blodgett and Bradley edition, p. 565.
42 For a detailed comparison of the 1805 and 1850 Snowdon texts, see *Borders of Vision*, pp. 327–31.

2

WORDSWORTH'S POEMS: THE QUESTION OF TEXT

STEPHEN GILL

'WHY can't you people get it right?' This question was put to me in exasperation after I had happily spent many summers 'working on' Wordsworth's texts at the Dove Cottage library in Grasmere. There I had discussed with more experienced scholars the priority of manuscripts, the significance of autographs, the difference between interlined and overwritten corrections, drafts, versions, states. I had shared the excitement of our little group when Professor so-and-so recovered through infra-red examination what the poet had obviously wanted to obliterate, and rejoiced when another professor found in a bookshop a previously unrecorded printing of *The Excursion*. Every summer brought new discoveries and promised more to occupy summers to come. To my questioner, however, the whole business seemed baffling. He knew Wordsworth's poems certainly as well as any of the academics assiduously transcribing manuscripts, but as a non-professional was prepared to recognize that if so many scholars needed to spend time on Wordsworth's texts there must be a problem. What he wanted to know was simply why such amassed brainpower couldn't put it right. Wordsworth had been dead for 125 years and eminent scholars had already spent years preparing multi-volume editions earlier in the century. What on earth was the difficulty?

It seemed to me at the time a reasonable question for anyone to put to an editor of Wordsworth, and it still does.

II

Since the distinctly muted centennial appraisals in 1950 critical interest in Wordsworth has returned in strength and he is once again the inevitable poet for anyone concerned with Romanticism. A very odd situation, however, currently exists. First, there is no authoritative edition of the poems. No edition records all of what he wrote, and even the magnificent work of Ernest de Selincourt and Helen Darbishire which comes nearest to that goal is, as is widely recognized, incomplete, inaccurate, and at times misleading.[1] Second, not one of the numerous compilations of the poems currently used by students can be recommended without most serious reservation. Can this be true of any other poet of Wordsworth's stature? Third, there is no bibliography. Exact information about what Wordsworth published, or authorized for publication, the prerequisite for any full edition of the poems, is not available. Booksellers refer to 'Healey' or to 'Wise', but these listings are catalogues of collections, not bibliographies, and even as such cannot be relied on totally for comprehensiveness or for accuracy.[2]

In recent years, of course, much textual work has been done, focused, as it must be, on the archive of Wordsworth manuscripts in the library at Grasmere. John O. Hayden has edited the complete poetical works in two convenient volumes. Jonathan Wordsworth introduced *The Ruined Cottage* and *The Pedlar* into the canon in 1969 and, with others, has published an edition of *The Prelude* which for the moment supersedes all others as a student text. The Cornell Wordsworth, under the general editorship of Stephen Parrish, has set the highest standards of accuracy and completeness in the presentation of selected texts.[3] These two latter editions present so much material, however, and reveal in their introductions and notes, as well as imply by their very format, such complexities in Wordsworth's manuscripts and published texts, that teachers, let alone their students looking for the cheapest reliable edition, can be forgiven for being confused and daunted.

Problems of text, however, face anyone reading Wordsworth, from scholar-critic to essay-writing student, and it is essential that all should understand the issues and what the significance is of decisions editors have made. What follows aims to be an elementary account of the major problems. It does not attempt to settle bibliographical or textual questions or to dictate the form of some future perfect edition, but attempts to map out areas of potential confusion and to explain why my friend's 'Why can't you people get it right?' is a good question, but one not easily answered.

III

During the last twenty years of the nineteenth century two professors were waging war over the text of Wordsworth's poetry. Both paid homage to the poet as 'teacher and inspirer during many years' and saw their labours as tribute due. William Knight issued his eight-volume edition of *The Poetical Works of William Wordsworth* between 1882 and 1886 and was answered by Edward

Dowden in seven identically titled volumes in 1892–3; he was counter-attacked in turn by Knight with another eight-volume assault in 1896.[4] In these prodigal feats of publishing the commentary was as civilized as the volumes were handsome, but it contained much designed to wound, for both scholars were zealots in a cause.[5] Their aim was to lay out texts for study in a manner which would most comprehensively, most appropriately, above all most effectively present the teacher-poet to a generation sorely in need of his ministry. Their disagreements were over method, but on one thing they agreed implicitly, that Wordsworth had to be saved from complexities of his own making. The conflict they began has not yet been decided, and as more material has become available, our awareness of those complexities has increased.

Between 1793 and 1849–50 Wordsworth published fifteen new volumes of verse (this count excludes reprint editions of *Lyrical Ballads*, *The Excursion*, *Yarrow Revisited*, selections, and pamphlets such as *Grace Darling*). From 1815 he also published nine collected editions (this count excludes reprints, American and other unauthorized editions). These collections, however, do not merely gather into uniform format poems published in the separate-title volumes, but include new work not previously issued. Thus, as T. J. Wise observed, each can claim to be an *editio princeps*, with the six volumes of 1849–50, which include new poems, claiming final authority as the poet's last revised text. Over this formidable number of editions and the ever-expanding quantity of verse Wordsworth exercised very great care in correction and revision, the editions of 1815, 1836, and 1845 moving him to particular labour and vigilance.[6] He clearly had a strong sense of the book, of the identity of, for example, *Poems, in Two Volumes* or *Yarrow Revisited*, but an even stronger sense of organization within the collected editions. From 1815 onwards arrangements designed to 'assist the attentive Reader in perceiving their connection with each other' determined the presentation of the shorter poems.[7] Exceptions to this non-chronological ordering were made for *Poems, Chiefly of Early and Late Years* (1842); new categories were added to those of 1815; poems were moved from one category to another; and by the collected editions of the 1840s the overall scheme was looking increasingly ramshackle. But such organization clearly was habitual to Wordsworth. A recently acquired Dove Cottage manuscript shows that as late as 1845 he was pondering on a series of 'Morning Voluntaries' to counterpoint the 'Evening Voluntaries' established ten years before and thinking of plucking 'To my Sister' out of *Poems of Sentiment and Reflection* to rest in the new category next to poems composed no less than forty years after it.[8]

Nothing could reveal more clearly than this continued labour at arrangement how steadily Wordsworth thought of his poetry as a unity, which might change shape, colour, and texture yet still remain 'workings of one mind, the features / Of the same face, blossoms upon one tree'.[9] His habits of revision suggest that he increasingly saw individual poems in the same way, as discrete entities on first publication yet open to evolution within the greater evolving order of the whole. That Wordsworth revised his work continually has always been commented on. His text, said Dowden, is of especial interest 'because it received from him the studious superintendence of a lifetime . . . Wordsworth's mode of poetical creation was one which favoured a return upon his own work.'[10] I do not think anyone, however, has pointed out not just the frequency of Wordsworth's revisions but their variety, or attempted to formulate the kinds of difficulty his habits of composition and publication can cause 'the attentive Reader', or an editor anxious to present the poems in the most intelligible and helpful way possible.

Wordsworth's practice of tinkering with published poems could be ascribed to what de Selincourt called 'the true artist's search for perfection'.[11] The less charitable (or romantic) might call it substitution, a way of avoiding sustained work on *The Recluse*. Whatever the cause, it was compulsive. His inability to leave texts alone caused illness, domestic friction, and personal fretfulness ('The annoyance of this sort of work is, that progress bears no proportion to pains, and that hours of labour are often entirely thrown away . . .'),[12] but revision did not stop. The new Dove Cottage manuscript referred to above contains phrases – no more – in the shaky hand of a seventy-year-old man, which are revisions for 'The Thorn', 'Goody Blake and Harry Gill', and other poems composed in that summer so movingly recalled in *The Prelude* XIII, 386–410, a summer now forty years past. Revision was compulsive and continuous. It could complicate publication at the very last moment, as the extensive revisions to the 'Ode to Duty' testify. While the printer was waiting for the copy for the 1807 *Poems, in Two Volumes,* which was being dispatched sheet by sheet as amanuenses completed them, Wordsworth transformed the poem even after a final text had been copied out. Revision, too, was immediate. It might begin as soon as a poem was published. J. E. Wells has demonstrated how Wordsworth seized the opportunity of a printer's error in the first issue of *Lyrical Ballads* (1800) to begin revising 'Michael' even before the poem had properly appeared.[13] For once, the poet was able to release a work and retrieve it almost simultaneously, satisfying a need which the usual exigencies of publishing could not meet. Normally at least a year would have to elapse – but no opportunity was missed. It is not true, for example, as Healey claims, that the six-volume 1843 collection is an unchanged stereotype reprint of 1841. 'The attentive Reader' will find that the poet could not resist the chance to make a change or two.

At its most severe, revision might mean temporary or permanent excision from the canon. 'The Convict', for example, was dropped after its first appearance in *Lyrical Ballads* (1798). 'Andrew Jones' existed from 1800 to 1815 but disappeared thereafter, a longer lifespan than that allowed to 'The Author's Voyage Down the Rhine', which was not reprinted after the 1822 *Memorials of a Tour*. 'Among all Lovely Things my Love has been' was not reprinted after 1807, perhaps as a result of the ridicule in *The Simpliciad*. 'Alice Fell', disparaged both by Jeffrey and by Coleridge in *Biographia Literaria* (1817), was excluded from the editions of 1820 to 1832. 'A Character' and 'The Sun has long been set' were likewise banished for many years after their first appearance in 1800 and 1807 respectively.

Revision might mean small but telling changes, such as that which produced as late as 1820 one of the most characteristically cadenced lines of Wordsworthian blank verse in 'Michael':

> There is a comfort in the strength of love;
> 'Twill make a thing endurable, which else
> *Would overset the brain, – or break the heart:*
>
> (my italics)

Or it might result in changes to the printed text as far-reaching as those which, unknown to Wordsworth's public, transformed poems in manuscript. The most remarkable of these, perhaps, is the revision in 1845 of the 1814 text of *The Excursion* Book I, which translates Margaret and the Pedlar from a world in which natural tragedy coexists with 'natural wisdom' available to the tutored mind, to one in which Margaret

> had ofttimes felt
> The unbounded might of prayer; and learned, with soul
> Fixed on the Cross, that consolation springs,
> From sources deeper far than deepest pain,
> For the meek Sufferer.
>
> (I, 935–9)

A change as dramatic as this one is, of course, full of implications for our understanding of Wordsworth's Christian faith, of his developing attitude to the exemplary nature of Margaret's suffering, even of the significance of the rest of *The Excursion*.

Even apparently minor alterations may affect interpretation, as Carl Woodring has demonstrated in drawing attention to a change which reveals how uneasy Wordsworth became about one of his most crucial declarations of faith, in 'Tintern Abbey' lines 95–100.[14] Variations in a single punctuation mark in successive editions open up difficult questions about Wordsworth's metaphysics:

> a sense sublime
> Of something far more deeply interfused,
> Whose dwelling is the light of setting suns,
> And the round ocean, and the living air,
> And the blue sky, and in the mind of man,
> A motion and a spirit . . .
>
> (1798–1802)
>
> And the blue sky, and in the mind of man
> A motion and a spirit . . .
>
> (1805)
>
> And the blue sky, and in the mind of man:
> A motion and a spirit . . .
>
> (1815–50)

Most of the revisions, however, have little impact individually and are unlikely to start many critical hares, yet their cumulative weight is a very considerable problem for any editor and can, if traced through their unfolding, affect the way any reader perceives a poem. Titles may change, and the gap between 'Old Man Travelling' and 'Animal Tranquillity and Decay' is not a small one. Our perception of 'Anecdote for Fathers' is altered, however slightly, when the plain epigraph of 1798, 'Shewing How the Art of Lying may be Taught', is replaced in 1845 by a quotation from Eusebius: 'Retine vim istam, falsa enim dicam, si coges.' Or, to give a final example, a text may change over many years, like a friend growing older in whom we can always see simultaneously the features as they once were and as they are now. Consider one of the greatest of Wordsworth's poems. In 1807 the very form of its printing marked it out as the culmination of the *Poems, in Two Volumes*. Simply entitled *Ode* on its own title-page recto separating it from the previous poem, it was reached via a brief epigraph on the otherwise blank verso. On its next appearance in 1815 it still stood alone, although next in sequence to 'Epitaphs and Elegiac Poems', but aggrandized by an interpretative title – 'Intimations of Immortality From Recollections of Early Childhood' – and prefaced, on a separate page, with lines from 'My Heart Leaps Up'. In 1820 four lines have been excised,[15] stanza numbering alters the appearance of the poem, and a page reference added below the prefatory poem tactfully reminds the reader that the poet is excerpting from another work of his which ought to be consulted. The process continues. In 1827 the prefatory poem, with page reference, is printed below the title 'Ode: Intimations. . .', and the whole poem itself is now numbered as XIV of the sequence 'Epitaphs and Elegiac Pieces'. Apart from the deletion of the four lines, these changes in presentation are all small, yet they undoubtedly affect how a reader *sees* the poem, in itself and as part of each collected edition, and point up the question: which text ought an editor to print and how ought it to be presented?

Knight and Dowden saw the problems and in their editions set a pattern which has been followed ever since. Taking to heart the poet's own declaration, 'You know what importance I attach to following strictly the last copy of the text of an author', they agreed on one principle, that the poet's last authorized edition, the six volumes of 1849–50, must provide the text, but disagreed fundamentally elsewhere.[16] Knight broke with Wordsworth's own arrangement of his poems, preferring to present them in chronological order of composition, in the belief that such a presentation 'shows us, as nothing else can do, the growth of his mind, the progressive development of his imaginative power'.[17] Dowden, on the other hand, citing evidence that Wordsworth detected offensive egotism in the idea of chronological arrangement of a poet's work, retained the classification begun in 1815. Modern editors have followed suit. De Selincourt and Darbishire work from the same premises as Dowden, while Hayden has followed Knight.[18] And despite the much greater inclusiveness and accuracy of these later editions they are open to the same objections as their Victorian predecessors.

Problems arise not just because of Wordsworth's care for the children of his imagination after they had first achieved independent life. This just demands of an editor the labour of recording the thousands of revisions to the printed texts. The greater problems arise from Wordsworth's methods of composition and from the imaginative husbandry with which he cherished his manuscripts over many years. Some poems, although revised towards eventual publication, remained unpublished for reasons which the poet explained or which can be inferred. *The Prelude* and *Home at Grasmere* are cases in point, both inextricable from Wordsworth's never-realized plans for the magnum opus, *The Recluse*. Others, however, were just not published. Some, perhaps, were thought too slight, like 'These Chairs they have no Words to Utter'; others, such as 'The Tinker', were dropped at the last moment because of exigencies of space. But it is difficult to imagine why a fine poem like 'St Paul's' remained unpublished, or why, when he felt able to issue the highly personal 'Elegiac Verses' on the death of John Wordsworth in a revised form many years after composition, Wordsworth did not also issue the equally poignant poem 'Distressful Gift', which is its companion in the manuscript collection of memorial verses compiled not long after his brother's death.[19]

Such poems as 'The Tinker' or 'St Paul's' clearly exist as finished works. An editor who adheres with Dowden and de Selincourt–Darbishire to the pattern of Wordsworth's last collection must print them in an appendix of non-canonical work, that is, as material not authorized for publication by the poet, whereas the Knight–Hayden procedure places them in chronological sequence. Neither method of presentation would really mislead a careful reader. A poem such as 'Elegiac Verses', however, poses a problem of quite another order. Composed in 1805 and, as the fair-copy manuscript shows, completed then, the elegy was not published until 1842 in *Poems, Chiefly of Early and Late Years*, and then only in a greatly altered shape. Such a gap between composition and publication is not uncommon. Judged unactable in 1797, *The Borderers* lay unknown until 1842.[20] Its first readers could not know how substantially the tragedy had been revised. The same volume contained *Guilt and Sorrow*, prefaced by a note which locates the poem in the war years 1793–4. Readers were not, of course, also told that it cannibalized two earlier long narratives, one of which Wordsworth had tried to publish in 1798, nor that the revised version subverted the polemical intentions of the earlier ones.[21] 'Address to the Scholars of the Village School of —', also published in 1842, is constructed from poems which had lain in manuscript for forty years. The late poem obliterates the separate identity of poems which were composed at the height of Wordsworth's powers and which still survive in manuscript. *Peter Bell* may serve as one final example. Conceived in the same year as 'Tintern Abbey' it was not released until 1819, when the glad assurance of that great ode had given way to the more sober tone of *The Excursion* and *The White Doe of Rylstone*.

Faced with the dilemma of how to present such poems de Selincourt and Darbishire, following Dowden, have to relegate to apparatus and notes all that precedes the latest revised text. The effect is to efface a poem's earlier existence, for what are presented as variant readings are in reality not minor revisions, gropings towards a final form, but the very substance of an achieved identity, poems which Wordsworth did not publish but could not leave alone. Hayden, following Knight, places them in the chronological scheme, thus alerting the reader to their significance for study of Wordsworth's development, but by printing the latest texts, which alter and disguise what Wordsworth had actually written at these points in his career, he completely destroys the usefulness of the chronological arrangement. To print under 1793 or 1798 poems actually constructed twenty or even nearly fifty years later, as de Selincourt drily observed, 'is not conducive to an intelligent study of the poet's art' (*PW*, 1, p. xi).

IV

Great though the change is between the elegies of 1798–9 and 'Address to the Scholars', or between *Salisbury Plain* (1793) and *Guilt and Sorrow* (1842), the identity of the earlier poem is still discernible in the later version. The original impulses of creation may only have been a memory to the poet who reshaped these works after the lapse of so many years, but the recognition remained that he had intended such and such a kind of poem, of a particular shape and in a particular verse form. Another very important category of poems exists, however, of which not even this much can be said. Even to describe them calls for utmost caution in terminology. I am speaking of passages of verse conceived when Wordsworth was working hard towards goals which he either could not perceive clearly himself or could only describe in the vaguest terms, passages which were temporarily discarded as these goals became clearer but which were later absorbed into other works linked to but not the same as the original goals of composition.

Examples will make clear why such hesitancy is appropriate. Dove Cottage MS 16, one of the richest notebooks of the entire collection, records much unfinished business from the period 1798–1800.[22] It contains (or contained on leaves where only stub remnants remain) fair copies of the second version of *Salisbury Plain* and the second full version of *The Ruined Cottage* – poems which Wordsworth had failed to publish in any form in 1798 – and a version towards the two-book autobiographical poem. A text of 'Nutting' is to be found, as are the description of the discharged soldier and the night piece, here just entitled 'Fragment'. The notebook also contains much excellent blank verse on themes appropriate to *The Recluse*, the poem in which, Wordsworth said, 'I contrive to convey most of the knowledge of which I am possessed. My object is to give pictures of Nature, Man, and Society. Indeed I know not any thing which will not come within the scope of my plan.'[23] One passage of seventy-five lines – also entitled 'Fragment' – discourses on the 'active principle alive in all things', and on the wealth of the human mind which partakes of this power. Another of 110 lines is a beautifully sustained declaration of the virtue of communion with the forms of Nature, beginning

> Not useless do I deem
> These quiet sympathies with things that hold
> An inarticulate language for the man
> Once taught to love such objects as excite
> No morbid passions, no disquietude,
> No vengeance and no hatred, needs must feel
> The joy of that pure principle of love
> So deeply that, unsatisfied with aught
> Less pure and exquisite, he cannot chuse
> But seek for objects of a kindred love
> In fellow-natures, and a kindred joy.

Another passage – again called 'Fragment' – considers that 'law severe of penury' which 'Blocks out the forms of nature, preconsumes / The reason, famishes the heart . . .' The theme is continued in a passage beginning 'For let the impediment be what it may / His hands must clothe and nourish them', which meditates on the destructive power of poverty. In a further seventy-two lines beginning 'There are who tell us that in recent times / We have been great discoverers', Wordsworth anticipates the Dickens of *Hard Times* in an attack on utilitarian theories of education which neglect the 'wiser spirit' ever at work, 'most prodigal / Of blessings and most studious of our good'.

I have listed enough of the contents of this manuscript to indicate its importance. Here are passages of such power that one sees at once why Coleridge was so convinced that Wordsworth had the genius of a *philosophic* poet. But the collection throws up knotty problems for reader and editor alike. How did Wordsworth's first readers know this verse – if at all? What was its significance when it was first written? How ought it to be presented to readers now?

Question one is easily answered. Some of the poetry was published early: 'There was a Boy' appeared in *Lyrical Ballads* (1800). Some appeared after many years: 'A Night-Piece' in 1815. Some was incorporated in *The Excursion* Books VIII and IX, and published in 1814, and some into *The Prelude* Books IV and V, not to be published until after the poet's death in 1850. And some remained unpublished until 1949.

To answer question two is much more troublesome, not least because it is so difficult to avoid the retrospective view. Wordsworth himself imposed a pattern on much of this material in the Preface to *The Excursion* (1814), when he explained:

Several years ago, when the Author retired to his native Mountains, with the hope of being enabled to construct a literary Work that might live, it was a reasonable thing that he should take a review of his own Mind, and examine how far Nature and Education had qualified him for such employment. As subsidiary to this preparation, he undertook to record in Verse, the origin and progress of his own powers, as far as he was acquainted with them. That Work . . . has long been finished; and the result of the investigation which gave rise to it was a determination to compose a philosophical poem, containing views of Man, Nature and Society; and to be entitled, The Recluse; as having for its principal subject the sensations and opinions of a Poet living in retirement.

This account is assured and in the logic of progress it offers convincing, but it is, as is now well understood, falsification. *The Recluse* was conceived before Wordsworth retired to his native mountains. Philosophical blank verse for that poem was written before the beginnings of the autobiographical poem, which itself was subsequent to the idea of *The Recluse* and not a preparatory work of investigation which gave rise to the idea of a philosophical poem. And yet even if we break down Wordsworth's coherent pattern, how difficult it is to avoid some retrospective interpretation. Faced with the blank verse in MS 16 one thinks of it naturally in its familiar setting. 'There is an active principle' became one of the Pedlar's most powerful declarations in *The Excursion*, so it is hard to detach it from the later poem as a whole. But it was not composed with *The Excursion* in mind, but with *The Recluse*, a work whose identity in 1798 was defined only in the haziest terms. The description of the discharged soldier was eventually incorporated into Book IV of the autobiographical poem – itself not even called *The Prelude* by Wordsworth – and so is naturally read, not as a free-standing poem similar to 'The Old Cumberland Beggar', but as part of the argument of a greater whole. Two 'Fragments', 'There is a Law Severe' and 'For let the Impediment be what it may' were not published by Wordsworth but first by Helen Darbishire in notes and appendices to her edition of *The Excursion*. But these very important passages were not written for that poem. Except in so far as they were conceived of as fitting somehow into the as yet unformulated plan of *The Recluse*, they were not written *for* any poem at all. They were composed as Wordsworth was considering very deeply the implication of convictions about God, Man, and Nature, which had produced the powerful affirmation of 'Tintern Abbey', but which were proving recalcitrant to extended expository treatment in *The Ruined Cottage*. To claim that they are free-standing fragments is, perhaps, not very helpful. To present them, however, as drafting towards a poem eventually published in 1814 is not very helpful either.

The case of 'There was a Boy' focuses the issues raised in this section. It was among the earliest descriptions of boyhood pleasures written in late 1798 and was grouped with other such passages in the manuscript in which Book I of the two-part autobiographical poem took shape. Not finding a place in the completed 1799 Prelude, it was published in *Lyrical Ballads* (1800), with a tailpiece which converted it into a unified memorial tribute, and retained its place in the canon until 1849–50. During the years in which it was appearing in successive editions amongst 'Poems of the Imagination', however, it also bore another identity as a section of Book V of *The Prelude*. Here the description of the boy serves to contrast the innocent and appropriate childishness of a 'favoured son' with the monstrous man-child produced by modern theories of education, just as it does in the satirical fragment preserved in MS 16 beginning 'There are who tell us'. Which then is the true identity of 'There was a Boy'? A very strong argument could be made for preserving both 'There was a Boy' and 'There are who tell us' since, at least for a time, the latter had quite as much independent existence as a shaped passage of verse as the former. And to see 'There are who tell us' among other poems of 1798–1800 is to see more clearly that Wordsworth was prepared then to advance his claims about the educative powers of Nature into the citadel of educational theory itself, going beyond statements of personal experience to make propositions of general truth.

V

I want in this section to consider an important implication of the issues raised so far. An editor who chose to print 'There are who tell us' as an independent piece in its proper place in a chronological sequence would, in a sense, be creating a poem. The lines were entered into the notebook in a completed state, but within four years had been absorbed into another evidently whole poem, which is now the centrepiece of the Wordsworth canon. There is no doubt, however, that its setting in *The Prelude* obliterates an earlier identity, and it has been the argument of the previous section that this earlier state is too important to be lost. It is so important, in fact, that an editor would be justified in restoring it to the canon of 1798–1800, for the sake of furthering understanding of the 'growth of [Wordsworth's] mind, the progressive development of his imaginative power'. To do so, however, would be to create a poem in a special way. It is clearly legitimate to rescue from oblivion poems Wordsworth excised from his canon or did not publish at all. *Home at Grasmere*, first published in 1888, or 'St Paul's', first published in 1947, are examples of such rescues. It is, perhaps, as clearly legitimate to print early versions of poems which were later revised into a very different state. Even the purist Ernest de Selincourt offered parallel texts of early and late versions of *An Evening Walk* and *Descriptive Sketches*, and few readers who have compared *Salisbury Plain* (1793–4) with *Guilt and Sorrow* (1841–2) would feel that the earlier poem should not be current. But these cases are not the same as the case of such passages as 'There are who tell us'. *An Evening Walk* was published by Wordsworth. Its first issued state was a completed poem. *Salisbury Plain* was not published, but the way it had been entered in a fair-copy manuscript and evidence of letters suggest that it was regarded as completed and publishable. For 'There are who tell us', however, the evidence is at best ambiguous. On the one hand, the fair-copy manuscript argues for completeness. On the other, the fact that Wordsworth used it after a short time in *The Prelude*, a poem whose origins date from the time of composition of the 'Fragment', might be taken to indicate that he regarded the passage as still unfolding towards a greater whole, and that the fair copy was made simply to preserve it during a pause in composition. An editor who printed a text of 'There are who tell us' would thus be exercising a judgment either that the poem had come to rest at a certain state of completeness, which would have made it publishable had circumstances permitted, or that the poem was still developing but that the interim state is too important to be suppressed. And in such a judgment not only textual and biographical but also interpretative and literary-critical considerations would play their part. How perplexing these considerations are can be seen from a look at the current status of *Home at Grasmere*. Two full versions exist. The later was constructed after the earlier had been pillaged for other works, but even so was not published by Wordsworth but left, in the words of the poem's recent editor, 'to die a peaceful death'.[24] Posthumous publication of the late manuscript in 1888 revealed the poem's existence but gave it only a dubious status as a non-canonical poem. No one quite knew what to make of it. The existence of an earlier manuscript version was revealed only in 1949, but even then the poem's identity and significance were obscured by its appearance – in a text of the late version – in an appendix to Vol. 5 of the de Selincourt–Darbishire edition. Beth Darlington's edition for the Cornell series at last presents all of the manuscript evidence and establishes *Home at Grasmere* as a very significant work from Wordsworth's greatest years.

Her scrupulous analysis of the surviving materials, however, reveals that exhaustive transcription of manuscript readings is not enough to place the poem in the Wordsworth canon, for doubts remain about the dating both of the poem's composition and of the manuscripts themselves. Helen Darbishire assigned the poem to early 1800. Later scholars, notably John A. Finch, have established that the early manuscripts almost certainly date from 1806, and the strength of the evidence is such that Hayden has printed a text of the later version under that date and made the poem current for student readers for the first time. Finch is probably right, but Hayden is wrong on two counts. The version he prints certainly does not date from 1806. More important, whatever the date of the manuscripts, the poem itself almost certainly belongs to a much earlier period, the years of Wordsworth's greatest confidence and power. As Jonathan Wordsworth has argued in a most persuasive article, '*Home at Grasmere* is, almost in its entirety, a poem of 1800 . . .'[25]

The case for dating *Home at Grasmere* must, perhaps, rest as not proven. What is clear is that problems remain for an editor presenting Wordsworth chronologically and for readers trying to make sense of Wordsworth's development. To print any version under 1806 is to risk seriously misleading students. Hayden's edition does just that. An editor who places it in 1800, on the other hand, may, by arguing from what we know of Wordsworth's activities, mood, and intentions at the time, be creating a poem which did not exist, at least not in the form in which it has survived. This point is only worth labouring because most readers can hardly be expected to be aware of how often editorial decisions are crucial or of how greatly such decisions over the presentation of Wordsworth's poems have recently altered our perception of his most fruitful years. It is not too much to say, in fact, that some of his finest verse at the centre of the currently discussed canon is, in some sense, a creation of modern scholarship.

Consider the case of *The Ruined Cottage* and *The Pedlar*. Conceived in 1797–8, the story of Margaret and the Pedlar survives in manuscripts which record work in 1797–8 and 1802–4. It was incorporated into Book I of *The Excursion* (1814) and revised for subsequent editions of that poem. When Helen Darbishire edited *The Excursion* in 1949 she recognized the importance of the early *The Ruined Cottage* and so presented a text of the MS B version in an appendix, together with other passages which she felt belonged with it. Readings from the later MS D were relegated to the apparatus. In the first full scholarly and critical account of the poem(s) in *The Music of Humanity* (1969), Jonathan Wordsworth reversed her judgment. His interpretation of the manuscript evidence and his critical sense of the literary merits of the poems led him to print *The Ruined Cottage* of MS D and, as a separate work, passages also from MS D which he entitled *The Pedlar*. James Butler's edition in the Cornell Wordsworth series (1979) reopens the question, however, by revealing how the poet's dissatisfaction with his work drove him to repeated revision, which culminated in a fair-copy manuscript of late 1803–early 1804 in which a narrative which has long pulled in two directions is at last unified.

Which text, then, ought to be available to non-scholarly readers? From manuscript evidence a case could be made for preferring the earliest full version called *The Ruined Cottage* or the latest pre-*Excursion* text, *The Pedlar*. On literary-critical grounds the intermediate MS D version of *The Ruined Cottage* might be preferred, and it is this text, in fact, which seems to have entered the canon for student readers.[26] Only those prepared to study all of the evidence in Butler's edition can be expected to realize that the text most readily available is, in the sense of the phrase used in this section, an editorial creation.

One final example is the two-part poem to Coleridge of 1799. Wordsworth conceived an autobiographical poem in 1798–9 and entered completed work in fair-copy manuscripts in later 1799. In late 1801 a process of expansion began which was to occupy the poet, fitfully at first, for the next four years, until the thirteen-book *Prelude* was completed. The poem was revised again and again until it was finally prepared for posthumous publication. In 1926 Ernest de Selincourt transformed our understanding of it by presenting parallel texts of the 1805 (manuscript) and 1850 (first printed) versions, and it is the 1805 text which has, at least in Great Britain, become the preferred text in any critical book not concerned with elucidating the poem's varying states. For de Selincourt the poem was Wordsworth's 'masterpiece', exhibiting 'not merely unity of design [but] something of epic character', and his very full account serves to demonstrate how the autobiographical poem detached itself from plans for *The Recluse* and unfolded gradually with its own unity, 'a unity which sprang from the poet's inner life'.[27]

Recent studies of the manuscripts, however, have fragmented the picture de Selincourt so confidently painted and have recomposed it rather differently. The poem of 1805 did not achieve its thirteen-book form by obedience to some inner logic but only after repeated struggles during which Wordsworth redefined what his purpose was. For de Selincourt all the surviving manuscripts tended towards the thirteen-book fair copies A and B, and so were presented as readings towards 1805 in his apparatus criticus, but recent scholarship has demonstrated how misleading this is. A five-book version of the poem is obliterated, as is the earliest completed version of 1799. The five-book poem cannot be recovered in a printable form, but the two-book poem does survive intact. Recently it has been extricated from the mass of other *Prelude* manuscripts and, in two editions, accorded its own status, not as a version of the opening books of the 1805 *Prelude* but as an independent poem, Wordsworth's great achievement between *Lyrical Ballads* (1798) and *Home at Grasmere* (1800). A new poem has entered the canon.[28]

The poetic quality of the 1799 *Prelude* is not in doubt. To Coleridge it was Wordsworth's 'divine Self-biography', and many readers will feel that it is his most powerfully sustained composition.[29] Nor is the status of the fair-copy manuscripts in question. In late 1799 Wordsworth was clearly ready to have his recently composed verse copied out and preserved. What is at issue is whether those manuscripts represent a completed poem. Of the thirteen-book poem Wordsworth was able to say in 1805, 'I finished my Poem . . . I was indeed grateful to God for giving me life to complete the work . . .' Dorothy spoke of preparing 'a fair and final transcript', and what she prepared was a text of a poem whose essential structure remained intact during the repeated revisions of the coming years.[30] But no such hard evidence survives for the two-book version, whose structural wholeness was being eroded by further composition within two years of its formation. All of the evidence is of a different kind, internal and aesthetic. The poem is clearly addressed to Coleridge and both parts conclude with addresses to him, the second being an affectionate farewell. The purpose behind the poem – self-examination as a stimulus for further work and an *apologia pro vita sua* for Coleridge – reaches out to *The Recluse*, a project we know Wordsworth intended to embark on in earnest around 1800. Within the stated limits of its intention the poem seems complete, and such evidence as there is persuades me that it was. But Wordsworth did not say it was. Even if it seemed complete to him, it only remained so for two years at most. He clearly did not feel that the concluding farewell was out of place when it became the end of the second book of a much larger work. On such evidence one could argue that the poem's existence as an independent work was of too short duration, or is simply too uncertain, for it to be printed as if it were a poem of the same status as, say, 'Tintern Abbey'. What readers ought to be aware of is that here, most strikingly of all, an *editorial* act has intervened decisively in the province usually claimed by interpretative criticism, the exposition of 'the growth of [Wordsworth's] mind, the progressive development of his imaginative power'.

Two observations might be made about the emergence of the poems discussed in this section. The first is, how strikingly the availability of these and other such texts has altered our perception of Wordsworth's most creative period. Not long ago an undergraduate course might properly have started at *Lyrical Ballads*, 1798 and 1800 with the Preface, have moved on to the lyrics eventually published in the 1807 *Poems, in Two Volumes*, and have concluded with the *The Prelude* of 1805. Now it is as likely that a course might begin with a glance at *Salisbury Plain* or *Adventures on Salisbury Plain*, move on to serious study of *The Ruined Cottage* and *The Pedlar*, jump from *Lyrical Ballads* (1798) to *Home at Grasmere*, the 'Prospectus' to *The Recluse*, and the two-part *Prelude* as the great achievements 1799–1800, and only then on to the familiar ground of the lyrics and the 1805 *Prelude*. The majority of the poems in this second course were difficult of access, realistically unavailable for undergraduate reading before the early 1970s.

The second observation is that in amplifying the corpus of studied poems, we are creating a revised Wordsworth canon in defiance of the poet's known wishes. It is one thing for scholars to discover a lost poem by a major writer, which is greeted with pleasure as a supplement to the existing canon, but quite another for scholars to reclaim works which the poet did not publish on such a scale that the existing canon is completely transformed. Criticism of course alters perception and tastes change. It may be that one day *Childe Harold* will seem more centrally Byron than *Don Juan*. But it is not, fundamentally, criticism or fashion that has altered the Wordsworth canon. Uniquely, I think, among the Romantic poets, it is editorial scholarship that has created the poet anew. That the poems thus rescued (or created) are of the highest quality or at least real interest should not allow us to lose sight altogether of the fact that the process by which they have emerged is not one that the poet would have approved.

VI

Since these reflections were first published some excellent studies have been published which take as their starting point the fluidity of the text of the particular poem(s) under discussion. The two articles I want to consider in this postscript, however, are ones which directly address general textual issues, directly or by implication taking up some of the points I raised in 1983.

In 'The Whig Interpretation of Literature' Stephen Parrish explicates lucidly the thinking behind the textual practices of the Cornell Wordsworth series, the magnificently ambitious project which he, more than anyone else, has brought into being.[31] Challenging the teleological thrust of all notions about a poet's 'final intention', Parrish argues that the Cornell editions are making available the materials for a critical approach in which 'the language of early versions, especially when those versions are complete, will be valued not for what it contributed to the late versions, not as a step in an inevitably evolving design, but for its own sake, as an achievement separate from the later history of the text'. No one is likely to dissent from this justification, but there is a problem. By what criteria does one judge that an early version is 'complete' and thus worthy of being printed as a 'Reading Text'? Acknowledging that this question enters the realm of what he calls 'editorial ethics', Parrish argues that Cornell editors have had to decide what 'divides legitimate from illegitimate editorial construction', but concedes that some readers will be troubled by judgments made in particular cases.

One such troubled reader is himself a distinguished editor, Jack Stillinger. In a wide-ranging article entitled 'Textual Primitivism and the Editing of Words-worth', Stillinger lays bare and challenges the editorial principles underlying the Cornell volumes, the Norton *Prelude*, and my own selection for the Oxford Authors series.[32] Demonstrating, *contra* Parrish and the Cornell editors, just what difficulties ensue from the pursuit of the elusive 'earliest' complete text, Stillinger returns repeatedly to what is his main worry, namely, that what he calls the current textual primitivism is effacing what the reading public has long known as 'Wordsworth'. The last authorized text of the poems, which 'were, after all, what put Wordsworth among the English poets', is being not just downgraded but effectively deleted.

Both articles are important, Parrish's for the lucidity and candour with which it lays out the editorial principles of the most important Wordsworth edition of our time, Stillinger's for the defence which it mounts of the poet's final text. What both agree on, though, is that criticism must recognize that Words-worth's poems exist in varying states and that it is neither responsible nor sensible to vest authority in a single version. Yes, Stillinger argues, readers of Wordsworth need the Cornell volumes, but 'We shall still need de Selincourt and Darbishire's *Poetical Works* or another, more accurate printing of the latest texts', and instead of pursuing the sterile debate about which text is the best, let us 'grant the legitimacy and interest, intrinsic or in connection with other texts, of *all* versions of *The Prelude* and the rest of the poems in the canon'.

Most Wordsworth scholars are likely to welcome such a generous invitation to future critical endeavours, not least because it precludes the possibility that debate about texts might degenerate into factional in-fighting. But it leaves me with a residual worry – what about the ordinary reader? All of the scholarly endeavours of the last twenty years have brought us no nearer agreement on what kind of edition we would want to be in the hands of schoolchildren, undergraduates, and other readers discovering the poetry for the first time. And surely it is the needs of those readers which ought to trouble the consciences of all of us, for if the result of our leisurely, grant-aided porings over erasures, interlineations, and paste-downs is, finally, to make Wordsworth's poetry inaccessible to all but doctoral candidates, we will have failed the poet we believe we are honouring.

NOTES

1 This comment is not meant to detract from the *Poetical Works of William Wordsworth* (Oxford, 1952–9). That de Selincourt and Darbishire achieved so much, working with a mass of manuscripts uncatalogued and largely untranscribed, is simply astonishing. Future references to this edition: *PW*.

2 George Harris Healey, *The Cornell Wordsworth Collection* (Ithaca, 1957); T. J. Wise, *A Bibliography of the Writings in Prose and Verse of William Wordsworth* (London, 1916). Since the first publication of this essay, Mark L. Reed of the University of North Carolina at Chapel Hill has begun the enormous task of preparing a Wordsworth bibliography.

3 John O. Hayden, *William Wordsworth: Poems* (Harmondsworth, 1977); Jonathan Wordsworth, *The Music of Humanity* (London, 1969); *The Prelude 1799, 1805, 1850*, ed. Jonathan Wordsworth, M. H. Abrams, Stephen Gill (New York, 1979); *The Salisbury Plain Poems of William Wordsworth*, ed. Stephen Gill (Ithaca, 1975); *The Prelude, 1798–99*, ed. Stephen Parrish (Ithaca, 1977); *Home at Grasmere*, ed. Beth Darlington (Ithaca, 1977); *The Ruined Cottage and The Pedlar* (Ithaca, 1979); *Benjamin the Waggoner*, ed. Paul F. Betz (Ithaca, 1981); *The Borderers*, ed. Robert Osborn (Ithaca, 1982); *Poems, in Two Volumes*, ed. Jared Curtis (Ithaca, 1983); *An Evening Walk*, ed. James Averill (Ithaca, 1984); *Descriptive Sketches*, ed. Eric Birdsall (Ithaca, 1984); *Peter Bell*, ed. John E. Jordan (Ithaca, 1985); *The Fourteen-Book Prelude*, ed. W. J. B. Owen (Ithaca, 1985); *The Tuft of Primroses*, ed. Joseph F. Kishel (Ithaca, 1986); *The White Doe of Rylstone*, ed. Kristine Dugas (Ithaca, 1988).

4 *The Poetical Works of William Wordsworth*, ed. William Knight (Edinburgh, 1882–6); *The Poetical Works of William Wordsworth*, ed. Edward Dowden (London, 1892–3); *The Poetical Works of William Wordsworth*, ed. William Knight (London, 1896). The quotation is from Dowden, 1, p. xvi. These years also saw published Thomas Hutchinson's *The Poetical Works of William Wordsworth* (Oxford, 1895), whose text remained the basis for the still widely used Oxford Standard Authors one-volume edition.

5 Both editors scored hits in their explanatory self-defensive prefaces, but the prize must be awarded to Dowden for this gentlemanly put-down of the grossly

inaccurate Knight: 'I desire to speak with great gratitude of Professor Knight's labours . . . But his collation in the earlier volumes of his edition, where collation was most important, is of a kind which cannot be called final' (I, p. xiv).

6 As Jared Curtis has pointed out in a detailed study of 'The Wellesley Copy of Wordsworth's *Poetical Works, 1832*', *Harvard Library Bulletin*, 28 (1980), pp. 5–15, Wordsworth believed that judicious readers would value the 1836–7 collection for the 'pains which has (sic) been taken in the revisal of so many of the old Poems, to the re-modelling, and often re-writing whole Paragraphs' (Wordsworth to Moxon, 28 January 1837). Curtis observes that the 'results of these efforts are essentially new versions of several poems, substantially revised versions of a hundred more, and pervasive changes in the details of presentation' (p. 5).

7 *Poems by William Wordsworth: including Lyrical Ballads and the Miscellaneous Pieces of the Author* . . . (London, 1815), I, p. viii. Wordsworth was concerned well before 1815 about arrangement and the cumulative effect to be gained from grouping poems: 'if individually they want weight, perhaps, as a Body, they may not be so deficient . . . these Sonnets . . . do . . . collectively make a poem on the subject of civil Liberty'. See whole letter to Lady Beaumont, 21 May 1807, in *The Letters of William and Dorothy Wordsworth: The Middle Years: Part I, 1806–1811*, ed. Ernest de Selincourt, rev. Mary Moorman (Oxford, 1969), pp. 145–51.

8 Dove Cottage MS 154. I am grateful to the Trustees of Dove Cottage for permission to use the manuscripts of the Wordsworth Library.

9 *Prelude* (1805), VI 568–9. In the Prefatory verses to *Poems, Chiefly of Early and Late Years* (1842) Wordsworth bids his volume:

> Go, single – yet aspiring to be joined
> With thy Forerunners that through many a year
> Have faithfully prepared each other's way –
> Go forth . . .

10 Edward Dowden, 'The Text of Wordsworth's Poems', *Contemporary Review*, 33 (1878), p. 735. Reprinted in *Transcripts and Studies* (London, 1888), pp. 112–52.

11 Ernest de Selincourt, *PW*, I, p. vi.

12 Wordsworth to Edward Moxon, [late December 1836] in *The Letters of William and Dorothy Wordsworth: The Later Years: Part III, 1835–1839*, ed. Alan G. Hill (Oxford, 1982), p. 337.

13 John Edwin Wells, '*Lyrical Ballads, 1800*: Cancel Leaves', *PMLA*, 53 (1938), pp. 207–29.

14 Carl Woodring, 'The New Sublimity in *Tintern Abbey*', in *The Evidence of the Imagination: Studies of Interactions between Life and Art in English Romantic Literature*, ed. Donald H. Reiman, Michael C. Jaye, and Betty T. Bennett (New York, 1978), pp. 86–100.

15 In *Biographic Literaria* (1817) Coleridge had remonstrated at the 'frightful notion of lying *awake* in his grave!' in commentary on the lines omitted from 1820:

> To whom the grave
> Is but a lonely bed without the sense or sight
> Of day or the warm light,
> A place of thought where we in waiting lie.

For evidence that Wordsworth attempted to revise the 'Best Philosopher' passage, which Coleridge also objected to, see Jared R. Curtis, 'The Best Philosopher: New Variants for Wordsworth's "Immortality Ode"', *Yale University Library Gazette*, 44 (1970), pp. 139–47.

16 William Wordsworth to Alexander Dyce [*c.* 19 April 1830] in *The Letters of William and Dorothy Wordsworth: The Later Years: Part II, 1829–1834*, ed. Alan G. Hill (Oxford, 1979), p. 236. Dowden stated his belief most forthrightly in his selection *Poems by William Wordsworth* (Boston and London, 1897), p. lxxxv: 'Among readers who have not carefully studied Wordsworth's text, an impression is common that he did his work much wrong. The impression, if we have regard to the final result, is certainly erroneous. A few poems suffered loss, but on the whole the gain is great. The latest text is the best text.' One might compare this with Jonathan Wordsworth's opening declaration in *The Music of Humanity*: 'On the whole poets are known by the best versions of their works: Wordsworth is almost exclusively known by the worst' (p. xiii).

17 Knight, *Poetical Works* (1882–6), Vol. 1, p. x.

18 Respect for the author's last revised text, however, clearly has its limits. Hutchinson, de Selincourt, and Hayden all restore to the 'Ode to Duty', within editorial square brackets indicating its uncertain status, a stanza which Wordsworth preferred to omit after 1807, because, in de Selincourt's words (echoed by Hayden), it is 'a valuable link in the thought'. This observation may be just, but acting on it breaches the textual principle of these editions quite unwarrantably.

19 Paul F. Betz discusses the poems to John Wordsworth in 'After the *Lyrical Ballads*: Wordsworth and Coleridge in 1801–1802', *Studies in Romanticism*, 12 (1973), pp. 580–9, and rightly concludes that 'This elegiac sequence is a buried masterpiece . . . which should be resurrected to assume its proper place in the canon of romantic poetry' (p. 585 n.). The poems are now printed from manuscript in *Poems, in Two Volumes, and Other Poems, 1800–1807*, ed. Jared Curtis (Ithaca, 1983), and in *William Wordsworth* [The Oxford Authors], ed. Stephen Gill (Oxford, 1984).

20 Hazlitt referred to the tragedy in *The Spirit of the Age* (1825) and quoted inaccurately from memory lines which Wordsworth added to *The White Doe of Rylstone* as an epigraph as late as the collected edition of 1836–7.

21 *Salisbury Plain* (1793–4) is a fierce attack on social oppression, war, and the unholy alliance of church and state. *Adventures on Salisbury Plain* (1795–9) is less direct but still highlights through its more complex story the evil of a society where a just man can be driven to murder. *Guilt and Sorrow* (1841–2), as its title suggests, focuses on the psychology of the central character and ends in muted stanzas which greatly alter the ending of *Adventures*. The poem was published in the very worst year of the 'hungry-forties' and it is clear from the Prefatory verses that Wordsworth hopes his words will be a balm 'Among a People mournfully cast down, / Or into anger roused by venal words', a very different hope from the one which inspired the original composition at the outbreak of the revolutionary war.

22 A full account of the manuscript will be found in Mark L. Reed, *Wordsworth: The Chronology of the Early Years* (Cambridge, Mass., 1967), pp. 325–8. He refers to it as 18A, its number before the Dove Cottage manuscripts were reclassified.

23 William Wordsworth to James Tobin, 6 March [1798] in *The Letters of William and Dorothy Wordsworth: The Early Years, 1787–1805*, ed. Ernest de Selincourt, rev. Chester L. Shaver (Oxford, 1967), p. 212. Future references to this edition: *EY*.

24 *Home at Grasmere*, ed. Beth Darlington (Ithaca, 1977), p. ix.

25 Jonathan Wordsworth, 'On Man, on Nature, and on Human Life', *RES*, n.s. 31 (1980), pp. 17–29.

26 This text of the poem was first made available in *The Music of Humanity* but has since been widely disseminated in the fourth edition of *The Norton Anthology of English Literature*, ed. M. H. Abrams, George Ford, and David Daiches (New York, 1979), Vol. 1, pp. 182–95, and in the *Oxford Anthology of English Literature: Romantic Poetry and Prose*, ed. Harold Bloom and Lionel Trilling (New York, 1973), pp. 130–42. The authority of the *Oxford Anthology* is placed behind the introductory declaration that of the various versions of the poem this text 'is by common scholarly agreement now considered the most effective'.

27 *The Prelude*, ed. Ernest de Selincourt (Oxford, 1926), p. xxvii.

28 For the two-part *Prelude*, see the editions by Parrish and by Wordsworth, Abrams, and Gill cited above, n.3. For the five-book version, see Jonathan Wordsworth, 'The Five-Book *Prelude* of Early Spring 1804', *JEGP*, 76 (1977), pp. 1–25. The two-part *Prelude* reached its widest audience in the *Norton Anthology*, 4th ed.

29 See *The Notebooks of Samuel Taylor Coleridge*, ed. Kathleen Coburn, Vol. 1 (London, 1957); entry no. 1801, 4 January 1804.

30 Wordsworth to Sir George Beaumont, 3 June 1805 (*EY*, p. 594); Dorothy Wordsworth to Lady Beaumont, 29 November 1805 (*EY*, p. 650).

31 S. M. Parrish, 'The Whig Interpretation of Literature', *Text*, 4 (1988), pp. 343–50.

32 Jack Stillinger, 'Textual Primitivism and the Editing of Wordsworth', *Studies in Romanticism*, 28 (1989), pp. 3–28.

3

"A POWER TO VIRTUE FRIENDLY": THE PEDLAR'S GUILT IN WORDSWORTH'S "RUINED COTTAGE"

JONATHAN BARRON AND KENNETH R. JOHNSTON

"There *is* guilt in this."   (*The Borderers*)

SPEAKING of revisions, there is a natural tendency to concentrate on the results, or product. But the process can be equally important, if viewed as "an ongoing endeavor" with its own "self-satisfying logic and rationale"[1] – especially when we are dealing with an author whose primary subject is the working of his own mind in the act of creation. *The Prelude* is the great document in Wordsworth's case, and its two main versions, of 1805 and 1850, constitute the grounds on which the permanently interesting debate about its revisions is conducted.[2] But "The Ruined Cottage" also has important claims in this regard, in their way as important, and certainly more manageable. If the various versions of *The Prelude* illustrate Wordsworth's changing conceptions of himself *as* subject, then his revisions of "The Ruined Cottage," which he continued throughout his career, may be said to represent his changing conception of one of his primary subject *matters*, human suffering, and how this subject might best be represented or narrated. *The Prelude* was at least published by the poet's direction (if posthumously and with a dubiously assigned title), but even in writing the title, "The Ruined Cottage," we are already working from manuscript evidence. As Stephen Gill has well said, any version of this poem is essentially an editorial creation.[3] Strictures can legitimately be made against mis-using manuscript evidence or "Reading Texts" if our object is the poet's finally intended art work. But if we are interested in the growth of his imagination, then we not only may but must make the widest possible use of the evidences of his work – his mind – in progress.

As far as Wordsworth's published intentions are concerned, the relevant product is Book I (titled "The Wanderer") of *The Excursion*, first published in 1814 and, typically for him, revised frequently thereafter until its final lifetime publication in 1849. This too is a good poem – for most readers of *The Excursion* (always a select company) it is the best part of the whole – but it is nearly twice the length of the early manuscript versions, and its traditional, religious context of explanation (expanded in post-1814 revisions), make it a very different poem from the philosophically and politically controversial documents Wordsworth produced in 1797–8 (and on into 1801, if we include other early versions called "The Pedlar"). It is the form and context of explanation for Margaret's suffering that constitutes what we may call the compositional drama of "The Ruined Cottage," but this tends to be lost if we only know it in *The Excursion* or in MS D (the effectively canonical version, since its publication in *The Norton Anthology of English Literature*) – or indeed in any single version.

MS D, with its "reconciling addendum" (493–538) placing Margaret's tale in a meditative context of nature's "calm oblivious tendencies," is a better balanced poem than MS B.[4] It presents a nice sequence through the poem's two parts, which can be represented as follows: Part I: introduction/tale/comment // Part II: comment/tale/conclusion. Furthermore, by omitting the Pedlar's biography (B.47–105) and adding his conciliatory final statement or moral, it has the virtue of showing us his wisdom in action rather than merely reporting it by way of characterization. It is true that few readers of alert sensibility, especially those of a modernist, post-Romantic cast, can bring themselves to accept on aesthetic, philosophical, or political grounds the cold comfort the old man offers his young auditor. But by rounding off the poem's terrific peroration (B.482–528; D.446–92) – "and here she died, / Last human tenant of these ruined walls" – the reconciling addendum gives us something to go on, even if, upon reflection, we cannot accept its comfort. Whereas MS B, ending with just those stark words (which everyone from Coleridge onwards seems to remember as the dominant experience of the poem[5]) leaves us almost literally nowhere, in an emotional vacuum, wondering what has hit us, and what we are to make of such a supposedly "common tale" of human suffering. It leaves us, in other words, in something very like Wordsworth's own position as creator: to find some point or explanation or motivation for such stories and, still more to the point, for the *telling, reading and hearing* of such stories. Nonetheless, a virtue of MS B's abrupt ending is that it engages us in the process of composition; it leaves it open to us, perhaps forces us, to experience the author's problem, to go back through the poem and see what conclusion or explanation we can assign to the powerfully disturbing experience we have just had. Here too we are engaged in revisions.

It is our contention that MS B, by open-endedly releasing us back through the poem (and thence forward through its subsequent revisions), brings us to another source of causal explanation, in addition to those already proposed by others,[6] for the power and meaning of these events. It allows us to see more clearly in the Pedlar's language and actions his feelings of conscience-stricken guilt for his role or participation in the sufferings of Margaret. It is these feelings which he now – perhaps for the first time – recounts to his chosen auditor, the unnamed young narrator who will, in the published version of the poem in *The Excursion*, be signally identified as "The Poet." Although MS B does not present a consistently more guilty picture of the Pedlar's role in the tale of Margaret, a comparison with MS D reveals that Wordsworth began there to revise the poem to create a more general feeling of guilt, while making it less personally applicable to the Pedlar himself – a direction he continued to pursue through all subsequent versions of the poem.[7]

Though everyone has something to say about the Ancient Mariner's guilt, very few have broached the question of the Pedlar's guilt. Indeed, given the Pedlar's evident function as moral instructor, it may seem bad taste to do so. But there are several things in the tale of Margaret, as he reports it, that might make him feel – now, in the present-tense telling of it – guilty, or conscience-stricken, and which give him a rationale (call it a program) for re-telling her story in expiation of these feelings. The responses of first-time readers can help us here. Part of their uneasiness with "The Ruined Cottage," as with "The Old Cumberland Beggar," arises from a sense that somebody should or could have done something for Margaret, despite her fixation on her absent husband. This might be called the literalist or "Antijacobin" response, since it recapitulates the satirical critique of the increasingly reactionary establishment press to the political "philanthropy" of much early Romantic writing.[8] But in trying to lead readers away from this "inappropriate" response, we may also come to appreciate its justice. Indeed, justice, or fairness, is the issue, and in raising it we expose a whole range of issues, or line-up of suspects – among whom we may also recognize the face of the very man who has reported the injustice to us.

Rounding up the usual suspects is an easy matter, and recent New Historicist readings of the poem have not scrupled to indict the author himself, principally for trying to cover up the guilt of the prime socio-historical culprit, the economic and military policies of William Pitt, representing the entire power structure of England, *c.* 1797–8.[9] The text itself cites causes rather too large to bring into custody: Nature ("two blighting seasons"), God ("it pleased heaven"), and Society ("the plague of war" – represented as a quasi-natural, quasi-divine event). Some readers have not been loath to blame Margaret for her own troubles, from De Quincey, who said she ought to have been prosecuted for criminal neglect of her infant (and the Pedlar subpoenaed as a witness for the prosecution),[10] to students, who are sometimes very hard on her for her unhealthy dependence on her husband and for failing to be an autonomous, self-actualizing individual. Robert, her husband, has escaped much scrutiny, and yet it might be said that his attempt to solve the family's problems by enlisting for the government's bounty did not, at best, show a very keen understanding of his wife's likely reaction, and, at worst, evinced an all too "masculine," selfishly uncommunicative, and narrowly material conception of what their problems really were.

With the mention of Robert's enlistment bounty, "a purse of gold" found by Margaret "on the third [day] by the first break of light" (B.321–3; D.262–4), we open up another range of guilty reference. This is not to say that Robert plays Judas to Margaret's Jesus, a dubious line of inquiry, but to recall that there are throughout the poem some powerfully free-floating religious references, to both the Crucifixion story and the Fall from the Garden of Eden. Stories, that is, in which the issue of guilt or responsibility is paramount. The oft-noted allusion to Ecclesiastes 12:6 in "The useless fragment of a wooden bowl" (B.145/D.91) can be extended to include the larger point of this famous chapter, which is not simply that "all is vanity" (12:8), but is rather to combat hopelessness with the assurance that "God will bring every deed into judgement, with every secret thing, whether good or evil" (12:13–14). Sharon Setzer has noted a pattern throughout *The Excursion* wherein idyllic gardens are invaded, or spied upon, by outside observers whose *function* (if not character) in the relevant passages may usefully be considered as "satanic."[11] This observation helps to explain the awkward way in which the narrator must "climb" the wall into Margaret's garden, as if it had no entrance-way from her cottage yard. It also gives point to the behavior of the "gaudy" sunflower and the promiscuous gooseberries and currants which hang over the garden's roadside wall in a way that has "tempted" many passers-by "to o'erleap" it, an even closer approximation of Satan's trespassing entrance into Eden. Hence we may well feel that some kind of guilt is also at issue, at a deep level of cultural intertextuality. The fact that it is "a young apple-tree" that Margaret fears "will be dead and gone / Ere Robert come again" (B.460, 464–5) may be more than a neutral botanical reference. Most of the signs of Margaret's decline and decay are in fact deduced from her garden rather than from her cottage, and a whole range of reference would be released immediately if the poem had been titled "The Ruined Garden."[12] But to whom does it refer?

There are events or effects here, and a wide range of causes, but we cannot draw a clear line between any one of the causes and the central event/effect of the story. We cannot even say unequivocally what that central event is. Is it Margaret's decline and death, or the effect of hearing about it? In addition to identifying causes inside or outside the story – all of which, from God to Pitt to Margaret to Wordsworth, may be said to have contributed something to the death of its protagonist – we propose that a literary version of Heisenberg's Uncertainty Principle is at work here, in that simply *observing* and *recounting* the events has a bearing upon the events themselves, changes their essence, and constitutes a kind of guilty implication in their meaning and denouement. We may say that the meaning of Margaret's story cannot be held constant to its narration, and that in the uncertain gap between the two we find traces of the Pedlar's implication in both – for which he attempts to exculpate himself, first by implicating his young auditor, then by educating him into a more flexible understanding of this dialectical relation between event and account. The account, as sequel to the event, invites a narration of its own.

The Pedlar's guilt responds to failed responsibility, to an inadequacy of response. Perhaps as much as the constant of human suffering, it is this failure that is the subject of Wordsworth's poem, and that characterizes the uncertainties of its narrative responses. We can find several reasons for the Pedlar to feel guilty about his role in Margaret's tale: not guilt for causing her troubles, but pangs of conscience for failing to respond to them. This evidence falls into four categories: (1) his failures to comfort Margaret, (2) his obtuseness about recognizing her misery, and (3) the language with which he comments upon it to the narrator. All of these depend on our recognizing (4) a special relationship between him and Margaret, and noticing the difference between his character in the frame story and in the tale itself. Although he appears to the narrator as the very mouthpiece of "natural wisdom," he is notably *un*wise in the story he tells, another similarity to Coleridge's Ancient Mariner.

The Pedlar offers effective consolation to the young narrator, but that is precisely what he could not give to Margaret. Each time he tried, he failed. On the first of the four return visits described in Part II, when Margaret breaks into bitter tears instead of giving the friendly greeting he anticipates, the Pedlar says, "I wist not what to do / Or how to speak to her" (B.309–10). A "strange surprize and fear" comes over him when Margaret asks about her husband, "And I could make no answer" (B.316). MS B is more definite about his inadequacy at this point. MS D's version, "Nor had I power to answer ere she told / That he had disappeared" (259–60), implies that he might have had something to say. After she tells her tale, "with many tears," he comments, "I had little power / To give her words of comfort." Not only that, *he* "was glad to take / Such words of hope from her own mouth as served / To chear us both" (B.333–7). And so it goes, more or less, with each visit: we never see that the Pedlar's wisdom and experience give Margaret any comfort, despite MS B's complimentary spiritual biography. At the end of his first return visit, Margaret

> sent a blessing after me
> With tender chearfulness and with a voice
> That seemed the very sound of happy thoughts.
>
> (B.345–7)

The doubt conveyed by that "seemed" is confirmed by her similar farewell after his second visit:

> I left her then
> With the best hope and comfort I could give;
> She thanked me for my will, but for my hope
> It seemed she did not thank me.
>
> (B.428–31)

The Pedlar knows the power of the One Life, but Paul Hamilton, reflecting the New Historicist critique of the political shortcomings of Wordsworth's philosophy, says that "the Oneness could hardly have consoled Margaret," and criticizes the Pedlar for "insouciantly abandoning the scene of Margaret's desertion."[13] Our point is that the Pedlar's shortcomings are less grand but more obvious: not only does he fail to give her any philosophical comfort, he pretty much fails to convey any effective sympathy even of the most ordinary, quotidian, conversational variety. But we also suggest that his philosophic – and narrative – effectiveness arises from his new sense of his former failures. Indeed, his biography pointedly suggests that the Pedlar's sensitivity has been too much inner-directed: "He had a world about him – 'twas his own, / He made it – for it only lived to him / And to the God who looked into his mind" (B.87–9). This in turn reinforces the possibility that his other-directed sensibility – of responsibility for others – has been dramatically heightened by his failings in Margaret's case, and that he now attempts to redeem the failure by passing on his experience to the narrator.

The Pedlar's unhelpful words of wisdom and comfort in the primary action of Margaret's tale are reinforced at the level of dramatic staging by the tardy deliberation with which he recognizes signs of decay in her cottage on each return visit, and his equally slow readiness to connect them to similar evidences in Margaret's person and family. These delayed perceptions may be explained as Wordsworth's effective drawing-out of the stages of Margaret's decline which, linked to the Pedlar's widely spaced visits, constitute the story's master-effect. But they also indicate a connection between the poem's aesthetic power and the Pedlar's ethical failures. For one whose message begins, "I see around me here / Things which you cannot see," the Pedlar was remarkably slow in coming to see them himself. On his second visit, it takes more than thirty lines for him to draw the proper conclusion, though most fresh readers of the poem see what's up immediately. To him, the cottage seemed "in any shew / Of neatness little changed, but I thought / The honeysuckle crowded round the door" (364–6). He strolls into the garden and then realizes "it was changed" (371). Finally, after waiting a couple of hours with "sad impatience" – since he always looks forward with pleasure to the greeting Margaret will give him – he begins to *feel* what's happened: "The spot though fair seemed very desolate, / The longer I remained more desolate" (386–7). And only then does he notice on "the corner stones, / Till then unmarked" (388–9) – though he's been sitting by them for hours – the blood stains and tufts of wool from the sheep that have started using the cottage as their night-time "couching place." In passing, he has heard, "from within / Her solitary infant [cry] aloud" (384–5), a detail, and a failure of responsive action on his part, so extraordinary that we would feel better ascribing it to the poem's unfinished state than to the Pedlar's lack of alertness, except for the fact that it remains even in *The Excursion*. On his next visit he is quicker to see signs in house and garden of what he calls "a sleepy hand of negligence," while pointedly noting that Margaret "seemed not changed / In person or appearance" (B.438–40), even though he had just called her "sad and drooping" (435). And he must have pointed out to him what even the slowest reader has again already divined, that Margaret *is* changed in person and appearance – as indeed had already been abundantly clear to him on his previous visit (B.414–24). The Pedlar's biography shows him to be insightful in giving "normal life . . . Even [to] loose stones that cover the highway" (B.81–2), but when it comes to human suffering, he is anything but a quick study. Yet that too may be an unelaborated point of MS B's biographical sketch, since it nowhere shows him *applying* his moral sensitivity to humankind, only to natural objects, despite the suggestion that he has *learned* some of it from human observation: "much had he seen of men, / Their manners, their enjoyments, and pursuits, / Their passions and their feelings" (B.59–61).

These two kinds of evidence of reasons for the Pedlar's retrospective guilt feelings toward Margaret are reinforced by qualities of tone and language in his tale. It is important to recognize that he is still upset by Margaret's pathos, even as he tells her tale, and that he is not simply an impassive dispenser of a Lucretian cold comfort nor of the resigned stoicism of Ecclesiastes.[14] When he asks, at the end of Part I, "Why should a tear be in an old Man's eye?" (250), it is not a rhetorical question, for there is a tear in his eye, as the next lines indicate: "Why should we *thus* with an untoward mind / And in the weakness of humanity / From natural wisdom turn our hearts away" (251–3; italics added). The "natural wisdom" and "natural comfort" he has achieved do not seal him from his emotions. He still feels for Margaret. The "untoward mind," "weakness of humanity," and "feeding on disquiet" he describes are his own, and could be nobody else's, strictly speaking, at this point in the poem.[15] Similarly, the famous "image of tranquillity" at the end of the poem is not a cold icon. It appeared to him "as once I passed" (a "once" which may be very close to the *now* of his narrative), and appealed to "the uneasy thoughts which filled my mind" – thoughts which, it appears, still come over him in thinking or telling about Margaret.

Further evidence of the Pedlar's residual guilt is to be found in the apparently inappropriate diction in which he summarizes her experience. It is surprisingly sexual or sensual language, and very effective as a subliminal heightening of the anguished empathy Margaret's story commands. In his first summary, the weeds and spear-grass of the later "image of tranquillity" appear to suggest something quite different: that the death of Margaret is something like Nature's rape or violation of the scenes of human affection. Margaret was a friend to every passer-by:

> no one came
> But he was welcome, no one went away
> But that it seemed she loved him. She is dead,
> The worm is on her cheek, and this poor hut, [his metonym for her]
> Stripped of its outward garb of household flowers,
> Of rose and jasmine, offers to the wind
> A cold bare wall whose earthy top is tricked
> With weeds and the rank spear-grass. She is dead,
> And nettles rot and adders sun themselves
> Where we have sat together while she nursed
> Her infant at her bosom.   (B.155–65)

Noticing the sensual connotations of these words may seem so inappropriate to the context as to make one feel guilty oneself, and even the Pedlar seems embarrassed when he says, "You will forgive me, Sir, / I feel I play the truant with my tale" (170–1). But to what is he "truant," that is, not attending? To his story's morality? Perhaps so, for he immediately introduces Margaret's husband to embody the moral life, "an industrious man, / Sober and steady" (172–3).[16]

This erotic diction is twice reinforced, both at crucial summary moments. At the beginning of Part II, before acceding to the narrator's request that he resume the story, the Pedlar warns that he should not tell it, nor the younger man hear it, in the wrong way; that is, sensationally:

> It were a *wantonness*, and would demand
> *Severe reproof*, if we were *men whose hearts*
> Could *hold vain dalliance* with the misery
> Even of the dead, contented thence to draw
> A *momentary pleasure* never marked
> By reason, *barren* of all future good.
>   (B.280–5; italics added)

This odd allusion to the *dalliance* of Courtly and Cavalier love poetry connotes a warning against promiscuity in literature, which is to say, against pornography.

The possibility is so foreign to the evident intention of the poem that we tend to efface it altogether. Yet it appears again at the end of MS D, when the young narrator turns aside "in weakness," almost as if sexually spent – an outrageous suggestion which nonetheless comes from the text itself:

> leaning o'er the garden-gate
> [I] Reviewed that Woman's suff'rings, and it seemed
> To comfort me while with a brother's love
> I blessed her in the impotence of grief.
>
> (D.495–500)

Such language is introduced by the Pedlar, then used by him as a warning to the narrator (who has given no signs of a tendency toward "vain dalliance"), and finally reappears in the narrator's reaction as an innocuous displacement (a brother's impotent love), thanks to the Pedlar's narrative innoculation. This sequence can be seen as arising from the Pedlar's realization that his language betrays his close relationship to Margaret, thus revealing his own "truancy," and tending toward a wrong lesson: that love is full of pain and its grief inconsolable. In these moments, the Pedlar realizes he is losing control of his language (and thus of his story), but he is strong enough to regain control in order to teach the right lesson. His diction would betray him but for his ability to master it.

Such language reminds us that a number of very intimate human relationships are invoked throughout the poem, and suggests that all three of its main characters may be guilty of misplaced tenderness. Most important to our thesis is the Pedlar's report with evident pleasure that Margaret always gave him "a daughter's welcome," and his corresponding claim that he "loved her / As my own daughter" (149–50). Everything points toward a special relationship between them, and nothing points toward the comfortably sociological deduction that Margaret was just one of many maids and wives he encountered on his rounds. Everything, that is, in the *story* (as distinct from its moral) points toward specificity rather than generality, and these pointers give still further definition to the Pedlar's guilt. This is made clearer in MS B by one key word describing the look on his face as he tells his tale, "With such a countenance of love" (B.268), altered in D to the much more general, "such a[n active] countenance."[17] As elsewhere, the shift from B to D is a shift toward a more distanced, less personally involved and responsible relationship between Margaret and the Pedlar.

Several critics have noted the trance-like or abstracted air with which the Pedlar opens what seems to be a general reverie on the human condition (129 ff).[18] This effectively elevated language continues beyond his most banal general statements ('We die, my Friend') as he gradually moves toward his specific subject, by way of "the waters of that spring" (135), to a rather belated introduction of the "she" upon whom all turns (147). The resonant echo and Biblical cadence of his repeated refrain, "She is dead" (157, 162), establishes an appropriately distanced perspective for what we can nonetheless begin to recognize as a confession about someone whom he "loved . . . as my own child" (149–50). But just when his reverie enters the direct narrative past tense – when he will be forced to confront his own failures in the case – he abruptly drops this more elevated diction. He is beginning to recall specific moments and places, "where I have seen her evening hearth-stone blaze / And through the window spread upon the road / Its chearful light" (168–70), when he suddenly stops: "You will forgive me, Sir, / I feel I play the truant with my tale" (170–1). "Truant" suggests he is erring from the kind of story he means to tell into a love story, rather than an instance of general human tragedy. But though the Pedlar swerves from his love story, we can still recognize his love for Margaret as a source of the guilt which causes him to tell her story in the first place. By admitting that he loved her, he also admits by implication that he failed her. A mere travelling salesman of either the best or worst sort might watch, however uneasily, a customer sink further and further into despair until both she and her child die. But for a lover, or a father, to watch with the same detachment would be immoral, "truant." This explains why the Pedlar restarts the tale not with Margaret but with her husband, to create an illusion of distance, and in a much more matter-of-fact, once-upon-a-time diction than the elevated rhetoric of his opening excursus.

But it soon becomes clear that the Pedlar and Margaret meant a great deal to each other, even in – or perhaps especially in – their absences from each other. We can easily miss this if we take the Pedlar's rounds merely at their functional value of creating the stop-time frames in which we observe the stages of the cottage's and Margaret's decay. When the Pedlar first returns after Robert's disappearance (unbeknownst to him), he expects to find the "chearful light" and happy woman he remembered:

> With many pleasant thoughts I cheered my way
> O'er the flat common. At the door arrived,
> I knocked, and when I entered with the hope
> Of usual greeting, Margaret looked at me
> A little while, then turned her head away
> Speechless, and sitting down upon a chair
> Wept bitterly.   (303–8)

To say that she weeps because he is not Robert is too thin an explanation.[19] Would a husband knock before entering? But if we accept that the Pedlar and Margaret have a close relationship, then the sight of him and memories of

73

former happy times might cause her, after "a little while," to break down Easier to remain unemotional with a stranger than with a friend. And now, for the first time, the Pedlar begins to feel, and report, his own shortcomings: "I wist not what to do / Or how to speak to her" (309–10).

Another aspect of their close relationship is the fact that from this point on, Margaret becomes increasingly dependent on the Pedlar, both for news of her husband and for emotional support. He feels this dependency and reciprocates it. Like all pedlars, he provides the services of something like a living newspaper circulating between his isolated customers. MS B touches on this function when it refers to his "wares for maids who live / In lonely villages or straggling huts" (B.45–6). Margaret believes that a man with such a range of contacts and acquaintance may eventually hear news of her husband. (De Quincey was almost beside himself in criticizing the implausibility that neither Margaret nor the Pedlar check with any of several likely sources for information about Robert's whereabouts: the war office, the local vicar, nearby army officers, a store-owner, or indeed almost any responsible citizen.[20]) But he does not, and because he so consistently disappoints her, he feels guilty. He begins to express his guilt immediately after this first visit: "I roved o'er many a hill and many a dale / With this my weary load" (348–9). This is not simply his pack of goods, but also the mixed bag of feelings he now carries with him. The new emotional state of his wandering is further emphasized by an echo from *King Lear*: "My best companions now the driving winds / And now the music of my own sad steps" (353–4). MS D weakens this mood by inserting between these lines a more conventionally picturesque allusion from Burns: "And now the 'trotting brooks' and whispering trees" (295). On the other hand, D removes an earlier reference to his "weary load" (B.106), thus strengthening the suggestion that his load has only now become "weary" and his travels "sad," as a result of his knowledge of Margaret's situation, and his own ineffectuality in alleviating it. His next return reflects his new mood, in its "restless steps" and "sad impatience" (379, 384). His growing despair is also contained in the fine Wordsworthian ambiguity of, "The spot though fair seemed very desolate, / The longer *I* remained more desolate" (386–7; italics added).

A further implication of the Pedlar in Margaret's behavior begins to increase with this visit, as it appears she has begun to model herself after him. A passing stranger says "that she was used to ramble far" (382), and Margaret admits the same in a confessional tone: "in good truth I've wandered much of late / And sometimes, to my shame I speak, have need / Of my best prayers to bring me back again" (399–401). MS D intensifies her self-blame for such behavior: "I have been travelling far, and many days / About the field I wander . . . / And so I waste my time" (D.347–52). Though plausibly explicable on other grounds as well, her wanderings are a distorted, perhaps even psychotic, imitation of how and why the Pedlar is important to her – and a reminder of his failure to bring the news she seeks. MS D alleviates some of his discomfort at this point with an interpolated "momentary trance" (D.369) that imagines her recovery, "when he shall come again / For whom she suffered" (D.374–5). With its strong religious overtones, this addition also allows the Pedlar to reassert Robert's responsibility as the cause of Margaret's sufferings, and to distance himself from his own failures to alleviate them. But MS B as usual refuses to temper anything, presenting a more Shakespearean drama, with stronger, more intense character-ization.

Margaret wanders with the Pedlar the last time he sees her – "went with me a mile" (478) – to give him his wandering/marching orders: [she] "begged / That wheresoe'er I went I still would ask / For him whom she had lost" (480–2). MS B at this point shifts directly into the poem's great peroration, "Five tedious years / She lingered in unquiet widowhood," but MS D adds a weak explanation for the Pedlar's sudden five-year absence, which is remarkable, given the seasonal regularity of his visits up to this point:

> We parted then,
> Our final parting, for from that time forth
> Did many seasons pass ere I returned
> Into this tract again.
>
> (D.443–6)

Though intended as an element of verisimilitude, the passage raises as many questions as it answers. Why did he wait so many years before returning to a "tract" that he had been traversing so regularly? MS B, by moving into the "Five tedious years" directly after Margaret's begging the Pedlar to always "ask / For him whom she had lost," opens the possibility that he does not return because he knows he cannot console her, cannot bring the news she wants, can only be what he has increasingly become, a source of disappointment rather than of comfort. In a sense, his guilty feelings lead him to abandon her – thereby increasing his guilt even more. We know he continues to ask others about her, for lines 485–528 are the excruciatingly reticulated, magnificently detailed tableau of Margaret's end. But their main burden – their "weary load" – is of her repeated requests to strangers for information, with results the Pedlar knows all too well: "when they / Whose presence gave no comfort were gone by / Her heart was still more sad" (504–6). He too has been a wandering man "whose presence gave no comfort."

It is true that the largest difference between the two versions, MS B's biographical sketch which D omits, does generally work in the opposite

75

direction from the one we have been pursuing, presenting the Pedlar as a wise man in whom there is no guilt, and little reason for suspecting any. Most critical attention to the Pedlar's background has centered on his philosophy, since isolating and defining Wordsworth's "nature philosophy" has for so long set the modern critical agenda. But attention to his literary gifts is also revealing, not only for understanding Wordsworth's development – since these passages are obviously way-stations toward *The Prelude* – but also for understanding the drama between the characters in "The Ruined Cottage." The Pedlar is not always philosophical. His biography contains hints of an alternative or parallel vocation for him, that of balladeer, a man of stories. Furthermore, this possibility is raised in connection with his prior knowledge of the young narrator. For, just as the Pedlar has a special relationship with Margaret, so he is given in the various manuscripts a special relationship to the young narrator. And this relationship, we think, is as important to the expiation of his guilt as his close relationship with Margaret is in causing it.[21]

In his youth, MS B tells us, the Pedlar loved to "repeat / The songs of Burns," "his eye / Flashing poetic fire" (B.70–2). That this is a thematic as well as a biographical detail is emphasized by B's epigraph – the only version to have one – from Burns's "An Old Scotch Bard":

> Give me a spark of nature's fire,
> 'Tis the best learning I desire.
>
> My Muse though homely in attire
> May touch the heart.[22]

As a textual figure closely impinging on "The Ruined Cottage," Burns's bard is significantly less learned than Wordsworth's Pedlar ("I am nae *Poet*, in a sense, / But just a *Rhymer* like by chance, / An' hae to Learning no pretence," lines 49–51), but also significantly more amorous ("There's ae *wee faut* they whiles lay to me, / I like the lasses – Gude forgie me!," lines 94–8). Since the Pedlar's biography informs us that "he was untaught / In the dead lore of schools undisciplined," but confidently asks, "Why should he grieve?" (74–6), we see immediately the symmetry between his "muse" and that of the author of "The Ruined Cottage": "nature's fire" kindles "poetic fire." Other versions of MS B, especially those which Butler identifies as the second and third stages of Wordsworth's expansion of the Pedlar's character (Butler, pp. 150n, 179n), give him a fairly complete literary background, amounting almost to a complete poetical biography. By contrast, MS D's poetical references are more decorative and less functional: the passing allusion to Burns's "trotting brooks" already cited, and the Pedlar's out-of-character sophistication in referring to the wisdom of "the Poets in their elegies and songs" when they call on Nature to lament the passing of a loved one (D.73–82).

He has the writer's basic "precious gift," a metaphoric imagination, constantly comparing his own ideas and impressions with those in nature (pp. 150–3). Though "few books were his," he has "gazed upon that mighty orb of song / The divine Milton," and spent what earnings he could spare on books, and reading others "while at the stall" in "the neighbouring town" (pp. 160–1). Even so,

> Small need had he of books; for many a tale
> Traditionary round the mountains hung
> And many a legend peopling the dark woods
> Nourished Imagination in her growth
> (p. 163, 6–9),

and "the rustic vicar" supplied him with the lives and deaths of the martyrs (Foxe's *Acts and Monuments*) and "straggling volume[s]" of "preternatural tale[s]": "Romance of giants chronicle of fiends" (pp. 163–5). The third-stage expansions take him even further in the direction of being not merely a reader but also a writer, or at least a singer of songs · his own as well as others. The young narrator avers that he still retains "an ear" (p. 181, 77) and "had an eye" (p. 185, 94) which made it "most sweet / To hear him tell of things which he had seen / To hear him teach in unambitious style" (p. 187, 18–20). Three stray lines at the end of this expansion indicate that he went beyond others" songs, traditional lore, and reports of what he had seen, to imaginative creations of his own:

> many a ditty sweet
> Which he had fitted to the moorland harp
> His own sweet verse and as we trudged along
> Together did we make the rock and hollow grove
> [Ring, etc.]   (p. 191, 8–11)

The young narrator is not merely acquainted with the Pedlar, they have made music together. Indeed, when we reflect that this young narrator becomes The Poet in *The Excursion*, we might almost think that the Pedlar's biography is his own. From epigraph to epitaph, various revisions of the poem skirt near suggesting that the Pedlar and narrator are one and the same person. This possibility, or Wordsworth's toying with it, is very much in keeping with a major line of his poetry's development from 1793 onwards: characters who *combine or divide* the alternate roles of narrator and sufferer (e.g., the narrator-*cum*-sailor of the Salisbury Plain poems or, in another way, the closely linked hero and villain of *The Borderers*).[23] The Pedlar first took up his vocation not as a job but as an avocation, "From impulses of curious thought" (B.68), and the narrator pleads to hear more of his story in an almost identical fashion, "impelled / By a mild force of curious pensiveness" (B.276–7) – neither detail appearing in MS D. So the Pedlar not only knows the narrator, he also knows that this young man is a poet. This is the aspect of the Pedlar's variously proposed biographies that helps to explain why their special relationship is important, and why, even, the Pedlar may have been looking for him.

He is, finally, something of a literary critic, for he knows the limitations of his tale, as his introduction to Part II indicates:

> 'Tis a common tale,
> By moving accidents uncharactered,
> A tale of silent suffering, hardly clothed
> In bodily form, and to the grosser sense
> But ill adapted, scarcely palpable
> To him who does not think.
>
> (B290–59)

That's what *he* says. But the tale we hear as readers is his tale as re-told by the young narrator, and some of these strictures no longer apply, for it has been made all too thought-provokingly "palpable," by "moving" characters rather than actions. And that may well be just what the Pedlar had in mind.

Given his guilt feelings, he wishes to create a "memorial" to Margaret: one of the commonest and most appropriate human responses to the death of a loved one, perhaps especially to those we feel we have not treated as well as we might have while they were living. When the Pedlar says, "very soon / Even of the good is no memorial left" (133–4), he refers not only to Margaret as "the good" but also to himself, for perhaps "very soon" he will be dead and gone. At the moment the story begins to unfold, *he* is that memorial, or epitaph, for he contains Margaret's tale, her biography, or biographical truth. Though it is a critical commonplace that the ruined cottage is Margaret's memorial and a symbol of her decline, the cottage is neither to the young narrator when he stumbles into the shade around it. It is merely "four clays walls / That stared upon each other" (30–1) – mutely, speechlessly, perhaps a bit stupidly. MS B here contains four lines of Gothic editorial comment to the effect that even "a wandering gypsey" might pass by such a place, preferring "the imperfect arch / Of a cold lime-kiln" to its bad aspect. As an uninterpreted object, it conveys nothing of the meaning with which the Pedlar wishes to invest it; quite the contrary. Certainly the cottage is a symbol, but it is a symbol created by the Pedlar, and then re-created by the narrator's tale. Until he can read its epitaph aright, the young narrator sees just a ruined cottage, and no very picturesque or inviting one, at that.

This epitaphic function of the Pedlar's tale is accented when we note the congruence between his character and behavior in the poem and Wordsworth's later definitions of the general nature and functions of epitaphs.

For the occasion of writing an Epitaph is matter of fact in its intensity and forbids more authoritatively than any other species of composition all modes of fiction, except those which the very strength of passion has created; which have been acknowledged by the human heart, and have become so familiar that they are converted into substantial realities . . . [They] should be instinctively ejaculated, or should arise irresistibly from circumstances . . . uttered in such connection as shall make it felt that they are . . . perceived in their compass with the freshness and clearness of an original intuition . . . [Epitaphs are] a record to preserve the memory of the dead, as a tribute to individual worth, for a satisfaction to the sorrowing hearts of the survivors . . . which record is to be accomplished, not in a general manner, but, where it can, in close connection with the bodily remains of the deceased . . .[24]

Where *is* Margaret buried, by the way? Perhaps very nearby: "She sleeps in the calm earth, and peace is here" (D.512).

When the Pedlar begins showing the narrator the "things which [he] cannot see," he suggests that everything around them contains some "memorial" significance of Margaret's life: "The waters of that spring if they could feel / Might mourn. They are not as they were; the bond / Of brotherhood is broken" (B.135-7). The "if" is tentative, but stronger than MS D's version: "Beyond yon spring I stood / And eyed its waters till we seemed to feel / One sadness, they and I" (D.82-4). MS B has already told us that the Pedlar can give "a moral life" to "Even the loose stones that cover the highway" (81-2). But the question for the Pedlar is, can the young narrator be brought to the same degree of sensitivity? The Pedlar's tale is not merely a "memorial" for a fellow-artist to record, but also a test of the narrator to see if he can feel it in the same way.[25] When, at the end of MS D, the narrator "Reviewed that Woman's suff'rings, . . . it seemed / To comfort me while with a brother's love / I blessed her in the impotence of grief" (D.498–500), we can say he has passed the test by restoring the broken "bond of brotherhood." Repetitions of the word "power" also suggest the need for each man to overcome a pertinent moral powerlessness. The Pedlar "had little power / To give her comfort," and this is nicely repeated in the immediate effect of the story on the young narrator: "nor had [I] power / To thank him for the tale which he had told" (D.495–6).) So too, his turning "aside in weakness," and "milder interest [in] that secret spirit of humanity" (D.495, 503) parallels the Pedlar's earlier and *apparently* generalized "weakness of humanity" (B.252), which we have suggested applies very personally to him.

The narrator is more than just an artistically inclined youth known to the Pedlar. He is also a candidate for election. The Pedlar, a singer in the oral tradition, wants to see if the young man is worthy to make the permanent, written record of Margaret's story, to turn it into history. And the narrator (though perhaps here one should simply say Wordsworth), besides recording her tale, also records, by no means incidentally, the effect of her tale on a first-time hearer: himself. This little meta-drama is embedded within the larger frames of the story, especially at the break between Parts I and II. The Pedlar, having recounted all the essential information that a casual inquirer might want to hear, stops with Margaret's words about Robert ("'Every smile,' / Said Margaret to me here beneath these trees, / 'Made my heart bleed'"; B.241–3), and then, looking up through the trees, asks an apparently general rhetorical question about why such stories make us so sad. Then he waits to see what will happen.

The narrator tries to imitate the Pedlar's apparent "easy chearfulness," and this works, at first: "that simple tale / Passed from my mind like a forgotten sound" (B.261–2). But the other "trivial things" they begin talking about become "soon tasteless" to him. "A heartfelt chilliness" comes over him and he, who so recently had sought this shade for coolness, now steps back out of it, "to drink the comfort of the warmer sun" (274). Then he returns and, "looking round / Upon that tranquil ruin" – no longer four bare, staring walls – "I *begg'd* of the old man that *for my sake* / He would resume his story" (278–9; italics added). The Pedlar had begun, abruptly, for *his* own sake, not giving the young man the chance to say a word before suddenly intoning, "I see around me here / Things which you cannot see." But now he has paused, having given the main outlines of Margaret's story (she's dead, she had a husband, their house is a ruin), and leaves it to the young man to ask for the details on his own. By reflecting on the story, and begging for it to be continued (in a situation created, staged, and directed by the Pedlar), the narrator shows that he also has that "power to virtue friendly" which arises from "mournful thoughts" based on emotional commitment rather than "momentary pleasure." He has passed the test, or the first part of it, for he must yet be warned against hearing it wantonly, without thought, and – especially important to the Pedlar – "barren of all future good" (285), since he must be the bearer of its good onto futurity. He must also learn to pass through the final stages of the Pedlar's mysteries, in the reconciling addendum (from impotent grief to "milder interest" [D.502] to natural cheerfulness), but he has already begun to enter into the community the Pedlar has in mind, because the Pedlar resumes Part II with a new pronoun: "we." *We* are not men whose hearts hold "vain dalliance" with the dead, because "we have known that there is often found / In mournful thoughts, and always might be found, / A power to virtue friendly" (B.286–8). The young narrator may not have known he knew that. Our first sight of him, irascibly making his way across the plain, does not seem to reveal any innate natural cheerfulness. But he is about to find out that he does have it, once properly stimulated and educated.

Finally, it is possible to suggest, on one accounting of the poem's time-frame, that the Pedlar has only just begun to tell this tale, that in fact his telling it to the young narrator may be his first, and certainly his most pointed, telling of it. For it is certainly the young narrator who is the "I" who tells it to us, who has created the verbal "memorial" which the Pedlar lamented might "very soon" be gone. That "very soon" could be almost immediately, for the Pedlar may have just returned to Margaret's cottage, banking on running into the young narrator whom he has seen "the day before" (B.40) or "two days before" (D.40), when they met and "had been fellow-travellers" (D.41). No one has ever accounted for Wordsworth's inclusion of this oddly circumstantial and apparently irrelevant detail, that the narrator and the Pedlar should now be meeting again after a hiatus of a day or two. But their meeting could have given the Pedlar a chance to learn that the narrator's hiking itinerary would pass by Margaret's cottage.[26]

The larger ramification of this possibility may be represented in a tabular subtraction which suggests that Margaret has died very recently indeed:

MS B	Line	Time
1	"'Twas summer"	Immediate Present
2–8	"pale steam," "clearer air," "deep embattled clouds," "sunshine interposed"	Immediate Present [clearing after recent rain?]
185	"some ten years gone'	c. year 10
186	"two blighting seasons"	autumn, years 10 and 9
199	"through those calamitous years"	years 10 to 8
200	"ere the second spring" [1st spring = year 9; second spring = year 8]	spring, year 8
297	"till that hapless year"	c. year 8
301–2	"green lane . . . lofty elms"	early spring, year 7 [Pedlar's first return visit]
319	"two months gone"	late winter, year 8
341	"it was then early spring"	early spring, year 7
349–53	"heat and cold," "wet or fair," "driving winds"	summer–autumn–winter, year 7
357	"towards the wane of summer"	late summer, year 6 [Pedlar's second return visit]
431–4	"Ere . . . the primrose flower"	early spring, year 5 [Pedlar's third return visit]
474	"beaten by autumn winds"	autumn, year 5 [Pedlar's fourth return visit]
482	"Five tedious years"	autumn, year 0 [immediately previous autumn = Pedlar's fifth return visit?]

| D.513–15 | "weeds, and high spear-grass," "mist and silent rain-drops" | previous autumn or present summer [recent rain?] |
| D.516 | "as once I passed" | "the day before"? (B.40) "two days before"? (D.40) |

The final deduction depends on whether we understand "five tedious years" to represent the whole course of Margaret's "unquiet widowhood" (483), in which case she has been dead two or three years (i.e., since Robert left her, *c.* year 8), or whether we understand the five years to refer to the time since the Pedlar last saw her alive. And this option, which brings us very much up to the present narrative moment, and is strongly inferrable in MS B, seems to be confirmed by D's narrative interpolation:

> We parted then,
> Our final parting, for from that time forth
> Did many seasons pass ere I returned
> Into this tract again.
>> Five tedious years
> She lingered in unquiet widowhood . . .
>> (D.443–7)

The Pedlar has returned at last, seen confirmation of the hearsay reports he has gathered of Margaret's end, and now waits for his intended auditor, who he knows is in the neighborhood, and who has the training and education to compose the appropriate "memorial" which he wishes to erect for her – the beloved's last responsibility.

We can clearly recognize that the two men represent two versions of Wordsworth's sense of his own development, the narrator being approximately his chronological age, while the pedlar may represent his philosophical *coming* of age. In this respect, the two narratives of "The Ruined Cottage" may be said to enact a Wordsworthian *rite de passage*, from one kind of Wordsworthian poet (and poem) to another, a passing-on of knowledge, and of a kind of tale-telling, "simple" and "common," but highly "palpable / To him who *does* . . . think" (B.294–5; italics added). The new kind of narrator created herein is very like the emergent narrator of Wordsworth's "lyrical ballads" of 1798, to which he now turned, in a fantastic outburst of experimental creativity between March and May. He there creates a narrator who excels at provoking the itinerant poor to reveal their painful life stories, but who offers remarkably – or sensibly – little by way of commentary upon them.[27] Such a change is

82

implicit even in "The Ruined Cottage," for the Pedlar's "lore" as well as his life has been changed by his experience. Comparing his present tale with his former repertoire, we may say that "The Ruined Cottage" represents a fundamental shift in the Pedlar's *œuvre* – as it does in Wordsworth's. His tale is now of a different sort from the kind he used to tell, of border ballads, traditional legends, or the songs of Burns. In short, the poem offers warrant to believe that the tale the Pedlar tells is not of the sort he always tells, or used to tell, but constitutes a revision. By his guilty involvement in Margaret's tale, he has become a specialist in fundamental human *change*, first as an observer, and subsequently (as a result) as an agent of change – revision – in others. He embodies a force in Wordsworth's writing, the need to retell and to account for the retelling. As Wordsworth reworked the implications of his poem, the Pedlar recreated his complicity in the past.

All these possibilities strengthen the otherwise weak explanation that the Pedlar just happened to be there, that the narrator just happened to be passing, and that this story is one of a hundred similar ones the Pedlar could draw from his literary pack to tell to anyone in any location. Like Leonard in "The Brothers," the Pedlar is no mere tourist in his return to this fated spot. *This* telling, on our accounting of the Pedlar's guilt and his knowledge of the narrator's literary sensitivity, is the one in which the Pedlar creates, not only a poem, but also a Poet.

NOTES

1 Jack Stillinger, "Textual Primitivism and the Editing of Wordsworth," *Studies in Romanticism*, 28 (1989), p. 28. The second quotation is from Stillinger's citation of Raymond Carney, "Making the Most of a Mess," *Georgia Review*, 35 (1981), p. 635.

2 See *The Wordsworth Circle*, 17 (1986) for a transcript of "The Great *Prelude* Debate" held at the 1984 Wordsworth Summer Conference.

3 "Wordsworth's Poems: The Question of the Text," *The Review of English Studies*, 34 (1983), p. 190.

4 All line references will be to the Reading Texts of MS B and MS D in James Butler's edition: *"The Ruined Cottage" and "The Pedlar"* (Cornell University Press, 1979).

5 See Butler, p. ix. Wordsworth himself was no exception: "Towards the close . . . stand the lines that were first written beginning 'Nine tedious years' & ending [']Last human tenant of these ruined walls'" (DCP, cited by Butler, p. 3). It is also probable that these lines were among the very first composed for the poem.

6 Much of the critical debate on "The Ruined Cottage" centers upon the Pedlar's biography which MS B includes and D excludes. No one has seriously proposed the Pedlar to be guilty or conscience-stricken in his feelings toward Margaret, though several have opined in passing that he does not offer her much substantial help. Roughly speaking, views on the Pedlar's character divide between the

psychoanalytical and the philosophical. Robert Marchant explores what he sees as the Pedlar's inordinate capacity for empathy, arguing that it creates an equally profound sense of despair which requires a psychological displacement. In order to deal effectively with his despair, the Pedlar seeks solace in the ruins of Margaret's cottage, respecting her tragic love for her husband because he recognizes it "essentially as something in himself" (*Principles of Wordsworth's Poetry* [Swansea, 1974], pp. 80–5). Evan Radcliffe suggests that the Pedlar empathizes so strongly as a substitute for direct action ("'In Dreams Begin Responsibility': Wordsworth's Ruined Cottage Story," *Studies in Romanticism*, 23 [1984], pp. 101–19). David Pirie agrees, and suggests that if the Pedlar appears to be cold and dispassionate it is because he chooses to moralize in order not to "deny the truth of his own feelings" (*William Wordsworth: The Poetry of Grandeur and of Tenderness* [London, 1982], p. 55). The opposite opinion is well represented by James Averill, who reads the Pedlar as an intellectual figure akin to Rivers/Oswald in *The Borderers*. Averill claims that the Pedlar uses Margaret simply as an occasion to "catechize" the narrator, taking him through seven distinct methods of dealing with despair (*Wordsworth and the Poetry of Human Suffering* [Ithaca, 1980], p. 122). In a similar vein, John Hodgson sees the poem primarily as a philosophical inquiry into "the One Life" (*Wordsworth's Philosophical Poetry 1797–1814* [Lincoln, Nebraska, 1980], p. 4). Jonathan Wordsworth unites these two poles of interpretation, "individual problems of the heart" and "philosophical exploration," by showing that the philosophy exists to explain the passion (*The Music of Humanity* [London, 1969], p. 256). Our view is that the philosophy is not commensurate with the suffering except insofar as we can see the Pedlar's implication in the latter.

7   In several other small ways, MS B is the more realistic of the two. For example, its cottage has "clay" walls where D's are "naked" (B.30/D.31). It also includes details of little thematic relevance that D omits, such as the moss and fungus on the cottage bench (B.37–8), and Robert's straightening out the buckles and nails in "an old household box" (B.224–9).

8   See selections from *The Antijacobin* reprinted by Marilyn Butler in *Burke, Paine, Godwin and the Revolution Controversy* (Cambridge, 1984), pp. 214–19. The journal parodies Southey's "The Soldier's Wife" as "The Soldier's Friend": "Come, little Drummer Boy, lay down your knapsack here: / I am the Soldier's Friend – here are some Books for you; / Nice clever Books by TOM PAINE, the Philanthropist."

9   Jerome McGann, *The Romantic Ideology* (Chicago, 1983), pp. 81–6; James Chandler, *Wordsworth's Second Nature* (Chicago, 1984), pp. 130–44; Marjorie Levinson, *Wordsworth's Great Period Poems* (Cambridge, 1986), p. 163, n33; Levinson, *The Romantic Fragment Poem: A Critique of a Form* (Chapel Hill, 1986).

10 "On Wordsworth's Poetry," *Tait's Magazine* (September 1845); reprinted in *The Collected Writings of Thomas De Quincey*, ed. David Masson (Edinburgh, 1889–90), Vol. 6, p. 304.

11 Sharon Setzer, "Surprised by Satan: Reading the Gardens in Wordsworth's *Excursion*," paper delivered at the 1988 Wordsworth Summer Conference.

12 See also the rhetoric of humanized Resurrection in MS D's description of the Pedlar's "momentary trance," where Margaret seems "A human being destined to awake /

To human life, or something very near / To human life, when he shall come again /
For whom she suffered" (372–5).

13 *Wordsworth: A Critical Introduction* (Atlantic Highlands, 1986), p. 23.

14 Even the allusion to Ecclesiastes is invoked to *contrast* that Preacher's resignation,
since the next line is, "It moved my very heart" (B.146).

15 MS D effectively rounds off the Pedlar's admission of continued emotion here
(B.245–56) with a very similar diction for his approval of the narrator's "penance" at
the end of the poem (D.508–25), especially in its repetition of words like "peace,"
"chearful," and "wisdom." The poem's mid-point commentary on the tale's effect
on its teller is thus recapitulated in its end-point approval of its effect on its auditor.

16 MS B lacks certain pauses in the narration, where the Pedlar admits to other
"truancies" of the tale's effect upon him: e.g., "my wiser mind / Sinks, yielding to the
foolishness of grief" (D.118–19). These have the effect of mitigating the Pedlar's
degree of responsibility: here, by admitting his grief yet judging it "foolish."

17 Wordsworth pencilled "active" into a gap left by Dorothy in copying out MS D
(Butler, p. 57n). Doubtless Dorothy left the space on purpose, thus indicating
Wordsworth's desire to change the emphasis here.

18 John Turner has proposed that the Pedlar's tale has two parts, a trance followed by a
rational moral lesson (*Wordsworth: Play and Politics*, pp. 104–6).

19 *Ibid.*, pp. 97–8. Yet Turner does stress the father–daughter relationship of the Pedlar
and Margaret (p. 91).

20 "To have overlooked a point of policy so broadly apparent as this vitiates and
nullifies the very basis of the story." De Quincey, *Collected Writings*, Vol. 6, p. 306.
Even if we accept De Quincey's observation, its point may be less that Wordsworth's
tale is implausible, than that such "oversights" again point toward some guilty
behavior shared by Margaret and the Pedlar.

21 Reeve Parker has made the strongest case to date for the special "elective affinities"
between the Pedlar and the narrator ("'Finer Distance': The Narrative Art of
Wordsworth's 'The Wanderer,'" *ELH*, 39 [1972], pp. 87–111). See also Turner,
Wordsworth: Play and Politics, pp. 109–13.

22 The ellipsis is Wordsworth's, slightly misquoting Burns's "*Epistle to J.L.* *****k*"
[Lapraik], *An Old Scotch Bard*, lines 73–4 (*Wordsworth: Play and Politics*, p. 42n). The
elided lines are: "Then tho" I drudge thro" dub an' mire / At pleugh or cart."

23 This process continues into the composition of *Lyrical Ballads*, and contributes to
Wordsworth's successful experiments there. (K. R. Johnston, "The Triumphs of
Failure: Wordsworth's *Lyrical Ballads* of 1798," in *The Age of William Wordsworth*,
ed. Johnston and Ruoff [Rutgers, 1988], pp. 133–59.)

24 "Essays Upon Epitaphs," in *William Wordsworth: Selected Prose*, ed. John O. Hayden
(New York, 1988), pp. 352, 354–5, 327.

25 Many critics have stressed the fact that the Pedlar teaches the narrator a lesson
(Averill, *Wordsworth and the Poetry of Human Suffering*, p. 58; Turner, *Wordsworth:
Play and Politics*, p. 107; Philip Cohen, "Narrative Persuasion in *The Ruined Cottage*,"
Journal of Narrative Technique, 8 (1978), pp. 185–99; Parker, "Finer Distance," pp.
97–8; J. R. Watson, *Wordsworth's Vital Soul: The Sacred and Profane in Wordsworth's
Poetry* (London, 1982), pp. 79–82). Pirie argues that the tale's emotional effects on the

narrator are deliberately created (pp. 52–59), though he does not suggest the Pedlar has deliberately chosen his auditor. Parker has anticipated us in suggesting that the Pedlar chooses his young auditor; he sees their relationship as a two-way street of "elective affinities" (pp. 97, 106–8). None of these authorities suppose an ingredient of guilt to be operating in the Pedlar's choice, and test, of the narrator.

26 Parker has pointed out the significance of fact that the Pedlar knew the young man was in the neighborhood ("'Finer Distance,'" p. 97).

27 See Johnston, "The Triumphs of Failure." It is perhaps more accurate to say that "The Ruined Cottage" is the end of one line of development, rather than the beginning of a new one: i.e., the last poem in which Wordsworth offers a comprehensive explanation and commentary on the suffering it represents. In *Lyrical Ballads*, this commentary is displaced, first to the experimental motifs of the "Advertisement" in 1798, and then to the much more comprehensive, but much more indirect, literary-critical terminology of the famous "Preface" of 1800.

4

REVISING THE REVOLUTION: HISTORY AND IMAGINATION IN *THE PRELUDE*, 1799, 1805, 1850

NICHOLAS ROE

BETWEEN 1805 and 1850 Wordsworth revised *The Prelude* so that the poem comprehended the development of his political and religious thought. Critical estimates of these revisions have varied, but in general terms the argument has contrasted the earlier *Prelude* texts of 1799 and 1805 with the published poem of 1850. Furthermore, the aesthetic quality of Wordsworth's poetry in these versions of *The Prelude* has sometimes been confused with the 'orthodoxy' or 'radicalism' of the poet's ideas.

'In later years', Norman Fruman has said,

Wordworth's opinions and feelings did change, about many things, from politics to religion to the proper language, technique, and subjects for poetry. And the consequence of these deep changes in feeling and thought was to impose upon the 1805 *Prelude* another consciousness. The result, as he would have predicted, was to injure the artistic, moral, and psychological unity of his great poem.[1]

Fruman's concern here was to point out that Wordsworth's 'deep changes in feeling and thought', as represented by his revisions to *The Prelude*, marred the aesthetic and intellectual coherence of his poem. Perhaps many would agree with him, but the relationship between Wordsworth's changing beliefs and poetic revision may have been more complicated than this paradigm of 'another consciousness' suggests.

The earliest readers of the 1850 *Prelude* were far from convinced about the poem's 'orthodoxy'. When in November 1850 *The Gentleman's Magazine* reviewed *The Prelude*, it recognized the French Revolution as the originating (and enduring) principle of Wordworth's poetry:

the French Revolution was an electric shock to his whole spiritual being, perversive in its immediate, and permanent in its remote effects. It led him, both in its transit and catastrophe, to meditate deeply on the destinies and capacities of man; upon the powers and duties of the poet; upon the relations of society and nature; upon all that keeps man little, and upon all that might render him great. The lyrical ballads, the critical prefaces, and the renown of Wordsworth, have wrought one of the greatest literary revolutions the world has ever seen: and the nerve and purpose to work it were braced and formed under the influence of a corresponding convulsion in politics.[2]

As this passage from the review indicates, *The Gentleman's Magazine* largely agreed with William Hazlitt's estimate of 'Mr Wordsworth' published a quarter century earlier in *The Spirit of the Age*. In Thomas Macaulay's opinion, however, the 1850 *Prelude* was less successful in describing the experience of revolution than *The Excursion*. But it was clear to him that the poem embodied the 'permanent' effects of the French Revolution nevertheless. 'I brought home, and read, the "Prelude"', he wrote in his journal:

The story of the French Revolution, and of its influence on the character of a young enthusiast, is told again at greater length, and with less force and pathos, than in the Excursion. The poem is to the last degree Jacobinical, indeed Socialist. I understand perfectly why Wordsworth did not choose to publish it in his lifetime.[3]

Macaulay's 'Jacobinical' reading of the poem, and his suggestion that Wordsworth suppressed the poem for political reasons, should make one pause to reconsider whether in fact the 1850 poem is ideologically and religiously orthodox. In effect, Macaulay links *The Prelude* with *A Letter to the Bishop of Llandaff*, the republican pamphlet that Wordsworth wrote in 1793 but also chose not to publish during his lifetime. His observations are limited to the revolutionary books of the poem, and these are not my concern in this essay. I want to look elsewhere in *The Prelude*, and in other poems by Wordsworth, to identify passages that might substantiate Macaulay's claim that the 1850 *Prelude* 'is to the last degree Jacobinical'. I shall do so by way of suggesting that the critical debate about the 1799, 1805, and 1850 versions of *The Prelude* has been polarized in a manner that has obscured the continuity of the revolution in Wordsworth's imagination over more than half a century.

VERSIONS OF 'THE BLIND BEGGAR'

Here is the 1805 text of the 'blind beggar' passage from *The Prelude* Book VII:

> How often in the overflowing streets
> Have I gone forwards with the crowd, and said
> Unto myself, 'The face of every one
> That passes by me is a mystery.'
> Thus have I looked, nor ceased to look, oppressed
> By thoughts of what, and whither, when and how,
> Until the shapes before my eyes became

A second-sight procession, such as glides
Over still mountains, or appears in dreams,
And all the ballast of familiar life –
The present, and the past, hope, fear, all stays,
All laws of acting, thinking, speaking man –
Went from me, neither knowing me, nor known.
And once, far travelled in such mood, beyond
The reach of common indications, lost
Amid the moving pageant, 'twas my chance
Abruptly to be smitten with the view
Of a blind beggar, who, with upright face,
Stood propped against a wall, upon his chest
Wearing a written paper, to explain
The story of the man, and who he was.
My mind did at this spectacle turn round
As with the might of waters, and it seemed
To me that in this label was a type
Or emblem of the utmost that we know
Both of ourselves and of the universe,
And on the shape of this unmoving man,
His fixed face and sightless eyes, I looked,
As if admonished from another world.
                        (*1805* VII, 595–623)[4]

   In this spot of time, an oppressive solitude – '"The face of every one / That passes by me is a mystery"' – gradually develops as a profoundly alienated state of mind, 'far travelled in such mood, beyond / The reach of common indications, lost'. Thomas De Quincey's brilliant criticism of 'There was a boy' serves to highlight the distinctive character of Wordsworth's imagination in the 'blind beggar' passage. Writing of the lines

        a gentle shock of mild surprize
    Has carried far into his heart the voice
    Of mountain torrents . . .

De Quincey says,

This very expression, 'far,' by which space and its infinities are attributed to the human heart, and to its capacities of re-echoing the sublimities of nature, has always struck me as with a flash of sublime revelation.[5]

In the 'blind beggar' spot 'far travelled in such mood' works in a similar manner, opening the border between outer and inner spaces. But instead of revealing the heart's sublimity, the phrase identifies the loss of 'common indications' with a surrender of the spirit, almost of life itself:

> all the ballast of familiar life –
> The present, and the past, hope, fear, all stays,
> All laws of acting, thinking, speaking man –
> Went from me . . .

Wordsworth's sense of 'desertion' even in the 'overflowing streets' is comparable to the abstracted mood that he had experienced during his earliest schooldays at Hawkshead: 'I was often unable to think of external things as having external existence . . . Many times while going to school have I grasped at a wall or tree to recall myself from this abyss of idealism to the reality.'[6] In *The Prelude* the 'blind beggar' spot reworks this childish anecdote as a disturbing encounter which shares the metaphysical desolation of *King Lear*. It is the 'view / Of a blind beggar' that recalls the poet from the 'abyss' of solipsism, although the reflex of his 'idealism' is a powerful estrangement of 'familiar life' transforming the man into a monitory presence 'as if from another world'. So the vision of a silent, solitary beggar amid the busy London streets becomes the measure of 'reality', an image of human suffering and alienation understood as 'the utmost that we know / Both of ourselves and of the universe'.

The beggar's closest relatives in Wordsworth's poems are the discharged soldier ('A mile-stone propped him') and the leech-gatherer: 'a Man from some far region sent; / To give . . . human strength and strong admonishment'. All three are monitory figures, their mundane existence defamiliarized by cosmic suggestion. I have emphasized the blind beggar's strange transfiguration ('As if . . . from another world') in the 1805 poem, for the 1850 passage has been significantly altered in this respect. In the 1850 *Prelude*, Wordsworth cut the lines about the loss of 'familiar life' (*1805*, VII, 604–7), and he made a number of other comparatively minor alterations. But the moment of confrontation,

>   'twas my chance
> Abruptly to be smitten with the view
> Of a blind beggar   (*1805* VII, 610–12)

was substantially rewritten in a manner that brings the politics of Wordsworth's revisions into focus.

Wordsworth's '*view*/Of a blind beggar' (my emphasis) resembles his drawn-out contemplation of the leech-gatherer: 'He being all the while before me full in view'. The poet himself was in no doubt as to the peculiar resonance of 'view' in his poems, and he emphasized this to Mary Hutchinson in a letter of 14 June 1802:

Your objection to the word *view* is ill founded; substitute the word *see*, and it does not express my feeling. I speak as having been much impressed, and *for a length of time*, by the sight of the old man – *view* is used with propriety because there is continuousness in the thing . . .[7]

'Abruptly to be smitten with the view / Of a blind beggar' modifies sudden disclosure with a durable intensity of contemplation, similar to the 'continuousness' described in the letter above. Inverted syntax ('Abruptly . . . smitten'), and the Biblical register of 'smitten' ('struck down' in battle or by the hand of God) both contribute to the sublime force of Wordsworth's line, transforming 'chance' encounter into supernatural revelation. If we turn to the 1850 text, however, something different happens:

> lost
> Amid the moving pageant, I was smitten
> Abruptly, with the view (a sight not rare)
> Of a blind Beggar . . .
>
> (*1850* VII, 636–9)

Wordsworth's run-on line 'I was smitten / Abruptly' is unchanged between 1805 and 1850, although in the later poem the force of revelation is dislocated by a momentary pause from its object in 'the view . . . / Of a blind beggar'. And as if to stress the ordinariness of the encounter, Wordsworth inserts a parenthesis – '(a sight not rare)' – one effect of which is to emphasize the beggar's extraordinary familiarity as a form of 'visionary dreariness'. My concern is not to question whether these changes render the 1850 spot 'better' or 'worse' than the 1805 passage. I shall use Wordsworth's revisions, instead, to show how the quotidian strangeness of the beggar relates to the poet's earlier democratic aspirations as an English Jacobin in the 1790s. My larger purpose will be to suggest that spots of time in *The Prelude* disclose a *continuousness* in Wordsworth's vision that substantiates Macaulay's criticism of his 'Jacobinical' imagination in 1850.

INTROSPECTIVE JACOBINISM AND THE SPOTS OF TIME

> It was in truth
> An ordinary sight . . (*1799* I, 319–20)

The common sight of beggars on the streets of London was an obvious focus for political protest during the revolutionary years. In 1793, for example, Wordsworth's acquaintance George Dyer argued that 'It is not always owing to idleness or to profligacy, that we see many a poor sailor begging his bread at the close of a long war.' That same year Wordsworth himself had looked forward in his *Letter to the Bishop of Llandaff* with 'a comfortable hope that the class of wretches called mendicants will not much longer shock the feelings of humanity'.[8] When Wordsworth added 'a sight not rare' to the 'blind beggar', therefore, he tacitly acknowledged the ineffectuality of his own revolutionary idealism in looking for an end to such poverty. And by reminding us of a world in which beggars are to be found at every street corner, the phrase affirms a link between revolutionary impotence and Wordsworth's later imagination of suffering in his poetry.

In protest poems and pamphlets the beggar was a stock figure of human misery, the cause of political complaint. But in the imaginative idiom of the spots of time the suffering figure (beggar, leech-gatherer, water-carrier, discharged soldier) initiates an inward process of psychic revolution and self-reproach:

> on the shape of this unmoving man,
> His fixed face and sightless eyes, I looked,
> As if admonished from another world.
>
> $(1805$ VII, 621–3)

Compare Wordsworth's encounter with the leech gatherer,

> the whole Body of the man did seem
> Like one whom I had met with in a dream;
> Or like a Man from some far region sent;
> To give me human strength, and strong admonishment.
>
> (116–19)

— and with the discharged soldier:

> Long time I scanned him with a mingled sense
> Of fear and sorrow . . .
>   Not without reproach
> Had I prolonged my watch . . .   (67–8, 83–4)

These monitory encounters might appropriately be described as an introspective Jacobinism. I'm not suggesting that the disappointment of France merely encouraged the poet's self-preoccupation as a retreat from a world that no longer accommodated his ideals. In each of these poems the poet's self-involvement is the condition for a sudden, intense revelation of ordinary existence. That instant of awakening marks the interpenetration of history and imagination, and the resurgence of visionary 'progress' that had been deadlocked in the public, political world. Manifest social 'injustice' (formerly the concern of protest literature) has been assimilated as an obscure sense of personal blame, and Wordsworth's former commitment to political enlightenment has been similarly involved as the personal revolutions of 'admonishment', 'reproach', and spiritual insight. Such moments constitute 'the growth of a poet's mind', stations in the poet's psychic development which correspond to the memorial celebrations of *Fédération* in the history of the French Revolution.

At the deepest level, then, Wordsworth's quest for the origin of his imaginative power was a fulfilment of revolutionary history. In this sublime aspiration Wordsworth stands close to Milton, who in *Paradise Lost* had undertaken to justify God's providence in the aftermath of the English revolution. Like Milton, Wordsworth had endeavoured to reform the world by political revolution. He concluded *The Prelude* by offering a 'lasting inspiration' which (like the will of God) would abide the vicissitudes of human history. The theatre of Wordsworth's latter revolution is not a Bastille or a National Convention, but the human mind in relation to nature. Its radical principle is to be found not in *The Rights of Man*, but in the imagination:

> Prophets of Nature, we to them will speak
> A lasting inspiration, sanctified
> By reason, blest by faith: what we have loved,
> Others will love, and we will teach them how;
> Instruct them how the mind of man becomes
> A thousand times more beautiful than the earth
> On which he dwells, above this frame of things
> (Which, 'mid all revolutions in the hopes
> And fears of men, doth still remain unchanged)
> In beauty exalted, as it is itself
> Of quality and fabric more divine.
> (*1850* XIV, 446–56)

These lines conclude *The Prelude* as published in 1850 after Wordsworth's death. The passage differs from 1805 in that 'sanctified / By reason, blest by faith' is perhaps more 'pietistic' than 'sanctified / By reason and by truth' in the 1805 version. '[W]e may teach' in 1805 becomes, more emphatically, 'will teach' in 1850; 'Of substance and of fabric more divine' becomes (less happily maybe) 'Of quality and fabric more divine'. Nevertheless, Wordsworth's claim for the divinity of the human mind is consistent between 1805 and 1850. In both poems it is the mind in its relation to the 'unchanging' forms of nature that sustains the hope for humankind that Wordsworth had first experienced in the 1790s. And this, I believe, was the cause for Macaulay's disquiet when he read the 1850 *Prelude*.

Macaulay was not preoccupied by the revolutionary books of *The Prelude*. In them Wordsworth had told the story of the French Revolution, Macaulay believed, 'with less force and pathos, than in the Excursion'. It was the poem's radical inspiration that he tried to neutralize by ridicule:

There are the old raptures about mountains and cataracts; the old flimsy philosophy about the effect of scenery on the mind; the old crazy mystical metaphysics . . .[9]

'Flimsy . . . crazy . . . mystical': if Macaulay believed this to be a true assessment of *The Prelude*, the poem would not have unsettled him. What troubled him, however, was that Wordsworth's poem had perpetuated an 'old, old, old' idealism for new (and possibly 'socialist') generations. In 'the old flimsy philosophy' he recognized the 'Jacobinical' theory of human perfectibility now manifest in negotiations between the idealizing mind and 'external existence'.

When William Hazlitt reviewed Robert Owen's *New View of Society* in *The Examiner*, August 1816, he insisted that Owen's plans for social reform were not original. He traced Owen's ideals to the Jacobin era of the 1790s and then to a more distant past, in terms that Macaulay may have remembered when he wrote about *The Prelude*:

> It is as old as the 'Political Justice' of Mr. Godwin, as the 'Oceana' of Harrington, as the 'Utopia' of Sir Thomas More, as the 'Republic' of Plato; it is as old as society itself, and as the attempts to reform it by shewing what it ought to be, or by teaching that the good of the whole is the good of the individual . . . The doctrine of Universal Benevolence, the belief in the Omnipotence of Truth, and in the Perfectibility of Human Nature, are not new, but 'Old, old' . . .[10]

The Prelude also belongs to this distinguished catalogue, in that it is a poem which announces the future redemption of mankind, 'how the mind of man becomes / A thousand times more beautiful than the earth / On which he dwells' (*1805*, XIII. 446–8). I want now to return to the source of Wordsworth's flimsy, crazy belief in the regeneration of man, to explore the intersection between politics and the composition of the early *Prelude* in 1798–9.

PERSECUTION AND PROPHETIC POETRY

In Book XIII of the 1805 *Prelude*, Wordsworth recalls the time when he had begun the poem:

> Call back to mind
> The mood in which this poem was begun,
> O friend – the termination of my course
> Is nearer now, much nearer, yet even then
> In that distraction and intense desire
> I said unto the life which I had lived,
> 'Where art thou? Hear I not a voice from thee
> Which 'tis reproach to hear?' Anon I rose
> As if on wings, and saw beneath me stretched
> Vast prospect of the world which I had been,
> And was; and hence this song, which like a lark
> I have protracted, in the unwearied heavens
> Singing, and often with more plaintive voice

94

Attempered to the sorrows of the earth —
Yet centring all in love, and in the end
All gratulant if rightly understood.

　　Whether to me shall be allotted life,
And with life power to accomplish aught of worth
Sufficient to excuse me in men's sight
For having given this record of myself,
Is all uncertain; but, beloved friend,
When looking back thou seest, in clearer view
Than any sweetest sight of yesterday,
That summer when on Quantock's grassy hills
Far ranging, and among the sylvan coombs,
Thou in delicious words, with happy heart,
Didst speak the vision of that ancient man,
The bright-eyed Mariner, and rueful woes
Didst utter of the Lady Christabel;
And I, associate in such labour, walked
Murmuring of him, who — joyous hap — was found,
After the perils of his moonlight ride,
Near the loud waterfall, or her who sate
In misery near the miserable thorn;
When thou dost to that summer turn thy thoughts,
And hast before thee all which then we were,
To thee, in memory of that happiness,
It will be known – by thee at least, my friend,
Felt — that the history of a poet's mind
Is labour not unworthy of regard:
To thee the work shall justify itself.

　　　　　　　　　　　(*1805* XIII, 370–410)

In both the 1805 and 1850 poems Wordsworth rearranges the historical sequence of events in 1798, and mentions the beginning of *The Prelude* in winter 1798 before alluding to the summer he had previously spent with Coleridge under the Quantock Hills. This reversal identifies *The Prelude* as a memorial to the 'happiness' and the creativity of 'that summer'. By contrast, however, Wordsworth's early work on the poem is remembered as a period of 'distraction and intense desire'. The lines immediately following allude to *Paradise Lost*, specifically to Eve's dream in which an angel tempts her to taste the fruit 'of interdicted knowledge':

　　　　　　　Forthwith up to the clouds
With him I flew, and underneath beheld
The earth outstretched immense, a prospect wide
And various: wondering at my flight and change
To this high exaltation . . .　　　　　(V, 86–90)

Eve's dream (which prefigures the fall in Book IX of the poem) had been inspired by Satan who, disguised as a toad, whispered in her ear as she slept. But why did this part of *Paradise Lost* return with Wordsworth's memory of the 'mood in which [*The Prelude*] was begun'? Unlike Eve's dream, Wordsworth's access to the ways of the imagination was entirely self-initiated:

> In that distraction and intense desire
> I said unto the life which I had lived,
> 'Where art thou? Hear I not a voice from thee
> Which 'tis reproach to hear?'

And Wordsworth's imaginative passage 'As if on wings' is wholly self-sustained, 'like a lark / Protracted'. The allusion to Milton serves to differentiate Wordsworth's imagination, orienting his poem upon its own creator: Wordsworth is his own Satan as he is his own redeemer, and his 'dream' in *The Prelude* is of himself,

> Vast prospect of the world which I had been,
> And was; and hence this song . . .

Here, as with all of Wordsworth's revisions of Milton, the supernatural causes of *Paradise Lost* are relinquished for the properties of the human mind: 'the image of man dominates' in the 1805 *Prelude*, as Herbert Lindenberger has said.[11] What, then, was the object of Wordsworth's 'intense desire'? It might plausibly be glossed as that 'other task', *The Recluse*, the philosophic poem Wordsworth and Coleridge had projected in spring 1798. But if that may have been the case, what was the 'distraction' which had perplexed the poet? Was it a sense of his own inability to tackle the greater philosophic poem? Or does Wordsworth's identity with Satan, implied by the allusion to *Paradise Lost*, offer an alternative solution?

If one glances back to the moment in *Paradise Lost* Book IV when Satan is discovered whispering at Eve's ear, inspiring her unearthly dream, this is what one finds: the angel Ithuriel touches Satan with his spear:

> up he starts
> Discovered and surprised. As when a spark
> Lights on a heap of nitrous powder, laid
> Fit for the tun some magazine to store
> Against a rumoured war, the smutty grain
> With sudden blaze diffused, inflames the air:
> So started up in his own shape the fiend.
> Back stept those two fair angels half amazed
> So sudden to behold the grisly king . . .
>
> (IV, 813–21)

Elsewhere in *Paradise Lost* Satan and the fallen angels are associated with gunpowder – indeed in Book VI they are credited with its invention. But the sustained metaphor here in the passage from Book IV also associates the destructive power of gunpowder with 'the grisly king' who emerges from the flames. 'Grisly', which we may understand as 'grim' or 'ghastly', was construed more emphatically in Milton's time as 'causing horror, terror, or extreme fear' – usually with reference to imminent death. The whole marvellous image of Satan restored to his true form in a blaze of gunpowder is republican in spirit, and this would not have been lost on Wordsworth. I want to suggest, then, that if we attend to Milton's presence in the 'Call back to mind' passage, Wordsworth's self-discovery as a man of imagination turns upon his 'desire' to prepare for *The Recluse* and also the 'distracting' presence of terror figured in a 'grisly king'. I want now to explore how 'terror' bears upon the origins of *The Prelude* in the winter of 1798–9.

Why in summer 1798 did Wordsworth, Dorothy, and Coleridge leave their homes in Somerset and set off for Germany? The trip was projected in March 1798, when Wordsworth wrote asking his friend James Losh about Germany. Coleridge was anxious to study at German universities and, at first, the Wordsworths planned to join him 'to furnish [themselves] with a tolerable stock of information in natural science' (*EY*, 213). The visit of John Thelwall in July 1797, and the Spy Nozy business the following month, had ensured that the St Albyn family would not renew the lease on Alfoxden House.[12] Perhaps one is justified, then, in speculating that the oppressive political climate in Britain was also a factor that encouraged Wordsworth to go into exile abroad. E. P. Thompson once suggested that both poets were 'dodging the draft' for the Somerset militia.[13] But there was another cause for Wordsworth's and Coleridge's political anxieties during 1798, that I believe had a direct bearing on their move abroad and Wordsworth's early work on *The Prelude*.

Two years after Coleridge's death, in 1836, George Dyer recalled that 'when Mr C. and Dr Southey were young men & first came to London they were in the habit of calling upon me & I remember introducing the former to Mr Gilbert Wakefield'.[14] Wakefield was a graduate of Jesus College, Cambridge, a brilliant classicist, unitarian dissenter, and a reformist of singular extremity. 'He was not one of those Socinians who brought to Coleridge's mind the image of cold moonlight,' E. P. Thompson says, 'for some strange stove raged inside him.'[15] In January 1798, three years after he first met Coleridge, Wakefield published a *Reply* to Richard Watson's defence of the Pitt administration in his *Address to the People of Great Britain*. On a previous occasion, early in 1793, Watson had provoked Wordsworth into writing *A Letter to the Bishop of Llandaff*. At the other end of the decade, Wakefield was 'almost the last public voice out of Jacobin England', as Thompson has put it. He was charged with seditious libel in his *Reply* to Watson, along with three booksellers who had sold the pamphlet: John Cuthell, J. S. Jordan, and Joseph Johnson. Jordan and Johnson were both well-known as radical publishers: in February 1799 they were jailed for one year and six months respectively. Cuthell was fined £20 and discharged. And on 30 May 1799 Wakefield was sentenced to imprisonment for two years: he was released in May 1801, and died four months afterwards.[16]

The imprisonment of Wakefield and Johnson, who had both figured in the radical careers of Wordsworth and Coleridge earlier in the 1790s, provides immediate evidence of the 'times of fear' that Wordsworth lamented at the end of the *Two-Part Prelude*. Johnson had published *An Evening Walk* and *Descriptive Sketches* in 1793. And while on his way to Germany in September 1798, Coleridge introduced himself to Johnson and arranged for him to publish *Fears in Solitude*.[17] At the close of the revolutionary decade the circumstances of Wakefield, Johnson, Wordsworth, and Coleridge represented alternative consequences of political repression: persecution and imprisonment or, on the other hand, exile and the imaginative introspection of poems such as 'Frost at Midnight', 'Tintern Abbey', and the early *Prelude*. Indeed, Wordsworth's 'Glad Preamble' (which dates from 1800 and stands as a preface to the 1805 and 1850 *Preludes*) defines his creative 'enfranchisement' in terms of an escape from

> a house
> Of bondage, from yon city's walls set free,
> A prison where he hath been long immured.
> (*1805* I, 6–8)

The association of city and prison was familiar to Wordsworth from the Old Testament, from Milton, Thomson, Cowper, and from Coleridge's poems.[18] But this full literary background for Wordsworth's metaphor is further enriched by the recognition that, as Wordsworth began his 'poem to Coleridge' in the winter of 1798–9, the poets' mutual acquaintances Wakefield and Johnson were both tried and imprisoned for their political opinions. In the 'Glad Preamble' to *The Prelude*, literary allusion places Wordsworth's imaginative investment within a context of political meaning. Wakefield was the 'last public voice out of Jacobin England', but the 'Glad Preamble' metaphorically associates political repression with the beginnings of Wordsworth's quest for himself in *The Prelude*.

The *Two-Part Prelude* is a poem of self-interrogation, written at a period when Wordsworth was very much aware of the contemporary realities of persecution and imprisonment, 'this time / Of dereliction and dismay'. And this enables one to see more precisely how his earliest investigations of his imaginative power may have constituted a *new radicalism* to supplant the failure of reform and revolution. Political change based upon the natural rights of man gave place, in *The Prelude*, to an exploration of essential human nature in the poet's own experience:

> There are in our existence spots of time
> Which with distinct preeminence retain
> A fructifying virtue, whence, depressed
> By trivial occupations and the round
> Of ordinary intercourse, our minds –
> Especially the imaginative power –
> Are nourished and invisibly repaired;
> Such moments chiefly seem to have their date
> In our first childhood.   (*1799* I, 288–96)

Wordsworth's imaginative virtue was radical, to the extent that it derived from the earliest experiences of his childhood. But while such moments retained a fructifying creative force, the formative emotion was typically guilt, fear, and alienation associated with childish exploits such as boat-stealing and bird-snaring or, more disturbingly, the death of the poet's father. The primary memory in all of these cases relates to childhood, but the traumatic experiences of terror and self-blame have a strange familiarity in adult life; for Wordsworth in *The Prelude*, childish trauma uncannily prefigures the violence of revolution he had known (and perhaps witnessed) many years later. To be specific, Wordsworth's bird-snaring spot of time (*1799* I, 27–49; *1805* I, 310–32; *1850* I, 306–25) draws some of its disturbing energy from a series of allusions to *Macbeth*. Shakespeare's presence here informs childish transgression with the politics of violence known in adult life, so that the child's misdemeanour and revolutionary mass-murder are mutually comprehended as human weakness overcome by 'strong desire'.[19] Wordsworth's glorious recognition that 'The Child is Father of the Man' was preceded, I think, by the darker intuition that the child had been father of violent revolution.

It may now be possible to see why Macaulay was provoked by 'the old raptures about mountains and cataracts . . . the old philosophy about the effect of scenery on the mind . . . the old . . . mystical metaphysics'. He recognized that *The Prelude* as a whole sought to comprehend (and, arguably, excuse) Jacobin excesses as a manifestation of flawed human nature, while perpetuating the visionary optimism which constituted the benevolent aspect of revolutionary idealism: 'The poem is to the last degree Jacobinical.' I want now to conclude with a return to Wordsworth's revisions in *The Prelude*, and to argue that Wordsworth's revisionism was in fact an effort to sustain this strong imagination of history.

REVISING THE REVOLUTION

The 1850 *Prelude* is indeed embellished with political and religious statements that are absent in earlier versions of the poem. In *1850* Book X, for instance, Wordsworth adds the following passage to the recollection of his return from France in December 1792:

> Twice had the trees let fall
> Their leaves, as often Winter had put on
> His hoary crown, since I had seen the surge
> Beat against Albion's shore, since ear of mine
> Had caught the accents of my native speech
> Upon our native country's sacred ground.
> A patriot of the world, how could I glide
> Into communion with her sylvan shades,
> Erewhile my tuneful haunt?
>
> (*1850* X, 236–44)

A footnote to this passage in the Norton edition of *The Prelude* comments: 'The plain statement of *1805*, "After a whole year's absence," is sacrificed in favour of poetic elaboration that is not even accurate. Wordsworth was in France late November 1791 – November/December 1792.' True. But was Wordsworth's 'poetic elaboration' in this passage simply a lyrical flourish? His rewriting sanctified the 'sylvan shades' of England, but it was also a revision of history and the reality that as a 'patriot of the world' he had been profoundly disaffected after his return from France. To describe his 'shock' when Britain entered the war with France, Wordsworth had created one of the most striking images in the 1805 poem:

> I, who with the breeze
> Had played, a green leaf on the blessed tree
> Of my beloved country – nor had wished
> For happier fortune than to wither there –
> Now from my pleasant station was cut off,
> And tossed about in whirlwinds.
>
> (*1805* X, 253–8)

The 'green leaf' and 'blessed tree' are removed in the 1850 *Prelude*. In their place Wordsworth imagines himself as a 'pliant harebell' growing 'on the ancient tower / Of [his] beloved country' (*1850* X, 277–80); from 'that pleasant station' he is torn and 'tossed about in whirlwind' (*1850* X, 282–3). The figure works in much the same way in both poems, representing the poet's alienation from his homeland. So why did he revise the 'green leaf . . . blessed tree' emblem in particular? The answer, I think, lies in Book VII of *The Prelude*, with Wordsworth's eulogy of Burke:

> I see him, – old, but vigorous in age, –
> Stand like an oak whose stag-horn branches start
> Out of its leafy brow, the more to awe
> The younger brethren of the grove.
>
> (*1850* VII, 519–22)

By removing the passage that would have the poet 'cut off' from the 'blessed tree / Of [his] beloved country', Wordsworth grafted himself back on to the trunk of English tradition represented by Burke. And to reinforce this allegiance, he claimed to have been 'thankful' and 'inspired' by Burke at the period when his *Letter to the Bishop of Llandaff* had lampooned Burke as a political drunkard, staggering unsteadily from liberalism to conservatism.

So the 1850 *Prelude* certainly does reflect Wordsworth's later opinions, to the extent that he was prepared to revise his own early history in order to align himself with Burke. The later poem consequently accommodates two sorts of radicalism. One is 'the allegiance to which men are born' (*1850* VII, 530), which derived from Burke. The other is the radical equality of humankind, which was the basis of Paine's political theory and an essential principle of Wordsworth's spots of time as representative human experience. The 1850 *Prelude* is, in effect, a synthesis of the great debate about the French Revolution which began with the publication of Burke's *Reflections* in November 1790. The poem embodies Wordsworth's creative effort, over nearly half a century, to come to terms with that argument in the light of his own experience of revolutionary optimism and defeat. To champion one or other version of *The Prelude* on the basis of politics, religion, or style is to lose sight of *The Prelude* in progress. It constitutes a narrowing of critical perspective, perhaps a scholarly dead-end. Wordsworth's revisionary imagination in *The Prelude* demonstrates that the texts of 1799, 1805, and 1850 together form a unity that is larger, and more complex, than any single 'early' or 'late' version. It is this greater poem that Wordsworth studies should now address.

NOTES

1 'Waiting for the Palfreys: The Great *Prelude* Debate', *The Wordsworth Circle*, 17 (1986), p. 13. Fruman's position in the passage quoted finds a precedent in Ernest de Selincourt's Introduction to *The Prelude* (Oxford, 1926), and in reviews of this first parallel edition of the poem's 1805 and 1850 texts.
2 *The Gentleman's Magazine*, n.s. 34 (1850), p. 466.
3 *The Life and Works of Lord Macaulay*, 10 vols. (London, 1896–7), Vol. 10, p. 280.

4 Quotations from *The Prelude* will be from the texts in *The Prelude, 1799, 1805, 1850,* ed. J. Wordsworth, M. H. Abrams, and S. Gill (London and New York, 1979). Unless indicated otherwise, quotations from Wordsworth's shorter poems will be from the Oxford Authors edition, ed. Stephen Gill (Oxford, 1984). Quotations from *Paradise Lost* will be from the Longman edition, ed. Alastair Fowler (London, 1968).

5 Thomas De Quincey, *Recollections of the Lakes and the Lake Poets,* ed. David Wright (Harmondsworth, 1970), 161. Lines from 'There was a Boy' are quoted from *Lyrical Ballads,* ed. R. L. Brett and A. R. Jones (London, 1963).

6 *The Poetical Works of William Wordsworth,* ed. E. de Selincourt and H. Darbishire, 5 vols. (Oxford, 1940–9), Vol. 4, p. 463. For three other accounts of Wordsworth's 'abyss of idealism' see Hugh Sykes Davies, *Wordsworth and the Worth of Words* (Cambridge, 1986), pp. 173–4.

7 *The Letters of William and Dorothy Wordsworth: The Early Years, 1787–1805,* ed. Ernest de Selincourt, rev. Chester L. Shaver, 2nd edn (Oxford, 1967), p. 364.

8 George Dyer, *The Complaints of the Poor People of England,* 2nd edn (London, 1793), p. 49, and *The Prose Works of William Wordsworth,* ed. W. J. B. Owen and J. W. Smyser, 3 vols. (Oxford, 1974), Vol. 1, p. 43.

9 *Macaulay,* Vol. 10, p. 280.

10 *The Complete Works of William Hazlitt,* ed. P. P. Howe, 21 vols. (London, 1930–4), Vol. 7, p. 98.

11 'The Great Debate', p. 2.

12 See my *Wordsworth and Coleridge: The Radical Years* (Oxford, 1988), pp. 234–62 for Thelwall and Spy Nozy at Nether Stowey. For the unhappy politics of the Alfoxden lease more particularly, see my essay 'Coleridge and John Thelwall: The Road to Nether Stowey', in *The Coleridge Connection: Essays for Thomas McFarland,* ed. R. Gravil and M. Lefebure (London, 1990), pp. 60–80.

13 E. P. Thompson, 'Disenchantment or Default? A Lay Sermon', in *Power and Consciousness,* ed. C. C. O'Brien and W. D. Vanech (New York and London, 1969), pp. 149–81.

14 Letter of 24 May 1836 to Dr Carey of the British Museum. Archives of Emmanuel College, Cambridge.

15 'Disenchantment or Default?', p. 164.

16 For the prosecution of Wakefield and Johnson, see Jane Worthington Smyser, 'The Trial and Imprisonment of Joseph Johnson, Bookseller', *Bulletin of the New York Public Library,* 78 (1974), 418–35, and chapter 5 in G. P. Tyson, *Joseph Johnson: A Liberal Publisher* (Iowa, 1979).

17 For Coleridge and Johnson in September 1798, see *The Letters of Samuel Taylor Coleridge,* ed. E. L. Griggs, 6 vols. (Oxford, 1956–71), Vol. 1, pp. 417, 420.

18 See Lucy Newlyn, '"In City Pent": Echo and Allusion in Wordsworth, Coleridge, and Lamb, 1797–1801', *Review of English Studies,* n.s. 32 (1981), pp. 408–28.

19 For a more extensive analysis of the politics of the 'bird-snaring' spot of time in *The Prelude,* see the final chapter in Nicholas Roe, *The Politics of Nature: Wordsworth and Some Contemporaries* (Basingstoke, 1992).

5

CROSSINGS OUT: THE PROBLEM OF TEXTUAL PASSAGE IN *THE PRELUDE*

KEITH HANLEY

THERE are signs that the long-running debate over the poetic superiority/ inferiority of the successive versions of Wordsworth's poems is returning to a consideration of the nature of his revisions.[1] The peculiarity of Wordsworth's case was established by Ernest de Selincourt, who observed: 'It is probable that no poet ever paid more meticulous or prolonged attention to his text than Wordsworth: certainly none has left more copious evidence of it.'[2] De Selincourt further commented on the growth of the revisionary 'obsession': 'as, with the passage of years, moments of vital inspiration became rarer, he strove to compensate for their loss by devoting endless pains to the revision of earlier work'.[3] What is in question is not simply the number of variants that encrust most Wordsworth texts but the whole compensatory scheme of his continuous rewriting.

Paradoxically, Wordsworth's alterations came to be addressed precisely to the denial and concealment of change, constantly seeking to make past utterance speak for an ever-present conviction. In the sense that all his work from the commencement of what was to become *The Prelude* can be seen as sharing in a repression of change, in which personal and political history are inscribed, Wordsworth was right in claiming in 1843 that 'No change has taken place in my manner for the last 45 years.'[4] Whenever he achieved a sense of conclusiveness, the latest version was published; if not, it remained part of a cumulative manuscript scrapbook in which texts were left somehow unresolved or moved around piecemeal into and out of different works that themselves might or might not prove finishable.

Notoriously, Wordsworth completely overhauled theological and political positions with little conscious acknowledgement: his poetry is traversed by a series of separable discourses – pantheism, associationism, Burkeanism, Anglicanism, neo-classicism, and so on – which, though their first insertions may be roughly dated, often overlap chronologically and sometimes contradictorily.

He was blinded to such discrepancies by an over-riding process of accommodation that sought to make the various discourses represent the same thing – a process that, in effect, he came to define as the imagination. It was during the composition of *The Prelude*, from 1798–1805, that a radical shift occurred, after which he came to believe that he could attach his own determinate meaning to given discourses.

However editors and critics value the effect that Herbert Lindenberger refers to as 'the struggle towards definition'[5] that characterizes the earlier phases of composition, it is undeniably very different from the kind of writing that Wordsworth came to prefer. The development is from a language of indeterminacy, of gestures towards something unsayable, to an attempted language of permanence and its pretence to finality of statement. The silence that invests the experiences which characteristically intrigue Wordsworth (which are offered as of primary interest and as prior to the language that displaces them) gives way to self-consciously conventional rhetorics. Wordsworth becomes generally less apologetic about the inadequacy of his poetry to provide 'Colours and words that are unknown to man',[6] and comes rather to assume poetry's representational potential.

But if the completion of poetic statement, the mastery of his own poetic discourse, became more urgent to Wordsworth than the evocation of a certain kind of private experience, communication with his ideal reader nevertheless continued to derive ultimately from a level of shared experience prior to social language, from 'quiet sympathies with things that hold / An inarticulate language'.[7] The Wordsworthian 'gentle Reader' particularly values a position enabled by the denial of language, and willingly summons up 'Such stores as silent thought can bring'.[8] But the poet's later public voice challenges them far more strenuously to recoup that 'pure principle of love'[9] behind the poetry which would discriminate what the discourse he used meant to Wordsworth. When Wordsworth wrote to Lady Beaumont that 'the voice which is the voice of my Poetry without Imagination cannot be heard',[10] he was demanding that sympathetic readers should conform to a peculiar appropriation of a given discourse that he believed would serve to institutionalize their common interest, and that he had come to see as his version of the creative imagination in completing the composition of *The Prelude* in 1804–5.

Yet what came to disturb Coleridge and other frustrated Wordsworthians was a discontinuity between private meaning and the apparently untransformed literalism of an established discourse that no longer drew attention to the characteristic force of the inexplicit, of 'the soul – / Remembering how she felt, but what she felt / Remembering not'.[11] As reported to their unofficial arbiter, Lady Beaumont, Coleridge's reaction to *The Excursion* reveals how the obscure purpose with which Wordsworth had adopted conventional discourses simply escaped other readers' comprehension:

As proofs meet me in every part of the Excursion, that the Poet's genius has not flagged, I have sometimes fancied that having by the conjoint operation of his own experiences, feelings, and reason *himself* convinced *himself* of Truths, which the generality of persons have either taken for granted from their Infancy, or at least adopted early in life, he has attached all their own depth and weight to doctrines and words, which come almost as Truisms or Common-place to others.[12]

Wordsworth might have countered that he was after all 'spreading . . . the depth and height of the ideal world around [discourses] of which, for the common view, custom had bedimmed all the lustre . . .'[13] More specifically, the 'depth and weight' that he attached to well established 'doctrines and words', making them so oddly impressive to himself, derived precisely from the exclusion of individualism that carries peculiarly personal and historical resonances. But for Coleridge, representatively, such institutionalized discourses remained after all unconstrained by Wordsworth's revisionary reading. They were too powerful for an inner reform of meaning, and were most likely to end up speaking effectively for unqualified social and political interests.

I

There is no space here to develop an argument that depends ultimately on Lacanian theory to elucidate the nature of Wordsworth's embarrassment with language. I have suggested elsewhere that this problem derives from a peculiarly dominant formation of a rudimentary sense of self that was caused and then reinforced by a series of crucial life-experiences.[14] It resulted in an ongoing interplay between that primary subject position and the subject subsequently inscribed in language.

Wordsworth's traumatic experience of the French Revolution reproblematized his original entry into the domain of language (the symbolic) during infancy – a trauma already reawakened in childhood by the death of his mother in his eighth year. The fixation that resulted during childhood on the imaginary order (of the 'mirror stage', when the infant has apprehended its bodily unity but has not yet become subjectified in the symbolic order of language), strengthened the primitive formation of the self, jubilant in its self-recognition and seemingly oblivious of any sense of alienation in the image of another self. The effect dictated not only an illusory oneness with natural objects but a marvellously satisfying self-inscription in imaginary languages of fairy-tale and romance. Throughout childhood and youth his relation to these imaginary languages informed his relation to literary discourse. It also suppressed the knowledge of his real social and economic subjectivity by representing a self-formation that was prior to and independent of the discourses of his historical moment.

But the traumatic revelation was inevitable that the symbolic domain (of the father and of history) had indeed been entered with the acquisition of language itself: of this a series of major 'shocks' made him reaware. The first was the death of his father. In his first important poem, 'The Vale of Esthwaite', written at the age of seventeen, Wordsworth recorded the trauma that had occurred less than three years before:

> Long, long, upon yon naked rock
> Alone, I bore the bitter shock;
> Long, long, my swimming eyes did roam
> For little Horse to bear me home,
> To bear me – what avails my tear?
> To sorrow o'er a Father's bier.[15]

Wordsworth was angry that the horse he expected his father to send to take him home for Christmas had not arrived; but his father was lying mortally ill from exposure at the time. It seems likely from this and the later *Prelude* version that 'a heavy load'[16] of guilt had resulted when impetuous expressions of vengeance had become self-fulfilling and obscurely self-enhancing: 'I mourn because I mourned no more.'[17] The retroactive 'shock' (Wordsworth obviously could not have known of his father's death, which took place ten days later) locates the oedipal trauma not so much in the news of his father's death as in the expression of his own bitterness that had turned out so potently self-affirmative.

In Part I of the two-Part *Prelude* of 1799 a later version of this episode inaugurates an important series of echoes from *Hamlet* that register Wordsworth's particular oedipal story. The list of 'spectacles and sounds' attached to the experience culminates in

> the mist
> Which on the line of each of those two roads
> Advanced in such indisputable shapes
>
> (365–7)

– revising the exchange of language invited by the ghost of Hamlet's father: 'Thou com'st in such a questionable shape' (I, iv, 43).[18] In the Wordsworthian encounter, the dialogue that initially seemed withheld by a paternal veto ('indisputable'), as the father refuses to share his power over the word, turns out to have been irrelevant to the fulfilment of a stronger desire, not for his father's death but for the correction of that desire and his own 'chastisment' (355). What resulted from this alternative desire was the triumphant return of the imaginary relation with nature that is credited not so much with a guilty victory over the father, and the appropriation of language, as with the sustained avoidance of conflict that the scene came to signify:

> All these were spectacles and sounds to which
> I often would repair, and thence would drink
> As at a fountain.   (368–70)

Wordsworth's access of power derives from the absence of that other, rivalrous self-formation that issues from a contest for the word of the father. The elemental violence of the storm (severe weather conditions had about that time actually killed his father) represents the threatened self-realization that had led to the diversion of his identification with his father's spirit (compare old Hamlet's 'I am thy father's spirit' (I, v, 8)) within the imaginary economy of nature:

> And I do not doubt
> That in this later time, when storm and rain
> Beat on my roof at midnight, or by day
> When I am in the woods, unknown to me
> The workings of my spirit thence are brought.
>   (370–4)

The lines below, written in 1798, and included in Part II of *1799*, suggest how the stormy confrontation of an '[un]common eye' (349) – or 'I' – with the father's ghost found expression in an imaginary language of nature:

> For I would walk alone
> In storm and tempest, or in starless nights
> Beneath the quiet heavens, and at that time
> Would feel whate'er there is of power in sound
> To breathe an elevated mood, by form
> Or image unprofaned; and I would stand
> Beneath some rock, listening to sounds that are
> The ghostly language of the ancient earth,
> Or make their dim abode in distant winds.
> Thence did I drink the visionary power.
>   (351–60)

For Wordsworth, the listener, the endless deferral of the otherness of social language effectively inflates the imaginary subject that keeps it at bay:

> the soul –
> Remembering how she felt, but what she felt
> Remembering not – retains an obscure sense
> Of possible sublimity, to which
> With growing faculties she doth aspire,

> With faculties still growing, feeling still
> That whatsoever point they gain they still
> Have something to pursue.   (354–71)

Throughout his youth, he piously dedicated himself ('else sinning greatly' (IV, 343)) to a special bond with what he came to regard as the imaginary language of nature, the climactic celebrations of which were his student trip to the Alps in 1790 and his ascent of Snowdon probably in the following year. But that key formulation – of the language of nature – was only arrived at later, after further shocks had brought him to realize that it was specifically his linguistic origin that he needed to retard.

Wordsworth's Revolutionary history was irrefutably self-alienating. In particular, his reaction to the sites of the September Massacres in 1792 would later seem to be to a premonitory text of the Terror to come, in which he was in danger of finding his own position misrepresented. '[W]ritten in a tongue he [could not] read' (X, 52), they stood for something other than the 'Revolution' he himself intended. Whether or not he saw it at the time, he was being hailed by a new voice from within – Macbeth's 'voice that cried / To the whole city, "Sleep no more!"' (X, 76–7), presaging the killing of the father of the *patrie*, 'le bon papa',[19] Louis XVI, the following January.

But it was not until the English declaration of war on France in February 1793 that his full implication in the other, novel meaning of the word as 'change and subversion' (X, 233) finally registered:

> No shock
> Given to my moral nature had I known
> Down to that very moment . . .
>   . . . that might be named
> A revolution, save at this one time.
>   (X, 233–7)

A disjuncture had opened up in what he had conceived to be the imaginary continuity from an English village community to the Revolutionary society he had formatively seen represented by the Fête de la Fédération of 1790, and through that gap he emerged 'at once / Into another region' (X, 240–1).

While this cumulative trauma raised the spectre of the word of the father, it was followed, according to the pattern established immediately after Wordsworth's mother's death, and repeated after his father's death, by a more powerful fixation on the imaginary. After the Revolution had again incited a subjectivity no longer representable simply by the imaginary relation with nature, Wordsworth discovered the alternative discourses of pantheism and associationism in which to redefine the imaginary relation of a de-centred and passive subject to the outer world. But these discourses contain a post–Revolutionary anxiety to scrutinize his own subjectivity and re-establish its imaginary position after it has been radically called into question. The powerful rhythms, for example, 'roll[ing] through'[20] the pantheism that was joyfully appropriated by a peculiarly overdetermined subjectivity had rendered a pre-established discourse historical and distinctively individual.

Coleridge, in providing these profoundly congenial discourses to foster Wordsworth's alternative subjectivity, had for a time become the father of a new imaginary language. But what unfolded from March 1798, when Coleridge handed over to Wordsworth the project of 'the first & finest philosophical Poem'[21] that was to become known as *The Recluse*, was a slow agon between Coleridge as the withholding father of the word, in which alienated subjectivity was inscribed, and Wordsworth's developing realization that his own, imaginary subjectivity could resolve this further conflict by reverting to his former languages of nature as the expression of a restored but different political idealism.

Coleridge radically misunderstood the nature of Wordsworth's originality, because the extraordinary 'Unity of Interest, & that Homogeneity of character which is the natural consequence of it',[22] which he readily recognized in Wordsworth's poetry, seemed to offer the basis for accomplishing his own conception of a philosophical poem. Eventually, he defined his idea of the contemplative 'genius of a great philosophical poet' which 'Wordsworth possessed more of . . . than any other man I ever knew, or, as I believe, has existed in England since Milton . . . His proper title is *Spectator ab extra* . . . [delivering] upon authority a system of philosophy',[23] which Coleridge later claimed himself to 'have been all [his] life doing'.[24] But rather than seeking, in Coleridge's way, a master discourse, that would transcend the dominant social and political discourses of the age, Wordsworth's 'peculiar dower'[25] was driving him to win over those discourses to the expression of an imaginary culture that, for him, was already there.

For six years after the transferral of the project to Wordsworth, he continued to look to Coleridge to present him with a culminating imaginary discourse, while he himself was effectively deflected into examining the origin of his own potentially creative subjectivity in what became *The Prelude*. But his revision of the Coleridgean project in a work that was referred to deferentially from spring 1801 as 'the poem to Coleridge'[26] required another shock finally to achieve its independence.

Wordsworth's self-scrutiny in the 'poem on [his] own poetic education'[27] was initiated late in 1798 by the repetition of the puzzling clause, 'was it for this' (see Figure 1.1, p. 28), and by the founding uncertainty about what the deictic gesture refers to: his inarticulacy, his inability to produce *The Recluse*, but also his fascination with the very act of writing about that inability. *Is* 'this' – this writing, and the project it is attempting – the appropriate upshot of his favoured experience? It is a question that while it hampered composition also, in radically problematizing his relation to language, insisted on a particular personal strength.

This fundamental ambiguity produced a continuing oscillation in the process of composition between the subjective alienation solicited by the Coleridgean programme and the retracting pull of the imaginary subject. The 'spots of time', which are identified in *1799* I, 288–96, record experiences in which the alienated subjectivity he was seeking to confirm had memorably emerged, but for all their momentousness they typically terminate in retreat, silence, and depression that intimate a return of the disrupted imaginary. In the 'glad preamble' of 1799–1800 he made another start, that while it advertised a sense of his capacity to proceed ('I am free, for months to come / May dedicate myself to chosen tasks' (*1799* I, 33–4)), nonetheless ended by celebrating the return to his imaginary relation with nature – 'A corresponding mild creative breeze' (I, 43) – as the destination as well as the origin of his recaptured power.[28] Each time he confronted the trauma of alienation, the renewed fixation resulted in an *impasse* to composition.

Wordsworth was able to proceed with poetic composition only by relying on a previously articulated subjectivity that had been innocent of the subsequent demand for alienation. With his work on *Lyrical Ballads* (1800), he was able to avoid the onus of original composition that was required for *The Recluse* by amplifying and working on a past achievement. When he did try to take up *The Prelude* in the spring of 1801, revising made him so ill that Dorothy was obliged to keep 'all the manuscript poems'[29] from him. Though at the end of the year he wrote some more of a '3d part',[30] the account of his Cambridge life with which he continued simply brought forward in time the adolescent assurance of his undisrupted inner life, when '[his] mind returned / Into its former self' (III, 96–7).

In the extended poetic debate between Wordsworth and Coleridge from the 1802 version of the 'Intimations Ode', through the various versions of 'Dejection', 'Resolution and Independence', and 'Ode to Duty', a shared sense of loss was acknowledged, analysed and, by Wordsworth, repeatedly repaired, over a trajectory that was giving his imaginary subjectivity, almost reluctantly, the upper hand: not only did 'primal sympathy . . . [remain] behind', but also 'other palms [were] won'.[31] Implicit throughout this sequence is Wordsworth's uneasy intuition that his own sense of dejection is closely linked to Coleridge's importunity for the alienating transfer of subjectivity into the symbolic domain, and Wordsworth's insistence on a 'second Will' who is 'more wise'[32] in espousing a tried moral discourse than inventing a discursive subjectivity in which, were it once out of imaginary control, he would recognize the image of his oedipal and Revolutionary self.

It was Coleridge's departure for Malta that was the major influence in removing the block to completing *The Prelude*. Over 1500 lines were possibly added in July–August of 1803, but, as Jonathan Wordsworth has noted, it was only with 'Coleridge's decision at Christmas 1803 to go abroad in search of health, and, more specifically, by Wordsworth's reading to Coleridge Part II of *1799* at Grasmere on January 4, 1804' that a 'new impetus was given'[33] to the composition. While one consideration was Wordsworth's urgent desire to produce an instalment, albeit marginal, towards realizing Coleridge's great philosophical conception, another impulse came from the indirect resolution of Wordsworth's dependence on Coleridge, as *The Recluse* was laid aside in the pursuit of *The Prelude*.

A sudden deterioration in Coleridge's health led to the crisis of Wordsworth's fear of the possible death of his former mirror and, more recently, antagonist, producing what he wrote to Coleridge was 'the severest shock . . . I think, I have ever received'.[34] With the absence of Coleridge imminent, Wordsworth was obliged finally to seize the initiative by insisting on his own version of imaginary discourse. He felt a characteristic 'load' of guilt over a victory he had not sought: 'I cannot say what a load it would be to me, should I survive you and you die without this memorial left behind.'[35] But the work he had effectively been substituting for the Coleridgean project, in the light of which his alternative had been minimized ('O let it be the tail-piece of the "Recluse"!'[36]), was on Coleridge's departure suddenly to expand and replace it. While Wordsworth's formulation of the imagination was necessary to complete the poem about his own creative subjectivity, so that in the sixteen months starting in January, 1804, he was to complete the eleven remaining books of *The Prelude*, it would always negate the possibility of writing Coleridge's *Recluse*.

II

The letter which revealed Wordsworth's fear that he was at last on his own in writing a work that was to revise the conception of Coleridge's philosophical poem was written on 29 March 1804. It marked the turning-point from which the alternative subjectivity that had been reactivated from the beginning of this crucial month would carry through the composition of *The Prelude*: 'I am now after a halt of near three weeks started again; and I hope to go forward rapidly.'[37]

As Dorothy mentions in the same letter, Wordsworth had begun the address to Coleridge which was to become *1805* VI, 246–331, assuring him of a continuing presence, 'with us in the past, / The present, with us in the times to come' (VI, 251–2).[38] By this point, the shift in precedence is conveyed in the wish to provide something for the good and guidance of Coleridge, rather than requiring something to further Coleridge's intentions:

> Throughout this narrative,
> Else sooner ended, I have known full well
> For whom I thus record the birth and growth
> Of gentleness, simplicity, and truth,
> And joyous loves that hallow innocent days
> Of peace and self-command.   (269–74)

Coleridge is effectively being exhorted to live up to his former correspondence with Wordsworthian subjectivity:

> twins almost in genius and in mind.
>   . . . framed
> To bend at last to the same discipline,
> Predestined, if two beings ever were,
> To seek the same delights, and have one health,
> One happiness.   (263–9)

Wordsworth now wishes that his 'more steady voice' (323) had influenced Coleridge much earlier, and he even offers an explicit critique of Coleridgean subjectivity, which detaches language from 'things', producing a mind beyond imaginary restraint:

> I have thought
> Of thee, thy learning, gorgeous eloquence,
> And all the strength and plumage of thy youth,
> Thy subtle speculations, toils abstruse
> Among the schoolmen, and Platonic forms
> Of wild ideal pageantry, shaped out
> From things well-matched, or ill, and words for things –
> The self-created sustenance of a mind
> Debarred from Nature's living images,
> Compelled to be a life unto itself,
> And unrelentingly possessed by thirst
> Of greatness, love, and beauty.   (305–16)

The break through this 'halt' in composition, as Wordsworth set off in his own direction, can be placed earlier in March. For up to eight weeks, from

January to early March, 1804, Wordsworth hoped to compose a new five-book version of *The Prelude*, but there is no extant fair copy of the whole, and, indeed, it seems likely that it became uncompletable in that form.[39] Though it was probably on 6 March that he assured Coleridge 'When this next book is done . . . I shall consider the work as finish'd',[40] earlier that same day he had written to De Quincey that the poem was no 'better [than] half complete'.[41] Perhaps the remark to Coleridge referred to what Wordsworth was already beginning to feel might be a sufficient accomplishment to send abroad with his sick friend, rather than to a belief that the work felt almost entire.

At that point, Jonathan Wordsworth writes, Book IV, the latest composed, comprised 'two clearly defined sections, the first concerned with the poet's experiences at Hawkshead during the Long Vacation of 1789' and 'the second with education and the beneficial influence of books'.[42] Certainly, there was nothing in his work so far that evidenced further headway in addressing his incapacity to produce a new (Coleridgean) discourse. The conjectural order of passages in the final book of the five-book poem as reconstructed by Jonathan Wordsworth is the Ascent of Snowdon, (*1805*, XIII, 1–65), followed, in the original version of MS W, by an aside to Coleridge, a passage on the power of 'higher minds' reflected in nature, (*1805*, XIII, 78–90), and a sequence of mind/nature analogies, that together with the aside to Coleridge and its sequel is omitted from a revised version in the same manuscript. The later version follows the Ascent of Snowdon with 'a shorter but probably coherent version of *1805*, XIII, 77–165',[43] and there are clear indications that the conclusion was to have been a version of the 'spots of time' sequence from the two–Part *Prelude* (*1799* I, 288–374 amplified into something closer to *1805* XI, 123–388).

During these weeks, Wordsworth experienced great difficulty with the physical act of writing that was symptomatic of his aversion to the pressure for fresh composition. In the letter to De Quincey on 6 March, he also complained about

a kind of derangement in my stomach and digestive organs which makes writing painful to me, and indeed almost prevents me from holding correspondence with any body: and this (I mean to say the unpleasant feelings which I have connected with the act of holding a Pen) has been the chief cause of my long silence.[44]

He needed constant encouragement, and at times to have the writing done for him, forcing him to join separate passages into the text that Coleridge awaited.[45] Though Wordsworth was planning to round off with the *1799* formulation of his imaginary relation to nature as it had been re-fixated following his renunciation of the Jacobin Revolution, such an effortless reversion would have obstructed the now urgent search for a conclusive discourse. The enigma remained, and around 10 March Wordsworth relinquished this version, that had achieved its solution in neither Coleridge's nor his own terms. He decided, as Jonathan Wordsworth has written, 'to reorganize his material and send Coleridge an incomplete poem to take with him to Malta'.[46] By 18 March he had completed in MS M, (almost certainly that prepared personally for Coleridge), the first five of the thirteen books of *1805*, for which Book IV of the five-book version was divided and refashioned into Books IV and V.

In the original version of the tentative final book of the five-book *Prelude* (in MS W), Wordsworth recapitulated his formulation of the language of nature which was the upshot of *1799*. His opening account of the Ascent of Snowdon figures the passage of the voice of an orphaned subject through what would be a psychic scission were it not resealed, as the language of nature gives powerful representation to a still unalienated imaginary subject. The voice of phallic and Revolutionary uprising is quelled by a scene that offers a fixed and superior self-expression:

> but in that breach
> Through which the homeless voice of waters rose,
> That dark deep thoroughfare, had Nature lodged
> The soul, the imagination of the whole.
>
> (MS W)[47]

Supported by this reaffirmation of the language of nature, the succeeding aside to Coleridge, in effect explaining the digression of the entire poem, is both deferential and self-assured. It requests Coleridge's submission to the terms of Wordsworth's own passage, textual and psychic, *back* to the continuing story of his imaginary subjectivity:

> Even yet thou wilt vouchsafe an ear, O friend,
> And something too of a submissive mind,
> As in thy mildness thou I know hast done
> While with a winding but no devious song
> Through [   ] processes I make my way
> By links of tender thought. My present aim
> Is to contemplate for a needful while
> (Passage which will conduct in season due
> Back to the tale which I have left behind)
> The diverse manner in which Nature works
> Oft times upon the outward face of things
>
> (MS W)[48]

In revision, Wordsworth cut the aside together with the sequence of six natural symbols of imaginary reorganization that proceeded from a further consideration of the Ascent:

> Oft tracing this analogy betwixt
> The mind of man and Nature, doth the scene
> Which from the side of Snowdon I beheld
> Rise up before me, followed too in turn
> By sundry others, whence I will select
> A portion, living pictures, to embody
> This pleasing argument.   (MS W)[49]

Though this developed reading of the Ascent suggests a new emphasis on the *language* of nature, seeing the scene as a whole as a symbol that offers the resistance of all self-representation ('Ris[ing] up before me'), the implication – of a re-encounter with discursive subjectivity – was obscured by the succeeding accumulation of natural symbols. His revised version, however, pursued the analysis of the creative imagination (that he had originally started in a passage which continued the aside and ended in the above consideration of the Ascent):

> I mean so moulds, exalts, endues, combines,
> Impregnates, separates, adds, takes away,
> And makes one object sway another so
> By unhabitual influence or abrupt,
> That even the grossest minds must see and hear
> And cannot chuse but feel. The power . . .
>   . . . is in kind
> A brother of the very faculty
> Which higher minds bear with them as their own.
> These from their native selves can deal about
> Like transformation, to one life impart
> The functions of another, interchange [?create],
> Trafficking with immeasurable thoughts. (MS W)

His expansion of this description shows Wordsworth distinctly less interested in the originating imaginary relation with nature than in the activity of a subject overdetermined by that formation but operating in the separate domain of the symbolic:

> Such minds are truly from the deity
> For they are powers and hence the highest bliss
> That can be known on earth in Truth a Soul
> Growing and still to grow a consciousness
> In a [?] they habitually infused
> Through every image and through every [?]

And all impressions hence religion faith
And endless occupation for the soul
Whether discursive or intuitive
And hence cheerfulness in every [?] of life
Hence truth in moral knowledge and delight
That fails not   (MS W)[50]

Wordsworth was allowing his formulation of the language of nature to be re-interrogated by the demand of Coleridgean subjectivity, but his recognition of the power of his own imagination was still embarrassed by the elision of his Revolutionary knowledge. His fixation on the language of nature, by which he had sealed the Revolutionary trauma, was and remained the basis of his rejection of a discourse of individualism, but that rejection was still a regressive evasion, appealing to a pre-Revolutionary formation, rather than an active control of undeniable alienation. Until he could retell the story of the Revolution in terms of the ascendency of imaginary subjectivity, the struggle for the Wordsworthian imagination would be incomplete.

As a result, in what remains of Book V, Wordsworth is studiously underplaying the reality of his alienation. He boldly dismisses the contamination of his own mind by a violent detachment from the 'soul of nature' (MS W) as a youthful 'presumption' (MS W). It arose, he writes, partly from picturesque faddishness, but more subtly from 'The domination of the eye' (MS W), the hyperactivity of which is impelled by the insecurity of a new self-consciousness, signalled by the symbolic subjectivity – the 'I' – that it echoes.

When, later in this section and for the first time in *The Prelude*, Wordsworth touches on the Alps, he claims that his visit in 1790 had marked the end of this 'transient . . . degradation' (XI, 250, 242) of imaginary control. Yet his previous treatment of the Alpine journey in *Descriptive Sketches*, published 1793, had illustrated the dangerous association of aesthetic arbitrariness with Revolutionary fervour that he had made since his visit of 1790, and 'Tintern Abbey' had later described the same savage passions haunting and propelling him over Salisbury Plain in 1793, at the time of his greatest Revolutionary turmoil.[51] Here, a major factor in the overdetermination of his alienation is suppressed by confining his view of the Alps strictly to that of 1790, resulting in a strangely inert kind of creativity:

In truth this malady of which I speak
Though aided by the times, whose deeper sound
Without my knowledge sometimes might perchance

Make rural Nature's milder minstrelsies
Inaudible, did never take in me
Deep root, or larger action . . .
      . . . I threw the habit off
Entirely and for ever, and again
In Nature's presence stood, as I do now,
A meditative and creative soul.   (MS W)[52]

III

Wordsworth's passage to his version of the creative imagination can be pursued in a crucial sequence of fragments towards *1805* VI, 488–548, that were jotted in MS WW after the five-book poem had been discontinued, probably in late March. In the course of the writing he realized his ability to overpower discourses of individualism by interpreting the prevailing discourses of his historical moment as representations of his own alternative subjectivity. The breakthrough, negotiated in this rough work that was the basis of his account of the Crossing of the Alps and of the questioning as to what that episode had come to mean to him, effected a textual passage into his sought-for discourse, initiating and enabling the final phase of composition, from March 1804–May 1805, in which Book VI and the whole thirteen-book poem were to be completed.[53]

The manuscript, twenty-three leaves cut from a notepad borrowed from Dorothy, is hastily written in extremely faint pencil, probably outdoors, with all the appearance of a first attempt, and 'remarkable', as Mark Reed notes, for its 'illegibility'.[54] The order of composition of the key leaves I wish to discuss (folios 25 recto–28 verso, here referred to as *1804*) is the episode on the Crossing (25 recto–26 recto), followed by the first version of the Cave of Yordas simile (26 recto–27 recto), followed, at some remove, by the Confrontation with the Imagination (28 recto, though the cut indicates that this last leaf was not immediately next to 27).[55] By *1805*, the episode of the Crossing is followed immediately by the Confrontation with the Imagination, which is followed by the Vale of Gondo description of the Simplon Pass, while the Cave simile is removed to Book VIII, 711–27.

1804 opens with a sketchy account of Wordsworth's having unknowingly crossed the Alps, ending:

[?Had] waited [?thus] a Pesant chanced to pass
[?From ?whom ?we ?learned] that we had mistook our [?road]

Which [——?——] the rivers bed
within

a few steps
For [?the ?short ?way] & [?then ?along ?the ?]

[?] course
In short that all the road [?before ?us ?]

the
Was downward, or to give [——?——] brief

the
     give [——?——] brief
The substance of this [?was ?the ?Alps ?were ?crost]
After a little scruple & short pause

of
[?] a rude [?shed] befor we [?in] this spot
Had waited long a peasan [chanced]   (25 verso–26 recto)

By *1805*, the experience is enlarged upon as one in which 'an under-thirst / Of vigour' (VI, 489–90) was checked, producing a feeling of 'dejection . . . A deep and genuine sadness' (VI, 491–2), that recurred throughout his Alpine experience as it is described in *1805*, and that had anti-climaxed in the bathos of his having crossed the Alps without noticing. The cause of this stultification, elaborated in *1805*, is already clarified by the original drafting of the Cave simile, that follows the Crossing in *1804*, and reveals it to be a disjunction between the expectations Wordsworth had attached to a discourse of the heroic – the Hannibalesque[56] and Napoleonic triumphalism of 'crossing of the Alps' – and his actual feelings. What was being most radically intimated, however, in this even more dejecting repetition of the effect of what a later manuscript refers to as the 'sudden blank of Soul, that shock'[57] of having previously seen the famous Mont Blanc, was the shock of his alienation in language.

In the Cave simile that explored this realization, the sense of loss that comes with the 'perfect view' (VIII, 726) of the interior is associated with the act of reading, indicating the way in which a formerly unopposed subjectivity ('As when a Traveller . . . / Looks up & sees the cavern chamber slowly spread / Widening itself' (26 recto)) has been reduced to language:

> And grieves at the remembrance of [?]
> [?Into] a clear and perfect [view in] which
> He [?reads] distinctly as a written book
> The vault of solid stone above [?& ?that]
> And grieves at the remembrance of his loss.
>
>   (27 verso)

1805 reads:

> Till, every effort, every motion gone,
> The scene before him lies in perfect view
> Exposed, and lifeless as a written book.
>
>   (VIII, 725–7)

There is an explicit opposition between the initial exhilaration of unbaffling indeterminacy and its termination in linguistic representation. That, ironically, the simile refers precisely to what Wordsworth is pursuing in his own poem – that is, textual completion, 'a written book' – manifests the origin of his writing block on the Coleridgean project as an embarrassment with language itself. Yet through the various textual stages of these passages we can witness the gradual emergence of an acceptable idiom of the imagination in which to write his own book (*1805*) from the originally impeded self-expression.

On the Alps, as Wordsworth spells it out in *1805*, he had found himself characteristically at cross purposes: the same words meant different things to himself and to his interlocutor, in this case a peasant passing by:

> And all the answers which the man returned
> To our inquiries, in their sense and substance
> Translated by the feelings which we had,
> Ended in this – that we had crossed the Alps.
>
> (VI, 521–4)

The variation of his 'feelings', which changed from elation to depression in relation to the same words, effected the 'translation' of an expression that had seemed to represent an indefinable self-assertion into a cliché. Language, contracted to a castrating literalism, drew attention to the self-alienation it most radically signifies.

The attempted passage on the Crossing that comes to an abrupt halt in *1804* retraces the quest of 1790 which had later become associated with his Revolutionary zeal. It is ostensibly in search of the articulation of Coleridgean subjectivity, only to discover that the completion of his passage into the symbolic to which it is alerting him is inscribed with precisely the same alienated subject that his imaginary subjectivity had repeatedly outlawed. From apparently achieving the object of a quest that is profoundly disappointing, Wordsworth gradually revises the realization of a failed triumph into the celebration of the alternative empowering that failure implies. He does so by writing through his final confrontation with the Coleridgean imagination, from the Confrontation with the Imagination drafted in *1804* to the completed version of *1805*, VI, 525–48. Between these versions, the subjectivity represented by the imagination is indeterminate until his former imaginary control of the aesthetic cravings of 1790 and of his Revolutionary commitment of the early 1790s returns to empower the confident formulation of his alternative, Wordsworthian imagination by the end of the *1805* version of the Confrontation.

It is not impossible that indications of the reversal of the mind's power from halted arrest into active inventiveness (as subsequently described in the extended Cave simile in *1805* VIII, 728–41) were contained in the leaves that are now missing in *1804* between the Cave simile and the Confrontation, but there is hardly any suggestion of such a *volte-face* in the first draft of the Confrontation. The text is almost indecipherable, painfully broken, and reiterative, making no explicit headway to the break-through recorded in *1805*:

> [?Both ?that ?word] must [?rest]
> A little while [?Imagination] crosd [?me ?here]
> Like an unfatherd vapour, & my [?verse]
> Halts in mid course [?& ? ?a ?cloud]
> [?But ?] [   ]
> That stoppd me, but tis cleared & broken up
> And populous shapes [?unfold] th[?] [?hid]
> before me the [?true ?pathway ?of ?my ?verse]
> Imagination [?! ?rising ?up ?]
> Like an unfatherd vapour here [?]
> Crossing & here I [?paused]
> I [?paused] was lost awhile as in a Cloud
>
> (28 recto)

Rather, the encounter with 'Imagination [?! ?rising ?up] . . . Like an unfatherd vapour' is an obstacle to his progress, as he is crossed rather than crossing on the true pathway of his verse. The familiar oedipal pattern of encounter with a spectral solitary associated particularly with Hamlet's father's ghost – he had re-read the play on 6 March – is even more verbally resonant in a later manuscript fragment: 'like the form / Ghostly and wan of some unfathered mist / vapour'.[58] In *1804*, the experience has not yet become disengaged from the inhibiting fear of linguistic castration that threatens the imaginary subject, and Wordsworth has not yet, as in *1805*, recognized the glorious recovery of the imaginary subject:

> Imagination! – lifting up itself
> Before the eye and progress of my song
> Like an unfathered vapour, here that power,
> In all the might of its endowments, came
> Athwart me. I was lost as in a cloud,
> Halted without a struggle to break through,
> And now, recovering, to my soul I say
> 'I recognise thy glory.'   (VI, 525–32)

The *1804* Confrontation is still wrestling with the word of the father, that has returned to be identified also in the traumatic demand of the Coleridgean imagination. At the same time, however, the recognition appeals to his own counter-formulation of the imagination in the five-book version represented by 'the scene / Which from the side of Snowdon [he] beheld / Rise up before [him]', with its claim to make the paternal voice rising from the mist issue in natural symbols of its own supremacy.

If there is any hint in *1804* that the imagination is about to emerge as something other than, in W. J. B. Owen's words, 'a paralyzing agent that halts activity'[59], and that it is already becoming involved in the power of the imaginary subject to retract the threatened self-alienation, it lies in the repeated word 'unfathered'. Wordsworth had previously used the phrase 'not . . . fathered' in Book III, when he had written of another disappointment – at not finding at Cambridge the inspiring literary culture of 'strong book-mindedness' (III, 404) he had anticipated. He had looked to find 'venerable doctors of old', sitting 'o'er their ponderous books . . . Like caterpillars eating out their way / In silence, or with keen devouring noise / Not to be tracked or fathered' (III, 460–7). Instead, he writes, 'Our eyes are crossed by butterflies, our ears / Hear chattering popinjays' (III, 456–7). In *1804* and *1805*, what crosses 'the eye and progress of [his] song' turns out, for all its forbiddingness, to be another vaporous vanity, as what had crossed his ears in 1790 was a local and touristic banality, and he is still fundamentally desirous of participating in an imaginary literary culture that can be entered without contest or the display of individuality – that is 'unfathered'.

That to Wordsworth the Coleridgean imagination is inscribed with alienated subjectivity is further evidenced from the verbal associations in the address to Coleridge of late March (which Wordsworth wrote he had written after 'a *halt* of near three weeks'; my emphasis), and in the *1804* version of the Confrontation and the *1805* version of the Crossing. The 'thirst / Of greatness, love, and beauty' attributed to Coleridge in the address echoes the aesthetic / Revolutionary rapacity of the 'under-thirst / Of vigour' (VI, 489–90) with which Wordsworth describes himself as seeking to conquer the Alps in 1790, and which was fated to result in the dejection that visits a mind 'self-created' by the substitution of words for things. Even Coleridge's 'gorgeous eloquence', seen in the address as 'the plumage of [his] youth', set incongruously 'Among the schoolmen' at Cambridge, ironically recalls Wordsworth's disappointment with the popinjays' disrupting his image of 'the venerable doctors of old' in Book III.

But it is the second half of the Cave simile (VIII, 728–41) that most helps to define the inchoate recognition of the non-alienating power of the counter-imagination in the *1804* Confrontation, and to account for the *process* of 'recovering' that is elided in the *1805* version. Indeed, it may even have been sketched in the missing leaves between those now marked 27 and 28. When, in the extended composition, the traveller/Wordsworth reads the literal text of the cave's interior, he finds that reading after all less compelling than former ways of perusing: 'But let him pause awhile and look again, / And a new quickening shall succeed' (VIII, 728–9). The ambiguity in the last word also implies that the mind represented has finally attained its passage and *successfully* realized its own kind of re-creative power:

> the senseless mass,
> In its projections, wrinkles, cavities,
> Through all its surface, with all colours streaming,
> Like a magician's airy pageant, parts,
> Unites, embodying everywhere some pressure
> Or image, recognised or new, some type
> Or picture of the world . . .
> A spectacle to which there is no end.
>
> (VIII, 731–41)

Once again, it is the Ascent of Snowdon that is determinative – this time of the return of the imaginary re-organization that Wordsworth had attributed to the scene after the aside to Coleridge in the five-book *Prelude*, describing

> The diverse manner in which Nature works
> Oft times upon the outward face of things,
> I mean so moulds, exalts, endues, combines,
> Impregnates, separates, adds, takes away,
> And makes one object sway another.

The 'magician's airy pageant' in the cave echoes Prospero's 'insubstantial pageant faded' (IV, i, 155), which in turn informs the 'Platonic forms / Of wild ideal pageantry, shaped out / From things well-matched, or ill' that Wordsworth attributes to the operation of Coleridge's alienated subjectivity in his address of late March. But Wordsworth is after all happier with his own pageant, because it displays his power to transform while insisting on imaginary self-reflection. The shock of discursive subjectivity is assuaged by the reassuring evocation of what look like the imaginary languages of fairy-tale and romance.

IV

The triumphalism of Wordsworth's celebration of the Confrontation with the Imagination in *1805* represents the victory of the Wordsworthian over the Coleridgean imagination:

                              In such strength
        Of usurpation . . .
                              . . . doth greatness make abode . . .
        The mind beneath such banners militant
        Thinks not of spoils or trophies, nor of aught
        That may attest its prowess, blest in thoughts
        That are their own perfection and reward –
        Strong in itself, and in the access of joy
        Which hides it like the overflowing Nile.
                              (VI, 532–48)

It also represents the confident revision of what Alan Liu has pointed out is a specific discourse of Napoleonic triumphalism.[60] Having experienced the return of imaginary subjectivity through the subordination of his linguistic alienation, Wordsworth had achieved a power over discourse as such whereby his imaginary self would always insist on its primary reflection in discursive otherness. Inasmuch as it was historically constrained by an event that represented the seemingly irresistible progression of individualism – Napoleon's crossing of the St Bernard in the brilliant Italian campaign of 1800 – the phrase 'crossing the Alps' had misled Wordsworth to a dead end. But, following this threat, the Napoleonic discourse of usurpation could after all be appropriated as one in which the take-over by imaginary subjectivity that it motivated is also inscribed.

The anxiety of subjective usurpation is latent in the Shakespearean echo in the Confrontation that de Selincourt observes is from *King John*: 'the eye and progress of my song' recalls 'Before the eye and prospect of your town' (II, i, 208). The phrase in question, spoken by King John, comes in the play from an elaborate parley before Angiers appealing to the town to settle the quarrel over legitimacy, as each party accuses the other of 'usurpation' (9 and 118): in the words of the French King Philip, 'let us hear them speak / Whose title they admit, Arthur's or John's' (199–200). The representation of the imagination in the Confrontation, 'lifting up itself / Before the eye and progress of my song', echoes King John's warning about French hostility:

        These flags of France, that are advanced here
        Before the eye and prospect of your town,
        Have hither marched to your endamagement . . .
        All preparation for a bloody siege
        And merciless proceeding by these French
        [Confronts your] city's eyes . . .   (207–15)

John also claims that it is the 'countercheck' (224) by his own power that has caused the French to offer words, instead of their planned attack, and to 'shoot but calm words folded up in smoke' (229), or breath, though talk may still be a smokescreen for residual hostility. There is a similar ambivalence in Wordsworth's encounter with a mist-enfolded language, that, rather than oppose violence with violence, seeks to convert its belligerence into an innocuous language. In the Wordsworthian echo, the town's eye/I is the locus of a contested subjectivity the struggle for which is also settling old political scores. The play's dynastic politics parallel Wordsworth's original view of the war against France in 1793. In both cases, an Anglo-French alliance (between King Philip and Prince Arthur in the play, and between the Revolutionary French and English radicals such as Wordsworth in 1793) represents a legitimacy that the official English regime (King John and Pitt's government) lacks. The Confrontation stages an initially indeterminate rivalry between John, who 'Crave[s] harborage within [the] city walls' (234), and the 'oppressed boy' (177) Arthur, who both have rights of abode in the citadel of the imagination:

> In such strength
> Of usurpation . . .
> . . . doth greatness make abode,
> There harbours whether we be young or old.
> (VI, 525–37)

A new legitimacy ensues, both in *King John* and in the course of the Revolution. As, in the play, the English lords who have revolted go over to the Dauphin, who is invading England, so, until the invasion of Switzerland in 1798, the anti-Pittite radicals, Wordsworth and Coleridge, remained implicated in the French cause and refrained from condemning Napoleonism as a betrayal of the Revolution. The discovery of the Dauphin's treachery and Napoleon's imperialist agenda, however, promotes the restoration of a united British nationalism in both cases.

The pursuit of the imagination was at last bringing Wordsworth face to face with his Revolutionary trauma, revealing both the origin of his discursive alienation and his power of relegitimizing it. The result is a containment and shaping of his Revolutionary history that will enable him to imagine it (as will be laid bare in Books IX and X) as the correction of rival British and French usurpations in his historical society by the legitimate power of the imaginary subject.

The path to Coleridgean subjectivity was abandoned when it led to blockage, but Wordsworth found his true direction in the fixation that follows trauma:

> The dull and heavy slackening which ensued
> Upon those tidings by the peasant given

> Was soon dislodged; downwards we hurried fast,
> And entered with the road which we had missed
> Into a narrow chasm.   (VI, 549–53)

The description of the Simplon Pass, between Brigg and Dovedro, that follows the Confrontation in *1805*, 549–72, represents the terms of Wordsworth's eventual entry into the symbolic domain – a domain that for Wordsworth is also the protraction of an imaginary borderland that need never be crossed, 'something evermore about to be' (VI, 542), like the spectacle in the cave 'to which there is no end' (VIII, 741): a pass *after* a crossing. Though the symbolic order has been entered, the imaginary subject goes marching on.

That the description of the Gorge of Gondo represents the climactic achievement of the Wordsworthian imagination is indicated by its separate publication in the section of 'Poems of the Imagination', 1845. Overall, the scene represents a powerful violence that can be infinitely delayed ('woods decaying, never to be decayed', 'stationary blasts' (VI, 557–8)). The bewildering contradictions of enraged confinement ('the raving stream' (565)) and ecstatic freedom ('The torrents shooting from the clear blue sky', and 'The unfettered clouds' (561 and 566)) are steadied by the gestalt of the originary self-reflection:

> Tumult and peace, darkness and light,
> Were all like workings of one mind, the features
> Of the same face, blossoms upon one tree.
>   (567–9)

But more to the purpose of Wordsworth's poetic project, the passage harnesses the empowering containment of elemental and Revolutionary violence in the language of nature to the appropriation of the Miltonic voice.

The voice of the father returns in the winds blowing through the skeletal 'hollow rent' (559), the muttering rocks, and the speaking crags ('As if a voice were in them' (564)). Moreover, the sounds of natural violence – the river is far noisier, even 'deafening', in some manuscripts:

> With dull reverberation never ceasing
> Audibly to attend the astounding uproar
> Of the vex'd flood, by drizzling crags beset[61]

– resound with the knowledge of historical disaster that had produced the conception of the language of nature that also informs this passage. The earthquakes around Brigg that had occurred at the time of the Lisbon earthquake easily resonate with the Revolution, for which they are the most common metaphor, as contemporary writers on the region demonstrate. Marc Théodore Bourrit, for example, who describes the most recent catastrophe that had been heralded by 'un bruit sourd qui venoit de la terre . . . un mugissement souterain, semblable au bruit d'un torrent qui descend avec rapidité dans un lit profond',[62] makes the point in writing of this region before the Revolution: 'il n'est pas jusqu'aux montagnes mêmes qui n'éprouvent, dans ce pays, des révolutions sensibles'.[63] Particularly, as William Brockedon writes, with a later knowledge of these scenes, the region had been a site of fierce anti-Napoleonic resistance:

During the years 1798, 1799, some severe battles were fought near Brigg. The Valaisians, and especially the inhabitants of the Upper Valais, a very brave race, resisted, with desperate courage, the invasion of the French; they fought to preserve their institutions from foreign interference, but were compelled by numbers to submit, and were at last united with France in the department of the Simplon.[64]

The Revolutionary overtones of the water's disturbing uproar is carried over to Wordsworth's subsequent description of what Brockedon describes as the 'strange and lofty building . . . which serves as an inn and a place of refuge for travellers', at the edge of the village of Gondo, where 'a few trees begin to relieve the horrors of the defile of Dovedro':[65]

> A dreary mansion, large beyond all need,
> With high and spacious rooms, deafened and shunned
> By noise of waters, making innocent sleep
> Lie melancholy among weary bones.   (577–80)

As Liu has pointed out, it prefigures the description of the 'high and lonely' room 'near the roof / Of a large mansion or hotel' (X, 57–8) in Paris, where in October 1792 Wordsworth, previously experiencing the sleeplessness of guilt, took in the impact of the September Massacres in the words of the regicidal Macbeth, who had murdered 'the innocent sleep' (II, ii, 33).[66]

Throughout the poem, Wordsworth appeals to the discourse of Shakespearean tragedy to dramatize his traumatic identification with alienated subjectivity in echoes of *Macbeth*, *Hamlet* and, shortly before this passage, *King John*. But only now that he has confidently contained this rival subjectivity is he in a position, in a moment of extraordinary ambition, to assimilate the univocalism of the epic poet, Milton, to the representation of imaginary subjectivity. The fixation, residing in the language of nature, now also enters poetic discourse, represented in

> Characters of the great apocalypse,
> The types and symbols of eternity,
> Of first, and last, and midst, and without end.
>   (570–2)

Following Milton's Adam and Eve, who had found the 'Unspeakable' represented in the 'glorious works' and 'universal Frame' of nature,[67] Wordsworth joins in a ubiquitous language of praise which is in effect self-reflective of divine creativity: 'On Earth joyn all ye Creatures to extoll / Him first, him last, him midst, and without end' (V, 164–5). Like Wordsworth's ascending vapour, Milton's elements provide an unalienated expression of authorship:

> Ye Mists and Exhalations that now rise
> From Hill or steaming Lake, duskie or grey,
> Till the Sun paint your fleecie skirts with Gold,
> In honour to the Worlds great Author rise.
>
> (V, 185–8)

What Wordsworth has appropriated in emulating Miltonic discourse is its monologic structure: the voice of a seemingly undivided subject. It was after all a version of the kind of subjectivity that Coleridge had advocated for the great philosophical poet, and indeed Coleridge was to describe Milton in terms reminiscent of his characterization of the poet of *The Recluse*: 'Milton is the deity of prescience: he stands *ab extra*.'[68] Coleridge's distinction between Shakespeare and Milton suggests a further resemblance to the dominance of Wordsworth's ideal ego, occupying a continuingly extra-symbolic position within the symbolic domain:

While the former darts himself forth, and passes into all the forms of human character and passion . . . the other attracts all forms and things to himself, into the unity of his own IDEAL.[69]

But one critical difference between Miltonic and Wordsworthian subjectivity is that Wordsworth's had Milton's to contend with. This ultimate struggle, with his poetic father, was compelled to issue in a voice through which his own priority would again emerge without struggle.

Looking back, Wordsworth's proceeding to this final usurpation of Milton's voice becomes clearer. The original intimation of the Wordsworthian imagination emanated from what is the distinctly Miltonic heroic simile of the Cave[70] – a sustained piece of metaphoricity that in itself promised the defeat of literalism, even as it was ultimately restabilized in the image of Wordsworthian subjectivity. The allusion to *Paradise Lost* in the description of the Simplon Pass is made in a phrase that did not originate in that poem but rather in *Revelation*: 'I am Alpha and Omega, the beginning and the end, the first and the last' (XXII, 13). Though Wordsworth emulates Milton's charging of it with Miltonic meaning (assimilating it to his own poetic discourse as Milton had absorbed it into his highly individualized later discourse), Wordsworth's own appropriation uncovers a different signified in a text that after all has priority over Milton's, but that seems to arise to speak more forcibly for Wordsworth's imaginary closure of the whole signifying chain, the alpha and omega, whereby all languages speak finally for the same, unchanging subject.

Rather than creating a master discourse, Wordworth had obliquely mastered those discourses – of Napoleonism and Milton – that challenged him to the containment of their alienating subjectivity. In the description of the Simplon Pass, Revolutionary millenarianism and the Miltonic voice are controlled by the second coming of the imaginary subject, that would thereafter find culminating self-representation in the post-Revolutionary communal discourse of British nationalism. The discourse in which he inscribed the Wordsworthian imagination was one that had already overwhelmed both rival discourses – of the Revolution and Milton – particularly as they were associated in the discourse of Miltonic republicanism.

After completing Book VI, he was to compose Books IX and X, 'Residence in France', '. . . and French Revolution', subduing his Revolutionary knowledge, and then Book VIII, 'Retrospect: Love of Nature Leading to Love of Mankind', to which the whole of the Cave simile was moved in order to re-imagine his entry on to the metropolitan scene of London, probably in 1788, as his passage into the national culture. In Book VII of *1850* he refers to this occasion, when he 'had felt in heart and soul the shock / Of the huge town's first presence' (66–7), and the simile enforces the familiar traumatic pattern of a text that, in presenting the enormity of its otherness, initially seems alienating, only to become unexpectedly empowering:

> but, at the time,
> When to myself it fairly might be said
> (The very moment when I seemed to know)
> 'The threshold now is overpast', great God!
> That aught *external* to the living mind
> Should have such mighty sway, yet so it was:
> A weight of ages did at once descend
> Upon my heart – no thought embodied, no
> Distinct remembrances, but weight and power,
> Power growing with the weight.
>
> (VIII, 697–706)

As with the Crossing of the Alps, the realization of the momentousness of the transition came not in 1788 but rather in the process of composition in 1805, when the imaginary subject fixed on the moment when it had become inserted into a discourse which had later returned to represent its victory over Revolutionary discourse:

> 'Twas a moment's pause:
> All that took place within me came and went
> As in a moment, and I only now
> Remember that it was a thing divine.
>
> (707–10)

The fantasy world in Wordsworth's extended account of the transformative imagination in the Cave simile might seem materially determined, in that the 'pageant' (734) of images derives so closely from the actual shapes created by the stalagmite and stalactite formations and the effects of light and shade they produce. But the high degree of conventionality that, as contemporary guidebooks make plain, influences Wordsworth's description of the interior in effect reflects popular interpretation. In his *A Descriptive Guide to the English Lakes, and Adjacent Mountains*, for example, Jonathan Otley describes how 'After proceeding a few yards, the cave seems interminable, as the eye is not quite accustomed to the gloom.'[71] Then he describes the appearances of the 'curious petrifactions' that cover the sides:

On the east, they are numerous, and give the idea of escutcheons, armour, and trophies, hung against the wall of some baron's hall. These are called 'The Brown Bear', 'The Coat of Mail', 'The Gauntlet', 'The Ram's Head', and 'The Organ'; – and the likeness to these different objects is very striking.[72]

He also refers to 'the "Bishop's Throne" in the north-east corner',[73] as does John Housman, in his *A Descriptive Tour and Guide to the Lakes, Caves, Mountains ... in Cumberland, Westmoreland, Lancashire, and a Part of the West Riding of Yorkshire*, where it is described among similar images 'in this natural edifice which the puny efforts of art may attempt to imitate, but in vain'.[74]

Wordsworth's description, that obviously alludes to several of these agreed likenesses:

> the warrior clad in mail,
> The prancing steed, the pilgrim with his staff,
> The mitred bishop and the throned king
>
> (738–40)

demonstrates the Wordsworthian imagination inscribing itself in the consensual discourse of nationalism that 'London' ('The fountain of my country's destiny / And of the destiny of earth itself . . . home / Imperial' (747–51)) signified to most readers:

the external universe,
By striking upon what is found within,
Had given me this conception, with the help
Of books and what they picture and record.

(766-9)

The panorama of London's 'majesty', evoked in the 'Ships, towers, domes, theatres, and temples'[75] of 'Composed Upon Westminster Bridge', written in

Figures 5.1-2   *The Cave of Yordas* and *Yordas – Looking Back*, from Jonathan Otley's *A Descriptive Guide to the English Lakes, and Adjacent Mountains*, 1842.

130

1802 to register the apprehension of an imaginary continuum from the deep calm of nature to that of the nation, is glimpsed in the 'Ships, rivers, towers' (738) within the cave. But the realm of bishop and king that the imagination re-establishes there supersedes the voice of Miltonic republicanism that Wordsworth had imitated in his 1802 sonnets, 'Written in London, September, 1802' and 'London, 1802', with their call for 'the good old cause'.[76] The appropriate discourse that represents communal modes of reading opposed to alienated individualism is that of an imaginary national tradition, 'not a punctual presence, but a spirit / Living in time and space, and far diffused' (763–4). It was a discourse of power that was, after all, already there.

NOTES

1 Stephen Gill's 1983 essay, reprinted in this volume, influentially weighed the different claims of different versions. Jack Stillinger argues for the appreciation of 'authorial intention residing in all the successive versions of a work', and lists the various contributions of Raymond Carney, Robert Young, Clifford Siskin and

Susan Wolfson to this reassessment in 'Textual Primitivism and the Editing of Wordsworth', *Studies in Romanticism*, 28 (1989), pp. 27–8.

2 *The Poetical Works of William Wordsworth*, ed. Ernest de Selincourt, rev. Helen Darbishire, 5 vols. (Oxford, 1952–9), Vol. 1, p.v. Future references to this edition: *PW*.

3 *Ibid.*, p. vi.

4 Quoted in *ibid.*, p. vii.

5 See *On Wordsworth's 'Prelude'* (Princeton, 1963), pp. 51–9.

6 *The Prelude* XI, 309. All references to this work, unless otherwise indicated, are to the 1805 version in the Norton Critical Edition, ed. Jonathan Wordsworth, M. H. Abrams, and Stephen Gill (New York and London, 1979). Quotations from the two-part version (*1799* in future references) are also from that edition.

7 From an addition to MS D of 'The Ruined Cottage', in *The Ruined Cottage and The Pedlar*, ed. James Butler (Ithaca, 1979), p. 372.

8 'Simon Lee', *PW*, Vol. 4, p. 63, lines 67, 66.

9 See note 7 above.

10 21 May 1807, *The Letters of William and Dorothy Wordsworth: The Middle Years, 1806–11*, ed. Ernest de Selincourt, rev. Mary Moorman (Oxford, 1969), p. 146.

11 *Prelude* II, 334–6.

12 *Collected Letters of Samuel Taylor Coleridge*, ed. Earl Leslie Griggs, 6 vols. (Oxford, 1956–71), Vol. 4, p. 564.

13 *Biographia Literaria*, ed. J. Shawcross, 2 vols. (London, 1907), Vol. 1, p. 59.

14 In 'The Imaginary Revolution: Wordsworth, Freud, and Lacan', *Revolution and Literature, DQR Studies in Literature*, ed. C. C. Barfoot and T. D'haen, 9 (1992), and '"A Poet's History": Wordsworth and Revolutionary Discourse', *Bucknell Review*, 36, 1 (1992).

15 *PW*, Vol. 1, pp. 279–80, lines 422–7.

16 *Ibid.*, line 429.

17 *Ibid.*, line 433.

18 This and future references to Shakespeare's plays are taken from *The Riverside Shakespeare* (Boston, 1974).

19 A phrase in a contemporary *poissarde* quoted by Simon Schama, *Citizens: A Chronicle of the French Revolution* (London, 1989), p. 461.

20 'Tintern Abbey', *PW*, Vol. 2, p. 262, line 102.

21 Wordsworth to Richard Sharp, 15 January 1804, *Collected Letters of Samuel Taylor Coleridge*, Vol. 2, p. 1034.

22 Coleridge to Sharp, 15 January 1804, *ibid.*, Vol. 2, p. 1033.

23 Phrases from 21 July 1832, *Specimens of the Table Talk of the Late Samuel Taylor Coleridge*, 2 vols. (London, 1835), Vol. 2, pp. 70–2.

24 *Ibid.*, Vol. 2, p. 71.

25 *Prelude* XII, 303.

26 The name by which the poem was known throughout Wordsworth's lifetime.

27 I.F. note to 'There was a Boy', *The Prose Works of William Wordsworth*, ed. A. B. Grosart, 3 vols. (London, 1876), Vol. 3, p. 38.

28 Indeed Stephen Parrish has shown that 'fragments of a preamble appear to [have

preceded]' the passage beginning 'was it for this' (*The Prelude, 1798–1799* (Ithaca, 1977), p. 8). The 'glad preamble' repeats the original checking of 'a superabundant flow of inspiration' (*ibid.*, p. 6).

29 Dorothy Wordsworth to Coleridge, 22 May 1801, *The Letters of William and Dorothy Wordsworth: The Early Years, 1787–1805*, ed. Ernest de Selincourt, rev. Chester L. Shaver (Oxford, 1967), p. 335. Future references to this edition: *EY*.

30 See Dorothy Wordsworth's entry in her Grasmere Journals for 27 December 1801, *Journals of Dorothy Wordsworth*, ed. Mary Moorman, 2nd edn (London, 1973), p. 74.

31 'Intimations Ode', *PW*, Vol. 4, pp. 284–5, lines 181–2, 200.

32 'Ode to Duty', *PW*, Vol. 4, p. 85, line 48.

33 The Norton Critical Edition, p. 516. Coleridge's departure re-enacted the circumstances of the composition of *1799*: 'There is in fact a sense in which *1799* shows Wordsworth moving *away* from Coleridge.' Jonathan Wordsworth and Stephen Gill, 'The Two-Part *Prelude* of 1798–99', *Journal of English and Germanic Philology* 72 (1973), p. 512.

34 *EY*, p. 464.

35 *Ibid.*

36 *Collected Letters of Samuel Taylor Coleridge*, Vol. 1, p. 538.

37 *EY*, p. 465.

38 Both de Selincourt (*EY*, p. 463, n.1) and Mark Reed (*Wordsworth: The Chronology of the Middle Years, 1800–1815* (Cambridge, Mass., 1975), p. 13) identify the passage referred to as VI, 246–331. Jonathan Wordsworth ('The Five-Book *Prelude* of Early Spring 1804', *Journal of English and Germanic Philology* 76 (1977), p. 5, n.16) confines it to VI, 316–31. The reversal I describe is implicit in the smaller section, whether it emerged fully around the time Wordsworth was making the other drafts for MS WW (see below) or during the following month of April.

39 My argument disagrees with Jonathan Wordsworth's conclusions about the five-book *Prelude*. Whether or not 'it is clear that Wordsworth did not expect his last book to give him any particular trouble' ('The Five-Book *Prelude*', pp. 15–16), I suggest that this version could neither be 'finished or within easy distance of completion' (p. 24) in the terms on which it was started.

40 *EY*, p. 452.

41 *Ibid.*, p. 454.

42 'The Five-Book *Prelude*', p. 11.

43 *Ibid.*, p. 17. But see note 53 below.

44 *EY*, p. 453. Wordsworth had experienced similar symptoms when beginning *The Prelude* at Goslar: see his letter to Coleridge, 14 or 21 December 1798, *EY*, p. 236.

45 See Wordsworth to Coleridge, 29 March 1804, *EY*, p. 465, for Wordsworth's acknowledgement that only the copying of MS M for Coleridge had preserved much of his composition.

46 'The Five-Book *Prelude*', p. 24.

47 My transcription. I am grateful to the Trustees of Dove Cottage for permission to use the manuscripts in the Wordsworth Library, and to quote from MSS W (DC MS 38) and WW (DC MS 43).

48 The draft material in this and the following passages quoted from MS W is

transcribed in the Norton Critical Edition, pp. 496–7.

49 An earlier version of this passage in MS WW (see below) refers to 'other [?scenes] which I [?will] [?unfold] / To my [?Friends] eye'. My transcription.

50 This passage has been in parts inaccurately transcribed by Robin Jarvis, 'The Five-Book *Prelude*: A Reconsideration', *Journal of English and Germanic Philology* 80 (1981), p. 545.

51 See *Descriptive Sketches*, ed. Eric Birdsall (Ithaca, 1984), pp. 114–16, lines 774–804, and 'Tintern Abbey', *PW*, Vol. 2, p. 261, lines 65–85.

52 Transcribed in the Norton Critical Edition, p. 428, n.9. It is an aspect of my argument that XI, 268–72 from this corresponding section in *1805* (about Wordsworth's 'deepest feelings that the mind / Is lord and master'), and his development of the murderer's name passage in the Penrith Beacon episode from *1799* in XI, 291–301 would only have been composed *after* the breakthrough to linguistic power examined in MS WW below.

53 My examination of this crux obviously follows in the tracks of Geoffrey Hartman, Harold Bloom, Thomas Weiskel, Jonathan Wordsworth, and Alan Liu. My differences are too intricate to specify in this place.

54 *Wordsworth: The Chronology of the Middle Years, 1770–1799*, p. 641.

55 In referring to this manuscript I use the bibliographical description that is employed by Mark Reed in his forthcoming Cornell edition of *The Thirteen-Book Prelude*. I am grateful to Jonathan Wordsworth for allowing me to use his unpublished transcriptions of MS WW. I have made some alterations, and have adopted several corrections and suggestions from Mark Reed, who has kindly reviewed my transcriptions.

56 Particularly through the writings of Polybius, Livy, and Gibbon.

57 *The Fourteen-Book Prelude*, ed. W. J. B. Owen (Ithaca, 1985), p. 127, app. crit., lines 530–41.

58 From a fragment transcribed in 'Emily Treven's Album', *The West Country Magazine*, 2, 3 (1947), p. 176.

59 *The Fourteen-Book Prelude*, p. 130, app. crit., lines 593–617.

60 See *Wordsworth: The Sense of History* (Stanford, 1989), pp. 24–31.

61 See *The Prelude, or Growth of a Poet's Mind*, ed. Ernest de Selincourt, rev. Helen Darbishire (Oxford, 1959), p. 210, app. crit., line 562.

62 *Nouvelle Déscription des glacières, vallées de glace et glaciers*, 3 vols. (Geneva, 1787), Vol. 2, pp. 216–17.

63 *Ibid.*, p. 216.

64 'Route from Geneva to Domo d'Ossola, by the Pass of the Simplon', *Illustrations of the Passes of the Alps, by which Italy communicates with France, Switzerland, and Germany*, 2 vols. (London, 1828–9), Vol. 2, p. 7.

65 *Ibid.*, p. 13.

66 See *The Sense of History*, p. 23.

67 *Paradise Lost* V, 156, 153–4. All references to this poem are to the text in *The Poems of John Milton*, ed. Helen Darbishire (London, 1961).

68 12 May 1830, *Specimens of Table Talk*, Vol. 1, p. 127. For a Lacanian consideration of Coleridge's contrast between Shakespeare and Milton, see Raman Selden, 'From Persona to the Split Subject', *Comparative Criticism*, 12 (1990), pp. 63–8.

69 *Biographia Literaria*, Vol. 2, p. 20.
70 Compare similes in *Paradise Lost* II, 488–95, 533–8, 636–43.
71 (Keswick, 1842), p. 201.
72 *Ibid.*
73 *Ibid.*
74 (Carlisle, 1802), pp. 37–8. Copies of this edition and of Otley's *A Concise Description of the English Lakes and Adjacent Mountains*, 6th edn (Keswick, 1837) from the Rydal Mount library were bought at the Stepping Stones sale. The latter is now at Cornell University library. Both have the bookplate of Wordsworth's son, William.
75 *PW*, Vol. 2, p. 38, line 6.
76 'Written in London, September, 1802', *ibid.*, p. 115, line 12.

6

REFLECTIONS ON HAVING EDITED
COLERIDGE'S POEMS

J. C. C. MAYS

THE origins of the *Collected Coleridge* lie in conversations between Kathleen Coburn and Rupert Hart-Davis during the 1950s. The project took off at the end of the decade, after the Bollingen Foundation agreed to sponsor the enterprise under the general editorship of Miss Coburn. Sixteen volumes were planned, some of them in as many as five parts, to encompass everything Coleridge wrote; only the letters and the notebooks were excluded, because they were appearing in other series. The first volume to be published, in 1969, was Barbara Rooke's edition of *The Friend*. Ten volumes have appeared to date, in whole or in part, and the remainder are in the press or at a late stage of preparation.[1] There have been many delays, but it is reasonable to expect that the project will be complete within the next few years.

I think it would be fair to describe the *Collected Coleridge* as an edition not much concerned with current discussions of text. Its aim has been to put an accurate readable version of all Coleridge's writing into the widest possible circulation, and the role of individual editors has seemed most obviously to use their knowledge to mediate what Coleridge has to say. The notes for editors ('Style Sheet') are concerned with harmonizing references and cross-references, not with how to handle variants. 'We print directly from xeroxed pages of the original,' the notes read; 'the text should be treated with caution and left basically as it is.'

The approach reflects the experience of Kathleen Coburn and the Associate Editor, the late Bart Winer, and is for the larger part appropriate and obviously successful. In Coburn's associated project of editing the notebooks, the problem is not textual, once the text has been deciphered, but one of annotation – how to make sense of fragments, trace references, and explain allusions. Similarly for much of the *Collected Coleridge*; the texts of titles like *The Watchman* and *Marginalia* are simpler or approximately as complex, but the process of editing is the same – ensuring the text is an accurate transcription and providing commentary. The extension of such an approach to the edition as a whole has resulted in historical introductions which are particularly rich, annotation of an amplitude, subtlety and range of cross-reference which is without parallel, and analytic indexes which are interpretive tools in their own right.

Some titles exist in more than one version, most obviously *The Friend* and less obviously some of the newspaper materials drawn on in *Essays on His Times*, but they are not compromised by the basic procedure. Other titles exist in annotated versions – *The Watchman* and *Lay Sermons*, for instance – but the revisions again can be considered accretions to or commentary on the base-text. Only material dictated to or taken down by auditors presents problems which are in any way complicated. In the case of the literary lectures edited by R. A. Foakes, the reported versions are different enough to be presented separately, like versions of *The Friend*, and their status is clear. But in the case of the philosophy lectures, the unpunctuated sentences of the 'original' manuscript in Toronto can often be combined in different ways; and in the case of *Biographia Literaria*, as Norman Fruman has argued,[2] there are grounds for a fuller display of alternative readings, even for a different choice of base-text.

I have described the approach to editing in the *Collected Coleridge* overall because it is the context in which I began my own work in 1976. George Whalley had been nominated editor of the poems when the project was inaugurated. By the time I took over the edition, he had assembled five large ring-files comprising a paste-up of Ernest Hartley Coleridge's two-volume *Complete Poetical Works* and pieces from Vol. 1 of the published notebooks. His interest focused on the canon of Coleridge's poetry, as he described it in an article for *The Review of Literature*.[3] The aim was to discover a formula which would delimit Coleridge's poetic *œuvre*, and Whalley reviewed and compared the separate collections of poems in the hope of discovering parameters for the new edition. Over the next year, we discussed the question of parameters back and forth, settling on one answer and then admitting so many exceptions to it that it had to be replaced, again and again.

I was at first too busy to think what I was doing. I accepted the aims of the edition overall – to be accurate, to be readable, to make available – and I appreciated the dilemma posed by George Whalley as to what collection 'best represented' our author. My brush with bibliography at Oxford – in the shape of Alice Walker and Herbert Davis – had left an impression of techniques addressed to Elizabethan problems and a vague feeling that Americans (Fredson Bowers, Charlton Hinman) did donkey-work one could make use of but actually went too far. I assumed that this bore on the Coleridge in that I should record all the versions of a poem but that my main task was to map the road to Xanadu. At the same time I reckoned the later question of how the materials were going to be arranged could remain undecided while I gathered together whatever materials I could find. Kathleen Coburn supplied me with a list of what she had noted on her own expeditions, and off I went. The manuscripts are all over the place, but one find led to another, and by the time Barbara Rosenbaum published her checklist,[4] there was little in it that was new. By now, I calculate I must have uncovered some twenty to thirty per cent more material than she lists. Minor poems and transcripts continue to surface; half a dozen have come to light in the interval since I wrote the first draft of this essay.

The printed material was often as difficult to lay hands on as manuscripts – copies of newspapers for specific dates, in particular – and I frequently wished there was an adequate bibliography which was more up to date than those by Thomas J. Wise.[5] The printed texts were also more difficult to analyse and piece together. There are occasions when one has to resort to ultra-violet light and police detection techniques to read a Coleridge manuscript, and one only gradually grows able to distinguish his hand from some copyists and amanuenses. However, to work out why the texts of *Remorse* vary as they do – there are three states of the first edition and two of the second – took me back to lessons taught by Alice Walker. It became important that the same play was printed by half-sheet imposition, and this made more sense of the records of the production scattered between the Garrick Club, the University of Melbourne, the British Library, and the Folger. It proved necessary to learn about nineteenth-century binders to fathom how an annotated *Remorse* was split surreptitiously into two copies by the collector, Stuart M. Samuel. And so on.

The amount and complicated inter-relation of the material revealed itself as I discovered it, otherwise it would have appeared overwhelming. At the same time, as I analysed and considered how each new piece of the jigsaw puzzle fitted in, my initial concerns did not seem as pressing. I had a separate cardboard file for each poem, and it did not matter that their separate histories did not conform to a pattern. Some, like the 'Ode to Chatterton', moved through separate stages each of which in effect constitutes a different poem.[6] It was clear that a large number of political poems was toned down when they were reprinted; other poems were re-directed; personal poems were generalized. Some poems were improved up to a point when Coleridge appears to have lost interest in them and allowed printer's errors to accumulate – for instance, 'The Garden of Boccaccio'. Others, like 'Frost at Midnight', underwent continuous improvement.

It was clear, also, as one mapped the relation between these versions, that changes of punctuation and capitalization were often, for Coleridge, as important as changes of wording. The difference was not as between first and second orders of significance, as implied by Greg's formula of substantives and accidentals. The several early transcripts of 'Christabel' by or authorized by Coleridge differ in these particulars more than in wording, and the differences work towards modified effects which are quite separate.

For example, it makes a difference whether or not direct speech is separated from its context by 'quotation marks'. To write Mary Mother, save me now!, without them, shares the appeal intimately between us and the person who speaks the words, and the omission controls the tempo as well as volume at which we register them. They elide with indirect quotations – And what can ail the Mastiff Bitch? – which thereby come out of a background of indistinct concern shared between author, character and reader. The capitalizing or non-capitalizing of nouns – not just Lady (Christabel), or Mother and Father, but intrinsically less significant nouns in such a context like Answer, Voice, Distress – modulates if only slightly the way they announce and contain their meanings. Similarly for the introduction of commas, or substitution of commas for semi-colons, or introduction or omission of hyphens, or doubled punctuation (viz., – ; – : –): this is not random but instinctive; it controls the pace at which syntax unfolds.

The process is subtle and was prompted by and engages instinct, so it is not possible to extrapolate a shared direction by applying the law of averages; each transcript of 'Christabel' communicates a different performance of the same words; parts move in different directions in each performance. The confusion in paragraphing in the printed versions makes as much difference to unfolding of the sense as many changes of phrasing, and again one such difference has a knock-on effect on others.

As more evidence concerning individual poems became available, the status of the separate collections in which they are gathered became more problematic. Analysis of the three late, three-volume collections and family manuscripts scattered between London, Toronto, and Texas revealed the part played by nineteenth-century editors. Similarly, analysis of the three early collections – 1796, 1797, and 1803 – revealed a complicated story of partially-rectified mistakes and missed opportunities. The proof copies of *Sibylline Leaves* at Yale and printer's records in the Bodleian, taken alongside the texts of individual poems, again make up a story of compromise. There is no 'core collection' which represents Coleridge's wishes transparently. Each collection arranges separate poems, which have separate histories, to make a different overall statement.

Meanwhile, as the files of Coleridge poems grew fatter, their number accumulated. A few titles needed to be removed from the previous collection by Ernest Hartley Coleridge, since they were included by pardonable mistake. Examples are 'To a Primrose', 'Thy Smiles I Note, Sweet Early Flower' (copied into a notebook from *Anthologia Hibernica*) and 'I Mix in Life, and Labour to Seem Free' (from William Preston). Also, besides the addition of previously uncollected or unknown poems, the limits of the *œuvre* began to blur. A number of adaptations of originals by Wordsworth, from 'Lewti' to 'Alcaeus to Sappho', deserve a place because of the intrinsic interest of Coleridge's modifications, but then there are revisions of poems by Charles Lamb, rewritings of Southey, poems Coleridge discovered by rearranging separate stanzas of Ben Jonson or by conflating passages of Daniel. In various ways, the body of Coleridge's poem is not separate as Yeats's is, or Wallace Stevens's. Though it contains a number of literary poems and other kinds beside – political, metrical experiments, whatever – its boundaries shift according to how you look at them. Nearly every quotation is modified – adapted and thereby 'creative' – and the wall between what is and is not his is eroded.

I arranged the files in chronological order as they accumulated because it was easiest to remember. Titles of individual poems changed and groupings of poems in volumes overlapped, and the notion of the sequence of composition appeared the most stable method of ordering them. By this stage, it did not matter that poems like the *Ancient Mariner* were composed over months, that the date of 'Kubla Khan' could only be guessed at, that the evidence for some other poems – like the sonnet 'It may indeed be Phantasy' and 'The Pang More Sharp Than All' – left them hanging between the 1800s and the 1820s. It is almost a virtue of the resulting compromise that its limitations are patently obvious.

What I have described constitutes the stage I moved through in the first half-dozen years. My bemusement about where the work would end probably helped me to continue it. It was a state of watchful discomfort whose balm was Kathleen Coburn's favourite Shakespeare phrase, which I also repeated to myself, 'The readiness is all.'[7] In fact, willy-nilly I was organizing the materials in the way they asked to be interpreted, moving towards an idea of poems growing and changing, even reversing their progress; looking for a method to record stages in their life which were discrete in a way which made the notion of their evolving, their succeeding one another, misleading. I evolved a Heath Robinson set of arrangements to record variants which would display the evolution of poems as I needed to sort them out myself. It was a framework to make sense of the very large amount of material I was uncovering, to keep it in place.

At about this stage, reading in bibliographical literature for practical assistance with the problems of collating and the like, I began also to pick up on the theoretical debate concerning the status of the New Bibliography. What was being said about how the different status of Romantic and Modern texts posed problems different from Elizabethan–Jacobean ones encouraged me to believe I was correct in not trying to force the Coleridge material into a Procrustean scheme. What I read by English and American bibliographers was largely negative or critical, however, pointing out the inapplicability of an old answer but not describing a new one. And when I discovered Hans Zeller's article in *Studies in Bibliography*,[8] it came with the force of recognition. It pointed the way to an answer I had been inventing separately in my ignorance, and, with certain modifications, it is at the heart of my new edition.

I suppose I must have discovered the article in about 1980, maybe before, and the time since has been spent assimilating it, pursuing the consequences of some of its suggestions and modifying them. It led to firming up the outlines of the work I had done as I added, revised and corrected. There was an uncomfortable interval when computer technology promised more than it could deliver, but the material is now (autumn 1989) in the state in which it would have been handed over to Bart Winer, if he were still alive. It will trickle onward through its processes – with further readers to check, copy-edit and design – and with luck might reach the bookstalls in 1992.

I have told how my contribution to the *Collected Coleridge* evolved because the story provides a perspective to understand how my volumes are organized. They differ from others in the series as I described it at the beginning, though not as much as they would if they were not part of the same.

The *Poetical Works* will make three volumes, and the volume in the middle will be at the centre in every way. It will contain all Coleridge's poems in chronological order, amounting to nearly 700, to which are added some 130 lost poems, poems of doubtful authenticity and poems for a long time supposed to be by Coleridge but since proved not to be. It is necessary that this penumbra of poems which are certainly or not quite his should be present in the sequence so they can be located in an expected place, and if the result is to blur the edges of his achievement that is precisely as it is.

A large number of the poems are collected, even published, for the first time. The new poems are in most cases occasional, and there are no 'Kubla Khan's among them and no third part of 'Christabel'. A contentious reviewer might argue that there is more poetry in many notebook entries or in an anthology such as *Inquiring Spirit*, but apart from *Allegoric Vision* and the prose part of *The Wanderings of Cain*, both of which Coleridge collected in his own *Poetical Works*, the criterion is metre.

Many kinds of poem and many levels of quality are represented, one following another sometimes incongruously. I have explained George Whalley's hope that some two-tier system could be devised to keep the lesser poems in a subordinate position where they would not take off from the greater, and how it could not be sustained. Such methods of organization failed because they were not democratic. They were overtaken by the large numbers of poems which fell between the categories of lesser and greater. The weight of exceptions eroded the fragile rules.

Within the sequence, the format of individual poems follows a pattern derived from Continental models. First there is discussion of the date, which, when a poem has been worked on over several years like 'Christabel', can extend to a couple of pages. Then follows a description of each of the texts which have been collated. In the case of manuscripts their relation to one another is explained; in the case of printed texts, annotated copies and reprintings are included under each heading; the sequence of texts is numbered and presented in continuous, chronological order. Then, in some cases in which further points arise, there is a general note. Thus, in a simple case like dated lines which appear only once in a notebook, what I have outlined fills only half a page. In a complicated case like *Religious Musings*, there are thirteen manuscripts and eight printed texts, several of which are emended in different ways, as well as the relation of some derivative versions which have to be set aside, to be described.

The body of the texts presents each line of a poem, with differences in the wording of versions shown as part of the line – that is, beneath the particular word or phrase. Thus, in line 101 of 'The Picture',

& 1   Each wild flow'r on the marge inverted there,

1   of   reflected

signifies that all the texts but manuscript 1 read as in the top line, and that the two words in the line beneath are substituted in manuscript 1. And in line 108 of the same poem,

1 1   In mad love-gazing on the vacant brook,

2–5   Love yearning by

signifies that printed-text 1 and manuscript 1 read as in the top line, and that the words in the line beneath are substituted in printed-texts 2 to 5. I originally hoped that differences of punctuation, spelling, and capitals could be shown ranged to the right of each line, but it was not possible within the *Collected Coleridge* page-width, and they have had to be positioned in a band at the foot of each page. Another band contains information concerning paragraphing, indentation, and Coleridge's textual emendations.

The aim was to cluster the variants in the body of the text, to display a situation in which a number of versions evolved, none of which is necessarily to be privileged above another. This is how, in a rudimentary form, I found myself recording variants as I assembled the texts, and how, far more elaborately, texts are presented in the new editions of Klopstock and Conrad Ferdinard Meyer.[9] I have not followed the Germans and the Swiss into algebraic notation because it confused me, though my display does become complicated when it encompasses omitted and deleted passages. Nor have I gone as far as the editors of the new Hölderlin edition in trying to reproduce typographically the exact contours of manuscript revision, though again a way has been found to register deletions and insertions within lines. I have taken heart from their example, but have not been persuaded to adopt their detailed solutions.

Despite the simplifications and the compromises, the method of display communicates a different supposition about what is going on than would the choice of one text rested on a pile of footnotes. The display communicates a process in which a number of versions have separate validity, described by the occasions in the initial notes on each text. Poems like *The Destiny of Nations* and *Religious Musings* are in fact several poems. Although large blocks of text are shared, carried across from version to version, they are put into new relations and given new meanings on each separate occasion. Thus, *The Destiny of Nations* exists as Coleridge's contribution to the revision of Southey's *Joan of Arc* in 1795, secondly in a newly-conceived but aborted form he worked on between 1796 and 1798, and lastly in a more integrated revision made during a period of rekindled interest in 1814–15. Also, the meaning possessed by each version of such poems is determined and modulated by a pattern of punctuation, spelling, and like particulars, as I described above with reference to 'Christabel'. A reader comes to see any one version as Coleridge would, if he could have recalled them all, as an emergent possibility against a background of several, often divergent or contradictory others.

Scholarly readers often read this way, I think, as do many writers. There are occasions, however, in which another kind of text is required. Though I have referred to the text in Vol. 2 as the variorum and the text in Vol. 1 as the reading-text, the variorum is essentially to be read and the reading-text is for speaking. The text of the poems in Vol. 1 rests on a series of choices which excludes alternatives, that is, each poem separately in the reading sequence rests on a decision about the evolution and special features of its more 'various' counterpart.

Unfortunately for tidy minds, there is no rule which distinguishes the version to be preferred. The evidence accumulated in the variorum points towards the necessity of making a fresh decision in each case, since each is quite different. As I said before, in some cases Coleridge continued to improve poems to the end. In others he patently lost interest and allowed mistakes to creep in. In others he was embarrassed or he changed his mind. There are other factors to be taken into account as well. Even if it can be demonstrated that some of his notes or prefaces are distractions, or that he took little interest in the second part of 'Christabel', readers have come to expect they will be present. In some cases, the issue can be fudged: one can provide a facing-text of both the earliest and latest versions of the *Ancient Mariner*, or provide the verse-letter to Sara Hutchinson and 'Dejection: An Ode' as separate poems. In some other cases, a choice must be made. It is not justifiable in this context to give three different versions of the Chatterton ode or *Religious Musings*: one version simply must be chosen.[10]

The texts are in every case but one complete single versions, that is, not cobbled together from several others. I have restored Coleridge's punctuation and spelling when it has been improved in ways which manifestly do not possess authority, and it follows from what I said about the importance of punctuation and spelling that these have been regularized hardly at all. A patina of consistency could have been imposed on all the poems, early and previously unpublished as well as late, such as Henry Nelson Coleridge attempted in 1834, but it would not have rested on a sound base and more would be lost than gained. What would be lost is the texture of the live performance and occasional effects which could be achieved in no other way. The policing would be for its own sake, just to satisfy tidy-mindedness. It would be like preserving a view through a wire fence.

The numbers assigned to poems in each sequence are the same, so they can be matched without trouble, and the reading text in Vol. 1 is accompanied by an editorial commentary in which the choice of text is justified and important variations or modifications are summarized or quoted. The commentary also includes originals of translations, or translations of Greek and Latin verses, as well as information about circumstances and persons and places. In the case of political or personal poems, such commentary often accumulates to an amount where it mediates an understanding of the verse, and the experience of following the reading-text approximates to the pursuit of the variorum, each word being heard through a hum of circumstance.

It is worth mentioning, because of the shadow cast by Lowes's *Road to Xanadu* on Coleridge studies in general and on the character of the *Collected Coleridge*, as well as on the approach to Coleridge's poetry in particular, that the annotation in these poem-volumes slightly differs from others in the series. I judged that more was lost than gained by exhaustive Lowes-type annotation of poems like the *Ancient Mariner* and 'Kubla Khan'. I have condensed it drastically and deliberately pointed to other matters of concern. In the same cause, I have restrained the impulse to barnacle the text with possible parallels and influences from Coleridge's reading, and to detail the many articles and books which take up particular points. Other, less literary poems and fragments often receive proportionally more annotation because I think literary readers will need it more. We shall see if I got the emphasis right when the first thousand ordinary readers send in their reports.

Vol. 3 contains the plays and also Coleridge's translations of Schiller's plays. The volume follows last in my description here and it might seem to complete the sequence with the air somewhat of an afterthought. In reality, it includes some of the most exciting new material in the set. Ernest Hartley Coleridge appears not to have taken the editing of the plays as seriously as of the poems, and there is a larger than usual number of errors to be corrected and additions to be incorporated. The opportunity is taken to clarify the relation between *Osorio* and *Remorse* and to add an acting-text of *Remorse*. The materials on the evolution of *Remorse* at Drury Lane and on its performances in the provinces are extensive. Besides being one of the most successful plays in a quarter-century period, it must also be one of the best documented. The story requires a number of received opinions about the early nineteenth-century stage to be modified.

The Schiller translations are presented facing the German originals for the first time. The manuscript of *Wallensteins Tod* is at Harvard, but the lost manuscript of *Die Piccolomini* has been reconstructed by Joyce Crick from other manuscript and printed sources. Both German texts differ considerably from the versions which Schiller published, and they will require estimates of Coleridge's habits as a translator to be revised. Again, though the work was undertaken to make money, it turned out to have larger importance. One consequence has to do with Coleridge's turn towards Shakespeare at this time, towards whom his views had earlier been for the most part conventional.

My other co-editor besides Joyce Crick, Lorna Arnold, is responsible for the Greek and Latin parts of the edition. The fully-annotated presentation of Coleridge's poems in these languages, many of them written when he was an undergraduate, together with a proper recognition of the Classical elements in his English verse, changes the way one understands his approach to verse in English in general and particularly his understanding of English metre. Again, his plans for translating both Anacreon and Renaissance Latin poets, although realized only in part, were as much a determining influence at the beginning of his poetic career as the sonnets of William Bowles.

I should complete this survey or preview of the *Poetical Works* by mentioning that, following the introduction, in which I go into many things touched on here at greater length, there are three extensive annexes. Annex A provides a description and analysis of manuscript collections of Coleridge's poems, Annex B of printed collections, and Annex C of annotated copies. The annexes complement the argument contained in the introduction, and reinforce both the grounds of the argument about the choice of reading-text in Vol. 1 and the relation between variorum texts in Vol. 2. The relation between annotated copies is often complicated and requires this separate presentation and discussion. There are twenty-three annotated copies of *Sibylline Leaves*, for example, and ten of *Zapolya*, as well as numerous related copies annotated by friends and contemporaries. They fall into different groups with different kinds of status and relevance, and make up, in effect, a further series of 'texts'.

Also, in the third volume, besides first-line and title indexes, there are comprehensive indexes of names and topics which cover the texts, the introductory materials and the commentary.

The story I told at the beginning, of how this contribution to the *Collected Coleridge* evolved, also provides a perspective on the comments to follow on some theoretical implications. It should be clear that I felt hard-pressed to get the job done. The practical difficulties loomed so large that I was luckily not aware of their scale until I had tunnelled through them. My over-riding conscious commitment was as a Coleridge editor, not as member of a centre for textual studies working on an exercise.

At the same time, I became aware of theoretical implications at a crucial stage, and, if I had not done so, I wonder if I would have had the confidence to finish as I did. Besides Hans Zeller's article and the editions mentioned above, I would add the discussions in Gunter Martins and Hans Zeller (eds.), *Texte und Varianten. Probleme ihrer Edition und Interpretation* (Munich, 1971); the special numbers of *Lili: Zeitschrift für Literaturwissenschaft und Linguistik*, 5 (1975) (Heft 19/20) and *Zeitschrift für Deutsche Philologie*, 101 (1982); *Les Manuscrits: transcrition, édition, signification* (Paris, 1976); *Avant-texte, texte, après-texte* (Paris and Budapest, 1982).

Although, as I came to realize, what I was doing was consonant with arguments applied to different circumstances by Jerome McGann, David McKenzie, Edwin Honigmann, and the editors of the Oxford Shakespeare, the methods current in French and German editing have not been applied to an English poet before. Such methods address problems which American and English textual critics have shown themselves to be aware of during the past twenty years, but have not been inclined to answer. In the course of turning over questions of multiple authoritative versions and final authorial intention – questions such as which version of Auden's or Marianne Moore's texts, early or late, actually constitutes their poems – the bibliographical consensus defended by Fredson Bowers and G. Thomas Tanselle has looked increasingly rickety. The importance of punctuation in writers like Emily Dickinson and Robert Frost has proved it to be a more than an 'accidental' quality. Questions raised by bibliographers of American literature, in particular, have proved awkward and unsettling.[11]

Hans Walter Gabler's three-volume edition of *Ulysses* (New York, 1984) is nevertheless the only example of a genetic presentation most English readers know, and its historical significance has been obscured by disagreement concerning individual readings and proper names and fixing on his decision to remove the first printed version of the complete text from a privileged place in the collation. Its true significance is that it constitutes an edition of an English (Irish) author which follows the procedures employed by the ongoing new editions of Flaubert, Proust, and Kafka, in which separate versions (*Fassungen*) can be read alongside one another.[12] My edition of Coleridge's poems is another application of the same method. It attempts to display a series of situations in which versions succeed one another in time but often have separate validity, and in which details work together to create the separateness of each different version. Sometimes a collected or later printed version is preferred, on its merits, but that does not alter the essential ground of agreement.

I suppose an essay such as this is expected to be provocative, so I will say that, in the light of what I have described, much Anglo-American editing looks to be stuck in a limbo, unable or unwilling to learn from answers which have proved successful elsewhere. The extensive re-editing of English Romantic poets, which the present collection of essays takes off from, often situates textual material in a Procrustean framework of Elizabethan–Jacobean dimensions, as I have said. The questions which originate from the odd match are unanswerable in the terms which prompted them. Who is to determine where *The Prelude* is among its versions? Or who can describe punctuation as 'accidental' at the close of 'Ode on a Grecian Urn'? The questions are raised as if they laid down a challenge, but then, abandoned, they continue to possess troubling life. They form part of a roster of like questions which have accumulated over the years, alongside examples as widely spaced as the three versions of *Piers Plowman* and the late rewriting of Henry James. There are signs that the recent, massive enterprise of re-editing Wordsworth has encouraged some awareness of the problem,[13] but the discussion has so far not moved towards a solution.

The gap between the Cornell Wordsworth and Harvard Keats, on the one hand, and the Düsseldorf Heine and Hamburg Klopstock, on the other, is therefore more than a difference of authors and language. The unanswerable questions on which Anglo-American editing gets stuck fade considerably in the different light which is cast on them. German Romantic editing makes available a way to show what is happening in the composition of poems like *The Eve of St Agnes* and to show how different versions of poems like Blake's *Songs of Innocence* co-exist. It does not matter that an author is disconcerted or embarrassed by the implications of what he has written, and that this is part of the meaning too need not be denied. A genetic or synoptic display does not of course answer the question of which version is to be recited on a school prize-day, nor should it be taken to suggest that all the versions displayed were present in an author's own mind at any one time, but it can present alternative versions so they can be understood together in the mind's eye with minimal distortion. A composite text displayed in such a way is inscribable, if not pronounceable. Any one text can be read in the light of several others, the strongest assertions sometimes in the light of their betrayal.

An example already exists in the Nonesuch printing of the 1798 and 1834 versions of the *Ancient Mariner* face to face. What the variorum does is to extend the principle beyond two texts, so that an example like the following presents a palimpsest in which three versions can be followed:

1. 1 Verse, Picture, Music, Thoughts both grave and gay,
   2 3   pictures,
2. 1 Remembrances of dear Friends far away,
   2 3   loved friends
3. 1 On   a pure ground   of virgin White display'd —
   2 3   spotless page
4. 1 Such should thy ALBUM be: for such are thou, fair Maid!
   2   art
   3   thine   sweet

I will not add the accompanying material, which records variations in the title and the different spelling, capitalization, and punctuation of the lines. The variants must be assessed in the light of the different status of each of the three manuscripts; and considerations like this are joined by extra-literary ones when the different persons to whom the lines might have been addressed are conjured up. A reader must imagine how the method can be extended from three to a dozen texts, each overlaying the other as if they were written on successive sheets of transparent paper, a dozen occasions connected.

Even a reader who finds such notions and practices unfamiliar will surely admit that Coleridge's poetry is constantly complicating a stable authorial viewpoint. The very life and nature of the Conversation Poems is tonal variation, shifting commitments, reversals. The animating presence of satisfy-ing recitable poems like 'Kubla Khan' is patently manifold, even contradictory, while the *Ancient Mariner* gloss – in all versions of the poem after 1817 – by itself frustrates monocular interpretation of the verses, contains further eddies of ambivalence. Political and occasional poems, which in other ways proceed more simply, are filtered like the album verses above by historical and personal circumstances which we, as readers, need to bring to them to elicit meaning. In other words, the habits of reading required by the variorum are not cast aside as one approaches the 'clean' reading-text. Even the few poems Coleridge wrote which aspire purely to literature do not allow a reading of the purely literary kind allowed by modern Objectivist lyrics.

The same feature bears on the editorial commentary. I remarked that suppositions engendered by Lowes's *Road to Xanadu* have cast a long shadow, and the peculiar range of verbal association in one kind of poetry Coleridge wrote has obscured other kinds of dialogue it enters into. The best-known personal encounters involve Wordsworth and Sara Hutchinson, but the same currents of feeling are modified differently at other times by, for instance, the Morgan family and Mary Evans. Equally important in a negative way are poems which turn on unnamed audiences comprising or affected by unsympathetic readers like Coleridge's brothers or Hazlitt. A footnote on the amaranth in the manuscript draft of 'Work Without Hope', for example, recalls Hazlitt's lament in *The Spirit of the Age*: 'Instead of gathering fruits and flowers, immortal fruits and amaranthine flowers . . .'[14]: the footnote is less elucidation than a distraction which reveals the pain the lines seek to alleviate. Very few poems even in the notebooks are written without a complicating dimension of self-consciousness, which often is as important to their full understanding as the echo of a book. Lautréamont told us 'Le plagiat est nécessaire,' and a welcome consequence of our present-day self-consciousness about intertextuality is that we can understand the workings of dialogic imagination, by echo and appropriation and encounter, in broader terms than in the past.

Coleridge's plays have been found to have literary shortcomings, but when they are read as they were conceived, in terms of particular actors and theatres and stage practices, their texture thickens. They communicate not solely as words privately on a page but as part of a context of meanings in which the verbal meaning is mediated. In short, there is a direct connection between the equipment necessary to read a political poem like 'The Bridge Street Committee', a personal poem like 'The Day Dream', and an aborted play like 'The Triumph of Loyalty'. It requires the literary aspect of the texts to engage with and circulate through non-literary kinds of understanding. The texts are in the hand, the work is in the language, or did Roland Barthes put this the other way round?

The arrangement of Coleridge's poems in an extended chronological sequence, instead of having them sorted according to subject-matter or levels of literary ambition, is not just a solution imposed by the material. It makes good sense for other reasons. George Whalley's interest in Coleridge's 'better poems' has to go into quotation marks because the phrase has deservedly come under examination. One result of the changing emphasis of literary studies over the past decades is that the concept of literariness has become more various and accomodating.

Wordsworth's lordly proclamation that satire 'would profane the sanctity of Verse' (*Prelude, 1805* X, 646)[15] is more questionable now than it might have seemed during the nineteenth century; even as the Kantian reading of Wordsworthian Imagination that Coleridge himself attempted has been proved a distortion. Many assumptions about poetry which Coleridge helped to establish bear an oblique relation to his own practice and partly misrepresent it. He is in reality not just the author of a dozen literary poems, or even several dozen, from which several hundred others of merely historical interest depend. The entire mixed sequence of his poems is best seen together, where they make up a dialogue with each other and with material not restricted to literature.

The European tradition of editing I have drawn upon answers some questions only to raise others, it is true. However, I do not worry about the forbidding appearance of some of the pages of the variorum Coleridge text because I know they are less ambitious and simpler than their German–French equivalent would have been and because they can be read easily when one relinquishes the ambition to speak them. Nor do I worry that each reading text represents a decision about, an interpretation of, the variorum material. It is better to make decisions which may be wrong in particular instances than universally to apply an empty rule. The variorum contains the material for readers to make up a different reading-text in each instance, if they feel moved to or as occasion demands.

Several poems will appear in Wordsworth's and Lamb's and Southey's and other writers' poetical works besides – such as the adaptations of Lamb's and Southey's sonnets or of Wordsworth's juvenilia for *The Morning Post*, or differently 'The Devil's Thoughts' (with Southey) and 'The Old Man of the Alps' (somehow with Wordsworth). Such poems have a different meaning in each context, like those unsigned canvasses by Picasso and Braque which belong to neither artist and to both. One also knows there will be a good many mistakes, however careful the checking, because statistically it is inevitable. One knows that in the interval between now and publication, new texts and titles will come to light and fresh information will be brought forward. One knows that such an edition is inevitably a product of its time, and that its basic working assumptions will limit it more than anything one can control or insert or remove in a revision.

I would see this as a counterpart to the theoretical consequence I named. Though *Poetical Works* is textually more elaborate than other titles in the

Collected Coleridge, it is textually less definitive. Each variorum text has to have an assumed point of balance on which the line-numbering can rest, and other readers might analyse individual cases differently. It is inescapably a matter of judgment as to when changes begin to betray rather than enrich the original intention, or which of several equally viable versions is to be preferred.[16] And just as different choices can justifiably be made for many reading-texts of the poems, so different criteria concerning normalization of spelling and punctuation can be applied. While the net has been cast very wide to include what Coleridge wrote in verse, it could be cast in other ways with different results.

Norman Fruman is doing another edition of *Biographia Literaria* on different principles from the *Collected Coleridge*, which I think is understandable and right. But several other editions of the poems are going forward at the same time as the *Collected Coleridge* edition, which is also proper and encouraging. Though I tried only to present the materials as they are, I was continually aware of having to make choices and to reject alternatives, often with regret. It is chastening to recognize that the parts of an edition which require the most care and which most consciously seek to be neutral are precisely those which will provide the justification for alternative editions.

I would only emphasize that recent developments in editorial practice and literary theory favour the presentation and understanding of Coleridge's achievement as a poet. The restricting of the claims of the (old) New Bibliography and the (old) New Criticism are closely related, and the presentation of Coleridge I have attempted provides the opportunity to consider characteristics previously seen as limitations neutrally or as strengths. The lessened insistence on particular kinds of purely literary effect may help retrieve his political and occasional poems. The breaking down of the myth of self-presence will aid an author who is present in his poems in typically evasive and contradictory ways, and the limits of whose *œuvre* are correspondingly fluid. The awareness of several separate versions of *Remorse* may aid the understanding of its special theatrical qualities.

At this stage, I feel inclined to retreat from the portentous claims I have been led to make. Though editors have a manipulative power which is no less for being concealed behind a wall of obscure information, their role is properly modest. The preparation of an edition like this is really no more than like arranging an exhibition. The paintings are brought out and cleaned, wrong attributions are removed and new attributions added, they are sorted and rehung in a way which one hopes will seem inevitable though one knows that it will soon appear dated and that the business will have to begin over again.

Of course, Coleridge is not writing according to a contemporary postmodern aesthetic any more than he wrote according to the old modernist one. Whatever theoretical implications we think we see in the way we choose to see him illuminate both writer and reader to the same degree. I have alluded to some contemporary theorizing in my discussion, but I hope in aid of an ultimately Romantic revision.

NOTES

1 The publishers are Princeton University Press in the United States, and Routledge in Britain. In the following list, I have marked volumes which have appeared with an asterisk and those which have appeared in part with a double asterisk: *1, *Lectures 1795: On Politics and Religion*, ed. Lewis Patton and Peter Mann; *2, *The Watchman*, ed. Lewis Patton; *3, *Essays on His Times*, ed. David V. Erdman; *4, *The Friend*, ed. Barbara Rooke; *5, *Lectures 1808–1819: On Literature*, ed. Reginald A. Foakes; *6, *Lay Sermons*, ed. R. J. White; *7, *Biographia Literaria*, ed. James Engell and W. Jackson Bate; 8, *Lectures 1818–1819: On the History of Philosophy*, ed. Owen Barfield; 9, *Aids to Reflection*, ed. John Beer; *10, *On the Constitution of the Church and State*, ed. John Colmer; 11, *Shorter Works and Fragments*, ed. H. J. Jackson and J. R. de J. Jackson; **12, *Marginalia*, ed. George Whalley; *13, *Logic*, ed. J. R. de J. Jackson; 14, *Table Talk*, ed. Carl R. Woodring; 15, *Opus Maximum*, ed. Thomas McFarland; 16, *Poetical Works*, ed. J. C. C. Mays.

2 'Review Essay: Aids to Reflection on the New *Biographia*', *Studies in Romanticism*, 24 (1985), pp. 141–73.

3 'Coleridge's Poetical Canon: Selection and Arrangement', *Review of Literature*, 7 (1966), pp. 9–24.

4 In *Index of English Literary Manuscripts, Vol. 4, 1800–1900. Part I Arnold–Gissing* (with Pamela White; London and New York, Mansell, 1982), pp. 505–661.

5 *A Bibliography of the Writings in Prose and Verse of Samuel Taylor Coleridge* (London, 1913); *Coleridgeana being a Supplement to the Bibliography of Coleridge* (London, 1919); *Two Lake Poets . . . William Wordsworth and Samuel Taylor Coleridge* (London, 1927).

6 Explained by I. A. Gordon, 'The Case-History of Coleridge's *Monody on the Death of Chatterton*', *Review of English Studies*, 18 (1942), pp. 49–71.

7 Compare *In Pursuit of Coleridge* (London, 1977), p. 14.

8 'A New Approach to the Critical Constitution of Literary Texts', *Studies in Bibliography*, 28 (1975), pp. 231–64.

9 Friedrich Gottlieb Klopstock, *Werke und Briefe. Historisch-kritische Ausgabe*, ed. Horst Gronemeyer et al. (Berlin/New York, 1974–); Conrad Ferdinand Meyer, *Sämtliche Werke. Historisch-kritische Ausgabe*, ed. Hans Zeller and Alfred Zach (Bern, 1958–). The Hölderlin edition referred to later in the paragraph is edited by Friedrich Beissner (Stuttgart, 1943–85). The Heine edition referred to in the last division of this essay, fourteen paragraphs from the end, is edited by Manfred Windfuhr (Hamburg, 1973–).

10 Though the severity of choice can again be mitigated in practice. The earliest version of any text constitutes the top lines in the variorum, and requires no extra practice to read. Two of the three versions of 'Chatterton' and *Religious Musings* are thereby available in easily-read form.

11 Among critics of the editing of American literature, see Hershel Parker, *Flawed Texts*

and *Verbal Icons: Literary Authenticity in American Fiction* (Evanston, 1984), but also the comments by Peter L. Shillingsburg 'An Inquiry into the Social Status of Texts and Modes of Textual Criticism', *Studies in Bibliography*, 42 (1989), pp. 55–79.

12 Gabler reflects on methodology in 'The Synchrony and Diachrony of Texts: Practice and Theory of the Critical Edition of James Joyce's *Ulysses*', *Text: Transactions of the Society for Textual Scholarship*, 1 (for 1981; published 1984), pp. 305–26. Compare also Jerome J. McGann, '*Ulysses* as a Postmodern Text: The Gabler Edition', *Criticism*, 27 (1985), pp. 283–306.

13 See Stephen Gill, 'Wordsworth's Poems: The Question of Text', *Review of English Studies*, n.s., 34 (1983), pp. 172–90; and Jack Stillinger, 'Textual Primitivism and the Editing of Wordsworth', *Studies in Romanticism*, 28 (1989), pp. 3–28 (as well as the references provided in Stillinger's notes).

14 *The Complete Works of William Hazlitt*, ed. P. P. Howe (London, 1930–4), Vol. 11, p. 37. Hazlitt's book was published in 1825, but had in fact been available since November 1824: see Herschel Baker, *William Hazlitt* (Cambridge, Mass., 1962), p. 433 fn. Indeed, the essay itself had been published in the *New Monthly Magazine* in January 1824.

15 Compare his relegation of satire to the sixth and lowest class of poetry in the 1815 *Preface: The Prose Works of William Wordsworth*, ed. W. J. B. Owen and J. W. Smyser (Oxford, 1974), Vol. 3, p. 28.

16 Charles Rosen, 'Romantic Originals', *New York Review of Books* (17 December 1987), pp. 22–31 makes the same point in smaller terms.

CREATIVE PROCESS AND CONCEALMENT IN
COLERIDGE'S POETRY

NORMAN FRUMAN

ON March 9, 1798, at the height of his *annus mirabilis* creative glories, Coleridge wrote to a friend, "People in general are not sufficiently aware how often the imagination creeps in and counterfeits the memory – perhaps to a certain degree it does always blend with our supposed recollections."[1] The most striking example of this in Coleridge's poetic career may well be the famous Preface to "Kubla Khan," where Coleridge set down an account of that poem's fabulous genesis which, despite its extraordinary particularity, has come to be widely doubted. "Counterfeiting" of various kinds, however, is pervasive in Coleridge's poetic career. For example, he gave false dates to many of his poems, in almost every case attributing them to his early years, in one or two cases assigning a poem written in middle age to his "schoolboy" muse. He published often under pseudonyms, although he once wrote, "I make it a scruple of conscience never to publish any thing, however trifling, without [my name]" (*CL*, 1, p. 259); and he often claimed in print, or in letters to friends, that a poem had been written in a burst of sudden inspiration when in fact he had worked very hard on it (as with the lengthy *Religious Musings*, labored upon for over a year, but published as the production of a single night). On several occasions he claimed as spontaneous work poems which were actually translations, paraphrases, or adaptations.

Poets, like other human beings, are not incapable of deliberately falsifying the past, and an endless number of motives, conscious and unconscious, can enter into the process of "counterfeiting the memory." Auden's revisions of several early political poems were obviously not undertaken solely for aesthetic reasons, but in many instances to repudiate or modify his youthful radical commitments, such as acceptance of "the necessary murder." The object of the poet's affections in some Byron poems has become decidedly problematical now that his active bisexuality has become known. "There be none of Beauty's daughters / With a magic like thee" – who could have suspected that these

"Stanzas for Music" may have been a compliment to a male college chum, or that "On This Day I Complete My Thirty-Sixth Year" was a love poem addressed to a Greek youth named Loukas?

The extent to which what is suppressed or designed to keep hidden is sometimes crucial to an understanding of poets like Auden and Byron (or Wordsworth) is a useful object of study, but in Coleridge concealment is an *insistent* need, one that regularly shapes his creative process and characterizes many of his revisions. Sometimes his poetic concealments are fashioned to obscure debts and are of aesthetic interest primarily in the study of his artistic development. In some cases his dependence on sources is so pronounced that his alterations and departures seem dictated by little more than a desire to muddy or obliterate the trail back to origins. Thus, for example, Bowles's sonnet "The Bells, Ostend" begins:

> How sweet the tuneful bells' responsive peal!
> As when, at opening *morn*, the *fragrant breeze*
> Breathes on *the trembling sense of wan disease,*
> So piercing to my heart their force I feel! . . .
> They fling their melancholy *music* wide . . .[2]

Here is the beginning of Coleridge's sonnet "Pain" (not published till the year of his death):

> Once could the *Morn's* first beams, the healthful *breeze*,
> All Nature charm, and gay was every hour: –
> But ah! not *Music's* self, nor *fragrant* bower
> Can glad *the trembling sense of wan disease,*
> Now that the frequent pangs my frame assail . . .[3]

"The trembling sense of wan disease" in both poems makes it difficult to suppose that Coleridge was not consciously following a model. The italicized words above identify identity of language, but is not Coleridge's "Morn's *first beams*" just as directly derived from Bowles's "*opening* morn"? Coleridge's "the frequent pangs my frame assail" is an almost grotesque paraphrase of Bowles's "So piercing to my heart their force I feel." Nevertheless, had Coleridge taken the trouble to eliminate the identical words and phrases that appear in both sonnets, who would be able to assert confidently that the one sonnet was dependent on the other? Who would even notice that a resemblance existed?

Coleridge was only twenty-four when he was accused of "a palpable imitation" in his "Lines on an Autumnal Evening" of a passage in Samuel Rogers's immensely popular "The Pleasures of Memory." Despite Coleridge's insistence that he had written his "Lines" "several years before I had seen Mr. Rogers' Poem," his "Autumnal Evening" verses *were* in fact a cunning pastiche of "The Pleasures of Memory." In this case, however, unacknowledged debts were not only to Rogers but also, surprisingly, to Wordsworth. Rogers's "Pleasures" was published early in 1792 and Coleridge's "Lines" in 1793. Is there evidence that STC wrote his poem before he had read Rogers's? An early draft of the "Lines" exists with the title "An Effusion at Evening." On the manuscript Coleridge wrote, "Written in August, 1792." If this is true, he could not have written the "Lines" *years* before he read Rogers, but he might not yet have read "The Pleasures of Memory." This would make the striking similarities of thought and phrase, however improbably, mere coincidence. However, the inscribed "August 1792" is a deliberate attempt to conceal the true date of composition, for the "Effusion" contains these lines:

> *When link'd with* Peace I bounded o'er *the Plain*
> *And Hope itself was all I knew of Pain!* (19–20)

In Wordsworth's "An Evening Walk," published in 1793, we find:

> *When link'd with* thoughtless Mirth I cours'd *the plain,*
> *And Hope itself was all I knew of pain.* (31–2)[4]

Coleridge never published this borrowing from Wordsworth, whom he had not as yet met. Thus his "Effusion" was clearly written *after* the publication of "An Evening Walk" in 1793 and *not* in 1792, as the manuscript clearly states. The young Coleridge who here went to such lengths to conceal the truth about the genesis of a minor poem strikingly foreshadows the mature poet, critic, and philosopher who deliberately falsified much of major importance about his creative and intellectual life.

While at Cambridge Coleridge sent his early love, Mary Evans, a poem entitled "A Wish, Written in Jesus Wood, Feb. 10, 1792" (*PW*, 1, p. 33). The sixteen-line verses are actually a translation of John Jortin's Latin "Votum," but the title (Coleridge was then a student at Jesus College) and the date surely led Mary, as they did Coleridgeans for generations, to suppose it an original effusion. Similarly, he sent Mary a little poem titled "On Bala Hill" (*PW*, 1, pp. 56–7). Since he had recently visited Bala Hill while touring Wales, Mary could hardly have guessed that "On Bala Hill" was really only a slight modification of a sonnet written by Southey.

These examples involve simple imitation. There are also early examples of concealment dictated by prudence or change of heart, for instance Coleridge's much maligned "To A Young Ass" (*PW*, 1, pp. 75–6). The poem originally concluded with a daring reference to "Handel's softest airs that soothe to rest / The tumult of a scoundrel Monarch's Breast'; the feeble change to "warbled melodies that soothe to rest / The aching of pale Fashion's vacant breast!"

destroyed whatever chance the poem might have had of winning respect for the young poet's courageous and publicly expressed indignation at entrenched and oppressive power.

Far more complex with respect to Coleridge's creative process and the poetic consequences of concealment is the "Ode to the Departing Year," written on the very eve of his stupendous flowering as a poet. In the Gutch Memorandum Book, analyzed with such infectious ardor by Lowes in *The Road to Xanadu*, one finds such mysterious and suggestive entries (made in September and October of 1796) as:

[a] Deep inward stillness & a bowed Soul −
[b] Searching of Heart −
     Fancy's wilder foragings −
[c] God's judgement *dallying* − investiture − retirement
[d] feeble & sore-broken − [etc.][5]

Just a bit further on, a single entry contains twenty-four short, fascinating, and mystifying jottings. Here are the first seven:

[a] Tame the Rebellion of tumultuous thought −
[b] ministration −
[c] sordid coherencies that cohabit with us in this Life −
[d] rolls round his dreary eye −
[e] outweighs the present pressure −
[f] Weigh'd in the balance of the Sanctuary −
[e] God's Image, Sister of the Cherubim − [*N*, 272]

For Lowes, and many others, these entries reflected a kind of creative frenzy, if not "chaos." Kathleen Coburn's researches, however, have demonstrated − at least to me − that Coleridge was not associating wildly or eagerly throwing down images arising from the bubbling alembic of the creative unconscious, but deliberately copying phrases from books open before him, reading with a falcon's foraging eye for what might prove useful. In 1797 he wrote Southey that "the metaphor on the diverse sorts of friendship" in "To The Reverend George Coleridge" had been "*hunted down*" [*CL*, 1, p. 334; STC's emphasis], and in his well-known letter on the epic he hoped to compose he wrote that he would not think of spending less than ten years to collect materials. A similar process seems to be at work with these lists. The items in the first series (and nine more not listed) all come from the Psalms and Aprocrypha and strongly suggest that Coleridge was purposefully accumulating phrases which might prove

useful in his writing (as indeed some did). The seven items in the second series (together with seventeen more not listed) are, in Professor Coburn's words, "almost, perhaps all, from Jeremy Taylor's *Sermons*" (*N*, p. 272n).

"Deep inward stillness & a bowed Soul" (item [a], series one above) appears the "Ode to the Departing Year" in line 6 as "With inward stillness, and a bowed mind." Related uses of these notebook entries need not concern us here, with the exception of Taylor's seemingly peculiar phrase (as given by Coleridge), "God's Image, Sister of the Cherubim." Involved in this instance is a variety of different concealments, on the one hand of literary debt, on the other of emotional life.

Coleridge was so smitten with this line that, slightly modified to take advantage of an alliteration, he confidently concluded his highly rhetorical "Ode" with it:

> Now I recentre my immortal mind
>   In the deep Sabbath of meek self-content;
> Cleans'd from the vaporous passions that bedim
> God's Image, sister of the Seraphim.
>
> (*PW*, i, p. 168)

But in what sense can God's image possibly be a *sister* of the seraphim (or cherubim)? Moreover, though vapors can well bedim an image, they make for a feeble adjective before *passions*. What Taylor had actually written was that the *soul* was "an angelic substance, sister to a cherubim, an image of the Divinity" (*N*, p. 272n). The *soul* surely can be thought of as a sister to an angelic creature, and as an image of God, but to think of God's image as a sister to anything is difficult.

That Coleridge was uncomfortable with this line is shown by the anxiously evasive variant in the collected edition of 1803, where the last two lines are collapsed as:

> Cleans'd from bedimming Fear, and Anguish weak and blind.

So gross a failure of poetic judgement is extremely rare in Coleridge, but it follows on the incoherence of the borrowing from Taylor and is indicative of fears it apparently intends to disclaim. It can be accounted for on the supposition that Coleridge wanted to conceal evidence of a discoverable debt to Taylor, but at work as well is a concealment persistent throughout STC's poetry, a desire to expunge *any* reference to ever having been possessed by any passions, vaporous or otherwise. Indeed, the quarto version of the "Ode," which appeared at the same time as its publication in *The Cambridge Intelligencer* (December, 1796) concludes:

> Cleans'd from the *fleshly passions* that bedim . . .

a strange oversight for Coleridge, who all his life was morbidly sensitive to any imputation of sensuality. By 1797 he had altered the line in a way that anticipates the 1803 version:

Cleans'd from the fears and anguish that bedim . . . (*PW*, I, p. 168, app. crit.)

thus getting rid of the passions, fleshly and otherwise, for twenty years, when the original ending of the "Ode" was restored for the collected edition of 1817.

Coleridge's extreme sensitivity to anything resembling an admission of personal sensuality in his poetry or a suggestion of sexuality in an admired character appears, for example, in one of the "Christabel" variants. In the first edition of 1816, at lines 28–9, Christabel has

> Dreams, that made her moan and leap,
> As on her bed she lay in sleep.
> (*PW*, I, p. 216, app. crit.)

This erotically suggestive passage, however innocently written, was erased by Coleridge in a copy of the first edition, never to reappear. Acute vigilance in such matters reveals itself again and again. The poet's love, in "An Effusion at Evening," has "dewy brilliance dancing in her eyes" (16). Who would suspect even the shadow of impropriety here? Nevertheless, in the expanded "Lines," what rather improbably dances in the charmer's eyes is "Chaste Joyance"! (15). In the very youthful "Honour," the "Enchantress Pleasure" is already "A hideous hag." "A slave to pleasure is a slave to smoke!" (*PW*, I, pp. 25–6, lines 59, 64).

"The Sensual and the Dark rebel in vain," Coleridge wrote in "France: An Ode," "Slaves by their own compulsion!" (*PW*, I, p. 247, lines 85–6). This appeared slightly modified in the *Morning Post* text of "Ode to Tranquillity" as "sensual France, a natural Slave" (*PW*, I, p. 360, app. crit.). "I do consider Mr. Godwin's Principles as vicious," Coleridge wrote to a newspaper in 1796, and his book as a Pander to Sensuality" (*CL*, I, p. 199). All his life Coleridge vehemently denied ever having indulged in sensual gratification for its own sake. "My sole sensuality was not to be in pain!" he exclaimed when charged with having taken opium for pleasure. "A Sensualist is not likely to be a Patriot," he wrote, strangely, to John Thelwall (*CL*, I, p. 214). In "The Destiny of Nations," "Fancy is the power / That first unsensualizes the dark mind / [and] Emancipates it from the grosser thrall / Of the present impulse" (*PW*, I, p. 134, lines 80–1, 85–6), and in "Dejection: An Ode," "Joy" is what can create

> A new Earth and new Heaven
> Undreamt of by the sensual and the proud (69–70).

"Sensual" and "dark" (when referring to the mind or secret thoughts) are words signalling massive disgust in Coleridge's poetry, and especially so when appearing proximately in any context. This explains why Coleridge deleted them from what was originally one of his most confessional poems. "The Pains of Sleep" first appears in a letter to Southey of September 11, 1802, but was not published until fourteen years later (together with "Kubla Khan" and "Christabel"). The revisions almost all represent suppressions and concealments. Thus in the original version sent to Southey, the dreamer is guilty of

> Vain-glorious Threats, unmanly Vaunting,
> Bad men my boasts & fury taunting
> Rage, *sensual Passion*, mad'ning Brawl . . .
> (*CL*, 2, p. 983)

To his intimate friend Thomas Poole, less than a month later, Coleridge sent on these lines as:

> Tempestuous *pride*, vain-glorious Vaunting,
> Base Men my vices *justly* taunting –
> (*CL*, 2, p. 1009)

For publication, however, Coleridge was hardly prepared to admit, even about a "wild" dream, that he could threaten and boast, feel fury, rage, pride, even *sensual* passion, and, moreover, that bad men could *justly* reprove him for his *vices*! He got rid of the first two lines of the passage as sent to Southey, together with the words *rage* and *sensual*, but rescued the couplet riming with *brawl* thus:

> Fantastic passions! maddening brawl!
> And shame and terror over all!

which is sufficiently vague. To Southey "all was Horror, Guilt & Woe" in the nightmare, to Poole "all was Guilt & Shame & Woe," but in the public text "all *seemed* guilt, remorse, or woe," a small but no doubt significant psychological revision.[6]

As described to Southey, the dreamer was "O'ercome by Sufferings *dark* & wild." In view of the power of the word *dark* for Coleridge, it is not surprising that the published text has "sufferings *strange* and wild." Finally, and perhaps most significant of all by way of creative process and concealment, in the lines to Southey (who was, it is rarely recognized, far more of a *confidante* to Coleridge than either Wordsworth or Poole), just before the final couplet, STC wrote:

> Frail is my Soul, yea, strengthless wholly,
> Unequal, restless, melancholy;
> But free from Hate, & sensual Folly!

These lines were expunged from the public text, which concludes famously:

> To be beloved is all I need,
> And whom I love, I love indeed.

In reading Coleridge's poetry it is tempting and surely often correct to suspect that mysterious details, or passages which elude plausible interpretation, or inexplicable gaps, derive from the wish to conceal something, or from unconscious pressure to express something forbidden. For example:

> The body of my brother's son
> Stood by me, knee to knee:
> The body and I pulled at one rope,
> But he said nought to me.
>
> (341–4)

What is the function of this odd stanza from "The Ancient Mariner"? It provides the only detail in the entire poem which humanizes the Mariner as a man who ever had a family. Why "knee to knee," and pulling "at one rope"? It has been suggested that there is an unconscious homosexual allusion here. The significance of the narrative detail seems particularly overdetermined, yet I cannot recall that any critic has ever paused to question the reason for the family connection.

And what to make of the strangely irrelevant "Conclusion to Part II" of "Christabel" (*PW*, 1, pp. 235–6)? Since the passage deals with the anger of a father towards a child, it has of course been argued that it is germane to the anger Sir Leoline feels towards Christabel. But surely this is specious, since the displeasure the elderly father in "Christabel" feels towards his mature daughter for her seemingly gross affront to the laws of hospitality is entirely different from the wholly unmotivated bitter words of the father directed at an innocent little child in the "Conclusion." Moreover, the "Conclusion" appears in none of the poem's several manuscripts and exists *only* is a gloomy letter of May 6, 1801 to Southey, where it follows this sentence: "Dear Hartley! we are at times alarmed by the state of his Health – but at present he is well – if I were to lose him, I am afraid, it would exceedingly deaden my affection for any other children I may have –" (*CL*, 2, p. 728). Immediately after the lines Coleridge wrote: "A very metaphysical account of Fathers calling their children rogues, rascals, & little varlets – &c –," which does not begin to describe adequately the explosive rage and paternal remorse the lines express.

Readers have been baffled by these twenty-two lines, not only because their connection with "Christabel" seems so remote, but because they are so transparently a rationalization of unacceptable behavior. We are asked to believe that the singing and dancing, happy little child so

> fills a father's eyes with light;
> And pleasures flow in so thick and fast
> Upon his heart, that he at last
> Must needs express his love's excess
> With words of unmeant bitterness.

Thus the published version, but in the original draft to Southey the last line read, "With words of *wrong* and bitterness." The remaining lines of the passage are suspiciously evasive, just as the comment about fathers calling their children "rogues, rascals & little varlets" transparently attempts to undermine the strange hostility to a loved child the "Conclusion" projects. Why did Coleridge add these lines to "Christabel" at all? Why indeed did he give Dr Gillman and his son Derwent two radically different accounts of how the poem was really meant to work itself out, with Geraldine in the one case an evil creature and in the other an agent working under the direction of beneficent forces? And why were lines 225–61 of Part I, in which

> Geraldine nor speaks nor stirs;
> Ah! what a striken look was hers!
> Deep from within she seems half-way
> To lift some weight with sick assay,
> *And eyes the maid and seeks delay* . . .

not published until 1828? In fact, they do not appear on any of the several manuscripts, but were written (in a hand other than STC's) into a copy of the first edition of 1816. Surely what they try to show is that Geraldine was *not* an evil agent, that she was acting under some kind of compulsion. And yet, in a little-known set of seven marginal glosses to the poem which Coleridge recorded on November 25, 1824, Geraldine is *definitely* an evil spirit. The fifth gloss, for example, reads: "As soon as the Wicked Bosom, with the mysterious sign of Evil stamped thereby, touched Christabel, she is deprived of the power of disclosing what had occurred."[7]

Despite the large number of "conversation poems" and others dealing with more or less personal matters, by far the most revealing of Coleridge's poems are the three most popular, "The Ancient Mariner," "Christabel," and "Kubla Khan," all of which *seem* uncanny because remote from personal concerns. And yet, as I have argued at length elsewhere, it is in these three great works that Coleridge's fears, conflicts, and repressed desires break through his normally vigilant censor. In each of these poems important gaps and fissures attest to the process, generally unconscious, of concealment. Thus, for example, in "The Ancient Mariner" we never have even the hint of a motive for the shooting of the albatross. We do not know why "a wicked whisper" makes the Mariner's heart "as dry as dust" when he tries to pray. As Wordsworth was to complain, the Mariner seems always to be *acted upon*, rather than to be an agent of free will in control of his acts. Even at the end of the poem his life is controlled by forces external to himself (as Coleridge often felt himself to be).

The Mariner is a being acting under *compulsion*, as is Christabel, a virtuous woman whose goodness and generosity lead only to enthrallment by a demonic creature. The Mariner cannot control his speech when possessed by the need to tell his story; Christabel's speech is wholly in Geraldine's power; and the father in the "Conclusion to Part II" is similarly unable to restrain "words of unmeant bitterness." In every case, I suggest, Coleridge's censor is permitting good people to behave very badly, but in each case what they do is either imposed upon them from without, or is inexplicable in view of their basically generous natures. The personal relevance all this had for Coleridge should be obvious. He was a man of intense religious convictions and exalted moral ideals, yet one who compulsively lived for the moment, and who was destructively self-indulgent and repeatedly tempted to various forms of dishonesty in both his intellectual life and personal relations. For a man with a basically generous and loving nature, his acts often seemed to himself explicable only in terms of humanity's collective fallen nature, or the mystery of visitations from an evil otherness having nothing to do with oneself. The self-image he presented to the world in his writings was an extreme version of his personal ideal, and this partly explains the almost hysterical anxiety with which he responded to any public threat to that image.

Coleridge's stormy relations with his wife (Southey's sister-in-law), and his long and frustrating love for Sara Hutchinson (Wordsworth's sister-in-law) led to the most *consciously* personal of all the poems he ever wrote, and the one most thoroughly revised so as to conceal personal matter. About great blocks (more than half) of the original verse-letter to Sara Hutchinson which Coleridge suppressed when he reshaped the material into "Dejection: An Ode," one can confidently say that the decisions were either aesthetic, or dictated by social realities – Coleridge was not a Byron to display his bleeding heart in public, nor was he capable of publicly humiliating his wife or advertising details about his conjugal miseries – but while most critics agree that the compact "Dejection" is a far greater work than the sprawling verse-letter, I share David Pirie's view that the passages which Coleridge retained, "lacking their original context and rearranged in a new order, [have] lost much of their power and most of their subtlety."[8]

Understandably, Coleridge deleted all reference to his love for Sara Hutchinson (he even went so far as to address the poem to an "Edmund" – a surrogate for Wordsworth – in its 1802 publication), expunged the long stanza about his children in which he "half-wished, they never had been born!" (*CL*, 2, p. 797), and cut everything clearly connected with domestic discord. The result is a poem in which the source of the speaker's dejection is generalized beyond the point of mere vagueness, a long poem which is never specific about the *cause* of "stifled, drowsy, unimpassioned grief," of "smothering weight" upon the breast, "viper thoughts, that coil around my mind, / Reality's dark dream!'", the loss of hope, of capacity to respond to the beauties of nature. What has *caused* the "afflictions [itself a significantly abstract word] that bow me down to earth" and suspend "My shaping spirit of imagination"? What the poet offers by way of explanation results in the most evasive passage in all of Coleridge's poetry:

> For not to think of what I needs must feel,
> But to be still and patient, all I can;
> And haply by abstruse research to steal
> From my own nature all the natural man –
> This was my sole resource, my only plan;
> Till that which suits a part infects the whole,
> And now is almost grown the habit of my soul.
> (*PW*, 1, p. 367, lines 87–93)

What is it that the speaker can't help feeling but mustn't think about? "Hence, viper thoughts," Coleridge writes in the next stanza, but the "viper thoughts," whatever they are, can hardly be what he mustn't think about, for we don't know what causes him to *feel* them. If the "viper thoughts" refer to a loss of imagination (and are thus not the *cause* of them), then what constrains Coleridge from thinking about that loss? And in any case, why should he bury himself in abstruse research? The reader who suspects that frustrated love for Sara Hutchinson is hovering unstated over the text, may surmise that Coleridge had tried to suppress erotic longings by fixing his mind on intensely demanding intellectual activity, such as abstruse research. But why should that lead to a general anesthetizing of all vivid bodily sensation, and thus destroy the "natural man"?

> Till that which suits a part infects the whole,
> And now is almost grown the habit of my soul.

What is concealed here, I suggest, is Coleridge's discovery in his thirtieth year that he was losing tactile sensation, especially sexual sensitivity, an affliction common enough among users of opium (though of course not understood in Coleridge's time). In later life Coleridge would write in one of his marginalia: "Opium is occasionally Aphrodisiac, but far oftener Anti-aphrodisiac. The same is true . . . I suppose of the whole tribe of narcotic Stimulants."[9] In a notebook entry of 1805, dealing, significantly, with "the influence of bodily vigor and strong Grasp of Touch in facilitating the passion of Hope," Coleridge writes, in a cipher code: "*Eunuchs in all degrees – even to the full ensheathement and the both at once*," an entry which surely implies that Coleridge knew from frightening and perhaps humiliating personal experience that it was possible to feel little or no sensation during coitus. The plausibility of this reading is greatly reinforced by the very next journal entry, which rather gingerly hints at genital contact and speculates upon "the imperfections of the organs by which we seem to unite ourselves with external things" (*Nos.* 2398–9 and notes). If these speculations are correct, then the "natural man" passage attempts to screen the real source of Coleridge's dejection. Not knowing that the cause of his "organ imperfection" lay in his extremely heavy use of laudanum, he attributed his affliction to an intense effort to suppress feelings about Sara Hutchinson, and believed that this effort, falsely asserted to have been successful – "that which suits a part" – had contaminated his entire affective life – "infects the whole" – and rendered him incapable of truly enjoying a sunset or the beauties of a moonlit night.

How much conscious self-deception there was in all this it is impossible to say. As a general rule it can be posited that vagueness of reference in Coleridge usually hints at some concealment. Thus, when he writes:

> For hope grew round me like the climbing vine,
> And fruits, and foliage, not my own, seemed mine
>
> (80–1)

we can be confident that Coleridge does not want to specify just what those "fruits, and foliage" might be, especially if, as I believe, he had in his despair come to believe that he was a brilliant imitator rather than an original poet, "an involutary Imposter," as he wrote to Southey in 1803 (*CL*, 2, p. 959). Just three years before, after the failed struggle to complete "Christabel," he had confessed to Poole: "[I am] convinced that I never had the essentials of poetic Genius, & that I mistook a strong desire for original power" (*CL*, 1, p. 656).

Finally, let us glance at a concealment so successful that it led John Livingston Lowes (and many others) to pore over innumerable old maps and to peruse numberless volumes, all in the hope of locating the elusive "Mount Abora" of "Kubla Khan," "unknown to any map," Lowes reluctantly concluded, "since time began."[10] When the only known manuscript of "Kubla Khan" came to light in 1934, the famous passage proved to read as follows:

> A Damsel with a Dulcimer
> In a Vision once I saw
> It was an Abyssinian Maid,
> And on her Dulcimer she played,
> Singing of Mount *Amara*.

Or possibly *Amora*, for the place-name, in Coleridge's handwriting, has a heavy stroke from the top of the *a* to the *r*, thus changing the letter to an *o*. Why should STC have wished to do this? The obvious reasons are aesthetic. *Amara* does not establish even a decent assonance with *Dulcimer* or *saw*, let alone an acceptable rime. Perhaps more important, the rhythm of the passage is horribly wrenched if *Amara* is accented by the reader on the first syllable, by analogy with Mount Ararat, thus unacceptably ending the musical line with two unaccented syllables. These problems alone would account for the change to Mount Amora, which provides the right rhythm and the right sound harmony with *saw*. Why then not leave it at that?

As all the world knows, Coleridge published "Kubla Khan" as a poem written in a dream, "without any sensation or consciousness of effort." He cited a very obscure volume, *Purchas's Pilgrimage*, as the immediate inspiration of this miraculously given poem, but it happens that "Kubla Khan" also reverberates with echoes of the fourth book of *Paradise Lost*, with Milton's roll-call of earthly paradises. Coleridge must have known this work practically by heart, for he quoted bits of it from memory in letters and imitated a portion of it in his early *Religious Musings*.[11] None of the echoes in "Kubla Khan" actually puts one in mind of *Paradise Lost*, with the sole exception of the passage now being discussed, which struck Lane Cooper long ago as a reminiscence of Milton's

> where *Abassin* Kings their issue Guard,
> Mount Amara, though this by some suppos'd
> True Paradise . . .
>
> (IV, 280–2)

It seems odd, to say the least, that Cooper's 1906 article[12] has made so little impression on discussion of "Kubla Khan," but with the manuscript before us we see that Coleridge's Abyssinian maid indeed did sing of Mount Amara. When Coleridge saw that for reasons of rhythm and sound *Amara* would not do, he made, apparently at once, the change to *Amora*, an especially attractive place-name in this context because of its possible connotation with a mount of love. Why, then, some time, perhaps years, later, another change? To a man with a memory so tenacious he had much of Milton by heart, it must have seemed inevitable that many readers would think of *Paradise Lost*'s *Abyssin* and *Amara* if confronted within the space of three lines with *Abyssinian* and *Amara*, or even *Amora*. And if *Amora*, could it not be viewed as a mechanical and arbitrary alteration, dictated by purely technical considerations? From *Amora* to *Abora* was but a single easy step (so it now seems), yet sufficient to obliterate for over a century the trail leading clearly to Milton.

There is a sad irony in all this. Coleridge, always so anxious to obscure or deny his intellectual obligations, has here in fact risen with a mighty hand superior to Milton himself, and created a paradise of greater beauty and power and resonance than anything in all of *Paradise Lost*. Here, as elsewhere, had he been less riven with tormenting self-doubts, had he not been so early and fatally infected with the romantic cult of originality, he might well have accepted what he dismissed in himself as mere "quickness in imitation," and have recognized it instead as a central aspect of his many-sided genius. Had Coleridge been less driven to present himself to the world as free of those ordinary failings with which most of humanity has always been afflicted (pride, ambition, sensuality, envy, lack of truthfulness), his life would surely have been much happier, and his career as a poet yet more productive and certainly far less problematical.

NOTES

1 *Collected Letters of Samuel Taylor Coleridge*, ed. E. L. Griggs, 6 vols. (Oxford, 1956–71), Vol. 1, p. 394. Hereafter cited in the text as *CL*.

2 Here, as elsewhere, italics are mine unless otherwise noted.

3 *The Complete Poetical Works of Samuel Taylor Coleridge*, ed. E. H. Coleridge, 2 vols. (Oxford, 1912), Vol. 1, p. 17. Hereafter cited in the text as *PW*.

4 See my *Coleridge, The Damaged Archangel* (New York, 1971), pp. 49–58 for specific documentation and a full discussion of Coleridge's "Lines" and Rogers's "Pleasures of Memory."

5 *The Notebooks of Samuel Taylor Coleridge*, ed. Kathleen Coburn (Princeton U.P., 1957–), No. 259. Hereafter cited in text as *N*. There are thirteen items in this series of jottings.

6 Just eleven days after sending "The Pains of Sleep" to Southey, Coleridge wrote Sir George and Lady Beaumont that *nine years before* a visitation of "Dreams with all their mockery of Guilt, Rage, unworthy Desires, Remorse, Shame, & Terror formed *at that time* the subject of some Verses, which I had forgotten till the return of the Complaint, & which I will send you in my next *as a curiosity*" (*CL*, Vol. 1, p. 993). The Beaumonts then knew nothing of Coleridge's opium addiction. In pretending that "The Pains of Sleep" had been written when he was but twenty-two years old, Coleridge was not only keeping his addiction a secret, but forestalling criticism of the "forgotten" verses as poetry, which were in any case only being sent along "as a curiosity." It will be remembered that "Kubla Khan" was published "rather as a psychological curiosity, than on the ground of any supposed *poetic* merits" (*PW*, Vol. 1, p. 295, italics in text). Another thread of connection with "Kubla Khan" is the claim to spontaneous composition: "I do not know how I came to scribble down these verses to you," Coleridge had written to Southey, "my heart was aching, my head all confused" (*CL*, Vol. 1, p. 984); and in the Preface to "Kubla Khan," "[I] could not have composed less than from two to three hundred lines . . . without any sensation or consciousness of effort." In 1814 Coleridge sent ("Not for the Poetry, *believe* me!") a nine-line fragment of "The Pains of Sleep" to an acquaintance under the title "Diseased Sleep," "a fragment from a larger poem, composed 1803. Written as a letter & of course never intended to be published, and which, I trust, never will be." It contains a new and characteristic couplet, "From low desires my Heart hath fled, / On Beauty hath my Fancy fed" (*CL*, Vol. 3, p. 495, italics in text). Two years later Coleridge, despite his seemingly strong wish to the contrary, published the poem.

167

7 See Barbara E. Rooke, "An Annotated Copy of Coleridge's 'Christabel,'" *Studia Germanica Gandensia*, 15 (1974), pp. 179–92.

8 "A Letter to [Asra]," in *Bicentenary Wordsworth Studies*, ed. Jonathan Wordsworth (Ithaca, 1970), p. 294.

9 *Coleridge on the Seventeenth Century*, ed. R. L. Brinkley (Durham, N.C., 1955), p. 454.

10 *The Road to Xanadu* (Boston and New York, 1927), p. 373.

11 Compare *Religious Musings*, lines 14–22 and *Paradise Lost* IV, 641–56. The connection was first pointed out in R. D. Havens, *The Influence of Milton on English Poetry* (Cambridge, Mass., 1922), p. 533, n. 2. See Also *CL*, Vol. 1, p. 223, and *PW*, Vol. 1, p. 321 and n. 1.

12 "The Abyssinian Paradise in Coleridge and Milton," *Modern Philology*, 3 (1906), pp. 327–32.

8

DOROTHY WORDSWORTH'S GRASMERE JOURNALS: THE PATTERNS AND PRESSURES OF COMPOSITION

PAMELA WOOF

THIS great Journal set off in 1800 with a devotion to almost daily writing; it was written in sporadic bursts towards the end of 1802, and in early 1803 it stopped. In between, it was subject variously to time: to the pressures of everyday activity and the presence of Wordsworth, and to the spaces created by either his sleep or his absence. It was subject to the selection, revisions, and afterthoughts of memory. It took into account ideas and talk, and stories told and retold in conversation. It reflected the concerns and writing of Wordsworth particularly, and of Coleridge too. The discussion here is of these pressures, both the practical ones of time and circumstance, and the more elusive influences of word and memory. The clear lights and colours of the Journal, their marvellous evocation of place and of the writer, these will be assumed; this discussion necessitates a return to the manuscripts, to some of those deletions and revisions, not all of them generally known, which reveal the Journal in the process of being written and the details that affected it. The minutiae in the end are important; they accumulate to a more intricate understanding of the writer and her words.

'I will take a nice Calais Book & *will* for the future write regularly &, if I can legibly, so much for this my resolution on Tuesday night, January 11th 1803.' Dorothy Wordsworth had not been writing at all regularly, and from the evidence of the final months of 1802, there is little to encourage us to suppose that she would change. Certainly no new notebook, such as might have been bought in Calais the previous August, no continuing Journal, has ever been found. That momentous journey of the summer seems to have disrupted the diary-keeping habit. Dorothy had managed a huge catching-up (possibly from notes) during the last week of October 1802 when she was confined the whole week upstairs 'in the tooth ache'; she had managed then to set down most of that journey to Gallow Hill, to London, to Calais to see Annette, back to London, to Yorkshire for the wedding and back to Grasmere. She finished the catching-up on Saturday, 30 October, and had time – 'William is gone to Keswick' – to give to that present day the attention, not of memory, but of the looking eye. Mary had gone with Wordsworth as far as 'the Top of the Rays. She is returned & is now sitting near me by the fire. It is a breathless grey day that leaves the golden woods of Autumn quiet in their own tranquillity, stately & beautiful in their decaying, the lake is a perfect mirror.' As she wrote this, Dorothy had time to savour her phrases: her first description of the golden woods of Autumn was 'tranquil & silent & stately'. These three adjectives were crossed out, and Dorothy achieved the formal beauty of 'quiet in their own tranquillity, stately & beautiful in their decay'. This last phrase was also crossed out, a tiny alteration made, 'beautiful in their decaying', and immediately, nature's ceaseless movement into decay was caught and poised against the tranquillity.

Now, finally, the Journal was up to date, as it had not been since 8 July, and the next day's entry, that for 31 October, has a fullness of detail that might suggest that it was written, in good diary fashion, on that very day. Circumstances were indeed favourable: Wordsworth was again away. He had gone to Keswick with Stoddart, and so, wrote Dorothy:

Mary & I walked to the top of the hill & looked at Rydale. I was much affected when I stood upon the 2nd bar of Sara's Gate. The lake was perfectly still, the Sun shone on Hill & vale, the Birch trees looked like large golden Flowers –

Dorothy made a precise revision: she inserted the word 'distant' before 'Birch trees'; only birch trees at a distance, across the valley perhaps, could look like large golden flowers. The entry continues to be detailed: the fields were 'of one sober yellow brown'; Dorothy 'could not' take a short sleep as Mary did, 'for I was thinking of so many things'; after Tea they 'sate nicely together . . . looking over old Letters. Molly was gone up to Mr Simpsons to see Mrs S who was very ill'. All these details of 31 October could have been recorded on that same evening, but they equally well could have been remembered a week later on 8 November when Dorothy seems to have been giving time to her Journal. For, despite the Journal's having no arrears by 30 October, Dorothy still appears not to have written on a daily basis. She made a new heading, for instance, for the day she had already dated as Saturday, 30 October, that 'breathless grey day' of autumn woods; she started again, 'Saturday 30th October' and wrote a summary of the evening events of the day. The very next entry to that Saturday, the full entry for 31 October, she miscalled Monday. These confusions imply a distance from the time of the original observations. The day's birch trees like large golden flowers, the old letters read over with Mary, these had remained in the mind and were recorded, I suggest, after a space of some days.

Why had that detail remained vivid? It is recalled precisely: 'I was much affected when I stood upon the 2nd bar of Sara's Gate'. 'Much affected . . .'; that strong feeling would account for the lively recollection, and the feeling was strong because memory was involved. Dorothy was surely remembering a walk of the previous autumn, 1801, when she and Mary 'walked as far as Saras Gate before Supper – we stood there a long time, the whole scene impressive, the mountains indistinct the Lake calm & partly ruffled – large Island, a sweet sound of water falling into the quiet Lake. A storm was gathering in Easedale . . .' They had then walked down to the village and 'stood long upon the bridge . . .' On that Wednesday, 18 November 1801, Mary Hutchinson had been in Grasmere a week (she was to stay till the end of the year), and she and Wordsworth must have declared their intention to marry. Two days before, on the Monday, Dorothy recorded that Molly 'has been very witty with Mary all day. She says "Ye may say what ye will but there's nothing like a gay auld man for behaving weel to a young wife."' Mary, so teased, had clearly to defend her choice of Wordsworth. By the following year, when she and Dorothy walked again to Sara's Gate, she had very recently become Wordsworth's wife. There was no storm gathering in Easedale in 1802; the distant Birch trees looked like large golden Flowers. They stood out in the landscape, 'distinct & separate' against the 'beautiful colours' that seemed 'melted into one another', and yet in 'an endless variety'. This is celebratory. Dorothy, standing on the second bar of the gate, and much affected, must have been conscious in that place, and with Mary, of the passage of time and its changes. For Dorothy, place was often the register that marked the ritual moment; towards the end of the long account written up in the last week of October, and when the Journal was moving out of the expanded narrative of the journey and into brief summaries of the Grasmere activities in the days after their return from the wedding, Dorothy still gave herself scope to mark the new relationship in terms of place: 'On Friday 8th we baked Bread, & Mary & I walked, first upon the Hill side, & then in John's Grove, then in view of Rydale, the first walk that I had taken with my Sister.' The events of 31 October 1802, the day of the second visit to Sara's Gate with Mary, a day on which they spent the evening 'looking over old Letters', was a day of complicated feeling for Dorothy. As such, it was one that would remain in the mind and could be recalled after a gap.

Certainly, the Journal seems not to have been picked up again until 8 November. The intervening days from 31 October are briefly, sometimes hazily, remembered: Dorothy is twice unclear in the entry for Monday, 1 November, as to whether Mr Bartholomew Simpson came to tea; she finally settled for Tuesday. One day was omitted, but on 8 November, when Dorothy was again bringing her Journal up to date, writing it in the evening, 'with a nice fire', there is detail. The description had to be from the window because, 'though the day was so delightful that it made my very heart linger to be out of doors, & see & feel the beauty of the Autumn in freedom', there had been no walking. Wordsworth had worked at Ariosto, Mary had been baking, Dorothy had read one Canto of Ariosto, and seen from the upstairs parlour window that one or two trees opposite were still green as compared with the 'yellow brown' ones on the other side of the lake.

Six and a half weeks go by before Dorothy takes up the Journal again, and there is no attempt to cover, even in brief summary, the omitted days. There is not even a remark on omitting them. The Journal was re-commenced on a day that was significant – it marked a passage. It was 24 December, Christmas Eve, and the eve of Dorothy Wordsworth's thirty-first birthday. It was '1/2 past 10 o'clock', Dorothy 'running the heel of a stocking', and she and Wordsworth repeating Wordsworth's sonnets to each other, Dorothy reading Milton to him, Mary 'in the parlour below attending to the baking of cakes & Jenny Fletcher's pies, Sara . . . in bed in the tooth ache'. Dorothy reports that 'Mary is well & I am well, & Molly is as blithe as last year at this time', though Wordsworth 'keeps his hand to his poor chest'. Coleridge had called in the morning on his way north, taking Tom Wedgwood home with him for a few days, and the Wordsworths had told him about the birth of his daughter (Sara). This leads Dorothy to mention her morning's walk with Mary up the Raise to meet Wordsworth who had been accompanying Coleridge part-way to Keswick. She then describes the landscape, 'no meltings of sky into mountains – the mountains like stone-work wrought up with huge hammers', and this stimulates the memory of another walk, the previous Sunday's to Rydal; Mary and Sara went on round the lakes, Wordsworth sat with Dorothy. Dorothy mentions the individual flowers she noticed, even to 'the topmost bell of a fox-glove'; the 'annual-report' aspect of the entry has dissolved. Dorothy makes an effort to catch up by a commentary on the week's weather and finishes the entry on Christmas Day, 'I am 31 years of age. – It is a dull frosty day.'

Up to date. But the jerky pattern continued. On 11 January 1803 she wrote, 'Again I have neglected to write my Journal.' Only one episode is dwelt on in the ensuing summary: the ride on 30 December to the foot of the hill nearest Keswick with Wordsworth, the potted beef and sweet cake eaten on horseback and the discussion about whether or not to pluck 'a tuft of primroses three flowers in full blossom & a Bud'. They did not, of course, pluck the flower, and it was still there when Dorothy returned on 2 January. Writing on the 11th, Dorothy remembered enough for 8, 9, and 10 January to give them separate entries. On 8 and 9 January Mary was not well, and Dorothy walked with Wordsworth to Rydal and to Brothers Wood, 'I was *astonished* with the beauty of the place, for I had never been there since my return home – never since before I went away in June!!' On 11 January 1803, when Dorothy resolved to take a nice Calais book and 'for the future write regularly', she did indeed begin well by recording full details for that day, how she, Wordsworth and Mary did not walk for 'the blackness of the Cold', what they each read, what letters, what plans, what writing, what each was going to have for supper. But after the next day's 'Very cold, & cold all the week', there is the entry for Sunday 16 January – the Journal's final entry – with its anecdote of Wordsworth's having a fancy for some gingerbread and Dorothy's putting on Molly's cloak and her own spencer, and their walking in the intense cold to the blind man's, Matthew Newton's, and buying six pennyworth, but really wanting the thick ginger-bread. Next day, when the woman came with some, 'just when we were baking', they bought only two pennyworth. And here the notebook is filled up. There is a drawing of a chair and the word 'Monday', and meeting this, from the other end of the book, are Wordsworth's extracts from Descartes. The final entry about the gingerbread, the anecdote of 16 January, can scarcely be adduced as earnest of regular or daily writing: it cannot have been written until Monday, 17 January, at the earliest. It is shaped into a story; it has setting, action, characters, feeling, direct speech, no intrusive pitying comment by the author; there is, rather, a thoroughgoing practical realism in the kindly but firm purchase of only two pennyworth of the thick gingerbread. Dorothy's pleasure in the story's neatness is shown even in the minute revision it needed. She had originally written, 'They were so grateful for the Sixpence when I paid them.' The phrase 'for the Sixpence' is crossed out as unnecessary as Dorothy realized that she had just written 'I bought 6 pennyworth.'

Despite the finish of this story, there is such a pattern of broken writing in the latter part of the Journal that Dorothy herself could not have felt too confident about the resolution to write regularly, legibly, and in a 'nice Calais book'. She had never before used a new book for the Journal. The four extant small Journal notebooks had been variously written in by both Wordsworth and Dorothy. The earliest one had rough jottings and accounts connected with the Goslar stay in 1798–9, pages were torn out of it, epitaphs copied into it, some of Wordsworth's verses tried out in it; the second has more sums, Dorothy's account of the journey to and stay in Hamburg, more verse drafts, more cut-out pages; the third similarly has a marvellous mixture – the conversation with Klopstock, Dorothy's account of the journey from Hamburg to Goslar, the great beginnings of *The Prelude*, part of an essay by Wordsworth and some of Dorothy's German grammar exercises; and so for the fourth: Descartes, drafts, torn-out pages. There was never any sense that Dorothy's Journal should have a book to itself. Nor any especial time to itself. It had to be fitted in, and Dorothy was best able perhaps to settle to an extended session with the Journal when Wordsworth was either away or asleep.

The Journal indeed owes its very beginning to the fact that on 14 May 1800 'Wm & John set off into Yorkshire after dinner at 1/2 past 2 o'clock – cold pork in their pockets', and were to be away some three weeks. Dorothy's resolve was to 'write a journal of the time till W & J return'. She wrote for three years, not three weeks. The first part of the Journal, written when Dorothy consistently had time to write, is for the most part detailed and generous, and Wordsworth surely, as Dorothy intended, would get 'Pleasure by it' when he came home. It is a wonderful evocation of the daily activities of a person alone in a country place that was new, in a first springtime, when the garden needed so many plants, the house so much attention, neighbours were still to get to know, the valley to be explored and delighted in. There is little revision in this part of the Journal; Dorothy's own orderliness, and the freedom, because she was alone, to be orderly, means that these entries were most probably written up every day. The most notable revision is for the evening of 6 June when Dorothy expected Wordsworth back: 'I slackened my pace as I came home fearing to hear that he was not come.' The word 'home' is crossed out and the phrase 'near home' substituted, bringing with it a more exact sense of Dorothy's rapid walking from Ambleside practically to Grasmere before she fearfully slackened pace.

Wordsworth returned very late the next night, 7 June 1800, and two days later his influence on the Journal is to be detected. Dorothy wrote a full account of her meeting with the tall beggar woman and her boys, a meeting that had taken place two weeks earlier on 27 May. On that day Dorothy had simply recorded, 'I walked to Ambleside with letters – met the post . . .' Now, on 10 June, on the day of the first walk there with Wordsworth – 'W & I walked to Ambleside to seek lodgings for C' – Dorothy describes at length an episode she had ignored in the entry for the day when it took place. Clearly, Dorothy talked about the beggars to Wordsworth during their walk over the same ground, and undoubtedly it was Wordsworth who wanted the experience preserved in writing. He was to use it in the middle of March 1802, almost two years later, when he wrote the poem 'Beggars'.

Interestingly, when he did write that poem, it must have been in the first place Dorothy's spoken words that he remembered, not the written words of the Journal, for he had 'half cast the Poem' before Dorothy read him her account. When he did hear it, its first effect was to inhibit him, 'he could not escape from those very words'. If in June 1800 it was Wordsworth's interest that encouraged Dorothy to write about something she herself had ignored, it must have been the desire to narrate well, the knowledge, perhaps even the agreed knowledge, that this was a possible subject for poetry, that made Dorothy so punctilious about detail; there is revision here, where in previous entries there had been virtually none. The points are small, but they reveal a care to get it right: 'I saw two boys one about 10', revised to 'I saw two boys before me one about 10'; '(The Boys were so like her' becomes, '(The Boys were so like the woman who had called at the door'; 'They had however sauntered so long at Ambleside' is changed to 'They had however sauntered so long in their road that they did not reach Ambleside before me'; 'On my return I met the mother' becomes 'On my return through Ambleside I met in the street the mother.'

We are probably indebted to a similar conjunction of events for Dorothy's description of the leech-gatherer. On 4 October 1800 Dorothy describes a meeting that took place on 26 September. The Journal was not indeed being written on 26 September, nor for several days before that; the last two weeks of September 1800 are summarized. They were very busy: Robert Jones stayed for a week, Coleridge for three days, John came and left, parting with Wordsworth and Dorothy 'in sight of Ulswater', there were visits and dinings with the Lloyds, calls from the Myers, father and son, and from Mr and Miss Smith. From the continuity of writing in the Journal (no concluding lines across the page) it would appear that the Journal was brought up to date on 2 October, probably while Dorothy was alone and waiting 'to receive the Lloyds'; the details of the Lloyds' visit, the walk, and the conversation about the manners of the rich were recorded either that night or possibly while little Sally was learning to mark next morning. Dorothy seems next to have taken up the Journal on 4 October, 'a very rainy, or rather showery & gusty morning for often the sun shines'; clearly she was writing the Journal at that moment. The chief events of the day before, 3 October, are recalled as well as the subject of Wordsworth's talk as Dorothy walked 'part of the way' to Ambleside with him: 'he talked much about the object of his Essay for the 2nd volume of LB'. After noting Amos Cottle's death in *The Morning Post*, Dorothy drew the concluding line after the entry. Her note that she wrote to S. Lowthian (the nursemaid who became part of the Wordsworth household at Cockermouth when Dorothy was born in December 1771) is remembered afterwards, for it is squeezed above the line as an insertion. The description of the leech-gatherer that follows, probably written on the morning of 4 October, must surely be a direct result of Dorothy's recollecting Wordsworth's talk about the object of his Essay. He had just finished this last, the Preface to *Lyrical Ballads* (1800); the entry for 1 October records, 'We corrected the last sheet' (though they were writing an addition on 5 October). One 'object of his Essay' must have been to provide an explanation for poems that were different from those a reader might expect; Lamb thought indeed that the explanatory essay would diminish the poems, making them appear as though specially 'written for *Experiments* on the public taste' (letter to Wordsworth, 30 January 1801). Wordsworth's explanation is well known: the poems were to make the incidents of common life interesting 'by tracing in them, truly though not ostentatiously, the primary laws of our nature . . . Low and rustic life was generally chosen because in that situation the essential passions of the heart find a better soil in which they can attain their maturity, are less under restraint, and speak a plainer and more emphatic language.'[1] Talk, during the October 3rd walk towards Ambleside, of such ideas, and quite conceivably of the leech-gatherer himself (Wordsworth had met him too) as a characteristic example of a man moving amongst 'the beautiful and permanent forms of nature',[2] surely led Dorothy the day after to write down the details she could remember about the man's appearance, history, work, and even very words. Editors of the Journals have not noted the quotation marks that frame the paragraph's final words: 'It was then "late in the evening – when the light was just going away."' These are not Dorothy's words indicating the time of day when she and Wordsworth met the old man, but his own 'plain' and 'emphatic' language about the time and light when he was himself wakening to consciousness, recovering after his accident 'from his first insensibility'.

In describing her encounter with the beggars, in writing an account of the leech-gatherer (also to have an important bearing upon a later poem, 'Resolution and Independence'), and in setting down other such stories, Dorothy must have had Wordsworth's purpose and poetry in mind. There are other instances: the story of Barbara Wilkinson's Turtle Dove (which Wordsworth asked her to set down, though he did not ultimately use it); the story of Alice Fell, originally a story told by Mr Graham to Wordsworth, then retold by Wordsworth to Dorothy, told again in the Journal by Dorothy, 16 February 1802, and retold in verse by Wordsworth 12–13 March; the story of Peggy Ashburner and the selling of the land, told by Peggy to Dorothy, probably retold by Dorothy to Wordsworth, written in the Journal and retold as the poem 'Repentance' by Wordsworth.

The Journal altogether confirms our sense of how much Dorothy and Wordsworth talked to each other, told their experiences; these might involve the extended stories of the wanderers on the roads, or they might concern quite insignificant and fragmentary things that nevertheless held truths about human history. Wordsworth for example, 'observed' some 'affecting little things' in Borrowdale, told Dorothy about them, and she wrote them down. One of them was an inscription on a decayed house; Dorothy, either not remembering the inscription, or not understanding it (if it were in Latin), left plenty of room on the page for Wordsworth to fill in the words, but he never provided the inscription. He was indeed busy in September 1800; he was writing the Preface, and shortly Jones and other visitors would come; but equally it is clear that Wordsworth was not in any regular fashion reading the Journal. He was talking to Dorothy. The other two 'affecting things' did not need his collaboration: in the churchyard, tall silent rocks seen through broken windows; and elsewhere, two ball-stones on gavel ends, one on a mansion carefully hewn, and the other, smooth from the river, placed on a nearby cottage. So close was Dorothy to Wordsworth's related experience, so alive was she to his spoken words, that an observation of his is recorded almost as though it were hers: on 4 November 1800 Dorothy walked a little way on the road with Wordsworth and Stoddart, who was leaving Grasmere, and then Wordsworth went on alone to Grisedale Tarn, 'afterwards to the top of Seat Sandal – he was obliged to lie down in the tremendous wind – the snow blew from Helvellyn horizontally like smoke – the Spray of the unseen Waterfall like smoke'. Dorothy was not there; she was walking to Rydal with Miss Lloyd, but it is as though she too were on top of Seat Sandal seeing Helvellyn with the blown snow like smoke and hearing that unseen waterfall, doubly unseen for her, yet with its spray seen as smoke. Snow that was like smoke was an old similitude of Wordsworth's. The lost child Lucy Gray set off with lantern in hand to light her mother, and she went blithely,

> Her feet disperse the powd'ry snow
> That rises up like smoke.

This 1798 poem is yet another that was 'founded on a circumstance', noted Wordsworth to Miss Fenwick in 1843, 'told me by my sister'. Again, an oral story that Wordsworth remembered; it is even just possible that that original snow like smoke was Dorothy's.

Influence in the sphere of telling and talking is elusive. It is also fascinating, and it is of course obvious that the Journal had to move away from the simplicity of its beginning when Dorothy for those three weeks was alone. There were indeed changes of mood during that early time, even to 'the deepest melancholy' (19 May 1800), but this was uncomplicated, unprobed; planting London Pride or lemon thyme, gathering mosses, walking for letters, feeling melancholy, these are all facts and aspects of busy days spent in the garden, the house, the length of the valley. Wordsworth returned on 7 June, and was at once more than an episode to be noted in Dorothy's days. The talking, the interaction, did, as I have indicated, complicate the stuff of the Journal. Practically, Wordsworth's presence made it more difficult for Dorothy to find time to write, and we can be grateful for such a day as 3 September 1800 when 'Coleridge Wm & John went from home to go upon Helvellyn with Mr Simpson. They set out after breakfast . . .' Dorothy 'accompanied them up near the Blacksmith's [by Tongue Ghyll]' and 'ironed till 1/2 past three' before going to the funeral of a pauper; she finished the ironing later. It was done by seven o'clock. 'The wind was now high & I did not walk – writing my journal now at 8 o clock.' The men were not back. Dorothy had time to write and so we have that funeral, its details of bread, cheese, ale, the corpse set down at the door, the psalm sung within the threshold, the carrying down the hill, the green landscape, the sun, the dark house. All is evoked so that we see it happen; but we see more than a ritual from social history. We see Dorothy too, an observer weeping at a pauper's funeral, 'no near kindred, no children'. Wordsworth's absences were as valuable as his presence in determining the texture of the Journal. He and John did not come home till ten o'clock (Coleridge continued on to Keswick).

Wordsworth's sleep also gave Dorothy useful spaces. He was more able than she to take snatches of sleep or periods of rest during the day. 'We dined', wrote Dorothy on 14 March 1802, '& then Wm went to bed. I lay upon the fur gown before the fire but I could not sleep – I lay there a long time – it is now half past 5 I am going to write letters. I began to write to Mrs Rawson – William rose . . .' The letter to Mrs Rawson was interrupted, but Dorothy had clearly used the time until then to bring her Journal up to date, and in more than summary fashion: the conversation about butterflies had taken place that morning at breakfast, and Dorothy records that she had told Wordsworth how 'I used to chase them a little but that I was afraid of brushing the dust off their wings'. This is a rare glimpse of Dorothy in early childhood, and we owe it to Wordsworth's being in bed that Dorothy had time to write down a little of the splendid conversation that informed the poem 'Stay near me, do not take thy Flight'. Sometimes, only a tiny detail makes us realize what a preservative Wordsworth's sleep could be: 'it is now 1/4 past 10 & he is not up . . . I have been in the garden. It looks fresh & neat in spite of the frost. Molly tells me they had thick ice on a jug at their door last night.' This was a Saturday morning, in the middle of May 1802; later in that same day Dorothy picked up her Journal, and she clearly forgot that she had already begun Saturday's entry. She made a fresh start, 'Saturday 15th. A very cold & cheerless morning. I sate mending stockings all the morning. I read in Shakespeare. William lay very late because he slept ill last night. It snowed this morning just like Christmas.' In some ways this has detail too: the stockings, Shakespeare, the snow like Christmas; but it is distanced even by the length of the same day. There is not that frustrated immediacy, '1/4 past 10 & he is not up' or the thick ice on the jug; that tone and that detail are both caught because Wordsworth had 'slept ill last night'.

A comment on Wordsworth's sleeping is perhaps in order since it has these literary consequences. His ill sleeping at night seemed often to follow a day during which Wordsworth had fallen asleep for a short or longer period.

However erratic Wordsworth's sleeping, Dorothy never tried to fix a pattern; she never woke him from daytime or morning sleep. On 3 June 1802, for instance, Wordsworth in the afternoon was 'sleeping – with the window open lying on the window Seat'. This was useful, as Dorothy gave her Journal some attention, but that night, Wordsworth 'slept miserably', and Dorothy, not to disturb his belated morning sleep next day, lay in bed herself so that there would be no household noise. During daytime sleeps she often quietly wrote, and these times were valuable for the Journal.

Wordsworth's sleep on the afternoon of 3 June gave Dorothy time to produce an intricate pattern of mood and memory. The Journal was not in fact in arrears that Thursday afternoon. Wednesday's entry seems already to have been finished at the comment on young oak tree leaves 'dry as powder'. A concluding line is firmly there beneath this comment, and the final insertion of that day, 'A cold south wind portending Rain' has been squeezed in (on Tuesday Dorothy had remarked the 'sad want of rain'; it came on Thursday morning). On Thursday afternoon, however, with time to write, Wordsworth sleeping on the window seat, Dorothy, despite the closure of Wednesday, did not begin with the rain of Thursday morning. She returned even to Tuesday: 'I ought to have said that on Tuesday June 1st in the ev . . .' Here she broke off, crossed out these words and within brackets squeezed into a half-line the stray memory, '([?saw] 13 primroses here & there in the Hollins)'. A period of silent and intense communion between brother and sister is then recorded; it presumably follows on from Wednesday's walk to Butterlip How when the dry oak leaves were noticed: 'After we came in we sate in deep silence at the window – I on a chair & William with his hand on my shoulder. We were deep in Silence & Love, a blessed hour. We drew to the fire before bed-time & ate some Broth for our suppers.' Another concluding line is drawn under this passage, and Dorothy returned once again to Tuesday: 'I ought to have said that on Tuesday evening, namely June 1st., we walked upon the Turf near Johns Grove. It was a lovely night . . .' and so on to the end of that entry, Dorothy reflecting in a leisurely way on the light upon clouds and mountains, on a new view of the lake, on the fairy-like yet alpine topography of White Moss. The line marking the end of this extended out-of-place Tuesday entry covers some three or four thoroughly illegible words, while a recollection of little John Dawson and his huge stick is squeezed in as an afterthought. The dated entry for Thursday, 3 June 1802 now finally begins, and Dorothy records items freshly heard and seen: the cuckoo's song, the small birds and the colours of leaves that she and Wordsworth had noticed as they sat sheltering in the doorway of a cow-house in Easedale that same morning. She even goes back over her writing to explain in an insertion why she had described the oak copses as 'brown as in autumn': 'with the late frosts' is added. She has reached in her entry almost the time of her writing:

We came home quite wet. We have been reading the Life & some of the writings of poor Logan since dinner. 'And everlasting Longings for the lost'. It is an affecting line. There are many affecting lines & passages in his poems. William is now sleeping – with the window open lying on the window Seat. The thrush is singing . . .

And from the upstairs window of the sitting room, Dorothy describes the honeysuckle she could see with all its 'thousand Buds' and only one in flower 'retired behind the twigs close to the wall & as snug as a Bird's nest'. She mentions John's Rose tree blended with the honeysuckle and then draws the line under the entry. But Wordsworth must still have been sleeping, for Dorothy went back once more to Tuesday and the encounter with little John Dawson: 'On Tuesday Evening when we were among the Rocks we saw in the woods what seemed to be a man . . .' Some twelve lines of detail and dialogue follow and another concluding line is drawn. There was still time for yet another recollection, now of Wednesday again: 'Yesterday morning . . .' and Dorothy re-tells the anecdote Wordsworth had told her after walking on Wednesday with Aggie Fisher as far as the Swan. Aggie 'was going to attend upon Goan's dying Infant' and told Wordsworth that she knew a woman who had buried four grown children in one year, and she had heard her say that when many years were gone by she had more pleasure in thinking of those four than of her living children. Aggie told how she could pass lightly by their graves. Dorothy, recollecting the thrice-told tale, had enough time to go over her writing and change the word 'pass' to 'trip': the mother could now 'trip lightly by their graves'. We cannot know whether Dorothy was improving the story or more precisely remembering it. The normal line is drawn under this anecdote. Wordsworth at this point must have awakened and it was presumably after an interval, perhaps a day's interval, that Dorothy, forget-fully, for a second time entered the date 'Thursday June 3rd'. This time she mentions two walks, before and after dinner, omits the reading of Logan and Wordsworth's sleeping but adds that while she was sitting in the window they received an 'affecting letter' from Mary Hutchinson and that she read 'Milton's Penseroso to William'.

Four separate accounts or starts for Tuesday, three for Wednesday, two for Thursday; any one of us with time to recall some two or three recent days might select, and then re-select as Dorothy does. It was clearly, for instance, on second thoughts that she decided to include the account of Wednesday's 'blessed hour' of 'deep silence'. This account of sympathy between brother and sister has been heavily crossed out; the parenthesis about the primroses (hitherto misread) is crossed out with it. Tuesday's false start is also crossed out but in an ordinary light sort of way. The 'blessed hour' deletion is as heavy as that, say, that crosses out the mention of William's being unwell on Wednesday or of Dorothy's illness imediately before the October marriage. It is not so heavy as the famous deletion of Dorothy's account of how she wore Mary's wedding-ring the night before Wordsworth's marriage, and how he reassuringly slipped it again on to her finger. But it is heavy, and has been done deliberately to obscure. The ink is iron-based, as is the rest of the ink of the Journal, and the deletion could have been done by Dorothy soon or later; it is certainly not difficult to see why the later Dorothy, secure and loved in the Wordsworth household, should prefer that such intense and personal moments remain private.

It is more interesting to ask, not why Dorothy deleted it, but why she so deliberately went back and included the 'blessed hour'. Logan is perhaps the key. Wordsworth and she had, before Wordsworth slept and Dorothy took up her Journal, been reading the 'Life & some of the writings of poor Logan'. Why does Dorothy refer to 'poor Logan'? Was it because he had died in 1788 at the early age of forty, an admired poet and popular preacher, but one, according to the 'Life' the Wordsworths read in Anderson's *British Poets*, 'always much elated, or much depressed', who had too 'eagerly snatched that temporary relief which the bottle supplied'? His history was not unlike that of those other poets, Burns and Chatterton (and, it could be feared, Coleridge), whose fates haunted the great poem, 'Resolution and Independence', which Wordsworth had recently finished in its first draft. It is not surprising that the phrase 'poor Logan' should be used by one or other of the Wordsworths. Again, Dorothy would associate Logan with their now far distant brother John who had particularly asked Dorothy to get Wordsworth to advise him on poems to read in Anderson, 'any good poems in Poets such as Logan for instance'.[3]

Having recorded that they had been reading some of the writings of 'poor Logan' that afternoon, Dorothy goes on, most unusually, to quote a line, '"And everlasting Longings for the lost"'. It is an affecting line. There are many affecting lines & passages in his poems. William is now sleeping . . .' The affecting line was from Logan's 'Ode, Written in a Visit to the Country in Autumn':

> O memory! how shall I appease
> The bleeding shade, the unlaid ghost?
> What charm can bind the gushing eye?
> What voice console the incessant sigh,
> And everlasting longings for the lost?

181

Of the 'many' lines and passages that Dorothy found 'affecting', surely some would be from the third poem in the slim Logan section in Anderson's *British Poets*. In 'Ode on the Death of a Young Lady', Logan laments the loss of the 'sister of my soul',

> Fair with my first ideas twin'd,
> Thine image oft will meet my mind;
> And, while remembrance brings thee near,
> Affection sad will drop a tear . . .
>
> No after-friendship e'er can raise
> Th'endearments of our early days;
> And ne'er the heart such fondness prove
> As when it first began to love . . .

This must surely have spoken to Dorothy.

Wordsworth was to marry at the beginning of October. It had only recently been decided that the marriage should take place in autumn. Though Dorothy welcomed the coming change, she seems to have been tense. Five days before reading Logan she had tried out three names on the remaining third of a page otherwise torn out and left empty (between entries 21 and 22 May); these were 'Dorothy Wordsworth, William Wordsworth, Mary Wordsworth May 29th 6 o'clock Evening sitting at small table by window. Grasmere 1802.' On that day, 29 May, Wordsworth had 'finished his poem on Going for Mary. I wrote it out.' Dorothy also wrote to Mary on that same day. The poem, 'Farewell, thou little Nook of mountain ground', hails the coming change by extending a welcome to Mary, but insists throughout, by the continuous use of 'we', 'us' and 'our', that Mary, in coming to their beloved garden, will be coming to them both; she 'will be ours'. This must have reassured Dorothy, for two days later, on Monday, 31 May 1802, when her tooth broke, she wrote of her other teeth, 'They will soon be gone. Let that pass I shall be beloved – I want no more.' Even so, there was further reassurance (and there continued to be, right up to the passing of the ring between brother and sister on the wedding morning in October[4]); and now, there was the 'blessed hour' of Wednesday, the 'deep silence at the window'. This was lovingly remembered and added to Wednesday's completed entry on Thursday. They were in the same places: they were again at the window, but Wordsworth now silent in sleep, and Dorothy writing her Journal with the affecting lines and passages of 'poor Logan' fresh in mind. The following day's (presumably) second, and much briefer, mention of Thursday's time at the window recalls only Mary's letter and Milton's 'Il Penseroso', a poem about a melancholy far tougher than Logan's, more intellectual, less exclusively of the feelings. In thus remembering Milton instead

Figures 8.1–6 Six pages from Dorothy Wordsworth's *Grasmere Journals*, 1–5 June 1802 (DC MS 31).

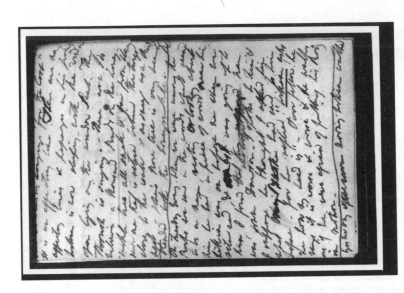

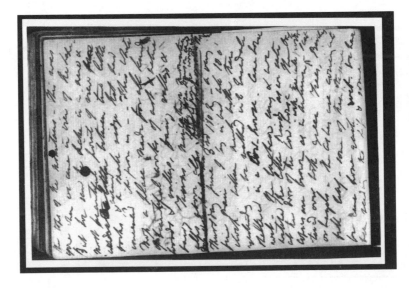

of Logan, Dorothy has already moved some distance from that pressure of feeling (encouraged by Logan) that had made her go back, interrupt her own writing, and add the 'blessed hour' account. Further distance would later prompt her to delete it.

This intricate entry for 3 June 1802 shows the Journal as a whole. It has the eye of the moment that sees the buds of honeysuckle, and it has the listening ear for the present singing of the thrush; in it, memory moves backwards and forwards; it has oral story, dialogue as well as description; it has openness to mood, the need to let the insistent feeling be expressed. Throughout its writing, Wordsworth is a subject Dorothy writes about, a sleeping presence as she writes, and a prospective reader of the entry.

Wordsworth's poetry too is an under-presence in her writing, a nuance beyond the many allusions, quotations, half-quotations from his poetry that she brings in. There is space here to discuss only one such half-hidden echo from Wordsworth, for it is also important to mention Coleridge; he too is written about in the Journal and his writing likewise is an occasional haunter of Dorothy's. First, the Wordsworth example. When Dorothy and Wordsworth walked one mid-May morning in 1802 through Brothers Wood amid unseasonable hail and snow showers, not surprisingly Dorothy wrote that 'there was no pleasure in stepping along that difficult sauntering Road in this ungenial weather'. This negative expression is strange: 'no pleasure', 'ungenial'. Dorothy more characteristically describes rough weather positively: a morning 'very dankish misty, wettish' (16 November 1801), or 'miserable clashy snowy' (17 February 1802), or speaks of a 'threatening windy coldish day' (30 June 1802). But here, in May 1802, she has 'no pleasure in stepping along the difficult sauntering Road in this ungenial weather' because the present is complicated by memory. She must be recalling Wordsworth's 'Point Rash-Judgment', a poem written eighteen months before, in October 1800, and describing a walk taken by herself, Wordsworth and Coleridge on this same 'narrow girdle of rough stones and crags,' this 'rude and natural causeway,' when they 'one calm September morning', according to the poem, 'Sauntered on this retired and difficult way' and came upon the peasant with rod and line and wasted limbs, fishing in hay-time. Dorothy is echoing Wordsworth's words and remembering that hot summer walk of July (not misty September to which Wordsworth changed it – it is in a July 1800 note that Coleridge records the shock of coming upon the 'thin, pale' man.)[5] Dorothy's 'difficult sauntering Road' must be a conscious echo of Wordsworth's line, and the July walk must be in her mind, for she goes on immediately in the Journal to voice regret for Coleridge's absence: William, walking backwards and forwards, was teasing 'himself with seeking an epithet for the Cuckow. I sate awhile upon my last summers seat the mossy stone – William's unemployed beside me, & the space between where Coleridge has so often lain.'

Coleridge in absence was often present in Dorothy's mind, and in ghostly fashion his words sometimes shadow hers. On 4 May 1802 Dorothy silently 'corrected' a phrase that Coleridge had used in his recent verse-letter to Sara (later, 'Dejection'), verses that thirteen days before, on 21 April, had so affected Dorothy and left her in 'miserable spirits'. They affected Wordsworth too, for they were in part released by questions he himself had asked in the four opening stanzas of his own recent and unfinished Ode:

> Whither is fled the visionary gleam?
> Where is it now, the glory and the dream?

Coleridge, in personal unhappiness, declared in answer in his verse-letter that the 'beauty-making Power' that confers glory on the earth comes from the joyous spirit of man himself, and that, to the man without joy, the earth must be a dead place. This was not to be Wordsworth's answer; in 'The Leech Gatherer' he reaches towards an alternative approach to the problem. The later title of the poem, 'Resolution and Independence', indicates that Wordsworth could find help for his own depression in the contemplation of men who could endure, and endure with dignity. These two poems, the 'verses to Sara and 'The Leech Gatherer', were much in the consciousness of Wordsworth, Coleridge, and Dorothy in early May 1802, and Dorothy's descriptions of the moon at this time become unusually allusive to the poetry of both men, but of Coleridge in particular. On 4 May, the first day of 'The Leech Gatherer's' composition (Wordsworth actually began it the night before), Dorothy appropriated and 'corrected' a phrase from Coleridge's verse-letter. After Wordsworth had written several stanzas of 'The Leech Gatherer's' and after Dorothy had written them out, and after, doubtless, they and the verse-letter to Sara had been among the verses 'Wm & C repeated & read' that day, Dorothy, commenting on the night walk home from Wythburn, recorded the moon as 'the crescent moon with the "auld moon in her arms"'. Now this had not been Coleridge's expression about the new moon in his verses to Sara. He had written 'I see the Old Moon in her Lap', and so the line was always to remain for him, his variant of Percy's 'with the old Moon in her arme',[6] but Dorothy, suddenly alive to the ballad surely because of Coleridge, quotes from Percy, only misremembering Percy's 'arme' as 'arms'.[7]

For descriptions of the moon for both 4 and 5 May, days when Wordsworth was 'very nervous' and working at 'The Leech Gatherer,' his 'answer' to Coleridge's poem, Dorothy returned again to Percy and to Coleridge. Indeed, without Coleridge it is unlikely that the moon would have received this literary attention. There is much in the Journals about the effects of moonlight on hills and water but there is less description of the moon itself (compare the Alfoxden Journal). The new moon has a handful of mentions earlier than May 1802. In five instances (i.e. most instances) it is simply the plain 'crescent moon'. Once, it is a 'beautiful crescent moon'. Once, a somewhat older moon is 'bowl-shaped'. Two months before, on Friday, 5 March 1802, Dorothy had as usual simply recorded, 'Beautiful new moon over Silver How', and only when she discovered that Wordsworth had seen this same Friday's moon at the same time, but in Keswick, not in Grasmere, did she return to that moon and offer an expanded and wonderfully precise description of the now significant moon – significant because Wordsworth had noticed it too:

8 March 1802 . . . On friday Evening the Moon hung over the Northern side of the highest point of Silver How, like a gold ring snapped in two & shaven off at the Ends it was so narrow. Within this Ring lay the Circle of the Round moon, as *distinctly* to be seen as ever the enlightened moon is – William had observed the same appearance at Keswick perhaps at the very same moment hanging over the Newlands fells.

In May 1802, it is Coleridge's verse-letter, as I have tried to show, rather than Wordsworth's conversation, that leads Dorothy to embellish her normally plainer references to the moon. The influence of the verse-letter continues from 4 May to the 5th. Wordsworth was again working at 'The Leech Gatherer' and the moon, wrote Dorothy, 'had the old moon in her arms but not so plain to be seen as the night before. When we went to bed it was a Boat without the Circle.' Now, Peter Bell as well as 'Sir Patrick Spence' is brought to mind, again, by way of Coleridge's poem. Coleridge had recalled Wordsworth's *Peter Bell* of 1798, where a bright little boat 'just like the crescent moon', 'a sweet and beautiful canoe' had offered the poet a magical plunge through the cosmos. Coleridge had written of the

> crescent Moon, as fix'd as if it grew
> In its own cloudless, starless Lake of Blue –
> A boat becalm'd! dear William's Sky Canoe!

Dorothy's new moon of May is the very next moon noted after hearing Coleridge's verse-letter, and on 6 May 1802, for the third day running, her moon recalls once more Coleridge's poem. This time Dorothy omits the ballad echo and emphasizes the *Peter Bell* element that Coleridge had quoted: 'The Moon was a perfect Boat a silver Boat when we were out in the Evening.' The allusiveness has now moved directly to Wordsworth's poetry.

On 9 May Dorothy copied out 'The Leech Gatherer'. It was, for the time being, finished, and so it, *Peter Bell* and Coleridge's verse-letter ceased to be at the forefront of the consciousness of both Wordsworth and Dorothy.[8]

Consequently, the moon too in Dorothy's Journal fell from prominence and had no more literary connections with Percy, Coleridge, or Wordsworth's poetry. Wordsworth's influence, however, remained. Only two out of the seven moons that remained before the Journal ended are mentioned; each time, Dorothy's attention was caught by Wordsworth rather than by the moon itself. On 13 June she records Wordsworth's observation 'that the full moon above a dark fir grove is a fine image of the descent of a superior being'; and on 8 July, the last night in Grasmere before the departure for Yorkshire and France, Dorothy recorded, 'The moon was behind. William hurried me out in hopes that I should see her.' This moon is the last moon in the Journal (though 'moonlight' is still twice recorded), and it combines with Dorothy's slightly unwilling submission to pressure, her being 'hurried' out, Wordsworth's 'pressing me to go out', to give us a final emblem of the pressures upon Dorothy in writing the Journal. They were generally positive (just as in this instance she valued the moonlit walk), whether they consisted in presence or absence or conversation or poetry.

But there are no rules, no models, for Journal composition. I have tried to discuss some of the pressures that lay behind the making of Dorothy Wordsworth's Journal. The Journal is so direct and various, so unassuming about itself, that the very words 'discussion' or 'pressures' seem too strong. It is perhaps possible to detect presences and directions here and there, yet after all that, to recall an entry that flies in the face of any formulation. Here, on 23 March 1802, Dorothy writes with Wordsworth awake, not asleep; present, not absent; the entry's delicacies belong to a room indoors, not the natural world; some literature, the faint ghost of 'Frost at Midnight' perhaps, might lie behind it, but these things are elusive. We read and acknowledge a sense of the passing of a day in time, of how a day can be passed well: in a house where there is love, and in reading and writing. Dorothy's sewing might seem less than idyllic to some, and there is anxiety for absent Coleridge, though it is unspoken. But these considerations, with time itself, as the entry insists, are notes in the whole composition:

A mild morning William worked at the Cuckow poem. I sewed beside him. After dinner he slept I read German, & at the closing in of day went to sit in the Orchard – he came to me, & walked backwards & forwards, we talked about C – Wm repeated the poem to me – I left him there & in 20 minutes he came in rather tired with attempting to write – he is now reading Ben Jonson I am going to read German it is about 10 o clock, a quiet night. The fire flutters & the watch ticks I hear nothing else save the Breathings of my Beloved & he now & then pushes his book forward & turns over a leaf. Fletcher is not come home. No letter from C.

NOTES

I am indebted to the Trustees of Dove Cottage, Grasmere, for permission to use manuscripts in the Wordsworth Library.

1 *The Prose Works of William Wordsworth*, ed. W. J. B. Owen and J. W. Smyser (Oxford, 1974), Vol. 1, pp. 122, 124.
2 *Ibid.*, p. 124
3 *The Letters of John Wordsworth*, ed. Carl H. Ketcham (Ithaca, 1969), p. 123.
4 The reassurance was needed. Compare Dorothy's own farewell to the garden, written at the moment of leaving it on 9 July, with Wordsworth's controlled poem. Dorothy's verbs of compulsion, the breathless present-tense sentences, almost cry out in panic at leaving: 'O beautiful place! – Dear Mary William – The horse is come Friday morning, so I must give over. William is eating his Broth – I must prepare to go – The Swallows I must leave them the well the garden the Roses all – Dear creatures!! they sang last night after I was in bed – seemed to be singing to one another, just before they settled to rest for the night. Well I must go – Farewell.'
5 *The Notebooks of Samuel Taylor Coleridge*, ed. Kathleen Coburn, 3 vols. in 6 pts. (Princeton, 1957–73), Vol. 1, n. 761.
6 The epigraph stanza of four lines, a single verse made out of two verses from Percy's 'Sir Patrick Spence', had as yet no place at the head of the poem. This, later, would indeed highlight Coleridge's variant, 'Lap', for in those lines the ballad was to be more correctly quoted:

> I saw the new Moon
> With the old Moon in her arms ['arme' in Percy]

7 The ballads in Thomas Percy's *Reliques of Ancient English Poetry* (1765) must have been well known to Dorothy; on 1 October at the beginning of the long German winter of 1798–9, she had noted in her Journal the purchase of a copy in Hamburg for 14 marks – probably the new edition, edited by Percy's nephew (1794).
8 The June–July revision of 'The Leech Gatherer' takes the poem further from Coleridge and the initial impulse of the verse-letter, and towards a remoter world on the borderline of consciousness, almost of dream. The new texture of the poem brings it closer to Spenser's 'Ruines of Time', and Shakespeare's 'Lover's Complaint.' This last poem was read by Dorothy to Wordsworth – 'very nervous' after 'Leech Gatherer' composition on 5 May; it 'left him composed'. Both these *rhyme-royal* poems (not far from each other in Anderson's *British Poets*), in situation, rhythm, and language, are of significance for the transformed 'Leech Gatherer', the poem 'Resolution and Independence' as we know it.

9

BYRON AND "THE TRUTH IN MASQUERADE"

JEROME MCGANN

I

LIKE all poets and artists, Byron is often found re-using earlier work in later circumstances – manipulating and changing it for different purposes. Normally these alterations take place as it were "in private," and readers only become aware of the transformations when they are brought to light by subsequent academic or scholarly investigation.

But there are also cases where textual manipulations are carried out as it were half publicly and half in secret. These are the cases – they are peculiarly Byronic – which I want to discuss here. We may recall for instance the several alternative uses to which the text of "When We Two Parted" was put.[1] Published in his 1816 volume of *Poems*, these verses were there dated 1808, with the obvious intention (we now know) – given Byron's circumstances in 1816 – of indicating that the lines had nothing directly to do with his wife or his recent domestic problems. The 1808 date would in fact have suggested, to those with knowledge of Byron's life, that the lines referred to Mary Chaworth. And in fact this is the way the poem was commonly read for over a century.

But the lines were not written in 1808 – that was a ruse of Byron's – they were written in 1815; and their immediate subject was Lady Frances Wedderburn Webster. Byron manipulated his 1816 text in order to hide that fact. But he was also manipulating another, altogether invisible text – a poem which he wrote in 1812 to Lady Caroline Lamb. This poem remained in manuscript until 1886, and its true addressee was not known for almost another hundred years. The connection between this poem to Lady Caroline Lamb and the 1816 "When We Two Parted" is that Byron used part of the earlier (manuscript) poem when he produced the text of the later (published) work.

When Byron published "When We Two Parted" in 1816 he also signaled his own textual manipulations, but he did so deceptively, in a kind of code. The date "1808" printed with the poem is a diversion, but one which, once registered as a diversion (or a possible diversion), points the reader toward other dates and other contexts of reading. And in fact Byron's London social circle – and his wife – would have been alive to those other possibilities. Lady Byron had made a copy of "When We Two Parted" for Byron in 1815, from a manuscript which she well knew had nothing to do with 1808. Furthermore, Lady Melbourne and her circle would have recognized at least some of "When We Two Parted" as a passage from an unpublished poem of 1812 – a poem written to Lady Caroline beginning "Go! Triumph securely, that treacherous vow." Several copies of that poem were in London circulation, and one or another of these copies was certainly known at least to Lady Caroline, Lady Melbourne, and Brummell. Furthermore, given what we know about the habits of the fast world of the Regency, and of the exchange value which Byron and his poetry had in that world, we can be certain that "the knowing ones," in this instance, were not confined to four people.

Thus that "false date" of 1808 would have signaled several very different lines of interpretation in 1816, depending upon the point of view adopted by the reader. 1808 would have been recognized as a mystification by Lady Byron and others as well, though in each case the search for "the truth" of the poem would have been carried out along different lines and from different premises. What may not have been recognized – what probably was not recognized – was the kind of deliberateness with which Byron carried out his mystification. That he anticipated and desired a disbelief in the date of 1808 by certain readers (not all) is clear not merely from the circumstances of composition and publication, but from Byron's 1823 correspondence with his cousin Lady Hardy, who was herself an intimate of Byron and his London world in the Years of Fame. In a letter to her of June 10, 1823 he told her that "the secret" of "When We Two Parted" was that it was written to Lady Frances Wedderburn Webster. But of course this only added a further level of mystification, or another direction from which the poem could be read.[2]

In the case of "When We Two Parted" we are dealing with a type of textual alteration and manipulation which seems to me extremely significant, and not merely for the reader of Byron's poetry. Let us pause for a moment to reflect on what is happening here – and also on what is *not* happening. It is one thing – a common thing – for poets, as for all artists, to plunder and re-use their work for different purposes and under different circumstances. And it is also one thing – an equally common thing – for poets to foreground their processes of writing, to make the act of writing a subject or topic of their work. It is quite another thing – far less common – for writers to manipulate their work so as to draw out and exploit the complicity of their readers and audiences.

The case of "When We Two Parted" shows, however, how readers can be imagined by texts, how they can be caught and defined by their own expectations and preconceptions. Acts of reading are always carried out by minds prepared to read in certain ways by their determinate social, personal, and institutional circumstances. More than most poets, Byron understood this, and his understanding led him into a mode of poetry where readers, along with their various preconceptions, are drawn into the theater of the poetry, and forced to confront, or refuse to confront, themselves. Byron manipulates "When We Two Parted" in order to call out certain lines of reading, certain interpretative options; and the poem then becomes an opportunity to learn to read – ultimately, to learn to read oneself – more self-consciously. The concrete equivalent of such a style is precisely the Byronic Hero, who

> had the skill, when Cunning's gaze would seek
> To probe his heart and watch his changing cheek,
> At once the observer's purpose to espy,
> And on himself roll back his scrutiny,
> Lest he to Conrad rather should betray
> Some secret thought, than drag that chief's to day.
> (*Corsair* I, 217–22)

To work in this way is necessarily to develop a clear initial sense of who is – and who is not – your audience. Byron's understanding of this necessity came to him very early, as his first five books (from *Fugitive Pieces* through *English Bards*) clearly show. In those books certain people and groups of people are addressed and others are not, and these inclusions/exclusions extend down to individual poems. *Hours of Idleness*, for example, has several homoerotic poems which are presented in coded forms that open and close different reading possibilities, depending on the point of view and context in which the reading occurs. And consider, for instance, a poem like the one titled in these early printings "Damaetas." It is a descriptive sketch of a schoolboy who has had an early education in vicious living, deceit, and hypocrisy. The title is itself a piece of code, referring back to Virgil and Theocritus. It is a cunning title which might, or might not, have homoerotic overtones. But the title is a diversion in another sense, as one discovers with a knowledge of the poem's manuscript (the autograph is apparently no longer extant). Byron's manuscript title was "My Character," not "Damaetas."[3]

"Damaetas" (or "My Character") is thus a deceitful poem, and part of its wit lies in its own deceitful execution. We cannot be absolutely certain that Byron's close schoolfriends were privy to these various levels of poetic equivocation, but it is difficult to believe – given the character of Byron's school friendships – that some of them were not. Who was or was not *in fact* a part of the audience of this poem's witty deceits is not, finally, the point. The point is that the poem is operating in such a rhetorical structure – even if, *in fact*, Byron was the only person at the time who knew what was involved in it.

This case is a nice illustration of how Byron uses different levels of poetic coding to define his audiences. It is a procedure which will achieve spectacular display in *Don Juan* and its associated poems, where Byron executes a many-leveled discourse comparable – in its own unregenerate secularity – to Dante's. As in all such writing, multiplying meanings entails playing with language, developing systems of punning and coded talk which require some kind of special knowledge to decipher. Such knowledge is both factual and procedural. "The grand Arcanum's not for men to see all," Byron says in a peculiarly important passage of Canto XIV, "And there is much that could not be appreciated / In any matter by the uninitiated." These lines are unusual only because of the way they have foregrounded this aspect of the poem at the level of conscious methodology.[4] *Don Juan* is of course a mine of such materials. What we sometimes forget is that the *Don Juan* manner is precisely designed *not* to disguise its own procedures of mystification. Rather, flaunting its doubletalk, the poem turns human hypocrisy and deceit (those sins against the human light) toward redemption by translating them into a poetic method – which is to say, by bringing them into the open. In Byron, poetry becomes not an Aristotelian "imitation of reality," where one side or the other of that transaction tends to be thrown into obscurity. Rather, it is what Byron calls "The truth in masquerade" (XI, 290), a situation where – to borrow a Yeatsian metaphor – body is not bruised to pleasure soul. When truth appears in masquerade, medium and message are placed on a new footing with respect to each other: not reconciled, certainly, and least of all married, but as it were living together in sin.[5]

"When We Two Parted" involves a comparable masquerade of its truth. As such, the poem exploits and even encourages its audience's awareness that there is more in the poem than might at first seem apparent. In this way it begins to develop a kind of social consciousness: on one hand, contexts of reading which transcend the immediate are being invoked, and on the other the audience is being made aware of itself as a participant in the construction of those contexts. The poem can be read in purely textual space, of course, but such a reading will not merely have missed certain relevant details, it will in the end have missed the point of the poem entirely.

We may well be reminded, in *this* context, of two important historical realities in the history of Byron criticism: that its dominant mode has always been heavily "biographical", and that the text-centered procedures of twentieth-century criticism have never been able to read Byron's work in interesting ways. Such text-centered criticism then declared Byron's work, and especially his non-satirical work, to be unimportant and uninteresting. But the fact is that Byron's poetry would be uninteresting *by definition* to this kind of criticism. And the real critical task is to assess the significance of Byron's procedures, on the one hand, and his execution of those procedures, on the other.

The first of those tasks involves a critique of the limits of a theory of autonomous poetry, and the development of an alternative theory. I want to examine a few examples of Byron's actual practice of installing the poetical experience as a social and historical event, rather than simply as an event in "language." In these cases we will again observe Byron manipulating his texts before his publics. But in these cases the stakes will be higher, the issues more important, the risks far greater. Indeed, we shall be looking at cases where, I believe, Byron crossed a watershed in his career as a writer, and where he first came to understand adequately the limits, the dangers, and the opportunities offered in a poetry of coded discourse.

II

A frequent charge against Byron – it has been especially prevalent in the twentieth century – is that his work lacks authenticity because he was too preoccupied with his audiences and their reactions. His poetry aims, it is judged, for cheap and factitious effects by pandering to the (presumably debased) expectations of his reading publics (and one must say "publics" because they were, as they always are, multiple, overlapping, and distinctive).

Now this is a highly problematic argument for two reasons. In the first place, all of Byron's universally acknowledged masterpieces – *Don Juan*, for example, or *Beppo*, or "The Vision of Judgment" – evoke and reciprocate audience expectations and reaction which are at once various and determinate. Why do those poems succeed where (let us say) *Manfred* and "Fare Thee Well!" are thought to fail? This is a question which Philip Martin, in his excellent recent book *Byron: A Poet Before His Public*, was never really able to answer.[6] And he was not able to answer it because his measures of critical judgment remain committed to the idea of the autonomy of the poetic event. For him, although poetry may engage itself with its audiences, its distinctively *poetical* character and value have to be judged through rather narrowly conceived aesthetic criteria.

Odd as it may seem, the correlative of this approach to Byron's poetry is the often-stated idea that to appreciate his work you have to take him in the gross (in both senses). Thus Don Reiman speaks for many when he says that

"Modern students who read *Manfred* without having waded through all of Byron's preceding volumes are probably unable to imagine the cumulative effect of his poetry."[7] This view assumes the social dimension of Byron's work and does not condemn it on that account; nonetheless, it is driven to apologize ("waded through") for the fact that appreciation of the work has to depend upon an awareness of audience reciprocities, or what Reiman calls here "the cumulative effect of his poetry."

Now I believe that these two scholars are correct to the extent that they force us to pay attention to the poetry's social and contextual dimensions. What I would like to argue, however, is that neither has elucidated how a poetry of "cumulative effect" actually works, and in what ways it moves beyond the autonomous resources of language (narrowly conceived).

To this end let us first look at a notorious work, "Fare Thee Well!", which Byron addressed to his wife at the time of the separation controversies in the spring of 1816.[8] The poem descends to us largely through one line of interpretation, which reads it as a *cri de cœur* from a heartbroken husband. This is the way the poem was read by many people in 1816. Madame de Staël, for instance, and Sir Francis Burdett, and various reviewers all read it this way and praised it extravagantly.[9] And Wordsworth read it this way as well, only he anticipated the common later judgment that the poem is hopelessly mawkish: "disgusting in sentiment, and in execution contemptible . . . Can worse doggrel be written . . . ?"[10]

But another, very different reading sprang up when the poem began circulating in 1816, like tares among the wheat of that first reading. Byron's friend Moore – who was later to endorse the sentimental theory of the poem – was at first deeply suspicious of "the sentiment that could, at such a moment, indulge in such verses."[11] Moore did not elaborate on his suspicions, but others did. The reviewer of *The Prisoner of Chillon and Other Poems* in *The Critical Review* of November 1816 paused to reflect on the earlier "domestic" poem:

for many who disapproved most of his lordship's . . . publication of his "Farewell" address, as inflicting a parting and lasting pang upon his lady, thought that the lines were most delightfully pathetic, and wondered how a man, who shewed he had so little heart, could evince such feeling. They did not know how easy it was for a person of his lordship's skill to fabricate neatly-turned phraseology, and for a person of his lordship's ingenuity to introduce to advantage all the common-places of affection: the very excellence of that poem in these particulars, to us and to others, was a convincing proof that its author had much more talent than tenderness.[12]

As it happens, Annabella herself, the person to whom "Fare Thee Well!" was most directly addressed, read the poem in just this insidious way. It seemed to her yet another instance of Byron's "talent for equivocation . . . of [which] I have had many proofs in his letters."[13] On February 13, a month before Byron wrote his poem, she explained this "talent" further and pointed out that she learned about it from Byron himself:

I should not have been *more* deceived than I was by his letters, if he had not pointed out to me in similar ones addressed to others, the deepest design in words that appeared to have none. On this he piques himself – and also on being able to write such letters as will convey different, or even opposite sentiments to the person who receives them & to a stranger.[14]

"Every day," she added, "proves deeper art" in her husband. What she most feared was "this ambiguity of Language in the Law," that it would give Byron an advantage over her in the separation proceedings.

Annabella went on to add two observations which are equally interesting and shrewd. Byron's skill in manipulating language reminded her of a passage in *Lara* (I, 504–9) in which the deportment of that Byronic hero is exposed as a text of such ambiguity that, reading it, one cannot be certain if it signals a heart filled with "the calmness of the good" or with a "Guilt grown old in desperate hardihood." And she added that this skill with words was one "he is *afraid* of" himself.

In a good recent essay W. Paul Elledge has revived a variant of this insidious reading of "Fare Thee Well!" The poem, he argues, is "a portrait of indecision, taut with antithetical tensions"; it "charts . . . the depth and configurations of the poet's ambivalence . . . toward reconciliation with his wife."[15] Although Elledge is, I believe, certainly correct in this reading of the poem, he does not go nearly far enough, either substantively or methodologically. In this respect the readings of both the *Critical* reviewer and Lady Byron seem to me more weighty and profound.

What Annabella and the *Critical* reviewer call attention to are the social contexts in which the poem was executed. Annabella was peculiarly alive to such matters because they touched upon her life in the most important ways. "Fare Thee Well!" was not simply a thing of beauty, an aesthetic object spinning in the disinterested space of a Kantian (or Coleridgean) theoretical world. It was an event in the language of art, specifically located, and she registered that event in particular ways. To her the separation controversy came to involve two primary matters. There was first the matter of the law, and who, in the complex legal maneuverings, would have power over the other to influence various decisions (Lady Byron feared, for example, that Byron would seek to deprive her of custody of their daughter Ada). And second there was the (closely related) matter of public opinion, and who would enter into and finally emerge from the separation proceedings with what sort of public image.

When Byron sent her a copy of "Fare Thee Well!" soon after he wrote it, Lady Byron was quick to read it as a shrewd ploy to gain power over her in the context of those two areas of interest which most concerned her. At first she emphasized the "legal" reading, for she felt, as we have already seen, that Byron's various communications were designed to construct a sympathetic self-image in order to improve his bargaining position. "He has been assuming the character of an injured & affectionate husband with great success to some," she remarked in mid-February.[16] When Byron sent her a manuscript copy of the poem late in March, she wrote ironically to her mother of its apparent tenderness, "and so he talks of me to Every one."[17] But the poem did not disturb her greatly until she learned Byron's intention to print and distribute it privately in London society. This act, she feared, would turn "The Tide of feeling . . . against" her,[18] but she was dissuaded from her first impulse – to publish a rejoinder – by the counsel of Dr. Stephen Lushington.

The significance of all this becomes more clear, I think, if we recall that "Fare Thee Well!" was initially constituted as three very different texts, only two of which were manipulated by Byron, while the other fell under the co-authority of persons and powers who were hostile to him. The first of these texts is the one which originates in the manuscript poem addressed to Lady Byron, and which Byron caused to have circulated in London in late March and early April. The second is the text privately printed and distributed in fifty copies on April 8, at Byron's insistence and over the objections of his publisher Murray. Byron's activities here are important to remember because they show that he was manipulating the poem, was literally fashioning an audience for it of a very specific kind. The original manuscript may have been addressed to his wife, but when copies of that poem began to be made and circulated, a new text started to emerge. The printed text in fifty copies represents the definitive emergence of that text, which was addressed past and through Lady Byron to a circle of people – friends, acquaintances, and other interested parties – whose "reading" and "interpretation" of the poem Byron wanted to generate, and of course influence.

In the most limited sense, Byron wanted his poem to be read as the effusion of an "injured and affectionate husband." Moore's later report in his *Life*, that the manuscript text he saw was covered with Byron's tears, represents in effect such an interpretation of the poem. But the fact that Byron was also managing a certain kind of circulation for the poem set in motion other forces, and other readings, which were only latent (so to speak) in the verbal manuscript text. The poem, that is to say, came to be widely seen – and read – as another event in Byron's troubled "domestic circumstances." It is this circulation of the verses which begins to change the meaning of the poem – indeed, which begins to change the poem itself. The words of the original manuscript do not significantly differ from the privately printed text; nonetheless, that first printed text has become another poem, and one which initiates a move toward the production of yet another textual change.

This new change is definitive when the privately printed text finally makes its appearance in *The Champion* on April 14 and thence throughout the periodical press. This is a new poem altogether. In the first place, it does not appear alone but alongside the bitter satire on Mrs. Clermont, a work which Byron had also put into private circulation in fifty copies several days before he began circulating "Fare Thee Well!" In *The Champion* text, "A Sketch" is presented as an exponent of the "real meaning" of "Fare Thee Well!", that is to say, it is used partly for the light it sheds on "Fare Thee Well!', as a way of exposing Byron's hypocritical malignancy. In the second place, the farewell poem is accompanied, in *The Champion*, by a long commentary denouncing Byron's character as well as his politics, and explicitly "reading" the two poems as evidence of his wickedness.

The Champion's text of "Fare Thee Well!" is, I would say, the definitive version of the (so to speak) *hypocritical* poem, just as the manuscript version sent to Lady Byron – which, interestingly, seems not to have survived – would be the definitive version of the *sentimental* poem. The "texts" which extend between these two versions dramatize this first, crucial stage in the poem's processes of transformation. But they do not conclude those processes. Even as *The Champion* text is completing that first stage of the poem's transformations, it has initiated a new stage, the one in which the two faces of this poem are forced to confront one another. And it is in this next stage of its textual development that "Fare Thee Well!" becomes most rich and interesting. This is the poem whose meaning focuses and culminates the controversies among the readers in Byron's day. The question is gone over again and again: is this a poem of love ("sentimental") or a poem of hate ("hypocritical")? The final contemporary text declares that in some important sense it is both. Byron himself produced the materialized version of this culminant text when he published the poem, with the telling epigraph from "Christabel," in his *Poems* (1816).

This is the text which Elledge has recently revived, a work full of painful and even frightening tensions and contradictions. And while I want to salute Elledge's success in rescuing Byron's poem from its impoverished sentimental readings, I must also point out Elledge's insistence – it stems from his New Critical background – that his is not a reading of a work of poetry so much as an exploration of a set of tense personal circumstances: "my concern is less with the poem as poem than with the dynamics of the relationship between poet-husband and audience-wife as Byron represents them."[19] He makes this statement because his notion is that "the poem as poem" is an abstract verbal construct, a "text" that not only can be, but must be, divorced from the social and material formations within which the work was instituted and carried out.

Such an idea commits one to a certain way of reading poetry which seems to me intolerable. But it is a way which is particularly destructive for a poet like Byron, whose poetical language is characteristically executed by invoking and utilizing its available social and institutional resources. More, Byron's work insists that this is the way of all poetry, though some poets and apologists for poetry argue that it is otherwise, that poetry operates in a space of disinterestedness and autonomy. "Fare Thee Well!" is therefore, in this respect, a meta-poem, a work which foregrounds Byron's ideas about what poetry actually is and how it works.

Byron himself seems to have recognized very clearly – that is to say, with pain and reluctance – the full significance of his poetic practice. In writing and circulating "Fare Thee Well!" he was the author and agent of the completed work, the one who finally would be responsible for all of the texts. Yet while Byron authored those texts, he could not fully control them – this, the fate of all poets, is sometimes called their "inspiration" – so that in the end he found that he too, like everyone else who would involve themselves with the poem, would have to trust the tale and not the teller. His discovery of this, a bitter revelation, would soon find expression in another of the "Poems on his Domestic Circumstances': the "[Epistle to Augusta]" which he wrote in the summer of 1816. Reflecting on that "talent for equivocation" which he flaunted before his wife, Byron would expose its equivocal character.

> The fault was mine – nor do I seek to screen
> My errors with defensive paradox –
> I have been cunning in mine overthrow
> The careful pilot of my proper woe.

(21–4)

Which is as much as to say of that most "cunning" of his poems to date, "Fare Thee Well!', that it tells more than one would have imagined possible, tells more than its own author wanted told.

I shall shortly return to indicate what I believe this kind of analysis signifies for a concrete "reading" of "Fare Thee Well!" But I want to reflect first on certain matters of general relevance for Byron's poetry. When we say that Byron's is a highly rhetorical poetry we mean – we should mean – not that it is loud or overblown, but that it is always, at whatever register, elaborating reciprocities with its audiences. These reciprocities, like all social relations, accumulate their own histories as time passes and more interchanges occur – and we then call these the "cumulative effect" of the work. New poetry is written – and read – within the context of those accumulations. The development of the various texts of "Fare Thee Well!" between March and November 1816 is a miniature example of how these reciprocities can get played out. Or Byron's employment of the "false date" of 1808 in "When We Two Parted" is an execution of poetic wit that utilizes the "cumulative effect" and history of Byron's work (the writing and the reading of that work, the entirety of its history).

I want to emphasize that Byron wrote this way throughout his life. The masterpiece of *Don Juan* is a work of, quite literally, *consummate* skill, because the whole of his life and career is gathered into it. Without an awareness of, an involvement in, that poem's "cumulative effect" one will be reduced simply to reading its words: as Eliot in this connection *might* have said, *not* to have the experience *and* to miss the meaning.

Related to this rhetorical framework of the poetry is Byron's habit of manipulating his texts. To present a work through a "cumulative" context is to open it to changes and modifications, in fact, to new opportunities of meaning: not so much, as Coleridge would have had it, the "reconciliation" of "opposite and discordant qualities" as their artistic exploitation. "Fare Thee Well!" did not bring about any reconciliations, poetic or otherwise; it raised a tumult of new discords and conflicts. Yet it is those very tumults, and their artistic significance, which turned the period of Byron's separation – from his wife, from England – to a watershed in his career, and in his understanding of what was involved, for him, in his methods of poetic production.

To understand this better we have to retreat in time, to Byron's years at Harrow and especially Cambridge, when he took his first lessons in the art of literary equivocation. Byron told his wife that he had a talent for that sort of thing, and Louis Crompton's recent book *Byron and Greek Love* has shown that it was a mode of writing practiced by Byron's circle of Cambridge friends – a deliberate and quite literally a *methodical* set of procedures for saying one thing and meaning something else. Briefly, they cultivated a mode of homosexual double-talk.

One of Byron's first epistolary exercises in this equivocal style was in his letter to Charles Skinner Matthews of June 22, 1809; Matthews's answer to this letter is important because of its explicit discussion:

In transmitting my dispatches to Hobhouse, my carissime Byron I cannot refrain from addressing a few lines to yourself: chiefly to congratulate you on the splended success of your first efforts in *the mysterious*, that style in which more is meant than meets the eye . . . [B]ut I must recommend that [Hobhouse] do not in future put a *dash* under his mysterious significances, such a practise would go near to letting the cat out of the bag . . . And I positively decree that every one who professes *ma methode* do spell the term wch designates his calling with an e at the end of it – *methodiste*, not method*ist*, and pronounce the word in the french fashion. Every one's taste must revolt at confounding ourselves with that sect of . . . fanatics.[20]

Byron's letter may in fact have been his "first effort" at writing in Matthews's particular dialect of "the *mysterious*," but it was a language he was already practiced in, and one which would receive its apotheosis in the incredible display of puns and coded talk that constitutes *Don Juan*.

Matthews's letter is also interesting because it suggests that the use of this kind of style is a game that can be played with, and that its practitioners should think of themselves as a kind of elite group with special gifts and powers. But it was also a style that ran grave risks for the user. Byron told his wife that he was afraid of his own skill with this method of writing. And well he might be, for it entailed the conscious deployment of duplicitous and hypocritical postures.

All of Byron's early tales are written in this equivocal style – which has become, in Byron's hands, a vehicle of immensely greater range and complexity than Charles Skinner Matthews would have imagined possible, had he lived to see Byron's displays. But the more Byron developed his talent for equivocation, the more he built a store of explosive and dangerous contradic-tions into his work. Those contradictions came to a head during the separation controversy, and in "Fare Thee Well!" they finally reached their flash-point.

That the poem is not what the commonplace "sentimental" reading has taken it to be is exposed unmistakably for us in the initial period of its production and reception. Many readers were alive to its duplicities. The opening four lines, in fact, signal the poem's method by installing a grammatical pun of fundamental importance:

> Fare thee well! and if for ever –
> Still for ever, fare *thee well* –
> Even though unforgiving, never
> 'Gainst thee shall my heart rebel.

The sense here urges us to take Lady Byron's as the "unforgiving" heart, but the grammar tells us that heart is Byron's own. The poem will operate under this sign of contradiction to the end. Noteworthy too is Byron's assertion that, though his heart is unforgiving, it will never "rebel" against hers: as if he were imagining their separate and mutual antagonisms succeeding to a second, darker marriage which would "never" be dissolved or put asunder.

In fact, the poem is replete with this kind of complex double-speaking. Ponder, for example, these four lines:

> Would that breast by thee glanc'd over,
> Every inmost thought could show!
> Then thou would'st at last discover
> 'Twas not well to spurn it so –
>   (9–12)

It is a nice question what the inmost thoughts of an unforgiving and yet *un*rebellious heart would look like. Blake wrote a great deal of poetry about just such a heart, and he always imagined it as dangerous and fearful. And if we merely "glance over" Byron's lines here we may easily fail to "discover" their full truth: that the passage does not merely tell about the dark truths of unforgiving hearts, it is itself executing them. "'Twas not well to spurn it so" is a warning of possible danger, but as coming from *this* speaker it carries as well a threatening message and rhetoric.

Of course the poem delivers these kinds of messages obliquely, but in doing so it only increases the volatile character of the text. Because more is meant here than meets the eye directly, the censored materials exert enormous pressure for their freedom of complete expression. The parallel text in Canto III of *Childe Harold's Pilgrimage* meditates the situation by comparing it to the fury of a storm breaking over the Alps:

> Could I embody and unbosom now
> That which is most within me, – could I wreak
> My thoughts upon expression . . .
>
> (st. 97)

And so forth: he longs for "one word [of] Lightening," one word of comfort that would "lighten" his heart of its weight of sorrow, one word of insight that would "enlighten" his understanding of his situation, and one word of power that would, like a bolt of lightning, "blast" and purify those places "where desolation lurk[s]" (st. 95).

Like Manfred – another creature of the separation – who begs from Astarte "one word for mercy" (II, iv, 155), Childe Harold's longings remain incompletely satisfied. In all these cases the very effort to achieve some kind of completion, to reconcile the various contradictions, only seems to install them more deeply and more firmly.

Charles Skinner Matthews wrote gaily of his "mysterious" style of discourse, but it was a style which Byron, its supreme master, came to fear as he developed it through his Years of Fame. And well he might have feared it since it was a style which forced into the open the hypocrisies of those who read and write poetry as if it were an amusement or an ideology, as if it were something that could be controlled – enlisted to the purposes of either those who produce it or those who receive it. "Fare Thee Well!" is Byron's farewell to the illusion that he could be the master of the artistic powers which were given to him. Written in hopes that it would allow him to control the dangerous cross-currents of his circumstances in 1816, the poem's bad faith – which is its genius – worked to undermine the actual despair latent in such petty hopes.

If "Fare Thee Well!" precipitated an "overthrow" of Byron's many self-delusions, it also drew him toward new, and ultimately more profound, experiments in his "style of the mysterious." One of the most important of these experiments was *Manfred*, where Byron exorcised his demonic quest for autonomy and absolute power.[21] The exorcism succeeds when Manfred finally both realizes and accepts his limitations: at that point the spirits of evil, who are wedded to Manfred precisely through his own pretences of supreme knowledge and power over them, "disappear" (as the stage direction at III, iv, 141 declares). The meaning of the play hinges on the meaning it gives to Manfred's death, which here becomes – as in Byron's related poem "Prometheus" – a "victory" because it represents a human life lived at last in truth rather than in deception.

Manfred's adherence to self-deception is most dramatically figured in his quest for "self-oblivion" (I, i, 144). His guilt with respect to Astarte so preys upon him that his entire life is dominated by his pursuit of "Forgetfulness" (I, i, 136), along with that structure of delusory power erected to secure his desired object. At the absolute height of his powers when the play opens, Manfred is gradually stripped of his grandeurs – is gradually naturalized and humanized – until, at the end, he finally appears, briefly, in a human form. Byron's play deconstructs a panoply of illusions.

It does not, however, counsel renunciation; on the contrary, it reveals the pursuit of knowledge as the foundation of human living. The forgetfulness sought by Manfred is an illusion of "mercy" revealed when he tries to execute his quest for oblivion. This is the "meaning" of Manfred's dramatic history. The significance of Byron's *play*, on the other hand, lies in its continuation of Byron's poetic programs in the teeth of their own failures and inadequacies. *Manfred* is yet another work in his equivocal style – is, in a way, more outrageous and bold than *any* of his earlier exercises in double-speaking.

At the heart of the play is, of course, Manfred's unspeakable secret sin. Because it is left to be reconstructed by the reader through scattered and fragmentary texts in the play, some have argued that Byron deliberately left the nature of the sin vague and mystified. But this is by no means the case, as various early readers show. Reviewing the play in *Blackwood's*, John Wilson found it "difficult to comprehend distinctly the drift of the composition" as a whole, but he had no difficulty at all in understanding Manfred's guilt: "Manfred had conceived a mad and insane passion for his sister, named Astarte, and . . . she had, in consequence of their mutual guilt, committed suicide."[22]

The play is not at all equivocal on these matters. What *is* equivocal, as readers from the beginning have also shown, is the existence, and the relevance, of biographical parallels. When the early reviewers call attention to the possibility of such parallels, as nearly all of them do, they shrink back. The work becomes untouchable: on one hand they register the play as somehow an exercise in Byronic self-expression, but on the other they fear to pursue or articulate the possibilities. This fear stems from an inclination to draw exact parallels, and to find in the drawing of such parallels the "meaning" of the play. Thus the *Monitor*: "we are almost afraid to express our belief that [Astarte] was Manfred's sister."[23]

These interpretive urgencies are responding, correctly, to "the cumulative effect" of Byron's work. Byron taught his public how to read his poetry, led them to see (for example) that more was meant in *The Giaour* and the other tales than met the eye of one who simply read them as exotic tales of adventure. Thus a framework of interpretation was gradually formed from 1806 onwards in which Byron's readers were trained *not* to take his works as textually autonomous structures. The works continually solicited the reader to observe, and elaborate, various referential connections: political, biographical, historical.

So in *Manfred* Byron continued to utilize the opportunities which a poetry of "cumulative effects" opens up. Indeed, the storm raised by "Fare Thee Well!", and the bitter insights it brought – far from making him more cautious – seem only to have deepened his original poetic commitments.

Perhaps nothing in the play illustrates so well the great artistic advance represented by *Manfred* as the so-called "Incantation" in Act I, whose full significance we may fail to appreciate from our (belated) historical vantage. The following observations in the contemporary *Critical Review* are important to recall: that the "fine incantation, published before . . . was generally understood to be a poetic imprecation against [Lady Byron]; and its introduction here will not repel that interpretation, for the incantation is utterly unintelligible in its present connection."[24] These remarks, a wonderful mixture of blindness and insight, deserve close scrutiny.

First we must notice that the reviewer is calling attention to the fact that the passage in *Manfred* had been published the previous year (1816) as one of the "Other Poems" printed with *The Prisoner of Chillon*. There titled "The Incantation," it carried this brief headnote: "(The following Poem was a Chorus in an unfinished Witch Drama, which was begun some years ago.)" Secondly, one observes that the interpretation of the 1816 "Incantation" as a curse on Lady Byron was commonplace at the time. Finally, one notes the puzzlement of the reviewer in face of the 1817 "Incantation." Recalling as he does the earlier text and interpretation, he registers a disfunction in Byron's employment of the same text in *Manfred*. In relation to the play the text seems "utterly unintelligible," so the reviewer decides simply to read it as if it were the same as the 1816 "Incantation." In making this decision he only confirms his sense of the text's unintelligibility in the context of *Manfred*.

The reviewer's difficulties are basically generic in character. That is to say, he has no problem reading the 1816 "Incantation" as self-expressive – despite its headnote – because the text in *The Prisoner of Chillon and Other Poems* is printed among those "Other Poems" as if it were, like them, personal and lyrical. In *Manfred*, however, he expects it to function "dramatically" because *Manfred* is a "play" and not a "lyric poem." That he has these generic expectations is plain from the rest of the review, which criticizes *Manfred* for its heteroglot mixing "of fabulous beings at once from Grecian, Persian, and Gothic mythology." This is a criticism which was leveled by other contemporary reviewers, and it has been revived in our own day by Philip Martin.

But it is a mistaken view, for it fails to see that *Manfred* is a syncretic text bent upon collapsing, and then manipulating, its divergent types of material. *Manfred* is every bit as personal and self-expressive as "The Incantation" published in 1816 – the whole of *Manfred*. This fact is underscored by the witty double-speak of the prose headnote to the 1816 "Incantation," which purports to represent that text as a fragment from an unfinished play. But no one reading the 1816 text failed to understand Byron's mystification – he was flaunting it – and most probably understood quite clearly the wicked overtones in the phrase "an unfinished Witch Drama, which was begun some years ago." Translated, that carries a domestic and not a bibliographical meaning: "the period of my married life with Annabella Milbanke."

Transporting the text of the 1816 poem to *Manfred*, however, worked an entirely new structure of meanings into the words. To see how this operates we have to begin by understanding that the character Manfred functions in relation to Byron precisely as the character of Childe Harold. These figures typify the way Byron uses his poetical creatures (they can be either fictional or historical beings, either Lara and the Giaour or Tasso and Dante). They are creatures with no independent existence, and Byron manipulates them in his poems. They allow him to objectify and explore certain ideas, attitudes, and situations; they are vehicles in an experiment for knowledge, puppets in what he would later call a "mental theater."

In *Manfred* the 1816 "Incantation" is changed. No longer a veiled curse on Lady Byron, it becomes in the play a mysterious "voice" delivering its imprecation over the unconscious form of Byron's hero, his surrogate self, whose fallen body, described in the text as "*senseless*" (I, i, 190), becomes a poetic figure of Byron's own hypocrisies and self-delusions, and hence of his need – his desire – for greater self-understanding. In the words of that relatively unveiled text quoted earlier: "I have been cunning in mine overthrow / The careful pilot of my proper woe."

Like Shelley's Prometheus, Byron's Manfred exposes, and suffers in, his own heart of darkness. In this respect, Byron's execution of the play is a confession of guilt and an act of atonement. It is an act carrying, however, neither absolution nor reconciliation. When atonement occurs, guilt remains, its dark double. Like *Don Juan*, the play simply sustains its contradictions and irresolutions to the end; for the goal of this, like all of Byron's work, is neither absolution nor reconciliation, it is simply – profoundly – knowledge itself: not absolute knowledge or ultimate Truth, which Byron regards as illusions, but knowledge as a living commitment to truth, the whole truth, and nothing but the truth. Such a goal must of course remain inconclusive, an achievement to be constantly renewed – which is why, for Byron, knowledge is "Sorrow," and vice versa (I, i, 10). And that is the play's ultimate contradiction, which Byron simply leaves in contradiction.

One final thing to note is how this kind of writing attempts to abolish the separation between the act and the meaning of the poetic event. As a quest for knowledge, the play argues that no knowledge worth having can ever be possessed: *not* because it does not exist, but because human knowledge is always a deed of knowing rather than a form of information or wisdom. Furthermore, in thus seeking to turn his work into a deed of language, Byron implicates his audiences, exposes the social reciprocities that are set in motion through every form of writing and language use.

Toward the end of the last, unfinished Canto of *Don Juan* Byron was to say: "I leave the thing a problem, like all things." It would serve as a fitting epigraph for all his poetry, which cultivates an engagement – his own or ours – with various riddles, puns, secret messages, and coded talk. The "interpretation" of such work does not lie, however, in exposing some "truths" which are presumed to be locked or hidden away. Byron does not want hidden truths in his work; he wants a plain text, a dance of apparitions. The reader's task, then, is not so much to arrive at his meaning – to decipher the text – as it is to describe and retrace his complex acts of encipherment. It is a great lesson not in the meaning of things, but in how those meanings are made, how they are fitted out, how they are revealed through repeated disguise.

NOTES

1 For another, related discussion of this poem see my essay "The Significance of Biographical Context: Two Poems by Lord Byron," in *The Author in his Work*, ed. Louis L. Martz and Aubrey Williams (New Haven, Conn., 1978), pp. 347–66.

2 See *Byron's Letters and Journals*, ed. Leslie A. Marchand, 12 vols. (London, 1973–82), Vol. 10, pp. 197–9.

3 See *Lord Byron: The Complete Poetical Works*, ed. Jerome J. McGann (Oxford, 1980–), Vol. 1, pp. 51–2, 367. Texts from Byron are taken from this edition.

4 For a good discussion of this passage see Cecil Y. Lang, "Narcissus Jilted: Byron, *Don Juan*, and the Biographical Imperative," in *Historical Studies and Literary Criticism*, ed. Jerome J. McGann (Madison, 1985), especially pp. 168–9.

5 These general points are also developed in an essay written correlatively with this one, "Lord Byron's Twin Opposites of Truth," published in my *Towards a Literature of Knowledge* (Oxford, 1989), chapter 2.

6 (Cambridge, 1982). See for example p. 174, where Martin makes it clear that he values *Don Juan* because he takes it to be a poem Byron wrote entirely for himself, and a poem which Byron brings "under complete control." On the contrary, it seems to me that *Don Juan* is every bit as involved with its audiences as the rest of Byron's poetry; furthermore, it is most definitely *not* a poem "under complete control." Byron himself *says* it is a poem whose every next word comes to him as a surprise, and most readers value the poem for its appearances of spontaneity. Indeed, *Don Juan* affects to be a poem written "under inspiration" rather than control, and is, in this respect, very like Blake's "dictated" works. Unlike Blake's, Byron's theory of "inspiration" is secularized, and indeed "inspiration" seems, in his poetry, precisely a function of his desire to solicit interactions with others in the making of the poetry.

7 See Reiman's *The Romantics Reviewed, 1793–1830: Contemporary Reviews of British Romantic Writers* (New York, 1972), Part B, Byron, IV, 1779.

8 The essential critical discussions of the poem are the following: *The Works of Lord Byron: Poetry*, ed. E. H. Coleridge, 7 vols. (London, 1898–1904), Vol. 3, pp. 531–5; David V. Erdman, " 'Fare Thee Well!' – Byron's Last Days in England," *Shelley and His Circle: 1773–1832*, ed. Kenneth Neill Cameron (Cambridge, Mass., 1970), Vol. 4, pp. 638–65; W. Paul Elledge, "Talented Equivocation: Byron's 'Fare Thee Well!,' " *Keats–Shelley Journal*, 35 (1986), pp. 42–61; see also *Complete Poetical Works, op cit.*, Vol. 3, pp. 493–4.

9 See Ethyl Colburn Mayne, *Byron*, 2nd edn, rev. (London, 1924), p. 256, and Erdman, p. 642 and n.

10 See *The Letters of William and Dorothy Wordsworth*, ed. Ernest de Selincourt, 2nd edn., rev. by Mary Moorman and Alan G. Hill (Oxford, 1970), Vol. 3, Part 2, p. 304. Wordsworth's reading is given in a letter to John Scott, who put out the unauthorized *Champion* printing of Byron's poem.

11 Quoted in Mayne, *Byron*.

12 *Critical Review*, 5th series (Dec., 1816), pp. 577–8.

13 Quoted in Malcolm Elwin, *Lord Byron's Wife* (New York, 1962), p. 394.

14 *Ibid.*, p. 400.

15 Elledge, "Talented Equivocation," p. 43.

16 Elwin, *Lord Byron's Wife*, p. 409.

17 Elwin, *Ibid.*, p. 448.

18 Doris Langley Moore, *The Late Lord Byron* (London, 1961), p. 164.

19 Elledge, "Talented Equivocation," p. 44n.

20 Quoted in Louis Crompton, *Byron and Greek Love* (Berkeley and Los Angeles, 1985), pp. 128–9.
21 In relation to the following discussion, two excellent critical essays are pertinent: Stuart M. Sperry's "Byron and the Meaning of *Manfred*," *Criticism*, 16 (1974), pp. 189–202 and Daniel M. McVeigh's "Manfred's Curse," *Studies in English Literature*, 22 (1982), pp. 601–12.
22 *Blackwood's*, Vol. 1 (June, 1817), p. 291.
23 Vol. 1 (1817), p. 172.
24 Fifth series, Vol. 5 (June, 1817), p. 624.

IO

DON JUAN AND THE REVISIONARY SELF

PETER J. MANNING

ASKED by John Murray, his publisher, to retouch *Hints from Horace* and the third and fourth cantos of *Don Juan*, Byron refused in a simile that seems a paradigm of Romantic spontaneity and independence: "it is all very well – but I can't *furbish*. – I am like the tyger (in poesy) if I miss my first Spring – I go growling back to my Jungle. – There is no second. – I can't correct – I can't – & I won't." And yet Byron buttresses this forceful expression of the naturalness of his writing by invoking precedent:

Nobody ever succeeds in it great or small. – Tasso remade the whole of his Jerusalem but who ever reads that version? – all the world goes to the first. – Pope *added* to the "Rape of the Lock" – but did not reduce it. – You must take my things as they happen to be – if they are not likely to suit – reduce their *estimate* accordingly.[1]

Despite the protest, revision was intrinsic to Byron's manner of composition, but Byronic revision takes the form of vital accretion rather than craftsmanly polish. The Texas variorum edition of *Don Juan*, which highlights in critical essays by T. G. Steffan the stages it presents of the poem's growth from manuscript, and the recent Clarendon edition by Jerome McGann witness a rapidity of second thoughts, new directions, and expansions for which the simile of the tiger seems wholly apt.[2]

The ideal of unmediated expression nonetheless conceals a history. Byron was chiefly adamant to reject any notion that he might tailor his work to suit public taste. From the start of his career, however, he had been unusually sensitive to the reception of his poetry. When some members of his Southwell circle objected to the erotic verses included in his anonymous and privately printed collection, *Fugitive Pieces* (1806), Byron burnt the edition; its successor, *Poems on Various Occasions* (1807), omitted the lyrics which had aroused censure. Likewise, the attack by the *Edinburgh Review* on his first published volume, *Hours of Idleness* (1807), prompted Byron to issue the second edition under the less provoking banner of what had formerly been the subtitle, *Poems Original and Translated* (1808), and to drop from it the offending preface.[3]

Byron might proclaim a lordly indifference, but he remained uncommonly attuned to the expectations of his readers. As his protest to Murray reveals, questions of revision were inseparable from those of the market-place. No one knew the connection better than his publisher; though Byron periodically castigated him for being a tradesman and no gentleman, Murray withstood the poet's fits of abuse, and for a decade shaped his career. Resourcefully cajoling Byron to continue in genres he calculated would sell and incurring accusations of negligence in order to discourage others, surreptitiously circulating or adroitly publicizing some poems while suppressing or excising others, Murray carefully fostered the image of the author from whom his wealth sprang.[4] Byron's circuit of revision passes through Murray and Murray's literary advisors to the public they represented, and it is the effects of this process of exchange upon the self produced in Byron's poetry, rather than particular textual changes, that this essay examines.[5]

Telling Murray in July 1812 of the "high pleasure" it had given him, Walter Scott described *Childe Harold's Pilgrimage* as "certainly the most original poem which we have had this many a day."[6] Six years later Scott took the occasion of reviewing the fourth canto of *Childe Harold* to locate the originality which had earned Byron instant fame in "the novelty of an author speaking in his own person." Byron was the first poet since the time of Cowper, Scott commented, "who, either in his own person, or covered by no very thick disguise, had directly appeared before the public, an actual living man expressing his own sentiments, thoughts, hopes, and fears."[7] Byron's dissolution of the boundaries between artistic merit and force of personality which the nascent profession of literary criticism was determined to uphold did not go unchallenged. "He has awakened, by literary exertion, a more intense interest in his person than ever before resulted from literature," conceded John Scott, the editor of *The London Magazine*, but he protested the endless slippage between the poetry and the man which had elevated Byron to one of the towering "objects" of the age. "Lord Byron's creations," Scott argued, "are addressed to the poetical sympathies of his readers while their main interest is derived from awakening a recollection of some fact of the author's life, or a conviction of an analogy to the author's own character."[8]

For John Scott the equivocation between life and art Byron exploited was a moral "confusion" to be resisted, but we may profit from his diagnosis to ask what kind of "person" is created by "literature." As an example of the obliquity of Byron's supposedly direct self-revelation, consider Childe Harold's "Good-Night." This ten-stanza lyric, placed after stanza thirteen in the first canto of

Childe Harold's Pilgrimage, shifts the perspective from the narrator and his lightly mocking Spenserianisms to the protagonist himself. The song, "pour'd" out "when no strange ear was listening," promises inwardness, and the conversations it briefly dramatizes figure William Fletcher and Robert Rushton, two servants who accompanied Byron on his journey.[9] Yet this confessional moment, authenticated by such autobiographical detail, is also thoroughly rooted in convention, as Byron advises in the Preface: "The 'Good Night', in the beginning of the first canto, was suggested by 'Lord Maxwell's Good Night', in the Border Minstrelsy, edited by Mr. Scott." If, to employ John Scott's terms, the Harold who Byron insisted was no more than a "fictitious character . . . introduced for the sake of giving some connexion to the piece" functioned as a lure to focus attention on Byron, it is also true that "Byron" was born (as "Childe Harold") through his revision of literary tradition.

The observation is not new, but it perhaps becomes more interesting if extended to *Don Juan*. "Adieu!, adieu! my native shore," exclaims Harold; "Yon Sun that sets upon the sea / We follow in his flight; / Farewell awhile to him and thee, / My native Land – Good Night" (I, 118–25). Seven years afterwards Canto II of *Don Juan* brings a recurrence of the *topos* in Juan's departure from Spain: "'Farewell, my Spain! a long farewell!' he cried, / 'Perhaps I may revisit thee no more, / But die, as many an exiled heart hath died, / Of its own thirst to see again thy shore'" (18). The prematurely jaded Harold, in flight to any fresh scene, is reversed in the homesick Juan, separated from his first erotic happiness with Julia. "Beloved Julia, hear me still beseeching!" cries Juan in *his* shipboard lyric, only to be cut off by the narrator: "(Here he grew inarticulate with reaching)" (20). This notorious parenthesis measures the worldly narrator's distance from Juan's youthful despair, but the echo casts back at the same time over Harold's.

Between these two instances comes another, at the opening of the third canto of *Childe Harold's Pilgrimage* (1816): "Once more upon the waters! yet once more! / And the waves bound beneath me as a steed / That knows his rider. Welcome to their roar! / Swift be their guidance, wheresoe'er it lead!" (2). The three form a series, which proceeds by turning upon a previous stage: Childe Harold on "Lord Maxwell's Good Night," the grandiloquent narrator of the third canto on the Harold of the first, the narrator of *Don Juan* on Byron's former excesses, whether embodied in fictional characters like Harold or Juan or *in propria persona*. At each stage, moreover, Byron recalls his readers to the previous ones. Canto III of *Childe Harold's Pilgrimage* simultaneously announces its connection to the first two cantos and encourages readers to note the distance Byron had travelled: "In my youth's summer I did sing of One, / The wandering outlaw of his own dark mind . . . in that Tale I find / The furrows of long thought, and dried up tears, / . . . Since my young days of passion – joy, or pain, / Perchance my heart and harp have lost a string, / And both may jar" (3–4). The melancholy grandeur of this canto *Don Juan* then subjects to counterpoint. The later poem repeats the "chiefless castles breathing stern farewells / From gray but leafy walls, where Ruin greenly dwells" of Harold's Rhine journey and the interpolated lyric "The castled crag of Drachenfels" (46–56), but hovers adroitly between meditation and brisk comedy:

> Ye glorious Gothic scenes! how much ye strike
>   All phantasies, not even excepting mine:
> A grey wall, a green ruin, rusty pike,
>   Make my soul pass the equinoctial line
> Between the present and past worlds, and hover
> Upon their airy confine, half-seas-over.
>
> But Juan posted on through Manheim, Bonn,
>   Which Drachenfels frowns over like a spectre
> Of the good feudal times for ever gone,
>   On which I have no time just now to lecture.
> (X, 61–2)

Through such self-reference Byron presents readers at each moment with a reminder of his entire career thus far, enticing them into the game of weighing continuities and contrasts, to construct from the play of speakers who are but temporary positions in the continuing process the personality they felt as Byron.

Rather than seeking to calibrate the distinction between such sly invitations to collaborate and the exhibition of sorrow John Scott condemned as merely a means "to tickle the idle, impertinent, and most unpoetical curiosity of the public," I should like to pursue what unites the two modes. Walter Scott's remark that in Byron readers experienced "an author *speaking* in his own person . . . an *actual living* man expressing his own sentiments" (emphasis added) provides the clue. These are the characteristics of an oral poet, and Scott's disdain for Byron's self-display can be reinscribed as the collision between a style with dominant oral traits and the aggressive print culture of the magazines and quarterlies.[10]

The clash was formulated in almost those terms by one of Byron's shrewdest critics, Francis Jeffrey. *The Corsair* and *The Bride of Abydos* led Jeffrey to propose a cyclical theory of literature, in which Byron's works mark a revolutionary return to the "strong sensations" of primitive poetry. As the progressive refinement of society becomes cloying, it generates the desire for a "more enthusiastic, authoritative and impassioned" literature. Poetry, Jeffrey argued, at such a moment in history "naturally goes back to those themes and characters which animated the energetic lays of its first rude inventors," revives "the feats of chivalry, and the loves of romance . . . with more than their primitive wildness and ardour," and imitates and surpasses "the old vulgar ballads . . . without dread of their coarseness." For Jeffrey Byron symbolized "this great transformation."[11]

The accuracy of Jeffrey's account matters less than that a founder and editor of *The Edinburgh Review* should have conceived Byron's appeal is at once a throwback and an innovative reaction to that diffusion of cultural standards of which his own journal was a principal agent. As an aristocrat Byron stood outside the pale of professional men, Whig or Tory, who oversaw the reviews; the invocations of his ancestors and their traditions of honor, the giving away of the copyrights to his poems and his contempt when Leigh Hunt spoke of literature as a "profession" instead of an "art" or "attribute" (*BLJ*, Vol. 6, p. 47), and the well-publicized amours which fascinated just in proportion as they violated the norms of the reading public beyond the Regency circles in which he moved, mark Byron's allegiance to an older code, personal and familial, whose supersession by the impersonal laws of commerce, state regulation, and respectability *The Edinburgh Review* was hastening.[12]

The exposure to an oral tradition provided by his experience in the East would have heightened Byron's predilection for a poetry with the immediacy of speech. Jerome McGann points out that in the final note to *The Giaour* Byron acknowledges a model in a story he had chanced to hear "recited by one of the coffee-house story-tellers who abound in the Levant, and sing or recite their narratives." McGann seizes this hint to interpret Byron's fragmented story, with its multiple narrators, as an imitation of the "virtuoso production" of such a performer: "*The Giaour* really has only one narrator, the ballad singer, who assumes different roles at different moments."[13] Byron met such virtuosity again at Milan in 1816, when the famous *improvisatore* Tommaso Sgricci "astonished" him by his fluency (*BLJ*, 5, p. 125); he heard Sgricci again at Venice in 1817, at the time of *Beppo*, and at Ravenna in 1820, in the midst of *Don Juan* (*BLJ*, 7, p. 47).[14]

Whether headlong and abrupt like the Turkish tales, declamatory like *Childe Harold's Pilgrimage*, or colloquial like *Beppo* and *Don Juan*, all Byron's poems proceed from a vividly dramatic narrator. Critics who read the flamboyance of this figure as the egomania of the author denounced his corruption and self-advertisement; John Scott, subtle enough to understand the Byronic narrator as a "highly charged and artificially quickened character," still accused Byron of factitious and hypocritical exaggeration.[15] In the oral universe, however, the boast is the expected gesture through which the hero affirms his glory; consider the vaunts of warriors in the Homeric poems, which contemporary scholarship was revealing as closer to ballads and tales than to the standards of epic pronounced by neo-Classicism. The hero anchors the oral world; statements about its nature originate from his perspective and are guaranteed by his presence. Nonetheless the identity of the hero of epic depends on the recognition won by his deeds; his status requires confirmation from others. This backdrop suggests the import of the contest between Byron and the journals; though obscured by the exotic surfaces of his work, the struggle enacted a significant debate over the location of knowledge and power. For the poet, they reside in the gifted individual; for the reviewers, they are to be fixed in the uniform discourses and structures of a growing commercial society.

Jeffrey recognized that the revival of primitive genres "in a late stage of civilization" did not produce exact copies. He saw that the moderns had joined to the "strong passions" which attracted them a psychological probing "of the i erior of human nature" alien to the originals: "The minds of the great agents must be unmasked for us – and all the anatomy of their throbbing bosoms laid open to our gaze."[16] Jeffrey thus explains the intense self-concentration others vilified in Byron as a symptom of the age, but without seeking to specify further the changes in literary production which reinforced it.[17]

The loose construction of *Childe Harold's Pilgrimage* and *Don Juan*, their episodic structure and additive, aggregative character, their repetitiousness and copiousness, are the natural means of imagining extended narrative in an oral context.[18] The seeming anomaly which needs to be resolved is that the conditions of literature in the early nineteenth century were scarcely those of an oral culture. As Jeffrey realized, in reviving an older mode in a new environment Byron inevitably revised it. Byron the best-seller, to borrow the title of a lecture by Andrew Rutherford, was a phenomenon possible only within a market supplied by organized channels of printing and distribution, fueled by competition and the sleights of publicity of which Murray was a master.[19] The organs which rebuked Byron spread his reputation while boosting their own circulation. The vastly enlarged and diversifying readership from which Murray and Byron profited, however, rendered it difficult for an author to know for whom he was writing. A mass audience, capable of purchasing ten thousand copies of *The Corsair* in a single day, but composed of myriad strata, different in education, taste, and values, is the antithesis of the cohesive community in which the oral poet thrives. But, as recent studies of nineteenth-century narrative have noted, the very absence of actual face-to-face encounter led writers seeking to control the uncertainties of reception to mime it within their work.[20] The amorphous audience is molded into ideal form by anticipatory representation in the text. To woo his largely unknown public the writer must simultaneously fasten its attention on him, seduce their affections, and sustain the attraction against the rival claims of others in a burgeoning field. Byron, "speaking in his own person" and laying open the anatomy of his "throbbing bosom," furnished the simulacrum of intimacy the new readership craved; the popularity of *Childe Harold's Pilgrimage* was capitalized upon in the repetitions-with-variations of *The Giaour*, *The Corsair*, *Lara*, and so on until "The Byronic Hero" became an established commodity.

Byron took advantage of the disparities between his oral manner and the medium of print to achieve some of his most typical effects. With the Siege of Ismail Byron offers an epic scene that equals Homer "in blood" (*Don Juan* VII, 80), but a surprising reference to polite literature breaks the intensity: the beleaguered Russian troops are said to have been "reduced, as is a bulky volume / Into an elegant extract (much less massy) / Of heroism" (VIII, 34). *Don Juan* is filled with devices which surround the voice to which we listen with insistent reminders that we are holding a book: strained rhymes carried across line endings, jokes for the eye such as the stanza made up of Latin prescriptions for Juan's illness (X, 41), puns dependent on spacing and typography, such as "I wonder . . . if a man's name in a *bulletin* / May make up for a *bullet in* his body?" (VII, 21). Consider again Byron's reflections at the outset of the third canto of *Childe Harold's Pilgrimage* on its precursor four years earlier: "in that Tale I find / The furrows of long thought, and dried up tears." Genuinely oral narrative has no past; whatever previous materials it needs must be brought into the present of the ongoing recitation. Byron's "I find," in contrast, points to the continued material existence of the first volume of the poem, available for Byron and his audience alike to reread. "I rattle on exactly as I'd talk / With any body in a ride or walk," says the narrator of *Don Juan* (XV, 19), but as the years went by such open-ended indeterminacy was stabilized by the books in which it was preserved. New publications were soon incorporated in Murray's expanding serial editions, physically embodying the past of the canon. "Hail, Muse! *et cetera*," the third canto of *Don Juan* begins: "We left Juan sleeping, / Pillow'd upon a fair and happy breast" (III, 1). Juan had been "left" two years before, but any reader needing to refresh his memory could easily fill the gap between Cantos I–II of 1819 and Cantos III–IV–V of 1821 by taking the first volume off the shelf.

The self represented in *Don Juan* advances by revisionary recurrence to its prior manifestations:

> Even I – albeit I'm sure I did not know it,
>   Nor sought of foolscap subjects to be king, –
> Was reckoned, a considerable time,
> The grand Napoleon of the realms of rhyme.

> But Juan was my Moscow, and Faliero
>   My Leipsic, and my Mont Saint Jean seems Cain
>   (XI, 55–6)

The wry, defiant identification with Napoleon even in defeat exemplifies Byron's heroic theatricality, evident as well in the enfolding into his current position of how he "was reckoned" by others in the past. His confidence that his readers were cognizant of the abortive staging of *Marino Faliero* and the outcries caused by *Don Juan* and *Cain* is performative: the allusions make Byron's past reception part of his self-representation.

From the very beginning of *Don Juan* Byron plays with the public perception of him. "I'm a plain man, and in a single station," says the narrator, but the poem was known to be Byron's despite appearing anonymously. The *persona*, and the subsequent clinching couplet – "Oh! ye lords of ladies intellectual, / Inform us truly, have they not hen-peck'd you all?" (I, 22) – rely for their maliciously witty particularity on the reader's awareness of Lady Byron's mathematical interests and the scandal of the separation. *Blackwood's* denunciation is merely the most violent testimony that Byron could draw upon his status as a public figure to underwrite his self-presentation. "Those who are acquainted, (as who is not?) with the main incidents in the private life of Lord Byron," *Blackwood's* revealingly declared, "will scarcely believe" that he has "commence[d] a filthy and impious poem, with an elaborate satire on the character and manners of his wife."[21] This flirtation at the borders between art and life, this calculated provocation of his audience, signals the continuous dialogue of *Don Juan* with its readers – (the author of *Childe Harold's Pilgrimage* "a plain man"?) – and how thoroughly the Byronic self exists in exchange with the social world around it. The quick satisfaction of the expressed need of "I want a hero: an uncommon want" by the half-capricious "taking" of "our ancient friend Don Juan" in the first stanza of *Don Juan* would be little more than a burlesque of the invocations of epic tradition were it not uttered by the author who had stamped his name on the Byronic hero and whose love affairs were public property.

A brief contrast with Wordsworth will accent the public and processual nature of the self in *Don Juan*. In *The Prelude* Wordsworth seeks to accommodate his experience to an overall design in which "in the end / All [is] gratulant if rightly understood" (XII, 384–5). Though the text subverts this program and betrays the shifting intentions of its prolonged composition, Wordsworth characterizes *The Prelude* as an effort to "fix the wavering balance of [his] mind" (I, 650), and to make the "rigorous inquisition" (I, 159) necessary before advancing to the "honorable toil" (I, 653) of his philosophic poem, *The Recluse*.[22] To compose *The Prelude* was also to compose his life and establish himself as The Poet. So grave a drama could be played only before an encouraging audience: the ideal reader projected by what Wordsworth referred to as "the poem to Coleridge" assumes Coleridge's attitude, "prompt / In sympathy" (I, 645–6). *The Prelude* engages the French Revolution and other public events, but remained private, unseen except by a circle of intimates and unpublished during Wordsworth's lifetime. Wordsworth confesses that it is a "Hard task to analyse a soul, in which / . . . each most obvious and particular thought – / . . . / Hath no beginning" (II, 232–7), but the project of *The Prelude* required grounding the self in formative childhood experience. In *Don Juan in Context* Jerome McGann has written wonderfully well about the serial character of *Don Juan*, which he aptly calls a poem "always in transition"; here I should like to stress simply that Byron gains his freedom to move forward unconstrainedly by forgoing such notions of origin.[23] Unlike Wordsworth, concerned to fashion an integrated self and a coherent narrative, Byron splits and multiplies into his characters. It is tempting to identify Byron with the narrator, but his upbringing with the widowed Mrs. Byron underlies Juan's with Donna Inez, and the strife of Inez and Don José echoes his marriage to Annabella Milbanke. No single voice is authoritatively "Byron," and indeed the self represented in Cantos I and II of *Don Juan* is not acknowledged as Byron's at all: the narrator is nameless and no link is admitted between him and Juan. Liberated from any fidelity to autobiographical actuality, Byron's past becomes the stuff for endless fictional revision. The Spanish cantos of *Don Juan* offer one oblique account of Byron's life in England, the English cantos, four years later, a revision, with the orphan Leila occupying the role of the innocent formerly taken by Juan. Truth in *Don Juan* is versional: "The very shadow of true Truth would shut / Up annals, revelations, poesy, / And prophecy" (XI, 37) proclaims the narrator, and shutting up is what he refuses to do.

Don Juan aims at unceasing invention, not stable and conclusive truth. This goal marks Byron's affiliations with the older oral traditions of a speaker in immediate contact with an audience whom he must arouse and persuade. The rhetor seeks not "truth," but what can be said. Despite the increasing presence of the narrator as *Don Juan* proceeds, Byron aims at diversity and abundance rather than the evolution and maintenance of a privileged perspective from which to order experience.[24] "I *have* no plan – I *had* no plan – but I had or have materials," Byron told Murray (*BLJ*, 6, p. 207); as the narrator admits (or boasts?), "I write what's uppermost, without delay" (XIV, 7), forsaking Wordsworthian meditative depth for immediacy. John Wilson Croker brilliantly captured, though he did not approve, the principle of Byron's "wonderful fertility of thought and facility of expression":

the Protean style of "Don Juan," instead of checking (as the fetters of rhythm generally do) his natural activity, not only gives him wider limits to range in, but even generates a more roving disposition. I dare swear, if the truth were known, that his digressions and repetitions generate one another, and that the happy jingle of some of his comical rhymes has led him on to episodes of which he never originally thought;

(Smiles, 1, p. 414)

As the text, so the self.[25] Pondering its fluidity, the narrator reflects: "I almost think that the same skin / For one without – has two or three within" (XVII, 11). The one that emerges at any given moment will have been summoned by the occasion. The self is not a static essence, but a relation revising itself in response to others. Not surprisingly, the view *in* the texts is consonant with the compositional history *of* the texts: even Byron's most apparently revelatory moments float within this collaborative circuit. Through the relationship between the protagonist and his sister in *Manfred* Byron teased a public tantalized by rumors of his incest with Augusta, but when Murray's advisors criticized the third act, the poet who said "I can't correct" agreed that it was "certainly d—d bad': "I will try & reform it – or re-write it altogether" (*BLJ*, 5, p. 211), and he did. Similarly, Byron dropped Childe Harold, once Childe Burun in the manuscripts, and the guise in which he had appeared "speaking in his own person," because, as he explained in the Preface to the fourth canto, he "had become weary of drawing a line which every one seemed determined not to perceive." The concurrent exchange of this sublime style for the worldly nonchalance of *Beppo*, which Jerome McGann has designated "essentially a very personal poem," was nonetheless sponsored by Murray.[26] "Give me a poem," he wrote Byron in January 1817, "a good Venetian tale describing manners formerly from the story itself, and now from your own observations, and call it 'Marianna'" (Smiles, 1, p. 372). Marianna Segati was Byron's mistress; the following August Byron heard from her husband the anecdote which became the basis for *Beppo*, written in October. The success of *Beppo* encouraged both Byron and Murray to continue in the same vein; in the same week of July 1818 that Byron began *Don Juan* his publisher wrote to ask "Have you not another lively tale like 'Beppo'? Or will you not give me some prose in three volumes? – all the adventures that you have undergone, seen, heard of, or imagined, with your reflections on life and manners" (Smiles, 1, p. 396). Murray fostered the personal qualities of *Don Juan* because he wanted a sensational work to "open [his] campaign in November"; the motto (subsequently canceled) Byron affixed to *Don Juan*, "Domestica facta," warned Murray that he was getting more than he bargained for, but such urgings make clear that the self-disclosures of *Don Juan* were of a kind Murray had stimulated to suit the market.

Even Byron's autobiographical *Memoirs*, deemed so frank as to be burnt after his death, arose in answer to his publisher. Since January 1817 Murray had been asking for some 'prose, which I will engage to keep sacredly secret and publish anonymously," requesting Byron to "keep an exact Journal of all you see, and write me faithful accounts of sights, curiosities, shows, and manners, etc." (Smiles, 1, p. 371). In July 1818 Byron replied: you "speak of prose – I think of writing (for your full edition) some memoirs of my life to prefix to them" (*BLJ*, 6, p. 59). Byron presented the *Memoirs* to Thomas Moore, and in April 1821 advised Murray: "As you say my 'prose' is good – why don't you treat with *Moore* for the reversion of the Memoirs" (*BLJ*, 8, p. 102). The seriocomic sequence in which the publisher consented to destroy the *Memoirs* in order to protect Byron's reputation from the indiscretions he had called forth shows the suspension of the Byronic self in the revisionary claims of literary production.

The personality known as "Byron" habitually developed through this give-and-take with his readers. In the final stanza of the first canto of *Childe Harold's Pilgrimage* Byron hinted that continuation depended on the favor of the "stern Critic" (I, 93); in the Preface to *The Corsair* he pledged no further to "trespass on public patience." These bids for applause produced their desired effect; Jeffrey concluded his review by declaring that "We hope he is not in earnest in meditating even a temporary divorce from his Muse.'[27] Byron orchestrated such displays, converting the periodicals into the chorus of his drama. McGann observes in DON JUAN *in Context* that *Don Juan* "is based upon the structure of human talk, which is dialectical without being synthetic" (p. 111), to which one should add that the actual context was formed by the reviewers, and Byron's talk was with them. When William Roberts, the editor of *The British Review*, was foolish enough to rise to the bait of Byron's jibe in *Don Juan* – "For fear some prudish readers should grow skittish, / I've bribed my grandmother's review – the British" (I, 209) – by printing a denial, Byron seized the opening it afforded to insert a "Letter to the Editor of 'My Grandmother's Review'" in the first number of *The Liberal*. Should Jeffrey complain that Byron's abuse of Southey "does no honour either to the taste or the temper of the noble author," he was sure to find the charge of injustice rebounded upon him:

> Some reckon women by their Suns or Years,
>   I rather think the Moon should date the dears.
>
> And why? Because she's changeable and chaste.
>   I know no other reason, whatsoe'er
> Suspicious people, who find fault in haste,
>   May choose to tax me with; which is not fair,
> Nor flattering to "their temper or their taste,"

> As my friend Jeffrey writes with such an air:
> However, I forgive him, and I trust
> He will forgive himself; – if not, I must.
>
> (X, 10–11)[28]

With such assurance Byron converted attacks into pretexts for further performance. One would not know from this insouciance that Byron never met Jeffrey. The staged camaraderie disguises the institutional relationship of author and reviewer, denying the primacy the quarterlies claimed and holding a contest carried out in print within the fiction of a conversation among friends.

The publication of *Don Juan* over several years enabled Byron repeatedly to situate his writing against the criticisms passed on earlier cantos. The continuous testing of, and influence by, the audience through which *Don Juan* develops is epitomized by Byron's explanation in Canto IV that, having "hear[d] that several people take exception / At the first two books having too much truth," he will "make Don Juan leave the ship" before Juan and the brunette with whom he is imprisoned become erotically involved, adding that "the publisher declares, in sooth, / Through needles" eyes it easier for the camel is / To pass, than those two cantos into families" (IV, 97). Byron never forgets, or lets us forget, that *Don Juan* is a text shaped within the literary market, subject to the pressures of opinion and the means of distribution. Byron described the third canto of *Don Juan* as "damned modest," confessing that "the outcry has frightened me" (*BLJ*, 6, p. 232), and such reminders built into his text trace the obstacles his writing navigates, making visible the conditions which shaped the particular form of his writing and the self represented in it.

The charges of sexual license provoked by *Don Juan* followed the accusations of cynicism levied against *Childe Harold's Pilgrimage*. The accusation, redoubled after the bleakness of the shipwreck in the second canto of *Don Juan*, Byron takes up and neatly reverses: "Why do they call me misanthrope? Because / *They hate me, not I them*: And here we'll pause" (IX, 21). Byron both perpetuates and repudiates the label of skeptic: "They accuse me – *Me* – the present writer of / The present poem – of – I know not what, – / A tendency to under-rate and scoff / At human power and virtue, and all that" (VII, 3). These gestures ask further analysis.

Some words of Gerald Bruns are apropos: "Is not skepticism, after all, the philosophical equivalent of a rhetorical habit of mind? . . . the motive for speech is the perpetual difficulty of making sense. Indeed the plenum of discourse rests upon the impossibility of a philosophical language."[29] Critics have often cited the couplet of the following stanza:

> Also observe, that like the great Lord Coke,
> (See Littleton) whene'er I have expressed

> Opinions two, which at first sight may look
>   Twin opposites, the second is the best.
> Perhaps I have a third too in a nook,
>   Or none at all – which seems a sorry jest;
> But if a writer should be quite consistent,
> How could he possibly show things existent?
>
> (XV, 87)

Self in this passage is only mercurial motion, its present state twinned by its opposite, and always about to be superseded by a third state, or perhaps by nothing at all. Byron balances the possibility of the abyss, however, by invoking the institution which stabilizes society, the law. Byron's insinuation that his most lawless behavior is perfectly lawful, or at least regular and lawlike, is a *jeu d'ésprit*, but one that contains an important truth. "Coke upon Littleton" was the standard authority on the law of property, but as its short title suggests, its authority evolved from layers of commentary and revision. Common law depends not on a transcendental origin, but on the adequacy with which it serves social ends. It remains inseparable from the human agents signaled by the proper names of Coke and Littleton and forever subject to, and available for, renewed interpretation.

Let me conclude by drawing together the various lines along which I have conducted this argument: the legal, the rhetorical, the oral, the journals. From its beginning with Alfonso's cuckolding by Julia *Don Juan* is concerned with the role of the law. That case exposes the inextricability of the private and passionate from the public and legal. Alfonso's lawyer, so "there were quarrels, / cared not for the cause, / Knowing they must be settled by the laws" (I, 159). As *Blackwood's* saw, Byron employs the story to present his side of the separation from Annabella, and he repeatedly emphasizes its double location:

> The nine days' wonder which was brought to light,
> And how Alfonso sued for a divorce,
> Were in the English newspapers, of course.
>
> If you would like to see the whole proceedings,
>   The depositions, and the cause at full,
> The names of all the witnesses, the pleadings
>   Of counsel to nonsuit, or to annul,
> There's more than one edition, and the readings
> Are various, but they none of them are dull
>
> (I, 188–9)

Don Juan is the poetic counter-argument to these legal records, an extra-legal *apologia* for Byron's worth. Unlike most defenses, Byron's shocks further, but it may nonetheless be seen as attempting to win over its audience, by the sheer dint of presence establishing the *ethos* of its speaker. The mockery of legal authority in these stanzas effects the transfer of the case from the courtroom to the tribunal of public opinion. But that tribunal was directed by journals such as *The Edinburgh Review*, of which the editor, Jeffrey, and major contributors, such as Henry Brougham, were lawyers.

Though Byron resists the claim to supremacy of the discourse of law, he inhabited a world in which those claims were inescapable. We might therefore think of his rhetoric as derived from the court and the *polis* as well as the realm of theatrical performance to which it is often assimilated, as here. Thomas Sloane has recently observed that reviving Ciceronian rhetoric would enable us "to see the forensic as paradigmatic of rhetorical thinking itself."[30] Byron's habitual proing-and-conning and trying out both sides of a case point to the broadly humanistic notion of truth as a process of testing, of discovery by challenge and debate. What Croker (another lawyer, instrumental to *The Quarterly Review*) apprehended as the merely random exfoliation of *Don Juan* belongs to a tradition of invention conceived as inherently dialogical, operating within shared but evolving conditions. Immersed in the particular situation, constantly assuming and addressing an audience, shying away from the universals and abstractions of philosophy, Byron aims always to persuade men to act, to decide, to approve: to approve his causes because approving him. His behavior, comprehensible in an oral hero or a pleading orator, comes to look like egotism only when traditional concepts of authority have yielded to the notions of originality and individual psychology which the reviews propagated: Byron's "genius" is the licensed exception against which the new norms can be articulated.

The endless self-revision of the Byronic self thus articulates a social process. "I don't know that there may be much ability / Shown in this sort of desultory rhyme," Byron disingenuously commented, "but there's a conversational facility, / Which may round off an hour upon a time" (XV, 20). Like Falstaff's wit, Byron's force propeled the contributions of others, not merely those of professional reviewers but also of all those who were provoked by his performance to enter the lists. Whether they were denunciations from "Presbyter Anglicanus" or witty rejoinders like "John Bull's Letter to Lord Byron," Byron engendered an ever-expanding literature that was the material body of his fame.[31] Byron provided the new print culture an icon to work upon; they provided him with material with which to sustain and transform his drama. Carried out in public, and enfolding the network to which it responds, Byron's textual self-revision bound his readers to him and illuminates the grounding of the self in dialogue and exchange. "Speaking in his own voice," the phenomenon his critics perceived as self-absorbed to the point of nihilism, Byron lays open to view the operations by which writers and reviewers together mapped the contours of the contemporary institution of literature.

NOTES

1 *Byron's Letters and Journals*, ed. Leslie A. Marchand, 12 vols. (Cambridge, Mass., 1973–82), Vol. 7, p. 229. Byron repeated the simile a year later in refusing to recast *Cain*; see Vol. 9, p. 54. Marchand's edition is hereafter cited parenthetically in the text as *BLJ*.

2 *Byron's Don Juan: A Variorum Edition*, ed. T. G. Steffan and W. W. Pratt, 2nd edn, 4 vols. (Austin, Texas, 1971); *Lord Byron: The Complete Poetical Works*, ed. Jerome J. McGann, Vol. 5, *Don Juan* (Oxford, 1986). I quote from the latter edition, and hereafter cite its various volumes as *Complete Poetical Works*.

3 See Leslie A. Marchand, *Byron: A Biography*, 3 vols. (New York, 1957), Vol. 1, pp. 114–52.

4 As an instance of Murray's careful manipulations, consider his treatment of "Lines to a Lady Weeping," studied in "Tales and Politics: *The Corsair, Lara*, and *The White Doe of Rylstone*," reprinted in my *Reading Romantics: Texts and Contexts* (New York, 1990). Murray's shrewd promotion can also be seen in his declining to publish *Waltz*, a satire in couplets Byron sent him in October 1812, which would have broken the mood of *Childe Harold*; it was published anonymously in the spring of 1813 by Sherwood, Neely, and Jones, a recourse which allowed Byron to deny authorship when it did not succeed (*BLJ*, 3, p. 41). Long after Byron had moved to Italy Murray was entreating him "to resume [his] old '*Corsair* style, to please the ladies'" (quoted in Ernest J. Lovell (ed.), *His Very Self and Voice: Collected Conversations of Lord Byron* [New York, 1954], p. 267).

5 I am particularly indebted to Thilo von Bremen, *Lord Byron als Erfolgsautor*, Athenaion Literaturwissenschaft, Band 6 (Wiesbaden, 1977). I should also acknowledge Keith Walker, *Byron's Readers: A Study of Attitudes Towards Byron 1812–1832*, Romantic Reassessment, 88 (Salzburg, 1979) and Herman M. Ward, *Byron and the Magazines, 1806–1824*, Romantic Reassessment, 19 (Salzburg, 1973). Two essays by Jerome Christensen have been particularly provocative: "Byron's Career: The Speculative Stage," *ELH*, 52 (1985), pp. 59–84, and "Perversion, Parody, and Cultural Hegemony: Lord Byron's Oriental Tales," *South Atlantic Quarterly*, 88 (1989), pp. 569–603.

6 Quoted in Samuel Smiles, *A Publisher and His Friends: Memoir and Correspondence of the Late John Murray*, 2 vols. (London, 1891), Vol. 1, p. 214. Hereafter cited as Smiles.

7 *Quarterly Review*, 19 (1818), pp. 215–32, reproduced in Donald H. Reiman (ed.), *The Romantics Reviewed*, Part B, Byron and Regency Society Reviewers, 5 vols. (New York, 1972), Vol. 5, p. 2049. That Scott could make such a remark, despite John Stoddart's enthusiastic advocacy of Wordsworth and Coleridge to him in 1800 and his meeting with Wordsworth in 1803, indicates how much less impact *Lyrical Ballads* made on the "public" than *Childe Harold's Pilgrimage*.

8 "Living Authors, No. IV: Lord Byron," *London Magazine*, 3 (1821), pp. 50–61, *passim*.

9 Quotations from *Complete Poetical Works*, Vol. 2, *Childe Harold's Pilgrimage* (Oxford, 1980), pp. 13, 4.

10 For a highly suggestive, succinct analysis of these distinctions, see Walter J. Ong, *Orality and Literacy: The Technologizing of the Word* (London, 1982).

11 Francis Jeffrey, review of *The Corsair* and *The Bride of Abydos, Edinburgh Review*, 23 (1814), pp. 198–229; Reiman, *Romantics Reviewed*, Part B, Vol. 2, pp. 848–9, rearranged.

12 On the importance of Byron's aristocratic status see also Jerome Christensen, "Theorizing Byron's Practice: The Performance of Lordship and the Poet's Career," *Studies in Romanticism*, 27 (1988), pp. 477–90.

13 *Complete Poetical Works*, Vol. 3 (Oxford, 1981), p. 423; Jerome J. McGann, *Fiery Dust: Byron's Poetic Development* (Chicago, 1968), p. 144.

14 Marchand, *Byron*, p. 719. In the stanzas which Byron added to the first draft of *Beppo* in mid-October 1817 he wrote of Laura's lover, the Count, that he "patroniz'd the Improvisatori, / Nay, could himself extemporize some stanzas" (33); the decisive cry of "seccatura" ascribed to him (31) Byron had relished when he heard it applied to Sgricci (*BLJ*, 5, p. 125). In Canto XV of *Don Juan* (written 1823) Byron remarks that his "irregularity of chime, / rings what's uppermost of new or hoary, / Just as I feel the 'Improvisatore'" (20).

15 The quoted phrase is from *The London Magazine*, 1 (1820), p. 124.

16 Reiman, *Romantics Reviewed*, Part B, Vol. 2, p. 850.

17 It is not surprising that the more conservative *Quarterly Review* should have repudiated Jeffrey's analysis in order to keep the question within the realm of individual moral responsibility: "the poetical cycle here described is purely imaginary ... [Scott, Southey, and Byron] followed the impulse of their own studies and habits, without dreaming that they thus completed a poetical cycle, or ministered to any taste or appetite peculiar to the present age or country ... this anatomical operation is essentially unpoetical." George Ellis, review of *The Corsair* and *Lara, Quarterly Review*, 11 (1814), pp. 428–57; Reiman, *Romantics Reviewed*, Part B, Vol. 5, pp. 2027–8.

18 On these hallmarks see Ong, *Orality and Literacy*, pp. 141–7.

19 Andrew Rutherford, *Byron The Best Seller*, Byron Foundation Lecture (Nottingham, 1964). The evaluative tendency which disrupts Rutherford's study of the "cultural phenomenon" (p. 7) of Byron's extraordinary popularity is still more pronounced in Philip W. Martin, *Byron: A Poet Before His Public* (Cambridge, 1982).

20 I am indebted to Jon P. Klancher, *The Making of English Reading Audiences, 1790–1832* (Madison, 1987), and Ross Chambers, *Story and Situation: Narrative Seduction and the Power of Fiction* (Minneapolis, 1984).

21 "Remarks on *Don Juan*," *Blackwood's Edinburgh Magazine*, 5 (1819), pp. 512–18; Reiman, *Romantics Reviewed*, Part B, Vol. 1, p. 145.

22 Jonathan Wordsworth, M. H. Abrams, and Stephen Gill (eds.), *The Prelude, 1799, 1805, 1850* (New York, 1979). I quote the 1805 text.

23 Jerome J. McGann, *DON JUAN in Context* (Chicago, 1976), p. 95.

24 Clifford Siskin has recently argued that Romanticism is constituted by a practice of revision as "a mutually *interpretative* relationship between parts and wholes," "Romantic Genre: Lyric Form and Revisionary Behavior in Wordsworth", *Genre*, 16 (1985), pp. 137–55; see also Siskin's *The Historicity of Romantic Discourse* (New York, 1988). By refusing to recuperate disjunctive experience by postulating an organic whole Byron eludes any such paradigm.

25 As text and self, so the world: Byron was fascinated by Georges Cuvier's speculation

that the world had been successively destroyed and recreated, a cosmological correspondence to the psychological notion of a continuously revising self. See *Don Juan* IX, 37–40, and the preface to *Cain*.

26 Jerome J. McGann, in *Shelley and his Circle*, ed. Donald H. Reiman, Vol. 7 (Cambridge, Mass. 1986), p. 246.

27 Reiman, *Romantics Reviewed*, Part B, Vol. 2, p. 863.

28 Jeffrey's remark occurred in a critique of *Sardanapalus, The Two Foscari*, and *Cain*, *Edinburgh Review*, 36 (1822), pp. 413–52; Reiman, *Romantics Reviewed*, Part B, Vol. 2, p. 445. Byron's quotation reveals that even in Italy he closely followed the notices of his work.

29 Gerald Bruns, *Inventions: Writing, Textuality, and Understanding in Literary History* (New Haven, 1982), pp. 2–3.

30 Thomas O. Sloane, "Reinventing *inventio*," *College English*, 51 (1989), pp. 461–73. I have drawn also upon J. G. A. Pocock, *The Machiavellian Moment* (Princeton, 1975), particularly pp. 49–80; Pocock's study illuminates the aristocratic republican doctrines which were Byron's Whig heritage. As this essay was completed there appeared Jerome McGann's *Towards a Literature of Knowledge* (Oxford, 1989); Chapter 3, "Lord Byron's Twin Opposites of Truth," extends McGann's formative criticism of Byron, and I am happy to find that this essay largely accords with what he there terms the "exchange structure" of Byron's poetry (p. 47).

31 'Presbyter Anglicanus" signed a "Letter to the Author of *Beppo*," *Blackwood's Edinburgh Magazine*, 3 (1818), pp. 323–9; for John Gibson Lockhart's pamphlet, see *John Bull's Letter to Lord Byron*, ed. Alan Lang Strout (Norman, Oklahoma, 1947).

I I

SHELLEY'S MANUSCRIPTS AND THE WEB OF
CIRCUMSTANCE

DONALD H. REIMAN

THOSE who pursue the study of Shelley's life, thought, and writings into his
surviving manuscripts soon unlearn much of what they were taught about
Shelley as a poet of idealized abstraction, out of touch with common human
concerns and too angelic for the realities of the mundane world. His
rough-draft notebooks themselves often contain confused drafts of several
works in verse and prose, interwoven with financial calculations, addresses,
drafts of letters, and other quotidian concerns. The often eccentric form of both
his surviving holograph fair copies and contemporary transcriptions by Mary
W. Shelley and Edward E. Williams reflects Shelley's constant struggle to reach
his publisher and his audience with a correct text but with minimal costs for
postage and for printing. Even the histories behind the survival and provenance
of these manuscripts reveal that the writings of Shelley, more than those of most
other poets, have always been enmeshed in the complexities of his struggles
with the world. Although Shelley's published works exhibit a careful, almost
symmetrical sense of form, the formless, inchoate nature of his drafts as they
developed teach us how hard he labored to shape and order his materials. In
these drafts, Shelley often shows anger, jealousy, and other less than angelic
emotions that, for the most part, he carefully excised before publishing his
works. Observing this process of suppression, we can sense also the cost to him
of shaping his works to conform to the spirit of his moral principles.

I

After Shelley was sent down from Oxford in March 1811, he pursued a rootless,
itinerant lifestyle that led to the loss of many of his books and manuscripts and
the accidental dispersal of others. When he separated from Harriet Westbrook
Shelley, for example, he lost possession of the manuscripts of his early poems,
many of them unpublished. A copybook containing many of these poems

remained in the family of Shelley's and Harriet's daughter Ianthe (later Esdaile), kept from the view of most Shelley scholars till the 1950s, and first fully published in 1964.[1] When Shelley returned to England from Switzerland in 1816, he left behind a small notebook containing transcriptions of "Mont Blanc," "Hymn to Intellectual Beauty," and two otherwise unknown sonnets; this notebook, apparently given by Byron to his friend Scrope Davies, who had presumably agreed to carry the notebook to Shelley, disappeared until 1976, when Davies's trunk was discovered in the cellar of the Pall Mall branch of Barclays Bank.[2] Shelley's loss of this notebook not only forced him to try to reconstruct texts of the longer poems from his drafts (creating serious textual problems in "Mont Blanc" and minor ones in "Hymn"), but also resulted in the loss of the two sonnets until the rediscovery of the notebook. In 1818, the Shelleys left books and manuscripts in Peacock's care at Marlow when they traveled to Italy; when Peacock moved to London in 1820, he in turn left many of these books and manuscripts in the care of Robert Maddocks (or Madocks). Later Maddocks retained (and eventually sold) them because Shelley owed him money for expenses and services in maintaining Shelley's house at Marlow. Among the hostages was at least one copy of *Queen Mab*, extensively revised by Shelley into a new version entitled "The Queen of the Universe," that had served as a draft of the passages published with the *Alastor* volume as "Superstition" and "The Daemon of the World."[3]

Shelley's alienation from his family also affected the very nature of his manuscripts. Because he was financially insecure and often poor, he frequently went to some lengths to save money on paper and postal fees – both relatively expensive during his lifetime. While he was in England, he wrote some of his long letters to Elizabeth Hitchener and Thomas Jefferson Hogg on huge folio sheets so that he could send a long letter for the minimum postage that the Inland Mail charged for a single sheet. When in Italy, he used every scrap of paper while drafting his works, and when mailing his poems to England, he often copied them (or had them copied by Mary W. Shelley) on very small slips of thin paper to avoid excess postal fees that, for overseas mail, were calculated by weight and paid by both the sender and the recipient. These inhibitions explain some basic differences between his manuscripts and those of Byron, for example, who could frank his mail in England, who was not burdened by lack of cash while he was abroad, and whose publishers were always glad to pay the postal charges because his poems were commercially successful.

Shelley wrote so uncompromisingly that most of his works were published by marginal, undercapitalized booksellers – particularly Charles Ollier, whose business failed soon after Shelley's death. Ollier could not afford to buy Shelley's copyrights and, thereby (according to the practice of the era), gain possession of his manuscripts, as John Murray acquired the manuscripts of

Byron. Nor did Ollier persuade the printers to save most of Shelley's manuscripts that served as press-copies during his lifetime; instead, they were discarded after the printing of the works they contained. Even Shelley himself made no effort to preserve the press-copy manuscripts of *The Cenci* and *Adonais*, which were printed in Italy under his supervision – perhaps because he lacked a safe place to store them.

The fervor with which Shelley battled against the establishment, however, eventually inspired an echoing enthusiasm in those who admired his writings, first in his wife, son, and daughter-in-law, and eventually among a coterie of their friends who preserved his surviving manuscripts and treated them with reverence. To gain access to the letters and literary documents, scholars were required to pass through what almost amounted to rites of initiation and tests of doctrinal purity.[4] When one of the few approved admirers appeared, Mary W. Shelley and, later, Sir Percy Florence Shelley and Jane Lady Shelley were liable to present him or her with a relic – usually a manuscript by Shelley. Among such documented cases, Mary Shelley presented Shelley's holograph press-copy of "Athanase: A Fragment" to a young journalist and aspiring poet from Canterbury named John Chalk Claris, who wrote Shelleyan poetry under the name of "Arthur Brooke." She also dispersed several leaves of the fair-copy manuscript from Canto I of *Laon and Cythna* (later *The Revolt of Islam*).[5] The hyper-reverential protection of the family's manuscripts at Boscombe Manor by Sir Percy Florence and Lady Shelley irritated such friends of Shelley as Edward John Trelawny. Neither William Michael Rossetti nor Harry Buxton Forman, the two nineteenth-century editors who took the strongest interest in the textual accuracy of Shelley's writings, was given access to most of these family manuscripts. At the same time, Sir Percy Florence and Lady Shelley gave away to such friends and advisors as Richard Garnett and the Reverend Stopford Brooke both loose sheets containing writing by Shelley and five of Shelley's rough-draft notebooks – including some of Shelley's most unusual compositions, such as his prose fragments on contraception and on Zionism (both of which remain to be published with his collected prose). The attitude at Boscombe Manor was itself circumstantially governed by the way private acquaintances and sensation-seeking journalists had misused the personal manuscripts of other Romantic writers (Byron and Coleridge, in particular) and through attacks on Shelley by John Cordy Jeaffreson and on Mary Shelley by an embittered Trelawny.[6]

II

A complicated interplay of human relationships, beginning with Shelley's alienation from his family that followed his expulsion from Oxford and continuing among Shelley's students and admirers even after his death, thus helped govern the dispersal of his manuscripts. But some of those same factors also, paradoxically, contributed to their survival and reassemblage and to recent advances in scholarly study of them. For while Shelley's status as a controversial figure, attacked by many in the literary and political establishments, led to the destruction of some of his manuscripts, it also helped to engender an enthusiasm for his works among others, who eventually drew most of his manuscripts into a small number of collections devoted to their study and dissemination.

Shelley's relative poverty, a result of his alienation from his wealthy father, led him to acquire numerous debts that creditors felt sure they would eventually collect; since many of these debts were never paid, or at least remained outstanding until after the value of Shelley's manuscripts became obvious, several kinds of legal and financial documents involving Shelley, of types uncommon among the papers of other poets of the period, survive intact. These documents include: a substantial portion of the cheques that Shelley wrote to his bankers, Brooks, Son, and Dixon, from 1815 through 1819;[7] correspondence and documents relating to Shelley's purchase (on credit) of a "chariot" from Thomas Charters, a New Bond Street coachmaker;[8] and a raft of papers related to his purchase on credit in 1817, from Messrs. English, English, and Becks of Bath, of furniture and draperies for Albion House in Great Marlow, materials that Shelley resold for a fraction of their value in 1818 before leaving for the Continent.[9] Though not of central literary interest, these papers supplement related letters to provide a substantial archive of materials relating one poet's creative life to the web of mundane fiscal affairs that competed for the time and energy of all the major Romantics. In Shelley's case, the discovery of such documents has proved beneficial in understanding what sort of a person he was. As I wrote in *Shelley and his Circle*, "Shelley shows himself to be neither angelic nor ineffectual. Our view of Shelley's genius as a poet is modified by a renewed sense of his practical awareness and intelligence . . ." (VIII, pp. 838–9).

Beyond the creditors who preserved Shelley's financial records, admirers of the poet outside the Shelley family who possessed the opportunity and the means became enthusiastic collectors and devoted themselves to seeking out his manuscripts with more than ordinary fervor. In the nineteenth century, substantial collections were assembled by the Shelley scholars Richard Garnett (who also collected on behalf of the British Museum, which he served as Keeper of Printed Books), Edward Dowden (who, as Professor of English at Trinity College, Dublin, left his collections to that institution), and – above all – Harry Buxton Forman. In America, the Brooklyn collector Charles W. Frederickson assembled a major Shelley collection that was finally dispersed at a sale in May 1897.[10]

Later in the nineteenth and into the twentieth century, the premier British collector was Thomas James Wise, but in America a substantial group that included J. Pierpont Morgan, Henry E. Huntington, A. Edward Newton, Jerome Kern (the songwriter), William K. Bixby, John A. Spoor, John Wrenn, Miriam K. Stark, Owen D. Young, the brothers Berg, and Carl H. Pforzheimer (1879–1957) all made significant purchases. Some of these, including Pforzheimer, began collecting Shelley in a substantial way at the sale of Harry Buxton Forman's great library at the Anderson Galleries of New York in 1920.[11] As the years passed, Wise's Ashley Collection was given to the British Museum; the Kern, Bixby, and Spoor libraries were dispersed at auctions (many of their important Shelley items ending up in the Pforzheimer Collection); the Pierpont Morgan and Huntington libraries both became great, multifarious institutions that emphasized other things; the Wrenn and Stark Collections became parts of what is now the Humanities Research Center at the University of Texas at Austin, which turned to the manuscripts of twentieth-century authors, as did the collection that Dr. Albert A. Berg (1872–1950) in 1939 gave to The New York Public Library (in memory of his brother Dr. Henry Berg) and enhanced by purchasing the distinguished collections of W. H. T. Howe (1874–1939) and Owen D. Young (1874–1962), submerging their fine Shelleyan holdings by specializing in English, Irish, and American literature of the later nineteenth and twentieth centuries.[12]

Following the deaths of Sir Percy Florence and Lady Shelley, their great collection at Boscombe Manor had been divided into three parts, one part going directly to the Bodleian Library, Oxford; another to Sir John Shelley-Rolls, heir to the Shelley baronetcy; and the third to Lord Abinger. In 1946, Sir John Shelley-Rolls, himself a notable scholar and enthusiast for Shelley's manuscripts, left his patrimony to the Bodleian.[13] After 1940, when years of Carl H. Pforzheimer's collecting and Emma Va. Unger's cataloguing were supplemented by the bibliographical finesse of William A. Jackson in the classic catalogue of the collection's holdings of *English Literature, 1475–1700*,[14] Pforzheimer centered his attention as a collector on the books and manuscripts of Shelley and his circle. By the mid-1950s, the Carl and Lily Pforzheimer Foundation had embarked upon an ambitious plan for a scholarly catalogue to tell the story of the Romantic age through the analysis of the documents of the leading figures represented in its collection up to the death of Shelley in 1822.[15] With eight volumes of this catalogue-edition *Shelley and his Circle* in print, the Pforzheimer Shelley and His Circle Collection was in December 1987 given by the Foundation to The New York Public Library, where it is now located across the hall from the Berg Collection. Meanwhile, in the late 1970s, Lord Abinger's manuscripts, which center on Mary Wollstonecraft, William Godwin, and

Mary W. Shelley, were put on deposit at the Bodleian, thereby reuniting the three portions of the Boscombe Manor Shelley family collection, together with more recent acquisitions by the Bodleian. Now the greater part of Shelley's literary manuscripts, as well as a clear majority of his letters and other documents, are located in either the Bodleian Library or the New York Public Library. A mere half-dozen other institutions in England and America – the British Library, Harvard, Pierpont Morgan, Library of Congress, Texas at Austin, Texas Christian University,[16] and the Huntington – contain most of the rest. The Keats–Shelley Memorial House in Rome possesses eight letters; no other institution or individual is on record as owning more than four letters, while a few autographs of single poems or poetic or prose manuscripts are scattered in half a dozen other British, American, European, and Japanese collections.[17] This concentration of Shelley's manuscripts, like Henry Folger's purchase of many copies of the folio editions of Shakespeare's plays, has brought together bibliographical, textual, and biographical researchers – many under the auspices of the Pforzheimer Foundation – and enabled them to make dramatic progress in these basic areas of study, as well as in literary criticism on Shelley and his circle, during the past forty years.

III

Just as the youthful Shelley's travels, in contrast to Wordsworth's settled life in the Lake District during his mature years, resulted in the loss or dispersal of most of P. B. Shelley's early manuscripts, as well as Mary Shelley's juvenilia, so the poverty of Shelley compared with Byron, whose large entourage packed and carried his papers around Europe, until he was ready to send them to John Murray for publication or to Douglas Kinnaird or John Cam Hobhouse for safekeeping, made it impossible for the Shelleys to compose chiefly on the kind of large loose folio sheets that were Byron's standard writing material.[18] Instead, Shelley often drafted his poems and prose alike in blank notebooks that served his contemporaries as diaries, or as commonplace, sketch, or account books. Given Shelley's financial problems, even these pocket notebooks were relatively expensive, and because he carried them around with him as he composed in the open air in Switzerland, at Marlow, and in Italy, he utilized pages in each notebook for a variety of purposes. He often interspersed in a single notebook not only drafts for several poems and prose works, but also ephemeral notes and memoranda concerning practical matters. For example, Bodleian MS. Shelley adds. e. 11 – which contains drafts, in poetry, for scenes for an abortive drama on the life of Tasso, "Stanzas written in Dejection, near Naples," *Julian and Maddalo*, and Act II, scene i, and Act III, scene iv, of

Prometheus Unbound, as well as prose drafts for "On Love," "A Discourse on the Manners of the Antients . . .," "On a Future State," and the Preface to *Prometheus Unbound* – also has on folio 124, verso, financial calculations and a receipt for a month's wages, dated April 20, 1819, in the hand of Vincenzo Gavita, who had served as the Shelleys" coachman since shortly before they left Naples.[19]

Besides a variety of works, a single notebook may contain materials of widely diverse tone and nature, with idealistic and even ethereal verses mixed with the most mundane and descendental notes and illustrations. An interesting example can be found in Bodleian MS. Shelley adds. e. 20, popularly called "Shelley's Last Notebook" because its extensive water damage is believed to have occurred when it sank with Shelley's sailboat "Don Juan" at the time Shelley drowned.[20] Folio 34 verso, amid very early rough drafts for *Adonais*, contains scattered lines of an uncompleted stanza, the first line of which reads, "Love weeps, – who ever knew Love weep?" and the last: "Thou mayst now weep anew." At the top of this page, Shelley has drawn three figures (see Figure 11.1). In the upper left-hand quarter is a fairly small sketch of a nude male, as seen from the rear right side (but with his scrotum clearly visible between his moving legs) who holds in his hands, outstretched before him, a large spear; this small figure has turned his face back to his right side and wears a pained or disgusted expression, because looming up directly before him are the abdomen and legs of a gigantic male figure (his waist is near the top of the page) who, with a large, semi-detached penis that seems to project backwards from his buttocks, is urinating on the little spear-carrier. Still farther to the right side of the page, where Shelley apparently accidentally spilled ink on the page, he has added a head and limbs to turn the ink-blot into a sketch of a devil, about the same height as the smaller nude human figure.

Shelley was doodling, and we would be mistaken to read too much either literary or psychological significance into these ephemeral sketches. If I were asked, however, to explicate these graphic figures in words, I would have to say that the smaller figure with the spear represents the young Keats, trying to confront the critics in their lair (see *Adonais*, st. 27) and encountering the headless giant, representing the anonymous critic of the *Quarterly Review*, who urinates on him. The figure of the devil who seems to be skulking away may, if related to the other two figures, represent Robert Southey, co-author of "The Devil's Thoughts" and the specific *Quarterly* reviewer whom Shelley blamed for anonymous attacks on Leigh Hunt and himself, as well as on Keats.

I come to this explication of Shelley's drawings largely through canceled passages in the drafts of the Preface to *Adonais* that appear on earlier pages, amid the fair copy of *A Defence of Poetry*, though the Preface was surely written later

Figure 11.1 Drafts related to *Adonais*, with Shelley's sketches: Bodleian MS.
Shelley adds. e. 20, folio 34 verso (quire VI, folio 11 verso).

than anything else in the Notebook. On folio 1 recto, Shelley writes (as I edit the draft on a very heavily canceled page):

The Editor of this ~~Quarterly~~ Review . . . amongst associates of the most splendid accomplishments, & the most honourable minds, certainly ~~has~~ in his employment one of ~~the most malignant~~ & [?un]principled slanderers (as I should have called him had he ventured one very broad insinuation) that ever prostituted his soul for twenty pounds *per sheet*[.]

Skipping some pages filled earlier, Shelley continues on folios 7 recto and 8 recto, where both the mention of Southey in the original text and a sentence written crosswise (and, therefore, later) suggest Southey as the target of Shelley's invective against Keats's reviewer: "Mr Southey, especially as the editor of the Remains of Kirke White knows feelingly what was done."[21]

In drafts for passages of the Preface that Shelley wholly deleted before publication, he alludes on folio 10 recto to his own relations with Keats: "No personal offence should have extr[acted] from me this public comment upon such stuff . . .; I knew personally but little of Kea⟨ts,⟩ having met him two or three ⟨?times⟩ at my friend Leigh Hunt's[,] but on the news of his situation I wrote to him suggesting the proprie⟨ty⟩ of trying the Italian climate, & invi⟨ting⟩ him to join me. –" Having introduced himself into the argument, Shelley momentarily loses sight of his ethical and rhetorical purpose, for on folio 11 recto he takes up his own quarrel with the reviewers and justifies his conduct:

I will allow myself a first & a last word on the subject of calumny as it relates to my own person[.] As an author I have dared & invited censure; if I understand myself I have written neither for profit nor for fame; I [have] employed my poetical compositi⟨on⟩ & publication simply as instruments of what sympathy between myself & others which the ardent & unbounded love I cherished for my kind, incited me to acquire[.]

Shelley then began a new sentence that he wholly cancelled before continuing: "~~I expected all sort of stupidity~~ ⟨⟩ |~~insolent contempt from those~~" – a strange way, one would think, for Shelley to demonstrate his "ardent & unbounded love" for his kind. Shelley himself obviously recognized this discrepancy: the next recto had already been partly used, along with all the verso pages early in MS. Shelley adds. e. 20, for the holograph intermediate fair-copy of *A Defence of Poetry*, and the next leaf (the one on which Shelley presumably continued the stricken angry thought) is missing from the notebook and may have been torn out by him, rather than lost through water damage. Folio 14 recto, the next surviving page, begins with incomplete and canceled continuations of the same kind of pained and hostile outcry, including an oblique complaint about the decision of the Chancery Court that deprived him of his children by Harriet:

"Persecution, contumely and calumny have been heaped upon me in a profuse measure. [D]omestic conspiracy and legal oppression combined have violated in my [person] the most sacred rights of Nature of humanity"; yet after Shelley continues with more canceled fragments about how badly his health and spirits have been affected by this persecution, he drops the subject at the bottom of folio 14 recto and on folio 15 recto (the next open page) he turns to the plight of Keats, beginning, "But a young mind panting after fame is the most vulnerable [prey]: he is armed neither with philosophy"; then, breaking off, he rephrases the thought, which continues on folio 16 recto:

But a young spirit panting after fame, doubtful of its powers & certain only of the aspirations is not [fitted] t⟨o⟩ assign its true value to the shews of this [deceitful] world [**FOLIO 16 RECTO**] He know not that such stuff as this is the [?parade] of the abortive & monstrous births which Time consumes as fast as it produces. He sees the truth & falshood, the merits & the demerits of his case inextricably entangled . . .

Here Shelley breaks off at the end of the page, turns from this ill-advised effort to describe Keats's youthful limitations, just as he had previously given up trying to portray his own virtues and the wrongs heaped upon him. Instead, he turns back to the cowardly reviewer and writes out a fair draft of what became the fourth paragraph of the published Preface, beginning: "It may be well said that these wretched men know not what they do.—"[22]

By analyzing what Shelley writes on each page of the manuscript in which these drafts appear, we observe that at the bottom of the small pages of this pocket notebook he rethought the direction of his argument, rereading the uncanceled passages before turning the leaf to determine how he wished to continue. Several of his ideas did not survive more than one or two turned pages in the drafts before he abandoned them to seek more viable lines of argument. In general, these changes steered him away from mentioning his own wrongs and Keats's vulnerability and toward depicting the evil of the *Quarterly*'s reviewers – particularly one, of whom he writes on folio 17 recto: "One of them, to my knowledge is [a] base & unprinci[pled] calumniator." This sentence as it appears in the published Preface is strengthened by the insertion of "most" before "base."

Shelley did not rid his Preface of hostility toward the *Quarterly* reviewers, or even of his personal animus toward Robert Southey, whom he believed to have been the author of three reviews that attacked him. But Shelley no longer described these feelings as "ardent & unbounded love." He did not eliminate all his condescending remarks about Keats's youth and vulnerability, but he began the Preface with his strong and sincere praise of "Hyperion" as being "second to nothing that was ever produced by a writer of the same years." The drafts of both the Preface and *Adonais* itself (extensive transcriptions from which appear as well in Anthony D. Knerr's *Shelley's* Adonais: *A Critical Edition*[23]) show us how much *art* went into what appear to be spontaneous outpourings of sentiment, how well Shelley succeeded in modulating his tone in order to bridge the gap between himself and his readers, and how carefully he constructed through the subtleties of language so that critics would have something worthy of being *de*constructed.

A comparison of all of Shelley's surviving drafts with his completed poetry and prose shows clearly that he, like Coleridge in composing *Biographia Literaria*,[24] could rapidly transfer raw feelings and thoughts into almost labyrinthine artifacts. This judgment, which was relatively novel thirty years ago when I began to champion it, has now become almost a truism. But the implications it holds for both textual scholars and literary critics of Shelley's writings have not yet been sufficiently appreciated.

IV

Although we have drafts of many of Shelley's mature works, we usually lack either his intermediate fair copy or else the carefully prepared press-copy transcript that directly preceded publication. With so much evidence of Shelley's process of composing most of his poems now lost, scholars will find it difficult to arrive at a consensus regarding the text of critically edited texts of Shelley's writings. Early work on the Bodleian Shelley manuscripts, together with my experience of editing both *Shelley and his Circle* and *Shelley's Poetry and Prose* (Norton Critical Edition), led me to suggest in "'Versioning': The Presentation of Multiple Texts" that for Romantic texts for which more than one stage of the process of composition survives, the most satisfactory solution might be to reproduce in facsimile and/or diplomatic transcription all the surviving textual authorities, so that scholars, critics, and students could compare the manuscripts and editions for themselves, note the changes that a work underwent during composition and publication, and determine the ways in which these changes affected the work's meaning.[25]

Upon further reflection, however, I am sure that even if all such textual authorities were available to scholars and critics, there would remain a strong need for critical editions. The history of Shelley scholarship and criticism shows that not only are most critics and some scholars too "busy" to consult primary authorities, but that even some who do are incapable of understanding their implications and value. Thus Neville Rogers, one of the earliest students of the Bodleian Shelley manuscripts, after surveying a number of very rough drafts, concluded that Shelley had no interest in details of orthography, punctuation, or even diction.[26] Similarly, Paul de Man, a casual reader of Shelley who drew conclusions based on his own ideology before he studied the evidence of the poet's method of composing and revising, tried to prove that Shelley's ideas led to defeat and despair; he read fragments and poetic efforts truncated by Shelley's untimely death (notably "The Triumph of Life") as though they were complete, public poems.[27] Clearly those who study Shelley's manuscripts with patience and understanding must point out to such amateurs and ideologues the difference between a draft (a private or confidential text, meant for the eyes of the author only or, perhaps, the author's intimate friends) and a press-copy or printed text approved as conveying the author's meaning into the realm of public discourse. Although discrepancies between private and public versions of a work may open vistas for psychoanalytical and deconstructive criticism, the public version of one poem and the private version of another cannot be discussed on the same scale without greatly distorting our understanding of an author's meaning and achievement.

After thirty years of pursuing the study of Shelley's life, thought, and writings into the surviving drafts of his poems and prose, I have arrived at a simple conclusion: A poet makes a better personal appearance wearing his clothes than he does naked. However interesting it may be to peek into Shelley's private papers, catching him off guard and *au naturel*, his polished writings teach us more. Shelley's literary stature appears greater when we focus on the poems that he finished and polished for publication. The scholar-critic can learn a great deal about Shelley's creative method by tracing his progress from the first, scattered and meandering jottings on a subject, then through his scattered rough drafts and (where they survive) his intermediate fair copies, and lastly to the few extant final polished manuscript copies that he sent to press. But in the end, the poet escapes our nets, exhibiting an elusive genius that proves at last what Shelley claimed in *A Defense of Poetry* – the superiority of the creative, synthesizing faculty to the process of analysis.

Ultimately, Shelley lures us into spending our time and expending our eyesight studying his manuscripts because his mind and sensitivity are greater than ours individually – and, perhaps, collectively. One mark of his superiority lies in the very fact that even when we can trace his progress through the sequential physical inscription of his texts, we cannot quite follow the trail of his mental processes that led him to make specific turns, or enabled him to mold a plethora of diverse pieces and fragments together into a beautiful and moving poem that is usually both organically unified and symmetrically structured. And just as Shelley outdistances most of his critics in his command of the formal aspects of poetry – in metrical subtlety and symbolic patterning, as well as in the larger structural ordering of his finished poems – so he shows himself superior in his moral vision.

F. R. Leavis criticized Shelley for "his weak grasp upon the actual."[28] Shelley's method was often to move, during poetic composition, from the precise and particular to the universally abstract; examination of Shelley's draft manuscripts shows that he often began with specific details that he later deleted because the references to specific individuals and groups conflicted with his moral vision of what poetry ought to be. In the drafts to *Peter Bell the Third*, for example, Shelley could be as wittily specific in his malicious thrusts at Wordsworth and Southey as Byron was, but – prodded by *internal* censors – he left the sharpest of these personal attacks on the cutting-room floor. Knowledge of his process of repressing what he termed, in a letter to Leigh Hunt, "the burr of self" that "will stick to one" may help us both to evaluate his intended meanings and to judge his moral success in expunging the record of his personal anger and reaching instead toward the ideal he enunciated in a note to *Hellas*: "it is the province of the poet to attach himself to those ideas which exalt and ennoble humanity."

Whether we personally prefer Shelley's poetic mode, which approaches Wordsworth's own ideal of avoiding mere "Personal Talk," or whether we enjoy the more realistic and satirical mode of Byron's greatest poems, we can still recognize, thanks to the evidence of Shelley's manuscripts, that he was neither naive nor blind to the world around him or to his own less noble emotions. Nor did he possess an ethereal, angelic nature. Shelley had vengeful thoughts and feelings that he often vented during the early stages of composition, but he was unusually successful in suppressing or sublimating them during the process of shaping his conceptions into poetic forms. The study of Shelley's manuscripts teaches us that in submitting his emotions and his ideal visions to the discipline of traditional poetic genres and fixed metrical forms, Shelley transformed his raw materials into aesthetic unities that suppress or chasten some aspects of the originating impulse in the interest of amplifying its positive values. Thus, though Byron may be the poet among the Romantics whose voice is most congenial to our age, Shelley's example may have more to teach today's poets who immerse themselves deeply in the waters of confessional spontaneity. Awareness of this possibility is at least one critical lesson taught by the study of Shelley's manuscript revisions.

NOTES

1 See *The Esdaile Notebook: A Volume of Early Poems by Percy Bysshe Shelley*, ed. Kenneth Neill Cameron (New York, 1964; corrected edn., London, 1965), and, for

additional corrections of the text and discussion of the evidence, *The Esdaile Notebook: A Facsimile of the Holograph Copybook in The Carl H. Pforzheimer Library*, ed. Donald H. Reiman (New York and London, 1985).

2 See Judith Chernaik and Timothy A. J. Burnett, "The Byron and Shelley Notebooks in the Scrope Davies Find," *Review of English Studies*, 29 (1978), pp. 36–49; Roland A. Duerksen, "Thematic Unity in the New Shelley Notebook", *Bulletin of Research in the Humanities*, 83 (1980), pp. 203–15; and T. A. J. Burnett, *The Rise and Fall of a Regency Dandy: The Life and Times of Scrope Berdmore Davies* (London, 1981).

3 On the revised copy of *Queen Mab*, see Kenneth Neill Cameron, "The Queen of the Universe: Shelley's Revised *Queen Mab*" and SC 296, in Cameron (ed.), *Shelley and his Circle*, Vol. 4 (Cambridge, Mass., 1970), pp. 487–568; on Shelley's books at Marlow and Maddocks's dispersal of them, see *Shelley and his Circle*, Vol. 10, ed. Donald H. Reiman (forthcoming).

4 For details and examples on these matters from a perspective sympathetic to Shelley, see Sylva Norman, *Flight of the Skylark: The Development of Shelley's Reputation* (London and Norman, Oklahoma, 1954); for a jaundiced view, see Robert Metcalf Smith *et al.*, *The Shelley Legend* (New York, 1945).

5 For details, see Donald H. Reiman, "Shelley as Athanase" and SC 582, Commentary, in Reiman (ed.), *Shelley and his Circle*, Vol. 7 (Cambridge, Mass., 1986), pp. 110–60; "The Composition and Publication of *The Revolt of Islam*", and related manuscripts and Commentaries in Reiman (ed.), *Shelley and his Circle*, Vol. 5 (1973), pp. 141–89, and 7 (1986), pp. 74–80; and Tatsuo Tokoo (ed.), *Bodleian MS. Shelley d. 3: A Facsimile Edition*, Vol. 8 of The Bodleian Shelley Manuscripts (New York and London, 1988).

6 Jeaffreson, *The Real Shelley: New Views of the Poet's Life* (London, 1885). For Trelawny's disgust with Sir Percy Florence and Lady Shelley, see William Michael Rossetti (ed.), *Rossetti Papers (1862 to 1870)* (London, 1903), pp. 399, 400.

7 See Appendixes H and P in Walter E. Peck's *Shelley: His Life and Work* (Boston and New York, 1927), Vol. 2, pp. 381–93 and 436–9.

8 See Cameron, "Shelley's 'Chariot,'" in *Shelley and his Circle*, Vol. 3 (1970), pp. 153–79.

9 See Reiman, "Shelley and the Upholsterers of Bath," in *Shelley and his Circle*, Vol. 8, pp. 827–42.

10 *Catalogue of the Library of the Late Charles W. Frederickson . . . To Be Sold at Auction Monday–Friday, May 24ᵗʰ.–28ᵗʰ. 1897 by Bangs & Co., 91 & 93 Fifth Avenue, New York*. This sale contained over sixty letters by Percy Bysshe Shelley, as well as a substantial number of letters by Byron, Mary W. Shelley, and others in their circles.

11 *The Library of the Late H. Buxton Forman* was sold in three parts at the Anderson Galleries: Part I, sale 1480, contained 1000 lots and occupied five sessions on March 15, 16, and 17, 1920; Part II, sale 1493, included 1228 lots in five sessions on April 26, 27, and 28, 1920; Part III, sale 1516, included 1344 lots in four afternoon sessions on October 4, 5, 6, and 7, 1920.

12 See *The New York Public Library . . .: Dictionary Catalog of the Henry W. and Albert A. Berg Collection of English and American Literature*, 5 vols. (Boston, 1969); *First Supplement*, 1975; *Second Supplement*, 1983.

13 On the division of the Shelley family's papers at Boscombe Manor, see Kenneth Neill Cameron, "The Provenance of Shelley and His Circle Manuscripts", in Cameron (ed.), *Shelley and his Circle*, Vol. 2, pp. 892–913 (see note 15).

14 *The Carl H. Pforzheimer Library: English Literature, 1475–1700*, 3 vols. (New York, 1940). The collection described in this bibliographical landmark is now in The Humanities Research Center, University of Texas at Austin.

15 After Carl H. Pforzheimer died in 1957, the Shelley collection continued to grow under the direction of The Carl and Lily Pforzheimer Foundation, led by Carl H. Pforzheimer, Jr. Kenneth Neill Cameron became editor of *Shelley and his Circle* in 1952, editing the first two volumes (Cambridge, Mass., 1961) and, after Donald H. Reiman succeeded him in 1965, completing the editing of Vols. 3 and 4 of the edition (1971).

16 See Lyle H. Kendall, Jr., *A Descriptive Catalogue of The W. L. Lewis Collection: Texas Christian University; Part One, Manuscripts, Inscriptions, Art* (Fort Worth, Texas, 1970).

17 The latest available listing of the locations of Shelley's letters, in Frederick L. Jones's edition of *The Letters of Percy Bysshe Shelley* (Oxford, 1964), was not fully accurate when it appeared and is badly outdated now. A number of the letters then in private hands have since been resold, and several of those are now in the Pforzheimer Collection, as are most of the new Shelley letters that have come to light since 1964.

18 For the large sheets of paper used by Byron for both the drafts and fair copies of his mature literary works, including *Beppo*, *Marino Faliero*, and *Don Juan*, see the bibliographical descriptions and facsimilies in both *Shelley and his Circle* and Garland's series The Manuscripts of the Younger Romantics (general editor Donald H. Reiman).

19 For facsimile, with full transcription and analysis, see The *"Julian and Maddalo" Draft Notebook: Bodleian MS. Shelley adds. e. 11*, ed. Steven E. Jones, The Bodleian Shelley Manuscripts, 15 (New York and London, 1990).

20 See *Shelley's "Last Notebook": Bodleian MS. Shelley adds. e. 20, together with Bodleian MS. adds. e. 15, and a Related Section of MS. Shelley adds. c. 4*, ed. Donald H. Reiman, The Bodleian Shelley Manuscripts, 7 (New York and London, 1989), pp. 81–379. In this essay, to clarify the more substantive changes in Shelley's argument, my quotations from the notebook drafts omit cancellations of primarily stylistic interest that are available in the facsimile edition.

21 *Ibid.*, pp. 162–3.

22 *Ibid.*, pp. 202–3.

23 Knerr, *Shelley's* Adonais: *A Critical Edition* (New York, 1984). Knerr's volume brings together a critically edited version of the published poem, transcriptions of the relevant pages in four different Bodleian notebooks and a variorum summary of critical commentary on the poem. He does not include facsimiles, or relate the *Adonais* drafts to the detailed information about other texts in these notebooks that appears in the facsimile editions The Bodleian Shelley Manuscripts series.

24 See Chapter 3: "Coleridge: The Will to Believe and the Art of Equivocation," in Donald H. Reiman, *Intervals of Inspiration: The Skeptical Tradition and the Psychology of Romanticism* (Greenwood, Florida, 1988), pp. 107–51.

25 See Reiman, *Romantic Texts and Contexts* (Columbia, Missouri, 1987), pp. 167–80.

26 Rogers set forth this doctrine in three issues of the annual *Keats–Shelley Memorial Bulletin*: 16 (1965), pp. 21–5; 17 (1966), pp. 20–30; and 19 (1968), pp. 41–6.

27 De Man, "Shelley Disfigured," in Harold Bloom *et al.*, *Deconstruction and Criticism* (New York, 1979), pp. 39–73.

28 F. R. Leavis, *Revaluation: Tradition and Development in English Poetry* (London: Chatto & Windus, 1949; first published 1936), p. 206. Leavis also writes: "There is nothing grasped in the poetry – no object offered for contemplation, no realized presence to persuade or move us by what it is" (p. 210).

12

SPACES BETWEEN WORDS: WRITING *MONT BLANC*

ROBERT BRINKLEY

[T]he silence [is] no silence at all. No word has come to an end and no phrase, it is
nothing but a pause, an empty space between the words, a blank – you see all the
syllables stand around waiting.
                                        Paul Celan, *Conversation in the Mountains*

IN the earliest version (Bodleian Ms. Shelley adds. e. 16, pp. 3–13), the draft in
the notebook that Shelley carried with him to Chamonix, 'Mont Blanc' has the
appearance of a palimpsest. A layering of passages – some in pencil, others in
ink; some ordered consecutively, others superimposed – the poem seems to be
structured by the breaks in composition. As a literary theorist, Shelley tended to
undervalue his experience as a writer – 'when composition begins, inspiration is
already on the decline . . . The toil and delay recommended by critics can be
justly interpreted to mean no more than a careful observation of the inspired
moments' (*A Defence of Poetry*, p. 504) – but what the Bodleian notebook
indicates is that much of 'Mont Blanc' was inspired as it was composed – *by*
intervals of thwarted writing and Shelley's subsequent 'observation' of 'that
verge where words abandon us' (*On Life*, p. 478). One might regard these
intervals as evidence of imaginative uncertainty, concrete expressions of
Shelley's skepticism. They punctuate textures of allusions and revisions.
Writing turns into silence. Mont Blanc itself appears in the notebook from
breaks in the writing, and in the notebook even its appearance is then cancelled.
'Mont Blanc ~~appears~~', the notebook reads. It is this texture that I would like to
consider, the insistent uncertainty in particular. If 'the mind in creation is as a
fading coal' (*Defence*, pp. 503–4), the uncertainty may live in the embers.

I   THE SEQUENCE OF COMPOSITION

At the time of publication (fall 1817, in *History of a Six Weeks' Tour* [H]) 'Mont
Blanc' was characterized as an 'undisciplined overflowing of the soul':

243

It was composed under the immediate impression of the deep and powerful feelings excited by the objects it attempts to describe; and as an undisciplined overflowing of the soul, rests its claim to approbation on an attempt to imitiate the untameable wildness and inaccessible solemnity from which those feelings sprang. (*H*, vi)

'[U]ntameable wildness' refers to the Ravine of Arve, 'inaccessible solemnity' to Mont Blanc itself, but this description obscures the revisionary nature of the composition.

Breaks in writing are indicated in e. 16 by shifts from pencil to pen and from pen back to pencil. Other interruptions may also have occurred (the last stages of revision probably took place more than a year later), but the following sequence of composition seems likely (reference is to equivalent lines in the published text; the notebook version of what became lines 25–9 follows a version of line 34):

(a) In pencil, lines 1–20 ('The everlasting universe of things . . . a feeble brook . . . Thus thou Ravine of Arve . . . thou dost lie / Thy giant brood of pines around thee clinging'). Followed by 31 ('A loud, lone sound no other sound can tame'), followed by 21–4 ('Children of an elder time . . . an old and solemn harmony'), followed by a second version of 31.

(b) In pen. Revision of 21–4, written over the pencil draft of the same lines. Addition of lines 30–4, also in pen, including still another version of 31 ('Thy caverns echoing to the Arve's commotion . . . Thou art the path of that unresting sound – / Dizzy Ravine'). Composition breaks off in the middle of 34.

(c) In pencil. Revision of 32–4, followed by completion of 34 ('Dizzy Ravine! and when I gaze on thee') and composition of 25–9 ('Thine earthly rainbows . . . Robes some unsculptured image . . . Wraps all in its own deep eternity'). Followed by 35–47 ('I seem as in a trance sublime and strange / To muse . . . In the still cave of the witch Poesy . . . Some phantom, some faint image'). Composition breaks off in the middle of 47.

(d) In pen. Completion of 47–8 ('till the breast / From which they fled recalls them, thou art there!'). Followed by 49–57 ('Some say that gleams of a remoter world / Visit the soul in sleep . . . do I lie / In dream . . . For the very spirit fails').

(e) In pencil. Revision of 57, followed by 58–63 ('Driven like a homeless cloud . . . Mont Blanc appears . . . Its subject mountains their unearthly forms / Pile around it, ice and rock').

(f) In pen. Revision of 63, followed by the rest of the poem, often heavily revised ('broad vales between / Of frozen floods . . . Thou hast a voice great mountain . . . Power dwells apart . . . a flood of ruin . . . Mont Blanc yet gleams on high . . . If to the human minds imaginings / Silence and solitude were vacancy?').

(g) In pen. Slight revision of lines 1–11.

(h) In pen over earlier pencil draft. Redrafting of 1–11, some revision.

In *H*, 'Mont Blanc' is dated July 23, 1816.[1] While composition probably began on that day (thus the date given in the text), lines 63f, which describe the Mer de Glace, are unlikely to have been composed before July 25, the day Shelley climbed to the surface of the glacier.[2]

Shelley left Geneva for Chamonix on July 21, 1816. He was accompanied by Mary Godwin (her name was not yet Mary Shelley) and by Mary's step-sister Claire Clairemont. The party arrived in Chamonix on the evening of the 22nd, having crossed Pont Pellisier, a bridge at the point where the Valleys of Servoz and of Chamonix meet. The notebook title for Shelley's poem was initially 'At Pont Pellisier', then **'The Scene of** ~~At Pont~~ **Pellisier, at the** ~~opening~~ **extremity** ~~of the valley~~ **of the Vale of Servoz',**[3] and it was presumably this scene that inspired the work. On the evening of July 22, Shelley wrote to Byron that 'it [the valley] exceeds and renders insignificant all that I had before seen, or imagined' (*Letters of PBS*, 1, p. 494). And with reference to the same valley, in the first entry of the journal-letter that Shelley wrote from Chamonix to Thomas Love Peacock (also on the evening of July 22; a version of the letter was published with 'Mont Blanc' in *H*):

> I never knew I never imagined what mountains were before. The immensity of these aerial summits excited, when they suddenly burst upon the sight, a sentiment of extatic wonder, not unallied to madness – And remember this was all one scene.
>
> (*Letters of PBS*, 1, p. 497)

But if 'Mont Blanc' originated in response to this scenery, it is also clear – given material in the letter to Peacock – that the poem was inspired by impressions from subsequent days: of the source of the Arveriron and the Boisson Glacier on the 23rd (recorded in the letter on July 24[4]), of the Mer de Glace on the 25th (recorded in the letter the same day). These impressions also find their way into a poem which is *not* all one scene but a sequence of images, a revision of different experiences and impressions over a period of days.

II '[T]HE ~~STREAM OF VARIOUS THOUGHTS~~ [ETERNAL] UNIVERSE OF THINGS'

The first break in the writing occurs in what will become the second verse paragraph of 'Mont Blanc' (in e. 16, this paragraphing does not yet exist):[5]

<pre>
                                    awful scene
          Where Power, in likeness of the Arve comes down
          From the ice ~~caves~~ gulphs ~~of his secret~~ that
               gird his [icy] secret throne
          ~~Bursting thro [these] dark mountains [like] the fire~~
               ~~like lightning thro the tempest~~
          Bursting thro these dark mountains like the flame
          Of lightning thro the tempest, thou dost lie
          Thy giant brood of pines around thee clinging
          [   ] to the Arve Arve sound can tame
          That with winds & stream   [with] thier high harmony
          [Thy charmed winds] [   ] ~~the with~~
                                        [all] its rocks
                                    [   ] [thy]
          Thy winds [   ]
                                    solemn
          [   ] sound   sound tame
               A loud   lone sound
                                    tame
                                    ceaseless
</pre>

(e. 15. 12–20; 31; 21–4; 31 revised. In pencil. All subsequent quotations of 'Mont Blanc', unless otherwise marked, from e. 16)

Not all of the writing is recoverable, but composition breaks off with 'the loud lone sound' of the Arve. When Shelley returns to the text, to revise and extend the passage, composition breaks off again with essentially the same image, the sound of 'the Arves commotion':

> **Thy caverns echoing to the Arves commotion**
> **A loud lone sound no other sound can tame**
> ~~**Thou liest**~~ **Thou art pervaded with** ~~**untameable**~~ **that**
> **unceasing motion**
> ~~**Some of Belonging to**~~ **Thou art the** ~~**cavern of**~~
> **path of unreposing sound**
> **Ravine of Arve. –**

(30–4. In pen. Here and in all subsequent quotations of 'Mont Blanc', text in pen is marked by bold-face type)

These lines are a revision. They rework a passage from the letter to Peacock (from the evening of the 22nd): the Ravine of Arve is

clothed with gigantic pines and black with its depth below. – so deep that the very
roaring of the untameable Arve which rolled through it could not be heard above.

(Letters of PBS, 1, p. 497)

Shelley's poem replaces silence with sound, presumably to fit the allusive
pattern in earlier lines – the pervasive sound of water:

> where from secret [caves]
> The ~~source~~ fountain of the mind ~~that~~ its tribute brings
> Of waters, ~~with a voice with a sound not all~~ – with a
>   ~~wild~~ sound ~~half~~ not all its own
> Such as a feeble brook will oft assume
> In the wild woods among the mountains lone
> Where waterfalls around it dash & fall forever
> Where woods & winds [contend], & a vast river
> Over its rocks [~~forever~~] ceaselessly bursts & raves
> Thus thou ravine of Arve, dark deep ravine –
> Thou many colored, many voiced vale. –

(4–13. In pencil.)

A simile for 'the fountain of the mind,' for the Ravine as well, the brook
provides a transition from the poem's opening lines: the fountain of the mind is
like the brook, which is like the ravine ('as a feeble brook will oft assume . . .
Thus thou ravine or Arve'); each has 'a ~~wild~~ sound ~~half~~ not all its own' – as does
the 'universe of things' in the mind, the image with which the poem opens.
These associations are not quite the equivalent of philosophical argument since
they develop a figure of speech, but they articulate a radical epistemology in
which things – and not their representations – are said to flow through the
mind. At the same time, the articulations echo Wordsworth, both 'Tintern
Abbey' (*TA*) and the 'Intimations Ode' (*IO*), so that epistemology becomes an
expression that is pervaded by allusion.

Neither the epistemology nor the allusion appear in the opening line as
Shelley first drafted it: 'In daylight thoughts, bright or obscure,' and below, 'In
day – the stream of various thoughts.' When he reworks this line, Shelley finds
a beginning in an allusion: 'In day – the [eternal] universe of things,' an echo of
Wordsworth and the 'life of things' (*TA*, 50), 'A motion and a spirit, that impels
/ All thinking things, all objects of all thought, / And rolls through all things'
(*TA*, 101–3).

> ~~In daylight thoughts, bright and obscure~~ In day – the
>   ~~stream of various thoughts~~ [eternal] universe of
>   things
> Flows thro the mind ~~reflecting rolls~~ & rolls its rapid waves

(1–2. In pencil.)

The radical philosophy emerges from a Wordsworthian allusion.

The remarkable syntactic blending of 'Mont Blanc''s opening lines (any opposition between universe and mind has been dissolved by the pronoun 'its' which has both for antecedents), the merging of mind and universe into the single phenomenal reality that a Wordsworthian image designates ('rolls its rapid waves') – these produce a revisionary equivalent: of 'waters rolling evermore' (*IO*, 170), of 'Tintern Abbey''s 'sense sublime / Of something.' Just below, the 'wild sound half not all its own' recalls 'the mighty world / Of eye and ear, both what they half-create, / And what perceive' (*TA*, 106–8), and Shelley's simile of the brook recalls 'These waters, rolling from their mountain-springs / With a sweet inland murmur' (*TA*, 3–4. 'The sounding cataract / Haunted me like a passion' [*TA*, 77–8]). A letter Mary Shelley wrote after her husband's death catches the revisionary quality of 'Mont Blanc'. Writing to Leigh Hunt from Lyons and with Mont Blanc in the background, she recounts her impressions of 'the ravines of the Alps': 'I felt his [Shelley's] presence more vividly . . . near the roar of the waterfalls & the "inland murmur" of precipitous rivers' (*Letters of MWS*, 1, 360). Mary may also recall one of Shelley's revisions for the Chamonix episode in *Frankenstein*, where the language of 'Tintern Abbey' becomes the language of 'Mont Blanc': in Mary's draft, Victor 'heard the sound of mountain streams and the dashing of waterfalls around,' but Shelley cancels the 'sound of mountain streams,' substituting in its place 'the river raging among rocks' (Abinger MS, 146). In 'Tintern Abbey', the 'inland murmur' had echoed Coleridge and 'The Eolian Harp', 'the stilly murmur of the distant Sea' (11). 'Mont Blanc' transfers the allusion from the English West Country to the Alps where it assumes the inland sound of its new surroundings – in the 'many voiced vale,' where the Arve 'ceaselessly bursts and raves.' At the same time, 'Tintern Abbey''s allusion to 'The Eolian Harp' is replaced by an allusion to a later poem by Coleridge, the 'Hymn before Sun-rise in the Vale of Chamouni' where 'the Arve and Arveiron . . . Rave ceaselessly' (4–5). It is with this allusion, however, that composition breaks off, with the 'loud lone sound' that the 'feeble brook' has assumed.

III   THE 'SUDDEN DEATH PAUSE OF THINGS'

Apparently in recreating an image, Shelley comes to the limits of its revision. The sound of water in 'Tintern Abbey' can be regarded as a symbol, a living part of the unity it represents, one that after five years Wordsworth can hear again. When 'mountain-springs' become the 'feeble brook' in 'Mont Blanc', the stress is not on unity but recurrence: the sound of waterfalls or of woods, winds, the River Arve, as they recur, perhaps are revised in the sound of the brook. At the same time, 'Mont Blanc' offers the sound of Wordsworth's poetry as it recurs, as it is revised and as it revises, so that 'Mont Blanc' has a sound but half its own 'such as a feeble brook will oft assume'. The brook then is an image for revision. When composition breaks off, the image becomes the source of further revisions.

Shelley contributed the entry for July 21 in the journal Mary was keeping at the time. Included in this entry is a description of two waterfalls:

Near Maglans, within a league of each other We saw two waterfalls. They were no more than mountain rivulets, but the height from which they fell, at least 200 feet made them assume a character inconsistent with the smallness of their stream.

(*Journals of MWS*, 1, p. 113)

The description provides a source for the simile of the 'feeble brook' (it too has assumed a character that is inconsistent with its size). When composition of the poem is blocked, Shelley returns to the same passage, to the description in this case of the first of the two waterfalls (the Nant d'Arpenas):

[It] fell in two parts; – & struck first on an enormous rock resembling precisely ~~those a~~ some colossal Egyptian statue of a female diety. It struck the head of the visionary Image & gracefully dividing then fell in folds of foam, more like cloud than water, imitating a viel of the most exquisite woof . . .   (*Journals of MWS*, 1, pp. 113–14).

Shelley writes in the poem:

> Mighty **Ravine ~~of Arve. – [   ] Thy~~** & when I gaze on thee
> Thine ~~earthly~~ earthly rainbows ~~hung [above] the~~
>   stretched across the arched ~~steep~~ steep & sweep
> Of ~~some~~ the ~~white~~ [   ] torrent which with its ~~strange~~
>   laced viel
> Robes some unsculptured image – ~~It the [path]~~ even the sleep
> The ~~momentary death~~ sudden ~~death~~ pause ~~of things~~ . . .
>   (16, 34; 25–7; line between 27 and 28 not in *H*. In pencil.)

'Momentary death' is revised to 'sudden death', then to the 'sudden pause of things.' Finally:

> The sudden pause which does inhabit thee
> ~~Which when the voices And when the woods & waves,~~
>   ~~sunbeams~~ Which when the ~~tumult~~ voices of the
>   desart fail
> And its hues wane, doth blend them all & steep
> Thier ~~tumult~~ periods in its own eternity.
> ~~[I seem] to gaze on my own [mind]~~ I seem as in a vision
>   deep & strange
> ~~I seem~~ to muse on my own ~~separate~~ various phantasy
> My own my human mind . . .
>   (line between 27 and 28; 28–9; 35–7. In pencil.)[6]

Both the image of the ~~white~~ torrent' and the image of the 'feeble brook' have the same source in the journal, the description of the same mountain stream.

Earlier Shelley had transformed mountain rivulets into a revision of Wordsworth by replacing sight with sound. Now he transforms the journal's 'visionary image', cancelling the simile of the Egyptian statue, *un*-sculpting the figure of speech and voicing a blankness in things. The goddess is replaced by an opening, an interpretative gap – the image that is not sculptured – which will eventually lead to a cave in the writing itself. Where the brook is associated with the universe of things and the world of eye and ear, the 'unsculptured image' is associated with sleep, death, 'the sudden pause of things' when the light of sensation fades. From the same realm, Mont Blanc will appear later as another 'unsculptured image' – in the same relation to the 'pause of things' that the ravine has had to the 'universe of things' – but what the poem will articulate first is the scene of composition in which this image has been sought.

Given the previous breaks in composition, the 'pause of things' may also reflect the sudden pause in the writing. The 1817 text will reorder lines to recall the figurative pattern with which the poem opened; traces of breaks in the notebook draft will be cancelled:

> Thou art pervaded with that ceaseless motion,
> Thou art the path of that unresting sound –
> Dizzy Ravine! and when I gaze on thee
> I seem as in a trance sublime and strange
> To muse on my own separate phantasy,
> My own, my human mind (*H*, 32–7)[7]

Gazing at this 'path of . . . unresting sound,' the poet imagines his own mind reflected, associating his mind with the mind the universe flows through in the poem's opening. What this reordering obscures is the association in the Bodleian notebook between the poet's mind and the ravine *which the unsculptured image inhabits* – for which the 'waterfall' is only a veil.[8] Connected with a revisionary 'pause' in both the writing and the mind, the image silences the voices of the ravine and turns the vale into a 'desart'. Shelley is left with the effects of revision: on the one hand, with a landscape whose 'wonders' are cancelled and replaced with a 'darkness'; on the other, with the scene of composition – 'in the still cave of the shade poesy' – where his poem becomes a self-referential allegory:

> thoughts whose wandering wings
> Now [land] rest float above they ~~wonders~~ darkness
>   – now rest
> ~~Where thou art surely no unbidden guest~~
> In the ~~weird~~ still cave of the shade poesy

[~~Seeking among the shadows on high thee~~] Seeking among
    the shadows that pass by
Ghosts of all things that are some shade of thee
Some likeness – some faint image [~~of~~] till ~~they till~~

                    (41–7. In pencil.)

In a cave that reflects the writing itself – the cave of a 'shade poesy' – and where the poet's thoughts may or may not be welcome (the line of welcome is cancelled), the search for a 'shade', a 'likeness', occurs, perhaps for a sculptured image. In the notebook draft, the writing is interrupted with the search still in progress.

IV   '[T]HOU ART THERE'

Shelley could not have known the Simplon Pass episode in *The Prelude* (*P*), but Wordsworth's narrative provides a close analogy. Here too an alpine setting is replaced by a scene of composition; here too the poet is confronted by the uncertainties of revision:

> Imagination! – lifting up itself
> Before the eye and progress of my Song
> Like an unfathered vapour; here that Power
> In all the might of its endowments, came
> Athwart me; I was lost as in a cloud,
> Halted, without a struggle to break through.
>   (*P* VI, 525–30)

In the earliest extant draft of the Apostrophe (MS WW), the text breaks off with a version of these lines: 'Imagination . . . Like an unfathered vapour . . . I [paused?] was lost awhile as in a cloud / A cloud which in my verse . . .'[9] Subsequent lines (not in MS WW, presumably composed some time later) seem to depend on Wordsworth's interpretation of the break in composition as a breakthrough, the discovery – in addition to past anxieties which the writing depicts – that the anxieties experienced while writing could produce a spot of time:

> And now recovering, to my Soul I say
> 'I recognize thy glory.' In such strength
> Of usurpation, in such visitings
> Of awful promise, when the light of sense
> Goes out in flashes that have shewn to us
> The invisible world, doth Greatness make abode
>   (*P* VI, 531–6)

While 'light of sense' refers to the experiential world that the narrative has been depicting, it also refers to the narrative depiction which has just been interrupted by its own imaginative power. Similarly, when the composition of 'Mont Blanc' resumes – in the cave of poetry, where the search for an image has been interrupted – Shelley celebrates the pause in the writing which has evidently just occurred:

> [~~Seeking among the shadows on high thee~~] Seeking among
>   the shadows that pass by
> Ghosts of all things that are some shade of thee
> Some likeness – some faint image ~~[of] till they till~~
>   **the breast**
> **From which they fled recalls them. – thou art there.**
>   (45–8; Revisions in pen.)[10]

When the search is abandoned and the writing breaks off, the pause turns out to be revelatory.

So long as Shelley searches for the image, the image eludes him. It only emerges in the pause between words, in the writing that no longer occurs or at least does not occur just yet. It might be tempting to imagine an image as the equivalent of this pause, but imaging requires that writing begin again, first with the deictic gesture that leaves the image unsculptured: **'thou art there'**. The reference can be interpreted as retrospective, to the Ravine, or prospective, to an image which will emerge. The location the gesture indicates can either be in the cave of poetry (the scene of composition) or outside the cave of poetry, in the phenomenal world – perhaps in both at once. As in the opening lines of the poem where mind and universe blend into the antecedant of the pronoun 'its' (2), so the phenomenal scene and the scene of composition merge as the referents of 'there'. They are each other, in the conflations of the deictic, and the uncertainty of the reference may perpetuate the search – for example, in the allusions which follow – as 'something about to be'.

V   'MONT BLANC ~~APPEARS~~'

> And now, with gleams of half-extinguished thought,
> And many recognitions dim and faint,
> And somewhat of a sad perplexity,
> The picture of the mind revives again . . .
>   (*TA*, 59–62)

> Whither is fled the visionary gleam?
> Where is it now, the glory and the dream?
>
> Our birth is but a sleep . . .
>   (*IO*, 56–8)

Immediately what follows are echoes from Wordsworth's poetry (transitions in which he revised what he had written). Recalling the Ode's myth of pre-existence, Shelley substitutes death for birth, evokes the realm of the unsculptured image, but then stops writing again:

> Some say that gleams of a remoter world
> Visit the soul in sleep – that death is slumber
> And that its shapes the busy thoughts outnumber
> Of those who wake & live – I look ~~above~~ on high –
> ~~Its~~ Has some unknown omnipotence unfurled ~~the~~
> The viel of ~~death~~ life & death – or do I lie
> In dream, & does the ~~world of sleep mighty earth~~ mightier
>   world of sleep
> ~~Outspread far Spread far around spread stretch inaccessibly~~
>   Spread far around & inaccessibly
> Its circles, ~~till the very~~ for the very mind is faint
> With aspiration.   (49–58. In pen.)

When the poem resumes, the final clause is replaced with still another allusion to a transition in Wordsworth's poetry: 'Nor, perchance, / If I were not thus taught, should I the more / Suffer my genial spirits to decay' (*TA*, 112–14).[11]

>   **for the very mind is faint**
> ~~With aspiration~~ For the very spirit fails
> ~~Climbing from among~~ Driven like a homeless cloud from
>   steep to steep
> ~~Which far above shapes~~ Which vanishes among the viewless
>   gales
> Far far above piercing the infinite sky
> Mont Blanc ~~appears & all its subject towers every pyramid~~
>   still, snowy & serene
> Its subject mountains ~~below & all around~~ their unearthly forms
> Pile round it, ice & rock – how hideously
> They overhang the Vale!
>   (57–63. Cancellations of pen in pencil. Text in pencil.)

This revision of Wordsworth apparently leads to the image that has been sought ('**thou art there**'), but in the notebook, the image has also been cancelled: 'Mont Blanc ~~appears~~'.

There is no indication that Mont Blanc was actually visible during Shelley's visit to Chamonix. According to the letter to Peacock, on July 22, in the Servoz Valley: 'Mont Blanc was before us but was covered with cloud, & its base furrowed with dreadful gaps was seen alone' (*Letters of PBS*, 1, p. 497). On subsequent days no view of the summit is recorded. What may have anticipated the image in the poem is Shelley's description of two waterfalls for Mary's journal. The second, he writes,

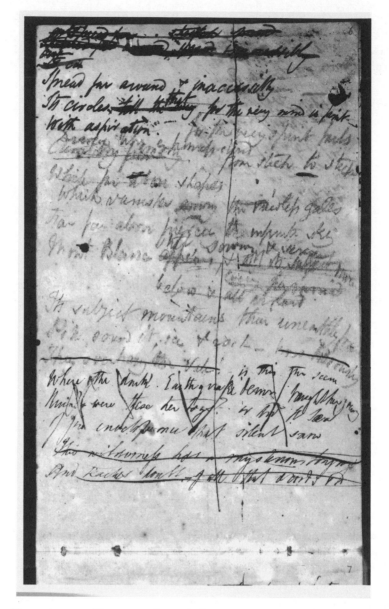

Figures 12.1–2 Two pages from Shelley's *Mont Blanc* MS: Bodleian MS
Shelley adds. e. 16, pp. 6–7.

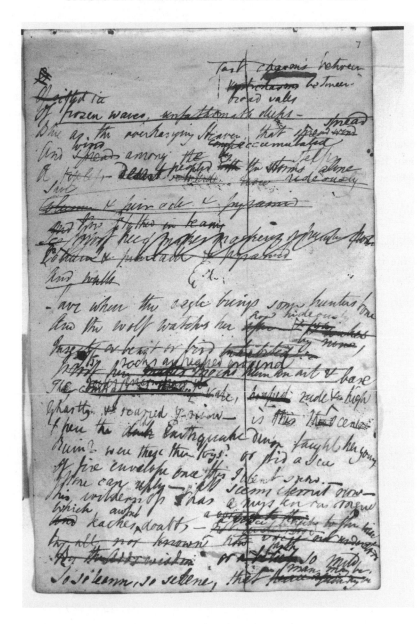

was more continuous, & larger [than the first]. The violence with which it fell, made it look rather like some shape which an exhalation had assumed – than like water – for it fell beyond the mountain; which appeared dark behind it as it might have appeared behind an evanescent cloud.   (*Journals of MWS*, 1, p. 114)

The mountain has the same relation to the second waterfall that the 'visionary image' has to the first. Both waterfalls are particular appearances that 'mountain rivulets' (the 'feeble brook') has assumed. In the journal a feeble brook veils the unnamed mountain like a cloud; in Shelley's poem the unnamed mountain is Mont Blanc. The 'evanescent cloud' becomes a simile for the spirit, and Mont Blanc appears when this cloud is dispelled.

VI   '[F]ROZEN WAVES'

Wordsworth had visited Chamonix in 1790. In retrospect, perhaps in reaction to the theology of Coleridge's 'Hymn', he remembered from the visit his experience of revision:

> That day we first
> Beheld the summit of Mont Blanc, and grieved
> To have a soulless image on the eye
> Which had usurped upon a living thought
> That never more could be   (*P* VI, 452–55)

In late revisions (perhaps after a reading of Shelley's poem), Wordsworth would call this 'soulless image' a 'shock of disappointment / That sudden blank of soul' (MS D), but verbal echoes in the Simplon Pass Episode connect the 'soulless image' with imaginative power ('In *such* strength / Of usurpation' [VI, 532–3; italics added]). The same echoes connect both passages with anxieties that live 'in the embers' and that Wordsworth learned to celebrate in the 'Intimations Ode':

> those obstinate questionings
> Of sense and outward things,
> Fallings from us, vanishings;
> Blank misgivings of a Creature
> Moving about in worlds not realized,
> High instincts, before which our mortal Nature
> Did tremble like a guilty Thing surprized . . .
>   (144–50)

These lines, which refer both to childhood uncertainties and to their recurrence in the poem Wordsworth is writing – the Ode is a texture of 'obstinate questionings' and 'blank misgivings' – locate the imaginative force of Wordsworth's writing in its revisionary moments of usurpation.

Behind the revisions in Wordsworth's Ode lie the traces of other poems: of Coleridge's loss of vision in the 'Dejection Ode' and the theological assertions of the 'Hymn' ('And still I gaze – and with how blank an eye' ['Dejection', 30]; 'O sovran Blanc . . . entranc'd in prayer / I worshipped THE INVISIBLE alone' ['Hymn' 3, 15–16]); of Milton's blindness in *Paradise Lost* ('But cloud instead and every during dark / Surrounds me . . . Presented with a Universal blanc' [*PL* III, 45–6, 48]). In 'Tintern Abbey' Wordsworth denied (not quite convincingly) that 'these forms of beauty' had been to him 'as is a landscape to a blind man's eye' (24–5) – he expressed the 'chearful faith that all which we behold / Is full of blessings' (134–5) – but in the Ode it is the 'questionings / Of sense and outward things,' the uncertainties and misgiving, which are full of blessing. They too are an 'inland murmur,' not of the natural sea, but of the ocean transfigured into the image of a nurturing power: 'Though inland far we be, / Our souls have sight of that immortal sea / Which brought us hither' (165–7). This image will recur in Shelley's poem.

With the appearance of Mont Blanc, another pause in the writing occurs – as if, having found the image he sought, Shelley must now begin to search for other images as well. At first Shelley works to articulate a questioning of his own, but the lines will be cancelled and once again the writing breaks off:

> Pile round it, ice & rock – how hideously
> They overhang the Vale! – **is this the scene**
> **Where the dark Earthquake demon taught her young**
> **Ruin? were these her toys? – or did a Sea**
> **Of fire envelope once that silent snow**
> **This wilderness has a mysterious tongue**
> **And teaches doubts – of all that words of**
>   (An initial draft for 63f. In pencil, then pen.)

This time the pause is followed by what may be the most radical of the poem's revisionary moments. On July 25, two days after composition of 'Mont Blanc' had begun, Shelley climbed to the surface of the Mer de Glace. He recorded what he discovered, first in the letter to Peacock and subsequently in the poem:

On all sides precipitous mountains the abodes of unrelating frost surround this vale. Their sides are banked up with ice & snow broken & heaped up & exhibiting terrific chasms. The summits are sharp & naked pinnacles whose overhanging steepness will not permit snow to rest there. They pierce the clouds like things not belonging to this earth. The vale itself is filled with a mass of undulating ice, & has an ascent sufficiently gradual even to the remotest abysses of these horrible deserts . . . It exhibits an appearance as if frost had suddenly bound up the waves & whir[l]pools of a mighty torrent. We walked to some distance upon its surface, – the waves are elevated about 12 to 15 feet from the surface of the mass which is intersected with long gaps of unfathomable depth, the ice of

whose sides is more beautifully azure than the sky. In these regions every thing changes &
is in motion. *(Letters of PBS,* 1, p. 500)

> Pile round it, ice & rock – ~~how hideously~~
> ~~They overhang the Vale! – is this the scene~~
> ~~Where the dark Earthquake demon taught her young~~
> ~~Ruin? were these her toys? – or did a Sea~~
> ~~Of fire envelope once that silent snow~~
> ~~This wilderness has a mysterious tongue~~
> ~~And teaches doubts – of all that words of~~
>   ~~vast chasms between~~
>   ~~vast chasms~~ broad vales between
> ~~Of rifted ice~~ Of frozen waves, unfathomable deeps –
> Blue as the overhanging Heaven, that ~~spread wind~~
>   spread
> And ~~spread~~ wind among the accumulated steeps
> A ~~lifeless desert solitude~~ desert peopled ~~with~~
>   by the storms alone ~~how hideously~~
> ~~Column & pinacle & pyramid~~
> ~~And Now clothed in beams~~
> ~~Ice Frost here makes mockery of human forms~~
> ~~Columns & pinnacle & pyramid~~
> ~~And walls~~
> Save where the eagle brings some hunters bone
> And the wolf watches her ~~after – it wakes by none~~
> ~~Insect or beast or bird Inhabited~~
> ~~Frost here makes mocks human art~~ how hideously
> ~~They compass the icy vale heaped~~ The ~~rocks encroach~~
>   Its rocks are heaped around rude & bare & high
>   Ghastly & Scarred & riven
>   (63–71. Pencil, then pen. Cancellations in pen.)[12]

'Our souls have sight of that immortal sea', Wordsworth had written, but in
'Mont Blanc' this vision is transformed into a desolate sea of ice.

The affirmations in the 'Intimations Ode' are also revisionary; they recall
'Frost at Midnight', 'the sole unquiet thing' (16) that 'fluttered on the grate'
(15), initially resisting but eventually affirming the 'ministry of frost' (72):
'O joy! that in our embers / Is something that doth live' (*IO*, 132–3).[13]
Wordsworth affirms only the resistance since frost has become an image for all
that is deadening and oppressive in life. The immortal sea is his alternative to a
frozen world: he 'hear[s] the mighty water rolling evermore' (170); he sees the
children nurtured by its shore. During the composition of 'Mont Blanc', on the
other hand, a desolating frost seems to revise what Wordsworth imagined.
'**Frost here makes mockery of human forms**' one cancelled line reads

(between 67–8, in pen), and '**Frost here ~~makes~~ mocks human art**' (between 69–70, in pen).

VII 'YE HAVE A VOICE GREAT MOUNTAINS'

Early in the composition of 'Mont Blanc', Shelley attributed a voice (or voices) to the Ravine of Arve: 'Thou many coloured, many voiced vale'. With the 'unsculptured image' and the 'sudden pause of things', the 'voices of the desert fail', but the desire for a voice that would replace them persists. With regard to the glaciers, in lines omitted from the poem: 'There is voice not understood by all / Sent from these desart caves' (Bodleian Ms. adds. c. 4, folio 72 verso, in pencil). And in cancelled lines from e. 16 that Shelley drafted immediately after the image of Mont Blanc (at first all Shelley imagined that this voice could nurture was doubt): '**This wilderness has a mysterious tongue / And teaches doubts – of all that words of**'. These lines are replaced by the description of the Mer de Glace (64–9), but subsequently they are redrafted, now with reference to faith as well as doubt and specifically in response to the glaciers:

> **This wilderness has a mysterious tongue**
> **~~And~~ Which teaches awful doubt, – ~~not understood~~**
> **   ~~a voice not understood a voice to the~~**
> **   a voice which to the wise**
> **~~By all nor known how~~**
> **~~By the~~ [——] wisdom or ~~a belief~~ faith so mild**
> **So solemn, so serene. that ~~there again may be~~ man may be**
> **~~with such a faith~~**
> **In such a faith with**
> **~~To such high thoughts of nature reconciled~~**
> **[Even] ~~with his with~~ [——] ~~nature~~**
> **~~But for such~~**
> **~~Mountains ye have a voice not understood~~**
> **~~By all but which the wise & great & good~~**
> **~~Interpret or make felt or deeply feel~~**
> **In such a faith with nature reconciled –**
> **Ye have a voice great mountains – to repeal**
> **Large codes of ~~woe vanity fraud & woe vain~~ fraud & woe:**
> **   not understood**
> **By all – but which the wise & great & good**
> **Interpret, or make felt, or deeply feel. –**   (69–83. In pen.)

In *H*, the 'mountains' become Mont Blanc – 'Thou hast a voice, great Mountain' (*H*, p. 80) – but neither in the notebook draft nor in the published text will any voice be heard. Shelley confronts the serene remoteness of power.

The passage concludes with lines that are cancelled, but which Shelley later redrafted:

> **Power dwells apart in its tranquility**
> **Remote serene & inaccessible! –**
> **And this – the naked countenance of Earth**
> **On which I gaze – even these primeval mountains**
> **Teach the adverting mind.**   (94–100. In pen.)

In subsequent lines, rather than the voice Shelley desired, the mountains nurture from their remote serenity an overwhelming sense of desolation.

Shelley had visited the source of the Arveiron and the base of the Boisson Glacier on the 23rd; he had described them for Peacock on the 24th. Now, after visiting the Mer de Glace and recreating his impressions in his writing, Shelley turns to the entry for the 24th, seeking additional revisions in what he has written:

The glaciers perpetually move onward . . . They drag with them, from the regions whence they derive their origins, all the ruins of the mountains . . . These are driven onwards by the irresistable stream of solid ice; and when they arrive at a declivity of the mountain sufficently rapid, roll down scattering ruin . . . The verge of a glacier, like that of Boisson, presents the most vivid image of desolation that it is possible to conceive. No one dares to approach it . . . [T]here is something inexpressibly dreadful in the aspect of the few branchless trunks which nearest to the ice rifts still stand in the uprooted soil. The meadows perish overwhelmed with sand & stones.   (*Letters of PBS*, 1:498–9)

With this descriptive passage available and with the remote serenity of the mountains as a context, Shelley will revise the opening imagery of his poem.

'Mont Blanc''s revisions of 'Tintern Abbey''s imagery recur –

> **All things are changed with tumult & with sound**
> **Wave rolling upon wave ~~with~~ in restless swell**
>   (Between 91–2. In pen.)

– but the revisions themselves are cancelled as Wordsworth's mountain-springs become a 'flood of ruin' (107). Shelley redrafts lines he has previously cancelled, and with them as a point of departure his revised Worthworthianism is extended:

> **~~The glaciers~~**
> **~~Rolling like snakes~~ The glaciers creep**
> **~~With~~ Thro thier own ~~desolation ruin clamity many a precipice~~**
> **   Like snakes that watch thier prey, from thier far fountains**
> **Slow rolling on – there many a precipice**
> **~~Which~~ Frost ~~has piled~~ & the Sun in scorn of human power**
> **~~Column & pinnacle~~ Have piled dome & pyramid & pinnacle**

A ~~city mountain~~ city of death, distinct with many a tower
~~Of~~ And wall impregnable of beaming ice
Yet not a city, but a ~~stream~~ flood of ruin
Is there – ~~the bran~~ [——] ~~fragments of before the giant pines around~~
  ~~it lay before it lay~~
~~Branchless & overthrown Uprooted & overthrown, or branchless stand~~
~~Infrequent in the desert soil and strewing~~
~~The~~ that from the ~~silence desarts~~ boundaries of the ~~air~~ sky
Rolls its ~~eternal~~ perpetual stream   (100–9. In pen.)

The glacial world is the source of the river that nurtures '**distant lands**' (124) and '**bears** [in *H*, 'rolls'] **its** ~~loud tribute~~ **loud waters to the Ocean waves**' (125; the cancelled phrase '**loud tribute**' recalls the 'tribute' of waters with which 'Mont Blanc' opens [5]), but Shelley underscores the destruction from which this nurturing originates, the desolation that is nurtured as well:

          vast pines are strewing
  ~~The path whic[ ] its fallen fragments The desart which~~
      ~~path, which it Its destined path, & rocks which in The~~
      ~~path~~ Its destined path, or in the ~~ruined~~ mangled soil
  Branchless & shattered stand, ~~and~~ the rocks drawn down
  ~~From the~~ From ~~the~~ yon remotest waste ~~all is life is all things~~
      have overthrown
  The limits of the dead & living world
  Never ~~to~~ to be reclaimed ~~again all is the spoil all is the spoil~~
      ~~and the as the spoil the wind~~ [——] [——] ~~insects & beasts~~
  ~~That dwelt~~ the dwelling place
  Of ~~many beasts & insects is the~~ insects beasts & birds becomes ~~its~~
      its spoil
  ~~Of the~~ thier food & thier retreat forever gone
  So much of life & joy ~~has fled~~ is lost – the race
  Of man flies far in ~~terror~~ dread, ~~while the~~ his work & dwelling
  Vanish ~~like~~ as smoke before the tempests stream
  ~~Amid the fields & woods Even with the fields & woods forests~~
  And their place is not known.   (109–20. In pen.)

The allusion to the Book of Job and Psalm 103 simultaneously repeats an allusion to the same Biblical passages in *The Excursion*: 'of the poor many did cease to be, / And their place knew them not' (I, 545–6). The dwellings the glaciers destroy recall Wordsworth's images of ruin – Margaret's cottage, the garden, 'the useless fragment of a ruined bowl' (493) – connect ruin to Wordsworth's intimations of immortality. In 'Mont Blanc' it is desolation that makes 'our noisy years seem moments in the being / Of the eternal Silence' (*IO*, 157–8).

VIII   'OBSTINATE QUESTIONINGS'

At times 'Mont Blanc''s impressions of eternity seem to intimate the absence of a Wordsworthian vision:

> The Clouds that gather round the setting sun
> Do take a sober colouring from an eye
> That hath kept watch o'er man's mortality
>
> (*IO*, 199–201)

> **the snows** ~~flakes fall~~ **descend**
> **Upon that mountain –** *none beholds them there*
> **Nor when** ~~the sunlight wraps thier flakes~~ **thier flakes burn in**
>   **the sinking sun**
> **Or the starbeams dart thro them** (131–4. In pen. Italics added.)

But while Shelley's revisions can be regarded as negations of Wordsworth, it may be more accurate to regard them as intensifications – of 'obstinate questionings' and 'blank misgivings' beyond the possibility of consolation (the negations may be Wordsworth's as well), of the turn in Wordsworth from Coleridgean pantheism to the burdens of the mind's imaginings.

The wilderness '**teaches awful doubt – or faith so mild / So solemn, so serene**', Shelley writes. Although critics have tended to associate this faith with Wordsworth, the doubt is Wordsworthian as well – including Shelley's doubt over how a Wordsworthian faith should be interpreted. Having cancelled '**but for such**' faith in e. 16, Shelley returned to this phrase in 1817.[14] Most recent editions have discounted his final choice, either by glossing 'but for such faith' as the equivalent of 'only for such faith', or by substituting the uncancelled line in the Bodleian manuscript for the language in *H*. These interpretations ignore, however, the force of Shelley's indecision. 'In such a faith' offers a conventional reading of Wordsworth's poetry; 'but for such faith', a reading more like Wordsworth's own in 'Elegiac Stanzas' (this 'light that never was, on sea or land . . . in the fond delusion of my heart' [15, 29]). That 'chearful faith' should *prevent* a reconciliation with nature suggests a sophisticated reading of natural religion. What Shelley seems to have recognized in 1817 is that Wordsworthian faith can nurture a mode of skepticism, and the wording serves to intensify a radical Wordsworthianism – its obstinate questioning of sense and outward things (questions addressed to the external world and questions addressed by the external world) – its ability to sustain the 'blank misgivings' of Wordsworthian poetry. In *Alastor* Shelley's narrator had hoped 'to still these obstinate questions' (26), but 'Mont Blanc' extends their range.

As Shelley's poem concludes and Mont Blanc '**gleams on high**' (127), the

image may recall the feeble brook: the mountain is also a revisionary image that
assumes the power of its surroundings:

> the ~~calm is there~~ Power is there
> ~~The solemn calm of power~~ The still & solemn power ~~of life &~~
> ~~death~~ of many ~~sounds~~ sights
> ~~And sound Death life Motion & sound~~ And many sounds, &
> much of ~~good & ill~~ life & death . . .
> . . . ~~Power the power~~ the secret
> strength of things
> Which governs thought, and ~~rules the starry the mute [is]~~
> ~~which overhangs this~~ to the dome
> Of Heaven is as a law, – inhabits thee   (127–9, 139–141. In pen.)

Shelley's revisions of 'the life of things' – the 'universe of things', the 'sudden
pause of things' – become 'the secret strength of things'. For a final time, Shelley
rewrites 'Tintern Abbey', its 'world / Of eye and ear' (*TA*, 106–7), turning it
toward the life in the embers of Wordsworth's ode. 'Mont Blanc' intensifies the
disquiet in Wordsworth's poetry, finding intensities in the questions that usurp.
In Wordsworth such questions can lead to affirmations – if 'blank misgivings'
are 'a sudden blank of soul', they also provide tokens of imaginative power –
but it is characteristic of Shelley's poem to be unsure:

> And what were thou, and earth, and stars, and sea,
> If to the human mind's imaginings
> Silence and solitude were vacancy?   (*H*, 142–4)

In the Bodleian notebook, even the final question is interrupted by cancellations, pauses in the writing. After the catalogue – mountain and earth, stars and
the sea – several rejected lines occur: Shelley writes, '**Pauses [Poet]**', and
cancels it; he writes, '**[   ] not the first**', and cancels that as well. Next
Shelley writes, 'When all the shapes', giving the final question the form, '**And
what were thou & Earth & stars & Sea / When all the shapes**'. The
adverbial clause is neither completed nor rejected, but below it Shelley adds the
question that provides his conclusion and that has emerged in all its uncertainty
out of the process of composition. To interpret it as rhetorical would be to
evade its suspension of belief.

> ~~What~~ And what were thou & Earth & Stars & Sea
> ~~Pauses [Poet]~~
> ~~[——] not the first~~
> ~~The~~
> When all the shapes
> If to the human minds imaginings
> Silence & solitude were vacancy
>
> (142–4. In pen.)

IX ADDENDUM: WRITING *FRANKENSTEIN*, 'THERE IS A VOICE'

For still I hoped to see the *stranger's* face
(*FM*, 41)

Wordsworth's 'blank misgivings' had revised the disquiet that the stranger reflects in 'Frost at Midnight' and that 'portend[s]' a break in the solitude: 'in this deep calm' a presence between 'the interspersed vacancies / And momentary pauses of the thought' (*FM*, 45–7), 'the arrival of some absent friend'. In 'Frost at Midnight', the friend is Coleridge's child Hartley; in the 'Intimations Ode', the child who fathers the man and is nurtured by the sea. Perhaps in 'Mont Blanc' the friend is Wordsworth himself, whose presence is pervasive in the vacancies, but it is tempting to imagine another as well – if not in 'Mont Blanc', then anticipated by the poem and realized in a work which constitutes a sequel, the novel that Mary Shelley was writing at the time.

The scene in *Frankenstein* on the Mer de Glace recreates the landscape from 'Mont Blanc' (I am quoting from the draft that Shelley edited; his contributions are in italics):

For some time I sat upon ~~the~~ the rock that overlooks the sea of ice. A mist covered both that and the surrounding mountains[.] Presently a breeze dissipated the mist and I descended on the ~~ice~~ glacier. ~~It is interpersed with rifts.~~ The surface is very uneven rising like the waves of a troubled sea descending ~~low~~, & interspersed by rifts that sink deep – The ~~width of the~~ *field of* ice is ~~merely~~ [in F, 'almost'] a ~~lege~~ league *in width* but I was [in F, 'spent'] nearly two hours *in* crossing it – The opposite mountain is a bare perpendicular rock. From that side where I now stood Montanvert was exactly opposite at the distance of a league and above it rose Mont Blanc in awful majesty. I remained in a recess of the rock gazing on this wonderful & stupendous scene. *The sea or rather the vast river of ice, wound among ~~the~~ its dependent mountains whose aerial summits hung over its recesses. Their icy & glittering peaks shone in the sunlight over the clouds.* (Abinger MS, 152–3; F; 93)[15]

Frankenstein revisits 'Mont Blanc' – perhaps in order to discover another presence in the landscape. In *Frankenstein*, this presence turns out to be the nameless creature who has made the glacier his home ('the desert mountains and dreary glaciers are my refuge . . . the caves of ice . . . a dwelling to me' [F, 95]). Perhaps the creature provides the voice which Shelley invokes in 'Mont Blanc' and that can 'repeal / Large codes of fraud and woe'.

'[T]he only unquiet thing' (F, 87), *Frankenstein*'s narrator revisits the Mer de Glace in search of a ministry of frost:

I remembered the effect that the view of the tremendous and evermoving glacier had produced upon my mind when I first saw it. It had then filled me with a sublime ecstacy that gave wings to the soul, and allowed it to soar from the obscure world to light and joy. (*F*, 92)

Frankenstein determines 'to go alone' since 'the presence of another would destroy the solitary grandeur of the scene' (*F*, 92). What finds him on the glacier, however, is precisely such a presence, Mary Shelley's radical revision of Milton's Satan. If, informing Shelley's Wordsworthianism, a source of 'Mont Blanc''s misgivings is Milton, his response to blindness and vacancy ('for the Book of knowledge fair / Presented with a Universal blanc'), then perhaps what *Frankenstein* reimagines is the politics haunting blindness (Milton's blindness with respect to Satan, the exclusion of the other that this political blindness allows):

I suddenly beheld the figure of a man, at some distance, advancing towards me with superhuman speed. He bounded over the crevices of ice . . . He approached . . . [an] unearthly ugliness . . . almost too horrible for human eyes . . . [He] placed his hated hands before my eyes . . . 'thus I take from thee a sight which you abhor. Still thou canst listen to me . . '. (*F*, 93–6)

In retrospect one might regard 'Mont Blanc' as an opening to this voice, as revision displacing faith with responsiveness to the stranger – to this 'presence that disturbs me' in 'the interspersed vacancies'.

NOTES

My thanks to the Bodleian Library for permission to transcribe portions of MS Shelley adds. e. 16 and c. 4. Unless otherwise noted, the text of 'Mont Blanc' will be quoted from the working draft in c. 16. Numbering, however, corresponds to equivalent lines from the published text in *History of a Six Weeks' Tour* (London, 1817; abbreviated in the essay as *H*). In my transcriptions from the notebook I have routinely reproduced cancellations and revisions in order to recreate the process of composition and revision. I have not tried to reproduce the look of the manuscript page. I have used brackets [   ] to indicate uncertain readings. Text drafted in pen is distinguished from text in pencil by bold-face type.

   My thanks to Lord Abinger for permission to quote from the *Frankenstein MS* (Bodleian MS Abinger Sep. c. 477); to the British Museum for permission to quote from the Scrope Davies fair copy of 'Mont Blanc' (Loan 70/8); to the Morgan Library for access to the manuscript of the Chamonix letter to Peacock (M. 1407); to Jonathan Wordsworth for sharing his notes on *Prelude* MS WW; to the Trustees of Dove Cottage for access to this manuscript.

   I have cited the following editions: for *History of a Six Weeks' Tour* (*H*), the Woodstock Facsimile, ed. Jonathan Wordsworth (1989); for Shelley's poetry and prose, the Norton Edition, ed. Donald Reiman and Sharon Powers (1977); for Shelley's letters, the Clarendon Edition, Vol. 1, ed. Frederick Jones (1964); for the 1818 text of *Frankenstein* (*F*), the University of Chicago Edition, ed. James Reiger (1974); for Mary Shelley's Journals, Vol. 1, the Clarendon Edition, ed. Paula R. Feldman and Diana

Scott-Kilvert (1987); for Mary Shelley's Letters, the Johns Hopkins Edition, Vol. 1, ed. Betty T. Bennett (1980); for *The Excursion*, the Clarendon Edition, ed. Ernest de Selincourt and Helen Darbishire (1940–9); for MS D of *The Prelude*, the Cornell Edition of the Fourteen-Book poem, ed. W. J. B. Owen (1985); for Wordsworth's other poetry, including the *1805 Prelude* (*P*), the Oxford Authors Edition, ed. Stephen Gill (1984); for Coleridge's poetry, the Clarendon Edition, ed. Ernest Hartley Coleridge (1935); for Milton's poetry, the Odyssey Edition, ed. Merrit Y. Hughes (1957). The epigraph is taken from *Conversation in the Mountains*, in Paul Celan, *Collected Prose*, trans. Rosemarie Waldrop (Manchester, 1986), p. 19.

An earlier version of this essay was delivered at the Wordsworth Summer Conference, Grasmere (1986) and appeared in *The Wordsworth Circle*, 18:3 (1987), pp. 108–14.

1 The date given in *H* is actually 'June 23, 1816', but this is clearly a misprint.
2 The revision in ink of lines 1–11 (stages g and h) probably dates from more than a year later. Since two pens were employed, composition presumably occurred in two stages. The first pen was also used to compose a number of lines for *Rosalind and Helen* over the pencil draft of 'Mont Blanc': '**well Helen – well / You love me strangely / I pray you cease such talk I feel.**' A continuation from p. 2 of e. 16, these lines are revised, then cancelled, on p. 13 – after the conclusion of *Mont Blanc* and as part of work toward lines 40–83 of *Rosalind and Helen*. The work on this poem dates from the autumn of 1817, the period when Shelley was preparing 'Mont Blanc' for publication. Perhaps as he composed *Rosalind and Helen*, he began to reread, then rework, the draft of 'Mont Blanc' in the notebook.

At first (stage g) the reworking involves corrections to match language that had already appeared in the fair copy of the poem, transcribed in Shelley's hand within a month of the visit to Chamonix, but subsequently lost and unavailable in 1817 (this fair copy, which came into the possession of Scrope Davies, was left behind when Shelley returned to England from Geneva). It is possible that Shelley corrected e. 16 from memory. It is also possible that he worked from another version which like the printer's copy of 'Mont Blanc' is no longer extant. In any case, after making two corrections ('fountain of the mind' becomes the '**source of human thought**' [5]; 'waterfalls . . . [that] dash & fall forever' become 'waterfalls . . . [that] **leap** forever' [9]), Shelley then, in another pen (stage h), transcribed the first eleven lines over the earlier pencil draft, in one case offering a new wording not to be found in Scrope Davies, but that recurs in *H*. In e. 16, the pencil draft (stage a), the 'feeble brook' has 'a ~~wild~~ sound ~~half~~ not all its own'; in the Scrope Davies fair copy: 'a sound not all its own'; in e. 16, the ink draft (stage h) and in the published text: '**a sound but half its own**' (6).
3 'At Pont Pellisier' is written in pencil, then revised in pen. In the Scrope Davies fair copy, the title becomes: 'Scene – Pont Pellisier in the Vale of Servox'. The focus of the title changes in *H* from the scene of inspiration to the scene of composition: on page 172, 'LINES / WRITTEN IN THE VALE OF CHAMOUNI'; on . 174, above paragraph 1 of the poem, 'MONT BLANC / LINES WRITTEN IN THE VALE OF CHAMOUNI'.

4 On July 24, the party attempted to climb to the Mer de Glace but was turned back by rain. Later in the day Mary worked on *Frankenstein* ('[I] write my story' (*Journals of MWS*, Vol. 1, p. 118)).

5 In e. 16, the only clear paragraphing occurs between what will become paragraphs 2 and 3 (lines 48 and 49) in *H*.

6 When Shelley drafted these lines in pencil, he also revised a number of previous lines:

> **Thy caverns echoing to the Arve's commotion**
> **A loud lone sound no other sound can tame**
> ~~Thou liest~~ **Thou are prevaded with** ~~untameable unceasing~~
> that unceasing **motion**
> ~~Some of Belonging to~~ **Thou art the** ~~cavern of~~ **path**
> **of** ~~unreposing~~ that unresting **sound**
> Mighty **Ravine**   (30–4. In pen. Revised in pencil.)

One phrase in the pencil draft that follows was subsequently revised in pen: 'Of ~~some the white torrent which with its strange laced~~ **the aerial waterfall whose** viel' (26).

7 In Scrope Davies, the reordering has already occurred.

8 The effect of the reordering in *H* is enhanced by revision of the poems opening line. Where e. 16 establishes a contrast between day and the aura of sleep, dream, death, that surrounds the 'unsculptured image,' *H* cancels the contrast. The poem no longer begins 'in day': 'The everlasting universe of things / Flows through the mind, and rolls its rapid waves' (*H*, 1–2).

9 Jonathan Wordsworth's transcription. In *Prelude* manuscript MS WW, the Apostrophe to Imagination is separated from the disappointment in the Simplon Pass by an initial version of the Cave of Yordas simile (in *P* VIII, 711–27) and by several missing notebook pages.

10 In Scrope Davies and in *H*, 'till the breast . . .,' but in e. 16 the word 'till' appears to have been cancelled.

11 As Beth Lau suggested during a conversation, it is unlikely that Shelley could have known the allusion to the same lines from *Tintern Abbey* in *Dejection: An Ode*: 'My genial spirits fail' (39). The only available text at the time would have been the version published in the *Morning Post* in 1802.

12 During revision in e. 16, what was initially a description of Mont Blanc's 'dependent mountains' ('how hideously / They overhang the Vale!') becomes a description of the glacier ('how hideously / Its rocks are heaped around').

13 See Lucy Newlyn, *Coleridge, Wordsworth and the Language of Allusion* (Oxford, 1986), p. 158.

14 In Scrope Davies: 'In such a faith.'

15 Mary was not much impressed with the glacier. Unlike Shelley's descriptions or her recreation of his writing in *Frankenstein*, what Mary's journal describes is a desolation without sublimity: 'This is the most desolate place in the world – iced mountains surround it – no sign of vegetation appears except on the place from which [we] view the scene – we went on the ice – It is traversed by irregular crevices ~~the~~ whose sides of ice appear blue while the surface is of a dirty white – We dine on the mountain' (Vol. 1, p. 119).

13

CORRECTING THE IRRITABILITY OF HIS TEMPER: THE EVOLUTION OF LEIGH HUNT'S *AUTOBIOGRAPHY*

TIMOTHY WEBB

LEIGH Hunt was in the first place a circuitous autobiographer. This may have been a result, in part at least, of the rather unfortunate and compromised circumstances in which he was propelled towards his first extended contribution to the emerging genre. After the deaths of Shelley and of Byron, Hunt found himself trapped in Italy, a country which he found essentially uncongenial and harshly out of keeping with the pleasant images conjured up by Italian prints and the *Parnaso Italiano*. The publisher Henry Colburn rescued Hunt from impecunious and irritable exile; Colburn agreed to look after Hunt's financial needs on the understanding that Hunt would produce a 'selection' from his own writings, preceded by a biographical sketch.[1] Not untypically, perhaps, Hunt returned to England but did not honour his side of the bargain. When Colburn eventually pressed him, the original plan was altered in the interests of expediency. Hunt's account of the book's evolution is somewhat contradictory. In the Preface to *Lord Byron and Some of his Contemporaries* (1828), which was the book's eventual title, Hunt at first seems to claim that the responsibility for the structural alterations was his own: 'I wished to make amends for loss of time: the plan of the book became altered; and I finally made up my mind to enlarge and enrich it with an account of Lord Byron.' The concluding paragraph suggests something rather different:

The account of Lord Byron was not intended to stand first in the book. I should have kept it for a climax. My own reminiscences, I fear, coming after it, will be like bringing back the Moselle, after devils and Burgundy. Time also, as well as place, is violated: and the omission of a good part of the auto-biography, and substitution of detached portraits for inserted ones, have given altogether a different look to the publication from what was contemplated at first. But my publisher thought it best; perhaps it is so; and I have only to hope, that in adding to the attractions of the title-page, it will not make the greater part of the work seem unworthy of it.[2]

The product of this negotiation and rearrangement was a large, if miscellaneous, book in three volumes whose title reflects some confusion of purpose: *Lord Byron and Some of his Contemporaries; with Recollections of the Author's Life, and of his Visit to Italy* (hereafter referred to as *LBSC*). This new disposition of material was dictated by the generous but shrewd Colburn, who had recently published Thomas Medwin's *Conversations of Lord Byron* and the anonymous *Life and Writings of Lord Byron* and who must have sensed the commercial possibilities of Byron's name. Colburn attempted to capitalize on the devils and Burgundy by arranging for extracts to be printed in *The Athenaeum* in advance of publication. Although contemporary reviewers did not ignore the autobiographical element (*Blackwood's*, for one, maintained its savagely judicial perspective), *LBSC* is largely identified not with Hunt's account of his own life or of his travels but with his uncharacteristically intemperate attack on Byron.

Yet in a strangely roundabout way Hunt's *Autobiography* had its origins in the misconceived, unfortunate, and largely forgotten book 'which Colburn called Lord Byron and his Contemporaries' and to which 'for obvious reasons, my name was suffered to be attached'.[3] When Hunt eventually produced his *Autobiography* in 1850 he did not make a fresh beginning but turned for much of his material to the earlier work. The first volume of *LBSC*, which was devoted to Byron, provided the basis for those parts of Chapter 19 in *Autobiography* on 'Lord Byron in Italy' and on 'Pisa', for part of Chapter 20 on 'Genoa' and for a few pages of Chapter 15, 'Free Again – Shelley in England'. Most of the material which had scandalized the reading public of 1828 by its malicious indiscretions was excluded; the rest now took its place in a chronological sequence which largely followed the course of Hunt's own life, while leaving room for chapters on 'Literary Acquaintance', 'Political Characters', and 'Keats, Lamb, and Coleridge', which were less obviously integrated into the narrative. These character sketches were based on the materials of the second volume of *LBSC*, where Hunt had given separate treatment to Moore, Shelley, Keats, Lamb, and Coleridge, and a composite chapter to Horace and James Smith, Fuseli and the others who feature under the heading of 'Literary Acquaintance'. The third volume of *LBSC* which bore the general title 'Recollections of the Author's Life', provided the foundation for the opening chapters of *Autobiography* and for the chapters on Hunt's 'Voyage to Italy' and on his 'Return to England'.

There were, of course, many other changes, exclusions, and additions. *Autobiography* is not in any simple sense that product of 1850 which many readers might take it to be. It draws on some but by no means all of those autobiographical materials whose exclusion from *LBSC* Hunt had so much regretted. It is also indebted to the *Letters from Abroad* which had appeared in *The Liberal* and to the two-part essay on the suburbs of Genoa and the country about London which had appeared in *The Literary Examiner* in 1823.[4] There are also various other self-borrowings from Hunt's periodical journalism and from letters. Yet in spite of these important exceptions, the book derives much of its being and its language from *LBSC*, of which it provides a revised and extended version.

LBSC is itself in many ways revisionary, and is often derived from Hunt's own earlier writings. For a number of years he had been in the habit of publishing essays in which he recorded various phases of his life or his experience. These might more properly be described as occasional memoirs rather than as exercises in autobiography, since for the most part they are concerned with impressions, character-sketches, and narratives and not with introspection, self-exploration, or auto-criticism.[5] At times, however, as in *The Wishing-Cap* essays for *The Examiner* (March–October 1824), they allowed Hunt to develop his autobiographical propensities while leaving room for 'any subject to which I feel an impulse, politics not excepted'. Although there is no fixed plan and no systematic development of autobiography, Hunt feels the need to defend at the outset the apparent egotism of the enterprise: 'I believe that if the first person we met in the street were to put down upon paper the experiences he has had in life, his schooldays, journeys, &c. they would be found interesting.' (This is only one example of what seems to have been a recurrent urge to apologize for the autobiographical vein and the use of the first person singular.)

The Wishing-Cap essays range over a wide variety of topics which feature both in *LBSC* and later in *Autobiography*: among other things, they touch briefly on musical evenings at Charles Lamb's house, the Volunteers (in which Hunt served), the literary dinners which Rowland Hunter inherited from Joseph Johnson the publisher, Christ's Hospital, the Thornton family in Austin Friars, Italian scenes, childhood memories of military music in St James's Park, and Hunt's imprisonment. All of these subjects are taken up in *LBSC*, quite often only glancingly but sometimes at greater length, and frequently the borrowing is direct. The longest and most impressive example of self-borrowing is provided by the two essays in which Hunt so memorably describes his imprisonment in Horsemonger Lane. Here for the first time he gave his celebrated account of how he transformed his grim surroundings into a pastoral *trompe-l'œil*: 'I papered the walls with a trellis of roses; I had the ceiling coloured with clouds and sky; the barred windows were screened with Venetian blinds; and when my book-cases were set up with their busts, and flowers and a piano-forte made their appearance, perhaps there was not a handsomer room on that side of the water.' This passage is usually quoted from the 1850 or, more usually, the 1859 version of *Autobiography* but it had first appeared in print as early as 1824. Even then, Hunt's frank response to the circumstances of his imprisonment had drawn upon a still earlier stratum of writings; his primary source was a remarkable sequence of leading articles for *The Examiner* which he had written from Horsemonger Lane immediately after his sentence and in which he had provided a very public reaction not only to his trial and sentence but to the everyday details of his incarceration.[6]

In addition to this, Hunt's portraits of contemporary writers drew heavily on the reviews and assessments of their work which he had published over the years. His accounts of Shelley, Keats, Lamb, Coleridge, Moore, and Campbell were a mixture of biography and criticism informed not only in their larger perspectives but in many of their phrases and formulations by the critical essays which he had contributed to *The Examiner*. The most complex and the most significant area of debt was constituted by the lengthy chapter in *LBSC* on Shelley. In composing this chapter Hunt was able to make use of a long sequence of essays and reviews in which he had defended Shelley against his critics and expounded the virtues of his life and work. These included a series of reviews in *The Examiner*, a number of which specifically defended Shelley against the moral strictures of *The Quarterly*; three further reviews which he had written in 1822 while waiting for calmer seas at Plymouth; passages from 'My Books' and the second essay 'On the Suburbs of Genoa and the Country about London' in *The Literary Examiner*; an essay intended for *The Liberal* but never published (and only recently identified); and a longer and quite different essay which was sent to *The Westminster Review* as a review of *Posthumous Poems* but was rejected.[7] The Shelley chapter was most heavily indebted to the review for the *Westminster* but it brought all this material to a focus. As we shall see, Hunt's version of Shelley not only involved a rewriting and recapitulation of his own interpretations but also a corrective revision of the prejudiced and critical attitudes of those who had pronounced judgment on Shelley without any personal knowledge of his life.

Hunt was in the habit of working by means of accumulation and accretion. In the case of *LBSC* the pressure to meet his obligations to Colburn may have encouraged him to draw upon his own miscellaneous efforts at autobiography and reminiscence. No doubt there was an element of convenience in this, and an element of opportunism, but publication in book form and assimilation into a larger structure might also have seemed to offer a more authoritative status to the piecemeal products of periodical journalism. On the other hand, we must remember, too, Hunt's publicly stated disappointment in both the structure of *LBSC* and his inability to make use of many of the autobiographical materials which he had prepared. Although a selective and organizing process was involved, the incorporation of earlier materials into *LBSC* was more cumulative than revisionary. Yet any study of the revisionary practices of *Autobiography* must take into account the methods and the circumstances which generated *LBSC*. As we have seen, *LBSC* itself provided a foundation for much of what was to become the *Autobiography* while in the case of the *Autobiography* itself Hunt's use of his materials was consistently revisionary and reflected not only his dissatisfaction with *LBSC* but several major changes of perspective.

To begin with, Hunt was now in a position to correct various errors and imprecisions and to put the record straight in a number of cases where he had not been able to do so previously. Some of these changes were made for the 1850 edition of *Autobiography* and some for the revised edition of 1859 which continued the process.[8] So, for example, he deleted in 1850 this confusing passage about his brother John who had set up a paper called *The News*: 'I say, the paper was his own, but it is a singular instance of my incuriousness, that I do not know to this day, and most likely never did, whether he had any share in it or not. Upon reflection, my impression is, that he had not' (*LBSC*, p. 401). Here he relieves himself from the shadow of Harold Skimpole, who had yet to be invented by Dickens. Elsewhere, he is careful to define in one instance his parents not as 'Republicans and Unitarians' but simply as 'Unitarians' (*LBSC*, 317; *Autobiography* [hereafter *A*], 1, p. 22) and in another to add the qualification that his mother had been 'perhaps' a Republican (*A*, 1, p. 34). The text of *Autobiography* does not tell us, as *LBSC* does, that while he was in prison Hunt daily took a 'stout' walk in his cell 'of I dare say fourteen or fifteen miles' (*LBSC*, p. 422; *A*, 2, p. 145). *1850* still prints the anecdotes concerning Shelley's chivalry to the seduced young lady at the ball (*LBSC*, pp. 183–4) and Keats's admission on a bench at Hampstead that 'his heart was breaking' (*LBSC*, p. 267; *A*, 2, p. 210), but neither story was retained in 1859. Both *LBSC* and the 1850 version tell us that when Shelley took his final leave of Hunt to return by way of Leghorn he was going 'to sign his will in that city', but the 1859 version does not (*LBSC*, pp. 17–18, *A*, 3, p. 14).

A fascinating example of Hunt's corrections is provided by a detail of the Sunday which Shelley and Hunt spent together in Pisa on the eve of Shelley's fatal voyage. It comes at the end of a passage where Hunt has been claiming that 'with all his scepticism', Shelley exhibited what Hunt calls a 'natural piety'. At this point in *LBSC* Hunt directly attributes to Shelley a view which is precisely in accord both with his own philosophy and with his attitudes to the effect of organ music: 'He said to me in the Cathedral at Pisa, while the organ was playing, "What a divine religion might be found out, if charity were really made the principle of it, instead of faith!"' (p. 176).[9] Here he is quoting, with minor verbal alterations, the account which had been written little more than two years after the event and which he had intended for *The Westminster Review*. In *Autobiography* the authority for this statement has shifted significantly and Shelley's relation to it is much less uncomplicated: 'He assented warmly to an opinion which I expressed in the cathdral at Pisa . . .' (*A*, 3, p. 20). The passage of time may have acted as an obscuring agency but it may also have allowed Hunt a greater objectivity which enabled him to discriminate between his own opinions and those of Shelley.

If the passage of time enabled Hunt to make some corrections and adjustments, it also gave him the opportunity to become less self-revealing and to make his work less directly a register of his own feelings. Perhaps because of the urgency with which it had been composed, *LBSC* is often unguardedly and embarrassingly frank. For example, there is Hunt's admission that he preferred Shelley to Keats and that he himself was 'the dearest friend that [Shelley] had' (*LBSC*, p. 190). There is his reaction to the loss of Shelley; 'From that time, Italy was a black place to me' (*LBSC*, p. 18). There is the account of his emotions on first encountering Christ's Hospital: 'I was not prepared for so great a multitude; for the absence of the tranquillity and security of home; nor for those exhibitions of strange characters, conflicting wills, and violent, and, as they appeared to me, wicked passions, which were to be found, in little, in this epitome of the great world. I was confused, frightened and made solitary' (*LBSC*, p. 360). Above all, perhaps, there is his gratitude to those who had befriended him during his imprisonment: 'Why must I not say every thing upon this subject, showing my improvidence for a lesson, and their generosity for a comfort to mankind? . . . I might as soon thank my own heart. Their names are trembling on my pen, as that is beating at the recollection' (*LBSC* p. 428). The image of Sir John Swinburne 'fills my whole frame with emotion. I could kneel before him and bring his hand upon my head, like a son asking his father's blessing' (*LBSC*, p. 427). Hunt reveals himself in the act of struggling against the desire to give thanks too openly: 'I am always afraid of talking about them, lest my tropical temperament should seem to render me too florid' (*LBSC*, p. 427).

None of these emotional outbursts was retained in *Autobiography*, and other uncomfortably self-revealing or self-regarding passages were also omitted. These changes are in keeping with a reticent polarity which was always in tension with the emotionalism of Hunt's 'tropical temperament' and with his autobiographical proclivities. The account of his life and character in *LBSC* may often seem disarmingly frank, yet it still is in some ways considerably less open and expressive than the manuscript narrative of his childhood and adolescence which he probably intended for Colburn before he was forced to compromise. Although this manuscript draft formed the basis for parts of *LBSC* and *Autobiography* and much of it was later translated into the printed text with minimal variations, many pages were abandoned and never published. Hunt is much more explicit in the draft about his adolescent infatuations; in *Autobiography* they are given a treatment which tends towards the composite and reduces their individuality and their interest. The draft is franker too about the sexual dangers of Hunt's tropical temperament (this phrase was one of his modes of referring to his West Indian origins, which he associated with indolence and sensuality).[10] Hunt also wrote 'An Attempt of the Author to Estimate his own Character', which he seems to have intended for *LBSC*. Actually printed, apparently for the first edition, but then never published,[11] the 'Attempt' contains 'matter, which no reputation for candour could render it agreeable to say, and which nothing could induce me to set down, if I did not believe that truth in society were the one thing needful'. Among other self-revelations, Hunt admits that 'I am not naturally a teller of truth. Impulse and fancy would tend to make me the reverse'; at the same time, he claims, 'I am more candid than others, and perhaps more voluptuous; but I demand also more refinement in my pleasures, and cannot separate them from sentiment and affection.' *Autobiography* does offer many insights into Hunt's character, but it is nonetheless significant that the 'Attempt' which was so near to publication remained unavailable to the reading public. There seems to be some conflict between the impulse which caused Hunt to write it and the caution which led him to withhold it and to describe his *Autobiography* as a 'most involuntarily egotistical book' (*A*, 2, p. 3).

LBSC was completed with some urgency. It was permeated by a vindictive animosity which seems to have surprised even Hunt himself. The rancorous tone is most evident in the first volume which is concentrated on Byron, but it also leaves its mark on the later volumes. Simply by omitting most of the Byronic material, Hunt achieved a decisive transformation of tone while at the same time abandoning the scheme which had been planned by Colburn and shifting the axis of the book from Byron towards himself. This revisionary tactic is unsurprising; what is much more significant is the way in which Hunt recasts so many passages in keeping with a new attitude which is less edged, less bitterly outspoken and less sharply judgmental. This more generous, less pointed perspective conditions many of the revisions in 1850. It can be traced through numerous minor deletions and adjustments of phrase. So, for example, Hunt thinks better of an earlier parenthetical side-swipe against Ives, the Governor of Horsemonger Lane: in a *Wishing-Cap* essay and in *LBSC* Hunt had called him 'the jailer' and had continued in a spirit of mock deference, '(I beg pardon of his injured spirit – I ought to have called him Governor)' (p. 426). This impulse of animosity is not given voice in *Autobiography*, nor is an attack in the earlier texts on the stinginess of the Royal Family. In *LBSC* Hunt had analysed a central and paralysing paradox in the nature of Coleridge, who was 'a mighty intellect upon a sensual body': 'Two affirmatives in him make a negative. He is very metaphysical and very corporeal; and he does nothing' (p. 301). *Autobiography* necessarily adjusts the tenses but it also substitutes for the final phrase an emollient and hesitantly qualified extension of the original paradox: 'so in mooting everything, he said (so to speak) nothing' (*A*, 2, p. 224). Again, there is the case of Hazlitt, with whom Hunt's relations were far from easy although they had much in common. In *LBSC* Hunt wrote of 'A living writer, who, if he had been criticizing in another what he did himself, would have attributed it to an over-weening opinion of his good word' (p. 404); the sting is slightly blunted by the courteous reluctance to use an identifying name. In 1850 the 'living writer', now dead for twenty years, was named as Hazlitt but the critical assessment was missing.

These small but indicative examples play their part in establishing through cumulative effect the ambience and native air of *LBSC* and of *Autobiography* respectively. Numerous changes are made on a larger scale and tend to arrange themselves around nuclear centres in the narrative. Byron, for example, not only plays a smaller role in *Autobiography* than in the book which bears his name but he also attracts far less authorial animosity when he does appear. Early in *LBSC* Hunt recalls how Byron had taken him into his confidence about his troubled relations with Lady Byron and had revealed that she had compared his own character to that of Giovanni in Hunt's recently published *Story of Rimini*: 'In all this I beheld only a generous nature, subject perhaps to ebullitions of ill temper, but candid, sensitive, extremely to be pitied, and if a woman knew how, or was permitted by others to love him, extremely to be loved' (p. 5). After recording that Byron had shown him a very personal letter from his wife, Hunt delivers his own devaluation of Byron's flattering act of seemingly particular friendship: '[T]he case was extreme; and the compliment to me, in showing it, appeared the greater. I was not aware at that time, that with a singular incontinence, towards which it was lucky for a great many people that his friends were as singularly considerate, his Lordship was in the habit of making a confidant of every body he came nigh.' In *Autobiography* the first, more generous, passage has been omitted, while the second has been revised to read: '[A] certain over-communicativeness was one of those qualities of his Lordship, which, though it sometimes became the child-like simplicity of a poet, startled you at others in proportion as it led to disclosures of questionable propriety' (*A*, 2, p. 178). For the directly personal engagement of the earlier version, *Autobiography* here substitutes a judgment which presents itself as more balanced and more objective, while it invokes the generalized experience of 'you' in place of Hunt's own disillusioned innocence. The intemperate pounce of 'singular incontinence' is also replaced by 'disclosures of questionable propriety' where the abstraction is perhaps excessively dignified.

Here Hunt rewrote his original and negotiated a precarious treaty with his own bitterness and disillusionment. Another instance of this endeavour to restore a juster balance is provided by his account of Byron's sudden and unaccountable fluctuations of mood after Hunt's glimpses of 'the proper natural Byron' during congenial evenings at the Casa Lanfranchi. 'Next morning', says *LBSC*, 'it was all gone. His intimacy with the worst part of mankind had got him again in its chilling crust' (68). *Autobiography* not only omits this criticism of Byron and his degrading connections but points its moralizing finger at Hunt himself. Hunt used to think that 'there was not a sacrifice which I could not have made to keep him in that temper'. Now he reflects:

But I ought to have made the sacrifice at once. I should have broken the ice between us which had been generated on points of literary predilection; and admired, and shown that I admired, as I ought to have done, his admirable genius. It was not only an oversight in me; it was a want of friendship. Friendship ought to have made me discover what less cordial feelings had kept me blind to. Next morning the happy moment had gone . . .

(*A*, 3, p. 67)

It is as if Hunt were making compensation for his own animosities and failures of charity and publicly confessing his own shortcomings; so the whole moral balance is shifted from censure to tolerance and from comfortable superiority to a rather cloyingly humble and tortuous self-criticism. On other occasions Hunt simply removes all traces of his earlier feelings. So in *Autobiography*, the young Byron is classified as 'a warm politician, and earnest in the cause of liberty' (*A*, 2, p. 311); this straightforward eulogy has removed the barb from the *LBSC* version of Byron as 'a warm politician, and thought himself earnest in the cause of liberty' (p. 3).

Hunt's evacuation of anger is even more noticeable and more significant in his treatment of Shelley. In this case, it may also have influenced fundamentally the received portrait of Hunt's friend. In *LBSC* Shelley, like everybody else, except the author, is overshadowed by the giant presence of the eponymous Byron; in *Autobiography* Shelley becomes the hero, the true moral centre embodying values antithetical to those of a Byron who has largely been displaced. While Hunt's animosity had been directed towards Byron, Shelley had been entirely exempted; instead, Hunt's anger had been focused on those who had misunderstood Shelley or misrepresented him or who had helped to constitute the inhospitable social element which hampered, frustrated, and rejected his unorthodox but practical Christianity. Hunt openly acknowledged this habit of attacking Shelley's enemies: he once told Shelley, 'I reckon on your leaving your personal battles to me.' The protective practice seems to have had its roots in the unprovoked public attack on Shelley's morality carried out by John Taylor Coleridge under the licensed anonymity provided by *The Quarterly Review*. Quite correctly, Hunt traced a connection between the assault on Shelley's private life and the reception of *The Revolt of Islam*; he was himself deeply involved since the first attack on Shelley had been made in the course of a review of his own collection *Foliage* and he knew that gossip had linked Shelley's allegedly scandalous behaviour with his own. On 3 October 1819 he addressed himself in *The Examiner* to the compromised morality of the 'reviewing Scribes and Pharisees' who were responsible for such calumnies. Since *The Quarterly* had called into question Shelley's Christian virtues, Hunt now employed a set of Biblical criteria and the example of Christ himself to demonstrate the hypocrisy of the Tory reviewers, two of whom occupied prominent positions in public life:

We will undertake to say that Mr Shelley knows more of the Bible, than all the priests who have anything to do with the Review or its writers. He does not abjure 'the pomps and vanities of this wicked world', only to put them on with the greater relish. To them, undoubtedly, the Bible is not a sealed book, in one sense. They open it to good profit enough. But in the sense which the Reviewer means, they contrive to have it sealed wherever the doctrines are inconvenient. What do they say to the injunctions against 'judging others that ye be not judged', – against revenge, – against tale-bearings, – against lying, hypocrisy, 'partiality', riches, pomps and vanities, swearing, perjury (videlicet, Nolo-Episcopation), Pharisaical scorn, and every species of worldliness and malignity? Was Mr Canning (the parodist) a worthy follower of him that condoled with the lame and blind, when he joked upon a man's diseases? Was Mr Croker, (emphatically called 'the Admiralty Scribe') a worthy follower of him who denounced Scribes, Pharisees, and 'devourers of widows' houses', when he swallowed up all those widows' pensions? Was Mr Gifford a worthy follower of him who was the forgiver and friend of Mary Magdalen, when he ridiculed the very lameness and crutches of a Prince's discarded mistress? Men of this description are incapable of their own religion.[12]

Here Hunt's indignation is in full unrestrained satirical flow. He does not resist the argument *ad hominem* and his rhetoric derives much of its strength from the naming of names and the specificity of the examples. When *LBSC* appeared just over eight years later, Hunt was still protesting against the hypocrisy of Shelley's critics and the self-contradictions of the Christian establishment, but the tone had lost something of its ferocity and, though his analysis was precise, it was also more safely and more charitably generalized. He presented the social circumstances which provoked Shelley's rebellion, but he admitted that not everybody who submits to such an element is tainted irrevocably by its moral contradictions. In spite of bad moral influences, there are still 'the honourable part of the orthodox' and those who 'by dint of a genial nature . . . turn out decent members of society'. Having made such concessions, he continued:

But how many others are spoilt for ever! How many victims to this confusion of truth and falsehood, apparently flourishing, but really callous or unhappy, are to be found in all quarters of the community; men who profess opinions which contradict their whole lives; takers of oaths, which they dispense with the very thought of; subscribers to articles which they doubt, or even despise: triflers with their hourly word for gain; statesmen of mere worldliness; ready hirelings of power; sneering disbelievers in good; teachers to their own children of what has spoilt themselves, and has rendered their existence a dull and selfish mockery. *(A, 2, pp. 281–2)*

In 1859 this analysis was removed from *Autobiography* together with Hunt's assertion that Shelley did not share the passivity of others who were prepared to 'see their fellow-creatures spoilt': 'He was a looker-on of a different nature.' Such a large deletion may have been motivated by the interests of verbal economy since the passage is largely a variation on a point which is powerfully enforced only two paragraphs earlier. Yet, for all the attempts at balance, this deletion also has the effect of limiting Hunt's own indignation and his tendency to identify with Shelley against 'the world'.

The passage in which Hunt partly anticipates this account of moral confusion and contradition is, in fact, a satirical portrait of that English country society into which Shelley, the young idealist, had been born. Hunt's rhetorical strategy equated the poet confronted by this confusing clash of signals with the force of Truth itself:

With what feelings is Truth to open its eyes upon this world among the most respectable of our mere party gentry? among licensed contradictions of all sorts? among the Christian doctrines and the worldly practices? among fox-hunters and their chaplains? among beneficed loungers, noli-episcoparian bishops, rakish old gentlemen, and more startling young ones, who are old in the folly of *knowingness*? In short, among all those professed demands of what is right and noble, mixed with real inculcations of what is wrong and full of hypocrisy, which have been so admirably exposed by Mr Bentham . . .
(p. 179)

Most of this was in fact derived from the review of *Posthumous Poems* which had been rejected by *The Westminster*. There the practices were *carnal* rather than *worldly* and 'among placements, among livings for younger sons' had been included after *chaplains*. The passage in *LBSC* was largely incorporated into *Autobiography* where the self-cancelling bishops disappeared from the text and the exuberant thrust of the rhetoric was qualified by the substitution after *knowingness* of a piece of charitable exculpation: 'people not indeed bad in themselves, not so bad as their wholesale and unthinking decriers, much less their hypocritical decriers; many excellent by nature, but spoilt by those professed demands of what is right and noble, and those inculcations, at the same time, of what is false and wrong . . .' (*A*, 2, p. 181). Such well-meaning and universal tolerance is hard to reconcile with the adversarial asperities of *The Examiner*. Whatever its moral virtue, Hunt's attempt to blame and not to blame remains unresolved. While *Autobiography* may be a more forgiving book than its predecessor, it tends to blur its own sharper perceptions through a desire to declare a general amnesty and forgiveness of sins.

The context of these passages is primarily religious rather than directly literary, since Hunt believed that many of the attacks on Shelley's poetry derived from a misunderstanding of his private life and especially of his attitude to Christianity. Hunt regularly claims that those who disapproved of Shelley's behaviour were not themselves true Christians whereas Shelley, paradoxically, was. This applied particularly to questions of sexual morality. Although Shelley was no libertine, his relations with Harriet were at the least a tragic tangle for which he bore heavy responsibility, yet Hunt, who had supported Shelley in the Chancery proceedings, entirely exonerated him from blame. In the *Posthumous Poems* review Hunt had even referred to Harriet as 'volatile and unfortunate' (in *LBSC* she was merely 'unfortunate' [p. 186]), and had treated her case so unsympathetically that this provided one of the main causes for the rejection of his review; yet this essay remained one of the main sources for the relevant pages in *LBSC*. In Hunt's eyes, Shelley was unhappy rather than culpable; culpability rested with the accusers to whom Hunt imputed precisely those moral enormities for which they had unjustly blamed Shelley. So in *LBSC* he exclaims with indignant and unsupported moral ferocity: 'Let the school-tyrants, the University refusers of argument, and the orthodox sowers of their wild oats, with myriads of unhappy women behind them, rise up in judgment against him' (p. 186).

In *Autobiography*, Hunt's essential position is still the same but the terms have been altered: 'Let the collegiate refusers of argument, and the conventional sowers of their wild oats . . .' (*A*, 2, p. 190). Similar assumptions about wild oats and double standards of sexual morality inspire another passage in *LBSC*: 'Had he now behaved himself pardonably in the eyes of the orthodox, he would have gone to London with the resolution of sowing his wild oats, and becoming a decent member of society' (p. 184). In *Autobiography* 'conventional in those days' replaces *orthodox*, thus shifting the focus from a point of view which is specifically identified with religion towards a viewpoint which is social and which is historically determined. *Autobiography* also adds another of Hunt's absolving parentheses: 'for it is wonderful in how short a time honest discussion may be advanced by a court at once correct and unbigoted, and by a succession of calmly progressing ministries; and all classes are now beginning to permit the wisdom of every species of abuse to be doubted' (*A*, 2, p. 188). Here Hunt conveniently fuses three of the concerns of his later years. He suggests that those who disagreed with Shelley were the products of a specific historical context for which they cannot be held responsible. He expresses a faith in progress or evolutionary meliorism which is one of the controlling dynamics of *Autobiography* and of its revisionary process in both versions; indeed, the progress of *Autobiography* from its starting-point in *LBSC* to its final version in 1859 is not only conditioned by this philosophy but comes to embody it in its own transformations. Hunt's addendum also celebrates the virtues of a Victorian court in a way which reminds us both that it was Hunt's criticism of the Prince Regent which had caused his imprisonment and that *Autobiography* was, among other things, a *curriculum vitae* of a possible candidate for the Laureateship; its author made it clear that in spite of certain sympathies he was not a republican and he included in its later pages a list of his publications in praise of the Royal Family.[13]

Shelley's Christianity was founded on admiration for Christ, 'for whose truly divine spirit he entertained the greatest reverence' (*LBSC*, p. 191); in *Autobiography* this religious commitment is qualified when 'truly divine spirit' is replaced by the much more guarded 'beneficent intentions' (*A*, 2, p. 194). According to Hunt, Shelley's reviewers were embittered by his interest in the epistle of St James and the Sermon on the Mount and by 'his refusal to identify their superstitions and worldly use of the Christian doctrines with the just idea of a great Reformer and advocate of the many; one whom they would have been the first to cry out against, had he appeared now' (p. 191). This passage not only castigates the blind conservatism of *The Quarterly* and other reviews, but it also very clearly reveals Hunt's tendency to identify Shelley with Christ which also features in the essays for *The Liberal* and *The Westminster Review*; in 1850 it was removed. At this point *LBSC* had continued:

His want of faith, indeed, in one sense of the word, and his exceeding faith in the existence of goodness and the great doctrine of charity, formed a comment, the one on the other, very formidable to the less troublesome constructions of the orthodox.

In 1850 this was subtly but significantly altered:

His want of faith, indeed, in the letter, and his exceeding faith in the spirit, of Christianity, formed a comment, the one on the other, very formidable to those who chose to forget what Scripture itself observes on that point.

The effect of these changes is to make Shelley into a Christian of more specific orthodoxy while once again removing the heat of the criticism from the orthodox themselves to the less challengingly pointed target of 'those who chose to forget what Scripture itself observes'.

In *LBSC* the next paragraph begins with a further insight into the unpopularity of Shelley's brand of Christianity: 'Some alarmists at Marlow said, that if he went on at this rate, he would make all the poor people infidels. He went on, till ill health and calumny, and the love of his children, forced him abroad' (p. 192). This did not appear in *Autobiography*, which only printed a pruned account of Shelley's pragmatic charities during his stay at Marlow. So *Autobiography* did not tell its readers that 'It was not uncommon with him to give away all his ready money, and be compelled to take a journey on foot or on the top of a stage, no matter during what weather' (p. 192). Yet even the *LBSC* version is less explicit than the account which Hunt had written nine years earlier for *The Examiner* and which had recorded that Shelley 'visited (if necessary) "*the sick and the fatherless*", to whom others gave Bibles and no help; wrote or studied again, or read to his wife and friends the whole evening; took a crust of bread or a glass of whey for his supper; and went early to bed'.[14] The frugalities of his life are also recorded, with slight variations, in *LBSC* and in *Autobiography*, but in these versions we are told that 'he visited the sick in their beds . . . and kept a regular list of industrious poor, whom he assisted with small sums to make up their accounts' (*LBSC*, pp. 186–7; *A*, 2, p. 190). In all cases Hunt is concerned to defend Shelley's reputation by claiming that, far from keeping a seraglio when he was at Marlow, he practised the Christian virtues.

In the earlier versions the tone is unmistakably controversial: Hunt is using the terms of Christianity against those unchristian Christians who have calumniated Shelley. One general effect of many of these changes is to make Hunt's account increasingly less adversarial, less immediately grounded in the urgently felt need to defend Shelley against his detractors. The most striking example of this is the story of how Shelley rescued a poor woman who was having convulsions near Hampstead Heath on a snowy winter's night. All the versions of this moral fable are centred on the contrast between the principled behaviour of the supposed atheist and the panic-stricken circumspection of a rich man whom Shelley approaches for help: '"God bless me, Sir! Dear me, Sir!" exclaimed the frightened wretch [the poor, frightened man (*Autobiography*)], and fluttered into his mansion' (*LBSC*, pp. 187–8; *A*, 2, pp. 198–200). In the *Literary Examiner* version Hunt had identified the house of this reluctant gentleman and had strongly hinted that it might be in his power to identify its owner, if he chose to remember his name. All the versions remark that 'the paucity of Christians is astonishing, considering the number of them' and that the 'real Christian had puzzled' the local gossips who hinted that Shelley, who was 'no Christian', had brought a disreputable female into the house. *The Literary Examiner* also remarked that 'their decent imaginations would never have got at the truth, had they carved it and Christianed it till doomsday'. Only

The Literary Examiner and *LBSC* provided the moralizing conclusion: 'Now go, ye Pharisees of all sorts, and try if ye can still open your hearts and your doors like the good Samaritan. This man was himself too brought up in a splendid mansion, and might have revelled and rioted in all worldly goods. Yet this was one of the most ordinary of his actions.'[15] This address to the Pharisaical reader is in fact a development of a sentence in an essay on 'Fellow-Creatures Suffered to Die for Want' which had appeared in *The Examiner* on 30 November 1817. This essay had focused on the face of charity and had taken as its two leading examples of charity in action Hunt's mother (whose gift of a flannel petticoat to a poor woman on Blackfriars' Road is also celebrated in *LBSC* and *Autobiography*) and Samuel Johnson. Hunt's account of one example of Johnson's practical Christianity bears a remarkable similarity to Shelley's action at Hampstead:

coming home one night, and finding a woman of the town in a most deplorable situation in the streets, with none to help her, [he] did not stand gaping, or walk off shaking his head at negligence in the police, or even at vice, but finding that charity was to take some decided measures, fairly took his fellow-creature up in his arms, carried her to his lodging (which he could ill afford to share), put her to bed, had her sickness cured, and sent her home to her friends in the country. Go, ye anti-Jacobins and lovers of Orthodoxy, and do so likewise.[16]

The shape and the resonance of the final sentence seem to have combined with the similarity of the two acts of charity to produce Hunt's direct appeal to the Pharisees in 1823 (repeated again in *LBSC*).

Hunt's attempts to Christianize Shelley were the result partly of an element which can be genuinely identified in the work and life of the poet himself; they can also be traced partly to Hunt's desire to defend Shelley against his enemies, and partly to his own psychological need to deprive Shelley's views of their radical and sceptical edge and to make them conform to a reading of Christianity which was increasingly sentimentalized. Even at an early stage in their friendship Shelley had already acquired angelic attributes when in 1818 Hunt warned Mary not to let Shelley out too much in the Italian sun for fear he should 'burn his wings'.[17] After Shelley's death the angelic features become more pronounced so that Hunt can claim without any apparent hint of irony that 'looking at you attentively his aspect had a certain seraphical character that would have suited a portrait of John the Baptist, or the angel whom Milton describes as holding a reed "tipt with fire"' (*LBSC*, p. 175). The next sentence anticipates the reader's objections by adding, 'Nor would the most religious mind, had it known him, have objected to the comparison.' By stressing the general and visual rather than the contextual force of the allusion, Hunt represses the fact that Milton's angel is a rebel and a master of artillery whose posture is both threatening and undignified: 'at each behind / A Seraph stood, and in his hand a Reed / Stood waving tipt with fire' (*Paradise Lost* VI, 579–80). While Milton deflates the revolutionary glamour by the rhetorical placement of words such as *behind* and *orifice*, Hunt tames the radical Shelley by aestheticizing and sentimentalizing him and rendering him socially acceptable. So Shelley scandalized society by his life and his work, but the 'generous reader will be glad to hear, that the remains . . . were attended to their final abode by some of the most respectable English residents in Rome' (*LBSC*, p. 202).

Hunt's attitude to Shelley is crystallized by the status which he accords to Shelley's heart. Hunt had always shown a tendency to identify Shelley with his heart; so, defending his moral character against the strictures of *The Quarterly Review*, he claimed that 'we believe him, from the bottom of our hearts, to be one of the noblest hearts as well as heads which the world has seen for a long time'.[18] The over-determination of this is symptomatic. Consequently, Hunt found himself in a peculiarly sensitive situation when he received for publication in *The Liberal* an account by Edward Trelawny of the cremation of Shelley's remains over which Trelawny had presided and in which Shelley's heart was rather publicly laid bare. Hunt himself wrote an essay which was intended as a framework for Trelawny's narrative; but, in the event, Hunt's own essay was never published and Trelawny's first appeared in *LBSC*, in a heavily edited and truncated version from which the physical details had been entirely eliminated. The manuscript in the British Library reveals a process which is more suggestive than this, since it shows Hunt's hand at work on Trelawny's prose. Here we can observe not the blank simplicity of total erasure but the much more indicative patterns of editorial intervention and revision.[19]

Hunt's main concern in this rewriting was to minimize the gruesome and the macabre, sometimes, perhaps, in the interests of accuracy but more often in the interests of good taste and tolerability. Trelawny is insistent and speculatively specific about the effect of fish on the watery corpses of Shelley and his friend Williams. For instance, he writes of Shelley that 'those parts exposed the face, hands, head had been so mauled by small fish so as not to leave a trace of what they had been' (*sic*). Hunt's version avoids the imprecision of *mauled* but also eliminates the fish altogether: 'though such parts of his flesh as were exposed, such as the face & hands, had been so destroyed & decomposed in the sea as not to leave a trace of what they had been'. Again, Trelawny's statement that the 'only parts of Williams's body eaten by the fish' were the hands, face, and head is tempered to read that these parts were the only ones 'disfigured or destroyed'. Likewise, where Trelawny records that the hands and one foot 'had been entirely eaten with all the flesh of the face by fish', Hunt emends the statement to read that the hands and feet 'were entirely gone'. It is likely that Hunt may have been motivated in part at least by stylistic considerations and by a desire to reduce the repetitive element in Trelawny's somewhat artless narration, but it is not without significance that the tendency of these revisions is to reduce the gruesomely physical specificity of the original.

This tendency is even more vividly in evidence in a larger intervention on Hunt's part. Trelawny offers a circumstantially detailed account both of the state of Shelley's body after it had been exhumed from its temporary place of burial in the sand and, most suggestively, of the reactions of the participants in the grim ritual:

The body was in the worst state of putridity and very offensive: the soldiers employed, were obliged to strengthen their nerves continually by drinking brandy and the officers retired from a sight so horrible. Both the legs were separated at the knees, the thigh bones bared and the flesh hung about in shreds; the hands were off and the arm bones protruded, the skull black & neither features nor face remaining.

Hunt's version of this is sanitized and deprived of its particularity: 'They were much decomposed & destroyed, like the others, from their long continuance in the sea.' Not only does this expurgate the anatomical comprehensiveness of the original but it also omits the gauge which Trelawny provides for measuring the intensity of the reactions experienced by those who actually participated. Nowhere else is the brandy mentioned or the withdrawal of the officers, and, once these details had been removed from the manuscript, they disappeared from the historical record as well.

Hunt's version of Trelawny also omitted a longish passage on the burning of Shelley's remains which pays particular attention to the durability of an organ which Trelawny identified as the heart:

it remained unaltered; a quantity of thin fluid still flowing and occasioning a bright blue flame . . . I took the heart out to examine it, and the oily fluid flowed freely from it; the only visible effect the fire appeared to have had was to change its colour to a dingy blue.

That Hunt should have cancelled this passage is not at all surprising since not only is it unpleasantly physical but it also focuses on the organ to which Hunt accorded a passionate and almost neurotic veneration. Hunt's eagerness to claim the prize of Shelley's heart from the flames and his reluctance to restore it to the widow are only too well attested. His unwillingness to acknowledge the heart as physical and material in its substance is indicated by the exclusion from the text of the 'thin' and 'oily fluid'. On the other hand, he retains the next part of the passage which emphasizes its almost preternatural ability to survive:

It is a curious circumstance that the heart, which was unusually large, together with some other vessels in that quarter seemed almost proof against fire, for it was still entire in figure and apparently in substance, though the intensity of heat was so great that harder substances were reduced to white dust.

Read in a context which minimizes the signs of physicality, these lines contribute to a sense of miracle. The tendency of Hunt's editing becomes even clearer when one notices that this is not precisely what Trelawny wrote. His version includes one minute but very significant variation: the heart was not, as Hunt would have it, 'unusually large' but rather it was 'unusually small'. What we are observing here is an editorial process, a consistent and extended metamorphosis whereby Shelley is dematerialized and his heart is transformed from an oleaginous organ to a symbolic property. This transformation may have answered to a psychological need; certainly, it was not impeded by the fact that Hunt was not present at the cremation but was safely ensconced in his carriage. This seclusion did not inhibit Hunt from correcting in Trelawny's version details of a scene which he had not witnessed. He consoled himself that through the circumstances of his death and cremation Shelley had escaped 'that gradual corruption of the body, which he seems to have contemplated with a dislike proportionate to his imagination'. Yet Shelley's imagination had allowed itself to dwell on the facts of bodily dissolution in *Adonais* and in his essay 'On Life', while Hunt seems to have forgotten, or allowed himself to forget, that even if Shelley's temporary burial had hastened the process of decomposition, his remains presented a spectacle of putrefaction so potent that the soldiers were forced to stiffen their nerves with brandy. The elision is curious but crucial. Protected in this way from uncomfortable tokens of human frailty, Hunt was more easily able to initiate a cult of Shelley's heart and the 'heartly' qualities of his life and work. It seems entirely appropriate that the motto he invented for Shelley's tomb in Rome should turn out to be 'cor cordium' (heart of hearts), not least because, whatever remains were interred in the Protestant cemetery in the shadow of the tomb of Caius Cestius, Shelley's heart was certainly not among them. In *Autobiography* but not in *LBSC* Shelley is characterized as 'that heart of hearts' (*A*, 2, p. 206) a figure of speech which both perpetuates the definition of the epitaph and simulates a characteristic Shelleyan trope ('soul of my soul').

The gradual dematerialization of Shelley and his translation into a disembodied organ of benevolence reflects the larger patterns of Hunt's own development. Thus he could respond to the demands of contemporary English politics in the year before the passage of the Reform Bill by claiming: 'The nobler morals of these times demand that a man should have a more enlarged heart, and a greater love of truth and his species.' It was no accident that when in the same year he issued a privately printed manual of devotion it should centre on the heart; when it was published in revised form in 1853 it was retitled *The Religion of the Heart*.[20] One of the features of this heterodox manual with its alternative Services and its 'exercises of the Heart in its Duties and Aspirations' was the inclusiveness of the texts which it recommended, not only more traditional writings but extracts from Wordsworth, Coleridge, Keats, Shelley, Tennyson, and Hunt himself.

Hunt's religion of the heart, with its emphasis on generosity and acceptance rather than on exclusiveness and judgment, is in keeping with his efforts both as a man and as a writer to eliminate anger and to cultivate charity and forgiveness. Hunt's writing shows a progressive tendency to invest in Shelley a set of values which were central to this philosophy. Shelley himself was not exempt from anger and it is fascinating to see the way in which Hunt negotiates this awkward (and too little acknowledged) fact. In the earlier accounts, Hunt had freely admitted that Shelley was susceptible to fits of temper. The essay intended for *The Liberal* put it this way:

Mr Shelley was naturally hasty and passionate; but his anger was soon over and he so repented it, that as it was said of some other person whose name we forget, it was a good thing, on these occasions for a servant to have offended him, or come in his way. He had made a very solid apology to a domestic for something said hastily a little before he died; and the poor girl spoke of him to us with a flood of tears, turning away her head and wringing her hands.

The vividness of this seems to indicate some authenticity. This anecdote was not retained in the review of *Posthumous Poems* or in *LBSC* or in any later account of Shelley, but in the essay for *The Westminster Review* and in *LBSC* Hunt did make a revelation which was not available to readers of *Autobiography*: 'He [Shelley] was naturally irritable and violent; but had so mastered the infirmity, as to consider every body's inclinations before his own' (p. 213). Hunt also specifically referred to Shelley's temper in the context of *The Quarterly Review*. The anonymous reviewer (in fact John Taylor Coleridge) who had been Shelley's contemporary at Eton remembered Shelley setting trees on fire with a burning-glass, while, in Hunt's words, Shelley recollected him 'as one of the school-tyrants against whom he rose up, in opposition to the system of fagging'. After quoting a passage from *The Revolt of Islam* which was the target of Coleridge's hostile review, Hunt continued: 'Mr Shelley retained all his kindness and energy, but corrected, as he here aspires to do, the irritability of his temper. No man, by the account of all who lived with him, ever turned it into greater sweetness. The Reviewer, by the usual process of tyranny, became a slave' (pp. 180–1). This passage did not appear in *Autobiography*. Perhaps this shows that Hunt himself had corrected the irritability of his own temper but it also deprives the reader of a vital insight into the tensions and complexities of Shelley's character.

In a letter of June 1841, Hunt expressed regret for his critical remarks on Byron not because they were not true, 'for they were', but because 'a better knowledge of myself has taught me that no one frail human being has a right to sit in that manner in judgment on another'.[21] Again, in *Autobiography* his account of George III conceded that 'with all his faults' he was 'a more estimable man than many of his enemies' and was followed by a passage which begins: 'Whatever of any kind has taken place in the world, may have been best for all of us in the long run. Nature permits us, retrospectively and for comfort's sake, though not in a different spirit, to entertain that conclusion among others' (*A*, 2, p. 56). Perhaps one is not being unjust in recognizing here something of that tone of voice which suggested to Dickens the character of Leonard (diplomatically altered to Harold) Skimpole. There is a striking contrast between this unfocused and all-embracing optimism and the pointed and energetically satirical accounts of the king which Hunt had contributed to *The Examiner*. As in other parts of *Autobiography*, the writing is compromised and weakened by the demands of the prevailing ideology: there is less and less of what Hazlitt had once pinpointed in Hunt's theatrical criticism as 'the true pineapple flavour'.[22] That Hunt himself was aware of this shifting of the balance is demonstrated by an essay which he published in *The Tatler* in April 1831: it gives an account of how in his younger days he had been bitten with admiration of wits and satirists but had been mellowed by suffering and experience.[23] In 1838 he provided another insight into his self-awareness when he wrote to S.C. Hall a letter which was intended as the basis for a biographical note in *The Book of Gems*: 'Time and suffering, without altering them, we understand, have blunted his exertions as a partisan, by showing him the excuses common and necessary to all men, but the zeal which he has lost as a partisan he no less evinces for the advancement of mankind.'[24]

This belief in a kind of evolutionary meliorism is evident both in his politics and in his religious philosophy of Universalism to which, as he tells us in *Autobiography*, both his parents had subscribed. The central tenet of Universalism was that in the final reckoning nobody would be condemned to hellfire or excluded from the circle of God's love. As Hunt himself put it in *The Religion of the Heart*: Universalism proclaimed 'the restoration of all mankind to happiness, without exception'.[25] The general tendency of Hunt's revisions both of *LBSC* and of *Autobiography* is in accord with this all-pardoning philosophy of Universalism and moves away from the censorious, the judgmental, and the satirical. Increasingly, it would seem, Hunt was driven by a desire to put the record straight which meant not so much a committed pursuit of historical authenticity as an understanding interpretation of what had once provoked his anger. Both versions of *Autobiography* retain passages which are sharply etched and which do not avoid satire or criticism, but there is a marked and progressive evolution towards what at the best is mellow and at the worst is bland. Hunt's philosophy of good cheer, the stoical optimism which carried him through the dark days of his imprisonment has now been translated into a kind of benevolent quietism which increasingly threatens though it never undermines the genuine achievement of *Autobiography*. This gradual process of revisionary evolution which is consummated by the closing pages of *Autobiography* (in both its versions) strongly suggests that for Hunt the process of revision was not only a matter of stylistics or even of truth to history and to self but an activity whose deepest resonances were moral and religious.

NOTES

A fuller account of the genesis and history of *Autobiography* and of its textual variations will be provided in my edition (based on the 1850 text), which is to be published by Oxford University Press.

1 Preface to *Lord Byron and Some of his Contemporaries* (London 1828), p. iii. Here and throughout this essay the text cited is the first edition folio which was also published in one quarto volume. The second edition, which was also published in 1828, was issued in three volumes with minimal textual variations from the first.

2 Preface. See also: 'as to my own biography, I soon became tired of that. It is true, I should have entered into it in greater detail, and endeavoured to make the search into my thoughts and actions of some use, seeing that I had begun it at all; but I was warned off this ground as impossible on account of others, and gladly gave it up.'

3 *The Correspondence of Leigh Hunt*, ed. Thornton Leigh Hunt (London, 1862), Vol. 2, p. 86; *The Autobiography of Leigh Hunt, with Reminiscences of Friends and Contemporaries* (London 1850), Vol. 2, p. 188.

4 *The Liberal: Verse and Prose from the South* (London, 1822–3), Vol. 1, pp. 97–120, 269–88, Vol. 2, pp. 47–65, 251–64; *The Literary Examiner*, Nos. 7 and 8 (16 and 23 August 1823), pp. 97–105, 113–20.

5 'Coffee-Houses and Smoking', 16 (1826), p. 50; 'A Schoolmaster of the Old Leaven', 14 (1825), pp. 599–600. *The Indicator*, 35 (7 June 1820), p. 278; 36 (14 June, 1820), pp. 285–6.

6 For the *Wishing-Cap* essays, see *The Examiner*, nos. 857, 859 (4, 18 July 1824), pp. 417–18, 449–51. For the earlier articles, see *The Examiner*, 259 (14 February 1813), pp. 97–99; 260 (21 February 1813), pp. 113–14; 261 (28 February 1813), pp. 129–30. While he was in prison, Hunt also prepared a memorandum which enabled him to rehearse on paper the topic of his imprisonment.

7 *The Examiner*, 527, 530, 531, 613, 614, 615 (1 and 22 February, 1 March 1818, 26 September, 3 and 10 October 1819), reprinted in *Shelley: The Critical Heritage*, ed. James E. Barcus (London, 1975), pp. 106–14, 135–47; *The Examiner*, 751, 752, 754 (16 and 23 June, 7 July 1822), pp. 370–1, 389–90, 419–21; *The Literary Examiner*, 1 (5 July 1823), pp. 4, 6; 8 (23 August 1823), pp. 118–19; British Library, MS. Ashley 915, catalogued as 'MS. of Leigh Hunt's account of the cremation of P.B. Shelley', transcription to be published with commentary and notes by Timothy Webb in *The Keats–Shelley Review* (1992); Payson G. Gates, 'Leigh Hunt's Review of Shelley's

Posthumous Poems', Publications of the Bibliographical Society of America, 42 (1948), pp. 1–40.

8 Hunt died before he was able to complete his revisions of *Autobiography*, so the book was prepared for the press by his son Thornton, who added some notes of his own. *1859* is more economical than *1850*, does not print some of the primary materials (such as articles in *The Examiner*), is much more selective in its use of literary quotations, and is generally less discursive. Throughout this essay *Autobiography* is quoted from the text of 1850 unless otherwise specified.

9 See, for example, Hunt's note to 'The Book of Beginnings', *The Liberal*, Vol. 2, p. 118 where he refers to the organ in the Portuguese Ambassador's chapel in South Street, Grosvenor Square, which was played by his friend Vincent Novello:

> I, to wit, one of the 'Satanic School' (Oh Bob!) have stood in that chapel, under the influence of that organ, and . . . have felt the tears run down my cheeks at the crowd of thoughts that came upon me. 'Aye,' quoth the Laureat, 'you were sorry that you had no longer a faith.' Excuse me; I have a faith, though not in your damnatory one, or your verses: but I was struck to think of all the miseries and bloody wars that had accompanied the spread of the kindest of doctrines: and wondered how it was possible for men to look upon the altar-piece before me, and hear the music that melted towards it, and not find out, that to injure and damn one another to eternity, was unbecoming even the wrath of charity.

The conclusion of this note is informed, among other things, by Hunt's Universalist rejection of the concept of Hell.

10 The manuscript now belongs to the Brewer–Leigh Hunt Collection in the University of Iowa Libraries. For a transcript and introduction, see *Leigh Hunt's Autobiography; the Earliest Sketches*, ed. Stephen Fogle (Gainesville, 1959).

11 The original quarto half-sheet from which this brief essay in self-analysis was first reprinted in *The Athenaeum* in 1893 is now in the Forster Collection of the Victoria and Albert Museum. It was also reprinted by Roger Ingpen in his edition of *Autobiography* (London, 1903).

12 Reprinted in *Shelley: The Critical Heritage*, p. 139.

13 Stephen F. Fogle, 'Leigh Hunt and the Laureateship', *Studies in Philology*, 55 (1958), pp. 603–15. Hunt's attempt to present an effective candidature led him to the following evasive reference to his imprisonment: 'the fancied indecorum of appearing in a place, where any previous connexions of it, however different from its existing connexions, may have been set by him in a disadvantageous light' (*A*, Vol. 3, p. 276; not in *1859*).

14 *The Examiner*, 615 (10 October 1819), cited in *Shelley: The Critical Heritage*, p. 143.

15 *The Literary Examiner*, 8 (23 August 1823), pp. 118–19; *LBSC*, pp. 187–8, where the anecdote is quoted in a footnote on the authority of *The Literary Examiner*.

16 *The Examiner* 518 (30 November 1817), pp. 753–5; *LBSC*, pp. 324–5; *A*, Vol. 1, pp. 32–3. Thornton Hunt remembered that Shelley and the woman's son had 'brought her on from the inhospitable mansion [of the rich man] to our house in their arms'. He added: 'I believe that, the son's strength failing, for some way down the hill into the Vale of Health Shelley carried her on his back.' 'Shelley. By One Who Knew Him', *Atlantic Monthly*, 11 (1863), p. 186.

17 *Correspondence*, Vol. 1, p. 116. See also, among numerous examples, references to Shelley's wings in *LBSC*, pp. 210, 212, and a letter to Horace Smith written shortly after Shelley's death: 'I cannot help thinking of him as if he were alive as much as ever, so unearthly he always appeared to me, and so seraphical a thing of the elements' (*Correspondence*, Vol. 1, p. 195).

18 *The Examiner*, 615 (10 October 1819), cited in *Shelley: The Critical Heritage*, p. 143. See also the following reference to Shelley and Keats: 'Finer hearts, or more astonishing faculties never were broken up, than in those two. To paint any man's heart by the side of Shelley's, is alone an extraordinary panegyric.' *The Literary Examiner*, 8 (23 August 1823), pp. 117–18.

19 Trelawny's manuscript is cited from British Library Add. MS. 39, 165, ff. 174–80; for permission to quote from this and from Hunt's essay I am indebted to the British Library. See also Leslie A. Marchand, 'Trelawny on the Death of Shelley', *Keats–Shelley Memorial Bulletin*, 4 (1952), pp. 9–34. A fuller account is included in my article for *Keats–Shelley Review* (see note 7 above).

20 Originally issued under the title of *Christianism: or, Belief and Unbelief Reconciled; being Exercises and Meditations*.

21 *Correspondence*, Vol. 2, p. 38.

22 *The Complete Works of William Hazlitt*, ed. P. P. Howe, 21 vols. (London and Toronto, 1930–4), Vol. 18, p. 381.

23 *The Tatler*, 195 (19 April, 1831), Vol. 2, p. 778.

24 Quoted in S.C. Hall, *A Book of Memories of Great Men and Women of the Age*, (London, 1871), p. 242. For an external assessment, see Charles Lamb's observation in a letter to Southey which appeared in *The London Magazine* in October 1823. Lamb noted that 'his political asperities and petulancies' were 'wearing out with the heats and vanities of youth'. *The Works of Charles and Mary Lamb*, ed. E.V. Lucas, 7 vols. (London, 1903–5), Vol. 1, pp. 232–3.

25 *Ibid.*, p. 219n.

14

FINDING MARY SHELLEY IN HER LETTERS

BETTY T. BENNETT

WHEN the first volume of my edition of *The Letters of Mary Wollstonecraft Shelley* was published in 1980, one reviewer suggested that Mary Shelley's letters were not worth publishing: Anyone interested might have requested microfilm from the Bodleian or xeroxes from the Pforzheimer Library and read the manuscripts for themselves. Reality raises the more obvious challenges to this simple solution: the manuscripts are scattered throughout the world in public and private collections; portions of letters are sometimes in two repositories; Mary Shelley's letters are often only partially dated or completely undated, thereby eluding contextual understanding; even after one accustoms oneself to Mary Shelley's handwriting, single words and phrases are often difficult to decipher. Nevertheless, the reviewer's suggestion, by its very failure to understand either Mary Shelley or the nature of editing letters, inadvertently raised several important questions for Romantic studies: did past biographies of Mary Shelley reveal all we needed to know about the author? Was her place in Romanticism insufficiently recognized not because her works lacked a philosophic basis but because we had not noticed or understood it? Can an edition of letters portray an author's life story sufficiently to add substantial depth and context to her works?

At least one school of criticism argues that the works themselves should tell us all we need to know about an author. But the fact is that until recent years scholars have generally regarded Mary Wollstonecraft Shelley as a result: William Godwin's and Mary Wollstonecraft's daughter who became Shelley's Pygmalion. The story goes that she was inspired when she was with Shelley to write the extraordinary *Frankenstein*, but that when his life ended, so did hers – the actual event not occurring for her until twenty-nine years later. Unhappily for her and for us, this narrative leaves both *Frankenstein* and all her other works in an intellectual straitjacket. Perhaps the best demonstration of this impact is that despite the phenomenal interest in *Frankenstein* in the last ten years, explanations of so significant a Romantic work are still limited by biographical interpretations based on either a Victorian filter or a Freudian filter; one as confining as the other.[1] Fortunately, there is another story. It is Mary Shelley's own, written in her own words, in counterpoint with her own era. A major part of that story is contained in her letters.

Some 1276 letters are collected in the three volumes of *Letters*, approximately doubling the size of the largest past edition. There is no question that many letters are yet unlocated that well might add further to understanding Mary Shelley's life and works. Nor, in any limited space, can one do more than suggest the richness of material in the *Letters* that await biographical and critical consideration in depth, but the letters tell Mary Shelley's story in her own voices, her own commerce with the world. From them, a new complex, intellectual, political Mary Shelley has emerged – one that had been there all along.

To establish Mary Shelley biography through her letters means recognizing and exploring the countless facts of her life that shaped their own intricate context, both biographical and historical. Her story has not been readily available partially because her Romantic existence was washed in the mores of the remainder of the century and because women's lives tend generally to be lost in historical accounts. But Mary Shelley added to this mask because she was, first to last, a private, introspective person who lived much of her life in the inner world of her own imagination.[2] Finding Mary Shelley in her letters, therefore, has called for searching beyond that which all letter-editors undertake. To paraphrase her much-admired Coleridge, it has required the willingness to suspend, as far as possible, beliefs and disbeliefs, to allow a constant testing of earlier concepts about the author against the evidence provided in the letters themselves. This testing process proves critical to editing Mary Shelley's letters because the letters do not support the relatively pallid image of Mary Shelley offered in preceding studies.

Even a factual outline of her life suggests a more complex person than was previously understood. From her birth in London on August 30, 1797, Mary Shelley had the possibility of a remarkable heritage. Mary Wollstonecraft Godwin, writer and radical, died ten days after giving birth to her namesake, but left her a written legacy of reformist theory and practice. From William Godwin she had both the written legacy of reformist theory and the living example of an unconventional philosopher-writer who advocated an egalitarian new world and was never quite at home in the world assigned him. In 1814, when Mary Shelley was almost seventeen, she eloped with Shelley, poet, radical reformer, disciple of her parents – and already married, leaving a trail of scandal that would follow her until she died. After his first wife committed suicide in

1816, the Shelleys married. Of their four children, the first born seven months after they eloped, only Percy Florence, their last child, survived both his parents. When Shelley drowned in 1822, his twenty-five-year-old widow was left to support herself and her son until Shelley's father's death in 1844 brought them Shelley's inheritance. During those years, Mary Shelley constructed a life of her own, committed to raising her son, continuing her own writing, and establishing Shelley's reputation through the publication of his manuscripts. At her death on February 1, 1851, she had succeeded at all three. Her literary activity included five novels after *Frankenstein* (1818): *Valperga* (1823), *The Last Man* (1826), *Perkin Warbeck* (1830), *Lodore* (1835) *and Falkner* (1837); one novella, *Mathilda* (1819, pub. 1959) two travel books, *A History of a Six Weeks' Tour* (1817) and *Rambles in Germany and Italy* (1844); two mythological dramas, *Proserpine* (1820, pub. 1832) and *Midas* (1820, pub. 1922); five volumes of biographical *Lives* (1835–9) of Italian, Spanish, Portuguese, and French writers for Lardner's *Cabinet Cyclopedia*; more than two dozen short stories; essays; translations; reviews; poems; and the precocious satire *Mounseer Nongtonpaw,* published in 1808. As Shelley's editor, she brought out Shelley's *Posthumous Poems* (1824), and the monumental *Poetical Works* (1839, four volumes and one volume), and *Essays, Letters from Abroad, Translations and Fragments* (1839, dated 1840).

Mary Shelley's place as a writer and editor was recognized by her contemporaries, but since that time even scholars for the most part have been unaware that she wrote anything of value beyond her first novel. In the interest of understanding the Romantics, we need to re-evaluate the intellectual and artistic life of an author who was in community with the leading figures of the era and who made her own significant contribution to that world. Unfortunately, biographies of women writers are generally the product of gender-biased interpretations that emphasize emotions and family life, and largely ignore the intellectual and artistic. At best this provides a sympathetic reflection of the critic's opinions and at worst a denigration of the writer's artistry. The letters, in contrast, provide a voice through which to establish a genuine biographical context, one which in turn allows a solidly founded basis for analyzing and interpreting the author and her works.

This is not to suggest that the letters are in and of themselves necessarily true. Or that the editor's character does not intrude to some degree in the final product. In the most reductive terms, works of fiction – and autobiography – are written for a larger, impersonal audience. Letters (with the exception of "literary letters" also intended for an impersonal audience) are written for one person or for the expanded, but particular audience, that their author has in mind. The "I" in the letters is the personal "I," whether in a love letter or a business letter, consciously engaging in dialogue with another person. Just as in oral conversation, that "I" may or may not be telling the truth; may be hiding or disguising intentions through style or diction; may only be partially aware of the implications of what is written. However, in compiling as many of the letters as possible, each separate voice, each separate "I," is set against another, finally bringing into focus the many facets that form their author.

Working with Mary Shelley manuscript letters provides two interdependent but distinct sources of information. The first, on the level of physical detail; the second, building on the physical properties, the ultimately significant, larger portrayal that results from amassing, interweaving, and comparing the contents of the letters. When accumulated and catalogued, the physical properties of the letters play an important role in constructing the sequence of a life. To begin with the most obvious: postmarks in Mary Shelley's lifetime reveal both the date a letter was mailed and the date received. These timelines are often vital in establishing chronological order because Mary Shelley omitted the year, and sometimes the numerical date and month, on approximately one third of her letters. Because postmarks are commonly only partially preserved or somewhat blurred and faded, working with the original document rather than a photocopy allows one not only to read more accurately but also affords the possibility, depending on the fragility of the paper (and the co-operation of the archivist), to refold the letter and fit what remains of the date marks together. This, hopefully matched with internal clues, can provide the otherwise missing information.

A brief example of how this methodology assists: In a one-line letter, dated only January 6, to her publisher Edward Moxon, Mary Shelley encloses "a letter to be inserted in the 2 Vol. of the Prose works at page 335." The pink stamp on the letter was first used only after May 1840. This establishes that the letter referred to the second, 1845 edition of the Prose, published five years after the first, which on p. 335 includes a letter to Keats's devoted friend Joseph Severn, with whom Mary Shelley had continued contact in the 1840s (III, January 6 [?1845]). Thus, the letter to Moxon establishes Mary Shelley's continuing activity as Shelley's editor.

An inventory of stationery can also contribute to construction of the chronological sequence. What color is the paper? The ink? What are its measurements? Is it laid or woven? Plain, gold-edged, black-edged, or torn from a larger sheet? Is there a watermark that includes the name of manufacturer and, as quite common then, the date the paper was made? Are there samples of a particular stationery that are dated, used only during particular years, that can, together with context, establish when an undated letter was written? Through this approach the letters involved in George

Byron's blackmail sale of forged Shelley letters have gone through a process of considerable editorial correction since they were first published in 1944. The first, important revisions, made in 1946, relied on matching stationery, thereby leading to three quite different letters than had been originally presented.[3] Further study of the stationery provided internal and external evidence that the blackmail negotiations were not concentrated in a brief period in October 1845, and then completed in September 1846, as previously believed, but that they stretched out throughout the period, one in which Mary Shelley was severely ill (III, October 28, 1845).

Working with manuscripts allows a variety of other revisions of past publications of the letters, illustrated in the following examples: (1) In the George Byron forged letters already referred to, previous editors mistook the number "8" for Mary Shelley's abbreviated "Yr" (for Your). As a result, they concluded that she had purchased and received eight Shelley letters early in the negotiation, confusing the possible provenance of those letters, miscounting the number of forged letters she actually received, and failing to appreciate Mary Shelley's assertive responses to George Byron's attempts to "borrow" further sums of money in exchange for additional Mary Shelley and Shelley letters. (2) Mary Shelley's concern for her son is quite differently interpreted when a comment that "the bustle of a school would develop his chances better" has been corrected to read that the bustle "would develop his character better" (II, May 5, 1831). (3) Her lengthy and informed letter to Abraham Hayward that discusses many contemporary issues both literary and political turns out to be an amalgam of two letters (III, 26 October 1840). (4) Mary Shelley's deleted passage at the end of her November 10, 1845 letter to Claire Clairmont, written after Mary Shelley had just escaped threatened blackmail by an Italian exile, repeats her injunction stated elsewhere to "Pray tell me that you [bu]rn our letters – the chief fear I have is there being other foreign [   ]." Clairmont replies that she does not reply sooner to Mary Shelley's letters because unless she responds at once, she forgets what is in them, being "obliged to burn your letters as soon as I have read them." Clairmont was obviously using this as an excuse and a bit of a complaint since actually – as in this case – she preserved almost all of Mary Shelley's many letters to her. The deleted passage results in another piece of evidence in the story of the troubled relationship between Mary Shelley and Claire Clairmont throughout most of their adult lives. A final example: (5) in a letter to Byron on [I, November 16, 1822] about *The Deformed Transformed*, which she had just copied for him, Mary Shelley writes that "The Critics, as they used to make you a Childe Harold, Giaour, & Lara all in one, will now make a compound of Satan & Caesar [   ] your prototype, & your 600 firebrands in Murray's hands will [   ] costume." The missing words "serve" and "be in" can only be supplied from snippets of the stationery that remain attached to the wax seal.[4]

The manuscripts also reveal Mary Shelley through a sentence structure that past editions of the letters have revised. In those editions, Mary Shelley's sentences almost always began with a capitalized word, have traditional punctuation in their expected place, and close with a period – all very proper. The manuscripts and her own testimony tell another tale. "A pen in hand my thoughts flow fast" (I, January 6, 1825), Mary Shelley wrote, and her letters support her self-description. She moves quickly along, her pace reflected mostly in dashes between phrases and sentences rather than full stops. She sometimes omits letters in words that she has already demonstrated she can spell. Her deletions, except for the relatively few meticulously blocked out, can usually be retrieved, allowing her correspondent at the time to read the thoughts that she had changed her mind about. When she completed a letter and had something more to say, she didn't rewrite – she added on. Her postscripts not only follow her signature, but appear in the margins of letters, upside down or right-side up at the beginning of letters, and when envelopes were invented, inside envelopes, and cross-written. In several letters she asked her correspondents not to cross-write to her because it made the letters difficult to read (I, March 7, 1823). This message she herself cross-writes. Does this indicate a contradictory character? A sense of humor? One should not make too much of such individual pieces of evidence in themselves. But taken together, such details help constitute the indices of a life.

Among the traces of Mary Shelley's life from the age of seventeen until a few months before her death, the letters offer the changes in her handwriting. Just after she eloped with Shelley, her handwriting was distinct for the squared nature of the individual characters, but during the couple's years together her handwriting came to strongly resemble his. Shelley and Mary Shelley editors have noted this, and it has often produced confusion, but what has not been noted is that after Shelley's death, her handwriting evolved again, moving from both her own juvenile script and its later resemblance to Shelley's. No doubt some interesting biographical arguments might be founded on this informa- tion, as well as another handwriting issue. In the last twelve years or so of her life, her script began at times to noticeably, even severely, slur. Letters flattened; words sometimes ended in a series of small bumps. A sign of advanced age or carelessness? Hardly, since Mary Shelley was only fifty-three when she died and other letters belied the notion of indifference. What the letters give evidence of, and what has not been recognized in biographical studies, is that the illness, which began in 1839 and which was coincident with her editing of the monumental Shelley editions, was not an isolated incident. Rather, it was the beginning of the illness that finally took her life. During the next twelve years, she reported she was ill, then mending and well, constantly believing – or wanting to believe – herself fully recovered. But the frequency and degree of her disturbed writing establishes a narrative of its own and suggests why Mary Shelley was a less prolific writer during the period. Her handwriting indicates that one of the major reasons she wrote less was not because she had lost interest in writing but because for much of that time she was ill with a tumor on the brain that caused severe head pain and partial paralysis, and eventually led to her death.

Each letter is therefore important, though obviously not equally so, in allowing the final image to piece itself together. Even seemingly trivial letters may help establish chronology, geography, as well as otherwise unnoted relationships, and these are critical particulars in composing a larger, more accurate narrative that would either confirm old perspectives or substantiate new ones. Such compendiums provide the context to revise Mary Shelley's image from that of a passive, conventional Victorian lady into a multidimensional, complex Romanticist. Among these accumulated trails of evidence, perhaps the most important from her readers' perspective are those that lead to a portrayal of Mary Shelley, author.

From the letters emerges Mary Shelley's fundamental consciousness of herself as author. The 1814–27 letters trace her growth from her early works (Shelley arranged the anonymous publication of *Frankenstein*, and sent Sir Walter Scott a copy; Scott, who gave *Frankenstein* an excellent review, assumed Shelley was its author) through new-found self-reliance, after Shelley's death, to continue not only to write but to take on the responsibility of becoming Shelley's editor and her own agent. In her letters, she frequently speaks of projects finished and unfinished, aspirations, feelings of failure and satisfaction, efforts to publish, reactions to reviews and friends' opinions, exhaustion from overwork, deadlines, lost manuscripts, revisions, self-reappraisal. Through introductions and recommendations by Godwin and friends such as Charles Lamb, Horace Smith, Leigh Hunt, she began, as she would for the remainder of her life, to negotiate directly and persistently for herself and others with many of the leading publishers and editors of the day. To the author Bryan Waller Procter, she sends her dramas to arrange for possible publication (I, May 9, 1824); to James Hessey, publisher of the *London Magazine*, she offers an unsolicited tribute to Lord Byron (I, May [?24–31], [1824]); she requires the return of two of her articles that were not published for publication elsewhere (I, [?June 1824–7]); offers a manuscript by her brother for publication (I, July 11 [?1824–7]). She arranged for the publication of her next four novels, biographical lives, and when publishers were slow, did not hesitate to remind that "an *immediate arrangement*" had been promised (II, December 12, 1829) or, on another occasion when kept waiting by a publisher, to wake him with a note beginning, "I hope your tiresome silence is not occasioned by your being dead" (II [December ?28, 1830]).

When Shelley's death left her with no income, she expressed confidence, based on earlier authorship of *History of a Six Weeks' Tour, Frankenstein*, and *Valperga*, in her ability to earn a living through her writing: "I think that I can maintain myself, and there is something inspiriting in the idea" (I, March 7, 1823). She found solace in continuing her habits of writing and study: "I study – I write – I think even to madness & torture of the past – I look forward to the grave with hope – but in exerting my intellect – in forcing myself to real study – I find an opiate which at least adds nothing to the pain of regret that must necessarily be mine for ever" (I, February 28, 1823). Protracted negotiations with Shelley's father, Sir Timothy Shelley, wrung from him, towards the close of 1823, only a modest allowance against Shelley's estate (I, see September 9–11, 1823, nn. 11 and 12). Dependent on her writing for additional income, Mary Shelley was aware, as professional authors necessarily are, that some works are motivated primarily by financial need. Her letters show, however, that she maintained her determination to develop and fulfill her understanding of herself as an artist. When she advised Leigh Hunt to write for magazines to earn the money he needed, she characterized her own situation: "I write bad articles which help to make me miserable – but I am going to plunge into a novel, and hope that its clear waters will wash off the [dirt] mud of the magazines" (I, February 9, 1824). Of *Rambles*, her last work, written when she was already a semi-invalid, she confidently asserted that her *History of a Six Weeks' Tour* had brought her many compliments and she had no doubt this new work would "procure me many more" (III, September 27, [1843]).

The years 1827–40 were Mary Shelley's most prolific as an author and editor. What do her letters present of her in these dual roles? Interactions with publishers are a pervasive theme. Her correspondence about *Lodore* is concerned mostly with efforts to find a publisher, negotiate a contract, and see the book through publication. New letters, however, reveal that a section of the book was lost, presumably in the mail or at the publishers, and that Mary Shelley was required to rewrite a considerable part of the novel. Other letters refer to Mary Shelley's many short stories, poems, reviews, and essays, and suggest that more shorter works were published than have been identified as hers. In dealing with matters of appropriate length of story, deadlines, payments, competing journals, contents, and editors, her letters provide considerable insight into contemporary publishing procedures and Mary Shelley's enterprise in that male-dominated world.

Another theme concerns her habits of reading and research, and complements the extensive records in her journals. Influenced by Godwin, Mary Shelley developed a lifelong habit of deep and extensive reading and research. The Shelleys had remained in Florence so she could locate Italian books for the materials she needed for *Valperga* (I, c. December 13, 1819, n. 4); when writing *Perkin Warbeck*, she wrote to Thomas Crofton Croker for Irish sources (II, October 30, 1828); to Sir Walter Scott for references to Scottish source material (II, May 25, 1829); and to Godwin and others for additional factual details that she could distill into her fiction. When she contributed five volumes to Lardner's *Lives of the most Eminent Literary and Scientific Men of Italy, Spain, and Portugal* (with others; 1835–7) and *Lives of the most Eminent Literary and Scientific Men of France* (1838–9), the work occasioned many letters to contemporaries, such as Sir John Bowring and Gabriele Rossetti, from whom she sought sources for biographical, historical, and critical materials.

Letters that propose topics for books and essays, whether undertaken or not, also demonstrate Mary Shelley's self-confidence and broadly based knowledge, which critics so often have failed to recognize. Among the subjects that interest her are: full-length biographies of Mahomet, Josephine, Madame de Staël (about whom a chapter was included in *Lives*); a history of manners and literature; lives of the English philosophers; a geological history of the earth; a collection of the lives of celebrated women; a history of women; and regular articles for the *Court Journal*.

Of those authors to whom she was closest, her letters not surprisingly speak most of Shelley and his works. One month after his death, she wrote: "The world will surely one day feel what it has lost when this bright child of song deserted her – Is not Adonais his own Elegy – & there does he truly depict the universal woe wh[ich] should overspread all good minds since he has ceased to be [their] fellow labourer in this worldly scene. How lovely does he [   ] paint death to be and with what heartfelt sorrow does one repeat the line – 'But I am chained to time & cannot thence depart'" (I, c. August 27, 1822]). In 1824, she edited and published his *Posthumous Poems*. Eventually she synthesized her judgments and observations of Shelley's works and his literary significance in the introductions and notes to her 1839 Shelley editions. She also continued to comment on Byron, often in relation to Thomas Moore's Byron editions. Her letters to Moore seem not to be extant, but his to her and hers to those who might assist Moore (including Teresa Guiccioli and Sir John Bowring) illustrate how material a contribution she made to Moore's editions. In reviewing Moore's volume, she comments that Byron

quitted England, feeling himself wronged – an outcast & a mourner – his mind took a higher flight – It fed upon his regrets – & on his injuries . . . As his mind became more subdued – he became more critical – but his school of criticism being of the narrow order, it confined his faculties in his tragedies & Lord Byron became sententious & dull –

except where character still shone forth . . . At Pisa he again belonged more to the English world – It did him little good . . . But, in the end, this war gave him a disgust to Authorship – and he hurried to Greece to get a new name as a man of action – having arrived at the highest praise as a poet.   (1 [June ?10, 1832]).

Her opinions of Godwin's works she expressed in letters and in her laudatory memoir of him for the Colburn and Bentley 1831 reprint of *Caleb Williams* (written simultaneously with her new introduction for the revised 1831 *Frankenstein*) and in her review of *Cloudesley* in *Blackwood's Edinburgh Magazine* (II, May 4 [1830]).

Among projects left unfinished was her life of Godwin, who died on April 7, 1836. His will appointed Mary Shelley his literary executor and requested that she determine which of his papers and letters should be posthumously published (II, April 20, 1836). She accordingly signed an agreement with Colburn to publish his memoirs and correspondence, for the benefit of his widow, whom, despite their differences over the years, she greatly assisted after Godwin's death. In the course of preparing Godwin's manuscripts, Mary Shelley began to annotate his early memoirs and to solicit his letters from friends and acquaintances, including Bulwer-Lytton, Josiah Wedgwood, Thomas A. Cooper, William Hazlitt, Jr. (for letters to his father), and Henry Crabb Robinson. She also attempted to enlist Robinson's aid in obtaining letters from Wordsworth and from Coleridge's executors. On January 26, 1837 she informed Trelawny that her "sense of duty towards my father, whose passion was posthumous fame," had readied her to "become an object of scurrility & attacks." She was determined to defer publication, however, until the completion of arrangements for Percy Florence Shelley's matriculation at Trinity College, Cambridge, that following spring, so that "a cry raised against his Mother" would not harm his career. She expected criticism not on the basis of politics but on that of religion, a subject that might well elicit public attack and scandal. Perhaps for this reason, the work was never completed. Or perhaps it was set aside in favor of first completing the Shelley editions and then was not resumed because she was unable to undergo again the acute physical and psychological stress that she endured in the preparation of her editions of Shelley's poetry and prose in 1838–9.

As editor, Mary Shelley became Shelley's collaborator, returning more than in kind the guidance he had given her when she wrote *Frankenstein* and other early works. She gathered and preserved his writings. She brought the experience of a professional author to the editing of his works. Finally, biographers and critics agree that Mary Shelley's commitment to bring Shelley the notice she believed his works merited was the single, major force that established Shelley's reputation as a poet during a period when he almost certainly would have faded from public view. Her intention to gather, preserve, and publish Shelley's works is repeatedly expressed in the letters, beginning almost immediately after his death.[5] After *Posthumous Poems*, her next major involvement with publishing Shelley was in 1829, when she assisted Cyrus Redding in editing Galignani's pirated *Poetical Works of Coleridge, Shelley and Keats*. Prohibited by Sir Timothy Shelley from bringing Shelley's name before the public in return for her repayable allowance, she obviously believed she could aid this French publication with impunity and thereby keep both her commitments: *she* would not bring Shelley forward, yet his works would be kept in the public notice. New letters and evidence supply fuller information than has formerly been available about the important contributions she made to the Galignani edition, including the fact that she read and gave her judgment of the Shelley memoir included:

I have only made one correction in the MS – The whole tone of the Memoir is to my mind inaccurate – but if this is the guise it is thought right that it should assume of course I have nothing to say – since it is favorable in its way & I ought to be content – I should have written it in a different style – but probably not so much to the Publisher's satisfaction – It is a mere outline & is as communicative as a skeleton can be – about as like the ⟨original⟩ truth as the skeleton resembles the "tower of Flesh" of which it is the beams & rafters.   ([? September–November 1829])

Ten years elapsed between the Galignani edition and Mary Shelley's 1839 editions. We have information now, however, from a previously unpublished letter that negotiations for her edition began at least as early as January 22, 1834, when she informed Edward Moxon of her willingness to publish with him once "family reasons" no longer prevented her. Mary Shelley's letters between 1834 and 1839 record the development of this project. They provide a wealth of information about the problems, constraints, editorial decisions, and exhaustive labor, as well as the ideals and objectives that shaped the volumes.

Among the most important aspects of these letters is how they illustrate the extent to which she went to try to prepare a text true to Shelley's intentions. For example, in trying to work with first editions when she did not have manuscripts, and at times finding herself without even those editions, she had to cajole grudging friends and strangers to borrow them. Thomas Jefferson Hogg said he had not a *Queen Mab*; but Mary Shelley asked,

yet have you not? Did not Shelley give you one – one of the first printed . . . Will you lend me your Alastor also – it will not go to the printer – I shall only correct the press from it. Sir Tim forbids biography – but I mean to write a few notes appertaining to the history of the poems – if you have any Shelley's letters you would communicate mentioning his ⟨author⟩ poetry I should be glad & thank you;. (I, December 11, 1838)

Has Miss Kent a *Queen Mab*? Has Charles Ollier? Who is Brookes; "two persons so uncivilized as to refuse to lend the book to *me* for *such a purpose* cannot exist" (II [December ?15, 1838]).

These letters also provide a far more accurate depiction than heretofore available of Mary Shelley's motives and actions and of contemporary publishing processes. For instance, Mary Shelley has been attacked almost universally for her omissions of the atheistical passages of *Queen Mab* in the four-volume *Poetical Works* (II, December 11, 1838). The letters disclose, however, that although she disagreed with atheism and believed that Shelley himself had changed his mind about this subject, she was persuaded by the publisher Edward Moxon to omit those passages to protect his copyright, which he could lose if found guilty of publishing a work containing blasphemy. Nor was her omission of the dedication to Harriet Shelley in *Queen Mab* the result, as critics have suggested, of her reluctance to relate Shelley's feelings for his first wife; rather, it was made on the reasonable editorial principle of authorial intent. Years before, she had decisive evidence that Shelley himself preferred the omission (II, February 11 [1839]).

The letters reveal Mary Shelley as a professional, deliberate editor. In addition to searching for first editions from which to publish and correct proofs, she inquired after additional manuscripts of Shelley's works and letters; and she sought advice and guidance from friends, including Leigh Hunt and Hogg. Her letters tell of her efforts in "turning over Manuscript books ... scraps ... unfinished half illegible" (II, November 11 [1839]); the questions of her claim to copyright (II, December 7, 1838; January 12, 1839); her impatience with the frustrations of the work; the injunction of her father-in-law, Sir Timothy Shelley, that she not include a biography of Shelley, which she circumvented through the notes she appended to the poems that trace their origins and history (II, December 11, 1838); the severe illness caused by the editorial and personal strains of preparing Shelley's manuscripts in context "chiefly produced by having to think of & write about the passed [past] ... It has cost me a great deal" (II, May 2 [1839]).

Her labors resulted in the 1839 publication of the four-volume *The Poetical Works of Percy Bysshe Shelley*, the two-volume *Essays, Letters from Abroad, Translations and Fragments* by Percy Bysshe Shelley, and the one-volume *Poetical Works* (with the complete *Queen Mab* and other poems added). This achievement was not merely the work of a wife seeking posthumous fame for the writings of a beloved husband, as has been suggested or implied by many critics. As is true for all editors, some decisions she made are open to criticism. But the letters show that even her most serious error, the failure to use first editions consistently as copy-text when manuscripts were not available, was the result not of amateurishness or indifference but rather of the inability to procure copies to work from despite an intense search (II, December 11, 1838; December 12, [1838] ff.). In fact, Mary Shelley's letters reveal that her editorial principles, stated or implied, stand up well even by modern standards that undertake to preserve all of a writer's works and present them as much as possible as the author wished (see, for example, her letters regarding the omissions of the atheistical passages in *Queen Mab* and the dedication to Harriet Shelley; and her many efforts, continued as late as 1845, to locate and publish Shelley manuscripts, II, December 11, 1838 ff.).

After the Percy Shelley editions, Mary Shelley wrote only one more full-length work, her two-volume *Rambles in Germany and Italy* (1844), published just seven years before her death. Very little has been written about *Rambles* or their place in Mary Shelley's works. Her own comments regarding *Rambles* are fragmented among a number of different letters. Read separately, the letters show an author sometimes anxious to write and other times reluctant to. Taken together, the many letters about *Rambles* interact with each other in a duel that takes them beyond their individual reports to create a complex, somewhat ambivalent picture of the author. They contain not only the expression of her attitudes towards writing in the ten last years of her life; they stretch in a continuum backwards to the young Mary Shelley, and give perspective to the nineteen-year-old who wrote *Frankenstein*, the earlier *History of a Six Weeks' Tour*, and all the works that followed.

In the 1840s, constantly fighting illness, Mary Shelley's letters indicate that she generally felt too weak to write another book. Despite her condition, wanting money to establish a home for herself and Percy Florence (III, May 17, [1843]), and anxious to assist the Italian expatriate Ferdinand Gatteschi, who in 1845 would use her frank and supportive letters as the instruments of blackmail (III, August 30 [1843]), she marshalled her writer's energy. Though she claimed she "wished never again to publish" she also felt herself destined to write: "one must fulfil ones fate" (III, November 10 [1843]), a fate she acknowledged as hers in her grieving 1822 *Journal*.[6] To Edward Moxon's invitation to write a new book, she indicated that her ill health at Florence had improved in Rome, and that she would be "glad to employ myself in that way this summer – but I [sca]rcely think I shall be able – we shall see" (III, May 7 [1843]). Mary Shelley did accept Moxon's offer and wrote at length about her journeys with Percy Florence Shelley and his friends to Germany (1840) and Italy (1841). Her first published book had been the *History of a Six Weeks' Tour* (1817), the record of her elopement with Shelley to the Continent. Now she came full circle, back to the Continent with another Shelley. Although the travelers, the events, and the years were different, throughout the *Rambles* there is an overlay of memories of earlier days, with occasional explicit references to those beloved and lost from a time long gone.

Her letters written during her 1840–1 travels also reflect those memories: "There is something strange & dreamlike in returning to Italy after so many many years – the language the mode of life the people – the houses the vegetation are as familiar to me as if I had left them only yesterday – yet since I saw them Youth has fled – my baby boy become a man – & still I have struggled on poor & alone" (III, July 20 [1840]). Those dreamlike memories also include deep grief: In Venice she reflects on the death of her dear Clara (III, October 1–2 [1842]); in Rome, on William's death and her initial discomfort at moving into Via Sistina No. 64, with its 1819 sad memories of Italy.

Just as her memories circle back, so, too, do the *Rambles* reflect Mary Shelley's basic methodology of *History of a Six Weeks' Tour*. Then, she drew on her *Journal* observations and her letters. Now, again writing in the first person, she worked from observation, calling upon the letters she had written to supply her with specifics. For example, she indicated to Claire Clairmont: "I am writing some thing that requires that I should refresh my memory with regard to our tour in 1840. If you have any descriptive letters from Percy & myself at that time I wish you would send them to me with all possible speed" (III, October 13–[16] [1843]). Like many other nineteenth-century travel books, *Rambles* is meant to be an actual guide to the regions explored as well as a compendium of her reflections. But Mary Shelley goes beyond the ordinary events of travel and sightseeing to comment on political suppression and the need for reform and liberty. Her letters and *Rambles* together provide important evidence of Mary Shelley's unabated interest and support of reformist politics, an interest that past biographers claim died with Shelley but that in fact was a preoccupation throughout her life (see, for example, her commentary on French politics, III, November 18 [?1840]; her letters to Alexander Berry regarding British and Australian politics; and *Rambles* for a larger perspective on her belief in political liberty and its contemporary condition in Italy and Germany).

For Mary Shelley, to write about a foreign country required thorough knowledge about the country and its people. Her letters indicate a good number of the research sources she studied in giving historical and socio-political context to the *Rambles*. As important, the letters shed light on the writer's self-attitude some twenty-six years after *Frankenstein* was published. Perhaps most revealing was the pain she suffered when a close friend told her she should not write because "it does no good to any body" (III, October 13–[16] [1843]). Her friend's remarks may have resulted from concern for how ill Mary Shelley actually was; Mary Shelley herself reported that she continued to work though "suffering in my eyes" (III, January 28 [1844]). But Mary Shelley reacted to the comment by feeling "guilty & wretched," unable to "assert myself" and momentarily wishing "that never my name might be mentioned in a world that oppresses me" (III, October 13–[16] [1843]). Wounded, ill, she claimed she would continue with *Rambles* only to assist Gatteschi. But this was not the first time she had been discouraged by others about her writing and nevertheless continued, as her earlier letters demonstrate.

Collected, Mary Shelley's letters are in many ways unlike Lamb's, Byron's, Shelley's or Keats's in their inclusion of domestic concerns from a woman's perspective. But they do share with them a creativity, reflectiveness, and overall perspective that places their author solidly in the Romantic tradition. By adding a different, equally important, voice, they provide us with a new source for understanding Romanticism. Her interaction with her father and her idolized mother; her early writing; her elopement and life with Shelley; the independent life she created for herself in widowhood; her confidence in the reciprocity of nature; her occasional ambivalence rooted in conflict between the role she envisioned for herself and that which her society called for; her own writing career, and her publications of Shelley's works – all are rooted in the Romantic defiance of conventions intended to constrain. The letters, in her own voice, reflect an individual in the process of struggling against, revising, and defying those conventions.

Because of her own varied interests and her sensitivity to the concerns of her correspondents, Mary Shelley's letters (except when brief or about business) are generally not confined to any one topic. A passage about literature may follow one about housekeeping; a discussion of the Tuscan landscape may precede an urgent request for combs or pencils. Though she occasionally played in her letters, she never posed. At times her self-awareness becomes maudlin, her candor chiding, her observations sentimental; but the voice that pervades is analytical, forthright, contemplative, and prophetic, at times darkly so.

NOTES

1 The Victorian filter interprets the work as free of the complex socio-political perspective that is fundamental to *Frankenstein*. The Freudian interprets the work as a *roman à clef*, with the creature and his creator interchangeably playing the role of Godwin and Shelley.

2 See, for example, December 2, 1834, *The Journals of Mary Shelley*, ed. Paula R. Feldman and Diana Scott-Kilvert (Oxford, 1987), Vol. 2, and her introduction to the second edition of *Frankenstein* (1823).

3 Theodore G. Ehrsam, "Mary Shelley In Her Letters," *Modern Language Quarterly*, 7 (1946), 297–98.

4 Frederick L. Jones (ed.), *The Letters of Mary W. Shelley*, 2 vols. (Norman, Oklahoma, 1944), Vol. 1, p. 202.

5 The first phase of this project, leading to the 1824 *Posthumous Poems*, is described in Vol. 1 of *Letters*; the 1827–40 letters in Vol. 2 detail the subsequent history of her plans that culminated in the 1839 editions.

6 See, for example, *Journals*, Vol. 2, pp. 431–2.

15

KEATS'S EXTEMPORE EFFUSIONS AND THE
QUESTION OF INTENTIONALITY

JACK STILLINGER

KEATS's original draft of his account of Madeline undressing, in the twenty-sixth stanza of *The Eve of St. Agnes*, shows the poet's creativity momentarily bogging down near the climax of his sensational narrative. Madeline's (soon-to-be) lover, Porphyro, is hiding in a closet, eagerly waiting to watch her prepare for bed, and Keats sets the scene with the celebrated stanzas 24–5 describing the triple-arched casement and the moonlight shining through to fall on Madeline at her prayers; stanza 25 concludes in the draft, "[Porphyro] grew faint / She knelt too pure a thing, too free from mo[r]tal taint."[1]

Now, after a line space in the manuscript, Keats launches into stanza 26: "But soon his heart revives – her prayers said / She lays aside her necl" – then cancels the last four words, rewrites the second line as "She strips her hair of all its wreathed pearl" (subsequently changing the last two words to "pearled wreathes"), sets down four more words of continuation in a third line ("Unclasps her bosom jewels"), but deletes this for a new third line, this time a full pentameter: "And twist[s] it in one knot upon her head." At this point he has an acceptable *a* rhyme for the first and third lines ("said"/"head") but alternative *b* rhymes in the second line (first "pearl," then "wreathes") that would, to meet the demands of the Spenserian stanza (*ababbcbcc*), require three more rhymes with the same sound in the fourth, fifth, and seventh lines. The prospects in either case do not seem promising: for rhymes with "pearl," in the first instance, "'girl" would not qualify – Madeline is not Fanny Brawne, *pace* the biographical interpreters – and while "curl" or "uncurl" could be used in connection with Madeline's hair (and "churl" in connection with Porphyro's behavior!), none of the other obvious possibilities ("hurl," "swirl," "twirl," "whirl") accords with the nearly still-life character of the painterly description; for rhymes with "wreathes" Keats would have been pretty much restricted to "breathes," "seethes," and, if the "th" is read as unvoiced, "heaths" and "sheaths," of which only the first ("breathes") relates to anything else mentioned so far in the poem.

Canceling, therefore, all of the preceding, Keats begins again with stanza 26: "But soon his heart revives – her prayers done" (subsequently changing the last three words to "her prayers soon done" and then "her praying done"), and continues: "Of all her [immediately revised to "its"] wreathed pearl she strips her hair / Unclasps her warmed jewels one by one / Loosens the boddice from her" – this last a line that has to rhyme with "hair" and seems destined to lead, sooner or later, to "bare." A flurry of divestings now takes place as Keats tries to imagine, and then cancels, one incomplete version after another of what Madeline is loosening: "her bursting," "her Boddice lace string," "her Boddice; and her bosom bar[e]," "her" (all these at the bottom of a page), and, beginning the line anew at the top of the next page, "Loosens her fragrant boddice and doth bare / Her "– at which point Keats again comes to a halt, deletes all that he has written of the stanza, and starts over.

The opening of the next attempt, this time headed with a stanza number (one of only three such numbers in the entire draft), repeats much of the preceding text just cancelled: "But soon [subsequently revised to 'Anon'] his heart revives – her praying done, / Of all its wreathe'd pearl her hair she strips / Unclasps her warmed jewels one by one / Loosens her fragrant boddice; and down slips / Her sweet attire." But now two more *b* rhymes are needed in the stanza to go with "strips" and "slips" in the second and fourth lines. Keats solves the problem by changing "strips" to "frees," rewriting "and down slips" successively as "to her knees" and "by degrees," then completing the fifth line with "knees": "by degrees / Her sweet attire creeps rusteling to her knees" (the last five words following two earlier attempts to describe the descent of the fabric: "falls light" and "creeps down by"). The remainder of the stanza takes shape somewhat more readily: Keats writes "Half hidden like a Syren of the Sea / And more melodious," then cancels the last three words, changes "Syren" to "Mermaid" and "of the Sea" to "in sea weed," and continues: "She stands awhile in thought [changed, for the sake of the pentameter, to "dreaming thought"]; and sees / In fancy fair Saint Agnes in [changed to "on"] her bed / But dares not look behind or all the charm is dead" (the last word a replacement for "fl" – the beginning of "fled").

The final text of the stanza in Keats's original draft is as follows:

> Anon his heart revives – her praying done,
>   Of all its wreathe'd pearl her hair she frees:
> Unclasps her warmed jewels one by one
>   Loosens her fragrant boddice; by degrees
> Her sweet attire creeps rusteling to her knees
> Half hidden like a Mermaid in sea weed
> She stands awhile in dreaming thought; and sees

> In fancy fair Saint Agnes on her bed
> But dares not look behind or all the charm is dead

Keats has written some twenty-five or more complete or partial lines to arrive at these nine, and the final wording here is very close to the text that we read in modern standard editions (there are five single-word alterations in later texts – "vespers" for "praying" in the first line, "pearls" for "pearl" in the second, "rich" for "sweet" in the fifth, "in" for "on" in the eighth, "fled" for "dead" in the ninth – and one lengthier change: "Pensive awhile she dreams awake" in the seventh line).

But this is not, in general, how Keats composed his poems. What is most interesting about this momentary failure of creativity – a fumbling with *b* rhymes, I suggest, rather than with lingerie – is its rarity. Keats almost never took so many lines to arrive at near-final text, even in the most difficult of the formal schemes that he used: the Spenserian stanza (as here), ottava rima (in *Isabella*), the sonnet, and the sonnet-like stanzas of his major odes. Manuscript after manuscript shows him getting *most* of the words right the first time. And for all the textual and biographical materials at our disposal, we really don't have the slightest idea how he managed to do this.

Those materials – which include Keats's own holographs, transcripts by relatives and close associates, the early printings of the poems, and Keats's and his friends" comments in letters, journals, and biographical and textual annotations, as well as the critical observations of modern scholars[2] – do allow some generalizations about the occasions and at least the mechanical procedures by which Keats's poems came into existence. I shall single out three points for discussion here.

In the first place, there is a remarkable degree of *spontaneity* – composition on the spur of the moment ("extempore effusion" in the title of this essay) – all through Keats's poems, from the very early "Stay, Ruby Breasted Warbler, Stay," which Richard Woodhouse noted "was written off in a few Minutes" when "some young ladies . . . desired fresh words" for an old tune they were singing,[3] to the very late ode "To Autumn," which Keats drafted shortly after an acutely pleasurable experience of the season's air and landscape while walking around Winchester: "this struck me so much in my sunday's walk that I composed upon it." The Chapman's Homer sonnet was drafted and delivered to Charles Cowden Clarke the next morning after Keats stayed up all night reading Homer with Clarke. The "Great Spirits" sonnet ("Addressed to the Same") is another next-morning product, composed after an evening with the painter Benjamin Robert Haydon that Keats says "wrought me up." According to a note by his brother Tom, the Vulgar Superstitions sonnet was "Written in 15 Minutes," very likely in the same circumstances that produced

"On the Grasshopper and Cricket," "To the Nile," and probably also "On Receiving a Laurel Crown": sonnet-writing competitions with Leigh Hunt (and on one occasion with Shelley as well) in which the allotted time was a quarter of an hour. In the first instance ("Grasshopper"), Keats "won as to time"; in the second ('To the Nile'), both Keats and Shelley finished "within the time" while "Leigh Hunt remained up till 2 oClock in the Morning before his was finished"; in the posited third instance ("Laurel Crown"), Keats appears to be making a sonnet out of the predicament of *not* being able to write a sonnet: "Minutes are flying swiftly; and as yet / Nothing unearthly has enticed my brain / Into a delphic labyrinth. . . . Still time is fleeting, and no dream arises . . ."

Keats wrote the dedicatory sonnet printed at the beginning of his *Poems* of 1817 ("To Leigh Hunt, Esq.") in circumstances that C.C. Clarke uses to exemplify "his facility in composition": "he was surrounded by several of his friends when the last proof-sheet of his little book was brought in; and he was requested to send the dedication, if he intended one. He went to a side-table, and in a few minutes, while all had been talking, he returned and read the Dedicatory Sonnet." "God of the Golden Bow" was produced "shortly after" an incident in which Keats felt he had acted foolishly in company at Hunt's; the Elgin Marbles sonnets were an immediate response to seeing the fragments at the British Museum; "On a Leander" was in effect a thank-you note for a gift from a friend. "Lines on Seeing a Lock of Milton's Hair" was written on the instant, when Hunt "surprised me with a real authenticated Lock of *Milton's Hair* . . . This I did at Hunt's at his request – perhaps I should have done something better alone and at home"; the first page of Keats's draft (at Harvard) is on a leaf in one of Hunt's notebooks. Keats wrote his *King Lear* sonnet when he "sat down to read King Lear . . . and felt the greatness of the thing up to the writing of a Sonnet preparatory thereto." A lesser reader might pour a coffee or a glass of wine in such a situation; Keats wrote one of his better-known sonnets.

"Hence Burgundy" is one of many instances of Keats spontaneously shifting into verse in his letters: "I cannot write in prose," he tells John Hamilton Reynolds; "It is a sun-shiny day and I cannot so here goes," followed by a flow of anapestic trimeters. Virtually all of Keats's poems from his walking tour in the summer of 1818 are occasional pieces, composed on the spot, often in letters to Tom or Fanny Keats: "On Visiting the Tomb of Burns," "Old Meg," "Ah! Ken Ye What I Met the Day," "To Ailsa Rock," and so on. One sonnet ("This Mortal Body") he wrote in the cottage in which Burns was born – "for the mere sake of writing some lines under the roof," he explains – and another ("Read Me a Lesson, Muse") on the top of Ben Nevis, while he was perched (as his friend Charles Brown describes the situation) "a few feet from the edge of that fearful precipice, fifteen hundred feet perpendicular from the valley below." He drafted several poems in the course of writing his longest journal letter, in the spring of 1819, including "Character of C. B.," "La Belle Dame sans Merci," "Song of Four Fairies," and the second sonnet "On Fame." And we have Brown's account of the circumstances in which Keats is supposed to have written "Ode to a Nightingale" (a poem that Brown classes with "fugitive pieces") in "two or three hours" while sitting in a "grass-plot under a plum-tree."[4]

These are just some of the better-known or more obvious examples of Keats's facility in drafting upon, or for, an occasion. Remarkably, there is practically no evidence that he wrote his longer or more ambitious poems in any other way.[5] The extant holographs of documented spontaneity – the enthusiastic responses, the entries in sonnet competitions, the drafts in the letters – are no different in appearance from the extant drafts of the best odes and narratives. (The long narratives were not, of course, written at single sittings, but they can easily be viewed as aggregations of shorter units: fifty- or sixty-line daily stints in *Endymion* and the other works in couplets and blank verse, and a page or two of stanzas at a time in *Isabella* and the other narratives in stanzas.) Regardless of category, the drafts are more or less messy according to the demands of the poetic form – messier in sonnets, odes, and Spenserian stanzas and, just as one would expect, cleaner in couplets (as in "The Eve of St. Mark" and *Lamia*) and blank verse (*Hyperion, Otho the Great*).

Keats theorizes about such naturalness in one of his axioms in poetry formulated in a letter of February 27, 1818 to his publisher John Taylor: "if Poetry comes not as naturally as the Leaves to a tree it had better not come at all" (*Letters*, 1, pp. 238–9). Woodhouse refers to this axiom near the beginning of the single most valuable comment we have on Keats's "mode of writing":

[Keats] has repeatedly said in conversation that he never sits down to write unless he is full of ideas – and then thoughts come about him in troops, as though soliciting to be accepted, and he selects. One of his maxims is that if Poetry does not come naturally, it had better not come at all. The moment he feels any dearth he discontinues writing and waits for a happier moment. He is generally more troubled by a redundancy than by a poverty of images, and he culls what appears to him at the time the best. He never corrects, unless perhaps a word here or there should occur to him as preferable to an expression he has already used. He is impatient of correcting, and says he would rather burn the piece in question and write another [on] something else. "My judgment" (he says) "is as active while I am actually writing as my imagination. In fact all my faculties are strongly excited, and in their full play. And shall I afterwards, when my imagination is idle, and the heat in which I wrote has gone off, sit down coldly to criticise when in possession of only one faculty, what I have written when almost inspired?" This fact explains the reason of the perfectness, fullness, richness and completion of most that comes from him. He has said that he has often not been aware of the beauty of some thought or expression until after he has composed and written it down. It has then struck him with astonishment – and seemed rather the production of another person than his own. He has wondered how he came to hit upon it. This was the case with the description of Apollo in the third book of *Hyperion* . . . Such Keats said was his sensation of astonishment and pleasure when he had produced the lines [specifically III, 81–2] . . . It seemed to come by chance or magic – to be as it were something given to him.[6]

As a matter of fact, the extant drafts do frequently show "correcting," and the scholarly recovery of what Keats wrote in the first place has sometimes been extremely useful in critical interpretation ("The real grass" in both the draft and the fair copy of *Endymion* IV, 622, for example, and "Was it a vision real" in the draft of "Ode to a Nightingale," 79). But typically these revisions are confined to single words and phrases (in Woodhouse's description just quoted, "a word here or there . . . preferable to an expression he has already used") and are concerned primarily with stylistic matters: logic and accuracy, sound effects, and the requirements of meter. (The accompanying illustration, the first page of the draft of the Nightingale ode, containing lines 1–26, shows several kinds of alteration, but also shows an amazingly high proportion of the words of the final text of these lines – 188 of the 199, or 94.5 per cent – present from the very first writing.) The revisions within the drafts, then, are of interest mainly negatively: they have so *little* to do with the creative process. Either some trial-and-error activity of initial composition took place in Keats's mind before he ever put pen to paper, or else we must believe what Woodhouse reported from conversations with Keats: there was never any significant amount of trial-and-error activity at all in the process – a large share of Keats's lines came "by chance or magic."

My second general point, which can be made much more quickly, is that Keats's revisions in fair copies and other manuscripts subsequent to the original drafts are similarly unrevealing concerning processes of poetic creativity. For works that he took seriously, Keats characteristically wrote two manuscripts, a draft and a fair copy. For many poems we either have both the draft and the fair copy, or else can reconstruct the text of one, or the other, and sometimes both, from transcripts and notes by Woodhouse, Brown, and others close to the poet.

With a single exception, the long narrative and dramatic works beginning in 1817 – *Endymion, Isabella, The Eve of St. Agnes, Hyperion, Lamia, The Jealousies,* and the co-authored tragedy *Otho the Great* – show no significant changes in plot, character, theme, or narrative method in the revisions that Keats made when he recopied the drafts in second or revised manuscripts. A clarifying stanza was added (and then, at his publishers' insistence, was dropped) near the beginning of *The Eve of St. Agnes*; an eighteen-line description of flowers, food, and rowdy behavior at the wedding-feast was cut from the middle of Part II of

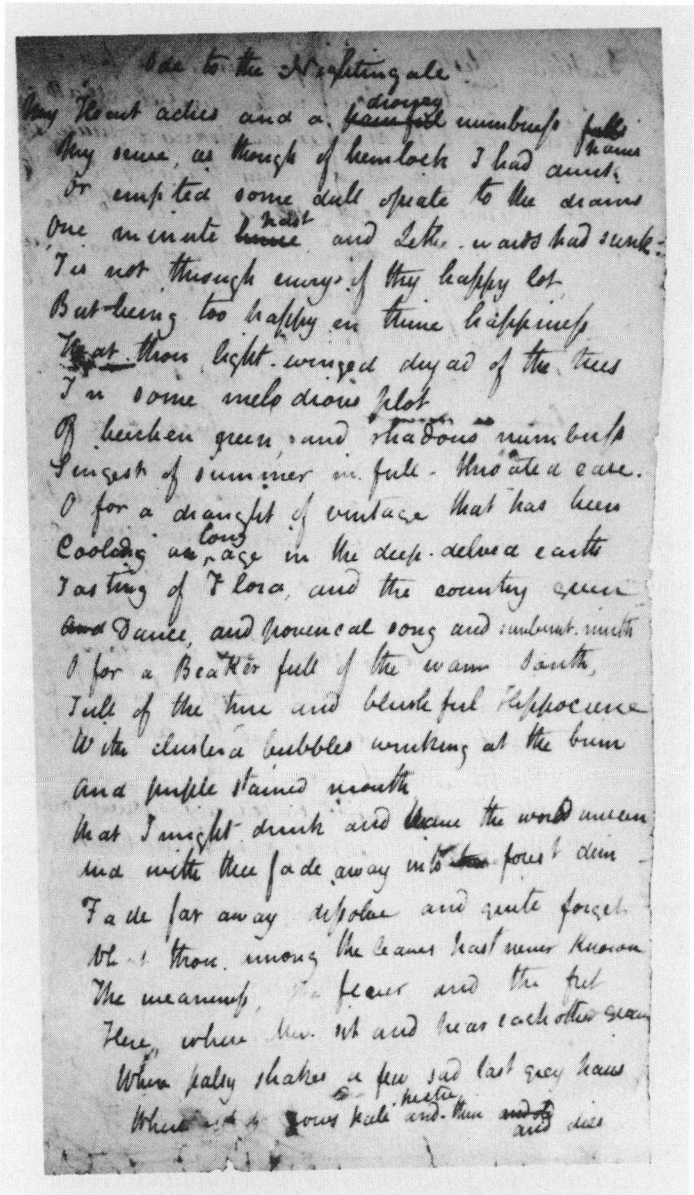

Ode to the Nightingale

My heart aches and a ~~painful~~ drowsy numbness ~~falls~~ pains
My sense, as though of hemlock I had drunk,
Or emptied some dull opiate to the drains
One minute ~~hence~~ past and Lethe-wards had sunk:
'Tis not through envy of thy happy lot
But being too happy in thine happiness
That thou light-winged dryad of the trees
In some melodious plot
Of beechen green, and shadows numberless
Singest of summer in full-throated ease.
O for a draught of vintage that has been
Cooling an long age in the deep-delved earth
Tasting of Flora, and the country green
~~And~~ Dance, and provencal song and sunburnt mirth
O for a Beaker full of the warm South,
Full of the true and blushful Hippocrene
With clustered bubbles winking at the brim
And purple stained mouth
That I might drink and leave the world unseen
And with thee fade away into ~~the~~ forest dim
Fade far away dissolve and quite forget
What thou among the leaves hast never known
The weariness, the fever and the fret
Here, where men sit and hear each other groan
Where palsy shakes a few sad last grey hairs
Where youth grows pale and spectre thin ~~and~~ and dies

Figure 15.1 The first page of the draft of "Ode to a Nightingale."

Lamia; the first scene of *Otho* was entirely rewritten. But for the most part, Keats's revisions in the second manuscripts of these poems are again confined to single words and phrases, with the main concerns pretty much the same as those of the reviewers of the day: style and expression. (The one exception is of course *Hyperion* – the subject of Jonathan Bate's essay in the present volume – which in revision, as *The Fall of Hyperion*, was changed so drastically as to become an entirely new work. In some technical sense, one of these Hyperion poems is a variant of the other, but nobody has ever suggested printing only one in an edition of Keats's works and relegating the distinctive readings of the other to a textual apparatus.)

The same generalization holds for Keats's second or subsequent manuscripts of his shorter poems, where the revisions almost always represent tinkering, polishing, and fine-tuning rather than a second session of genuine creativity. (The addition and then cancellation of a stanza in "Ode on Melancholy" and a possible rearrangement of stanzas in "La Belle Dame" are the most extensive among the recoverable alterations.) So also with the handful of poems that appeared in magazines before they were published in one of Keats's books – three sonnets in *The Examiner* ("O Solitude," "Chapman's Homer," and "To Koskiusko") and two odes in *Annals of the Fine Arts* ("Nightingale," "Grecian Urn"), where the variants between the earlier and later printed texts are again mainly isolated words and matters of expression.

Thus the Keats canon, *texturally* as well as textually, is vastly different from the canons of poets like Wordsworth and Coleridge who repeatedly rewrote their poems during careers spanning many decades. Wordsworth's "obsessive" revising has been a point of critical controversy surrounding the ongoing Cornell University Press edition of his works, and there continues to be debate over *which* of the four or five versions – 1798–99, 1804, 1805, c. 1819, or 1850 – is the "real" *Prelude*. Coleridge's successive revisions of *The Rime of the Ancient Mariner* (from old spelling with "Argument" to modern spelling with "Argument," modern spelling without "Argument," poetic text alone, text with Latin epigraph and marginal glosses) are well known, as are the significant structural and philosophical changes, along with stylistic revisions, that he made in "The Eolian Harp," "Frost at Midnight," and "Dejection: An Ode." The texts and apparatus of E.H. Coleridge's Oxford English Texts edition of 1912 reveal (or perhaps conceal) at least ten separate versions of "Monody on the Death of Chatterton" produced over a period of forty-four years; J.C.C. Mays, who is editing the poems for the Collected Coleridge (his essay in the present volume emphasizes the plurality of *versions* in the canon), has surely discovered several additional ones among the manuscripts.

Keats's entire poetic career was only four years long, and he died at twenty-five, little more than a year after writing his best poems. Obviously he never had the chance to revise over a span of decades, or a succession of editions, in the way that Wordsworth and Coleridge did. From his practice while alive, however, and the statement quoted by Woodhouse in the note given above on Keats's "mode of writing" ("And shall I afterwards . . . sit down coldly to criticise . . . what I have written when almost inspired?"), it may seem rather unlikely that Keats, had he lived, would ever have produced radically altered versions of *The Eve of St. Agnes*, "La Belle Dame," the major odes, or *Lamia*. Keats was a fundamentally different sort of poet from Wordsworth and Coleridge, and it should be plain that one of the many differences lies in his attitude toward revision.

My third general observation based on the textual and biographical materials is that others besides Keats had a hand in the revision of his poems.[7] *Isabella* is a useful example, because we have an extraordinary amount of information about it in letters, extant holographs of the poem, and transcripts (including the copy used by the printer of the first published text, in Keats's volume of 1820, *Lamia, Isabella, The Eve of St. Agnes, and Other Poems*). J.H. Reynolds proposed an alteration when he read Keats's fair copy. Woodhouse began tinkering with the text, pointing to faulty rhymes and meter and suggesting improvements, when he made a shorthand transcript of the fair copy, and he introduced further changes in two successive longhand transcripts based on the shorthand. The publisher Taylor also made changes in the final transcript (the setting copy); and Keats, responding to queries and suggestions in the transcript, also introduced new readings at the last minute. Keats of course remains the nominal author of *Isabella* (as well as the actual author of a high proportion of the words), but Woodhouse and Taylor between them are responsible for the title (Keats's own heading was "The Pot of Basil," which became the printed text's subtitle), for most of the punctuation and other "accidentals" throughout, and for some of the wording of about sixty of the 504 lines – roughly one line out of every nine in the poem.

Earlier Taylor had made significant revisions in both pencil and ink while editing Keats's fair copy of *Endymion* for the printer, marking vaguenesses and inaccuracies in wording, faulty rhymes, and passages of physical and rhetorical extravagance (an awkward reference to "Leda's bosom," for example, too much physical intimacy between Endymion and his sister, and phrases like "maddest Kisses" and "hot eyeballs . . . burnt and sear'd"). Later both Woodhouse and Taylor, dismayed by the sexual explicitness of some of Keats's revisions in *The Eve of St. Agnes*, worked over the poem in Woodhouse's transcripts and produced a composite version (still our standard text) of readings of Keats's draft, readings of his revised fair copy, and new readings that do not appear in any manuscript and, as a consequence, are more likely to be inventions of the well-meaning editors than of Keats himself. Woodhouse and Taylor also had a hand in printer's-copy alterations and proof-changes in *Lamia*. And all along, with shorter and longer poems alike, Keats routinely handed his manuscripts over to Woodhouse and Charles Brown for transcribing, punctuating, and correction of the spelling and other details. There is abundant evidence that he considered their transcripts (rather than the holographs from which they were taken) the principal finished versions of the poems before publication. Indeed, for some of the pieces Keats had *only* Woodhouse's and Brown's transcripts available when he collected his poems for the volume of 1820.

The known facts of the revising, editing, and printing of these poems give us a rather attractive overall picture of Keats, Woodhouse, Taylor, Reynolds, and Brown all pulling together to make Keats's lines presentable to the public; and for the most part, though not always, Keats welcomed his friends' help, indeed regularly depended on it, and was gratefully aware that his poems were the better for it. But the attractive picture does entail some theoretical problems relating to diffusion of authority in the texts. Practical critics, and frequently theorists as well, tend to rely on single authorship to validate their interpretations ("this is what *the author* meant"), and editors of the Greg–Bowers–Tanselle persuasion take single authorship, "final" or otherwise, as an inviolable standard ("this is what *the author* intended us to read"). In both realms – interpretation and editing – Keats scholars are having to adjust to the fact that Woodhouse, Taylor, and others are responsible for small and occasionally larger effects all through some of Keats's best-known poetry.

On the present occasion, however, I wish to call attention to an even more basic problem concerning intentionality in Keats's poetry, a problem that goes back to the way Keats drafted his pieces in the first place, and to Keats's and Woodhouse's remarks about naturalness, "chance," and "magic" in the process of composition. The heart of the problem is whether Keats, characteristically writing even his greatest poems in the manner of extempore effusions, can have had any specific intentions *at all* in the sense in which scholars interpret and edit according to the standard of authorial intention.

There is an enormous body of books and essays on the subject of intentionality in art and literature, especially on the place of authorial intention in literary criticism and interpretation. W.K. Wimsatt and Monroe Beardsley's essay "The Intentional Fallacy" (1946) is an early landmark, provoking considerable debate at the time and repeated citation and discussion in the four decades since it first appeared; E.D. Hirsch's *Validity in Interpretation* (1967) is another landmark, twenty years later, that continues to be at the center of the controversy; and in this decade Steven Knapp and Walter Benn Michaels's "Against Theory" (1982) has set off another extended flurry of special issues and symposia.[8] The point of contention (stated in the simplest possible terms) is whether or not the "meaning" of a text is the same as the author's intended meaning. Wimsatt and Beardsley said, or thought they intended to say, that the question was beside the point, while Hirsch and Knapp–Michaels argue, in different ways, that the meaning of a text *has* to be the author's intended meaning. Significantly (for present purposes), all principal sides in this controversy routinely assume that authors do in fact have intended meanings.

A better view is that some poets have such intentions in drafting their works, while others do not, and that Keats in general belongs in the latter class. Perhaps the distinction should be made between a poetry of themes and ideas, on the one hand, and what might be called a poetry of subject-matter, on the other. Wordsworth and Coleridge frequently appear to be centrally concerned with ideas as ideas: Wordsworth especially, in prefaces and notes to his poems, makes a point of explaining just what the ideas are, and Coleridge too, in prefaces and notes, evinces a similar emphasis by, in effect, apologizing for his poems' lack of serious thematic intention. Both writers' prefaces and notes (like their revisions of the texts themselves) come after the initial drafting, of course, and can be seen as their own critical interpretations as they become readers of what they created. But such interpretations do impart an air of high intellectual and moral purpose to the works.

Keats, by contrast, seems to operate more like the artist depicted by R.G. Collingwood in *The Principles of Art* (1938): "the artist has no idea what the experience is which demands expression until he has expressed it. What he wants to say is not present to him as an end towards which means have to be devised; it becomes clear to him only as the poem takes shape in his mind."[9] *Endymion*, as Keats described it before he had got very far into it, is a perfect example of Collingwood's artistry without prior intention: the poem was to be "a test, a trial of my Powers of Imagination and chiefly of my invention . . . by which I must make 4000 Lines of one bare circumstance and fill them with Poetry" (*Letters*, 1, pp. 169–70). *Isabella* and *Lamia* can be seen as similar tests of invention in the retelling of stories in Boccaccio and Burton. *The Eve of St. Agnes* represents inventions based on "a popular superstition," and a principal effect of "The Eve of St. Mark" was to "give [the reader] the sensation of walking about an old county Town in a coolish evening" (*Letters*, 2, pp. 139, 201). "Ode to Psyche" was written to atone for history's neglect of the goddess, and "To Autumn" to celebrate the beauty of the slow-dying season.

I do not advocate reversion to the anti-intellectual position of Garrod ("I think [Keats] the great poet he is only when the senses capture him, when he finds truth in beauty, that is to say, when he does not trouble to find truth at all").[10] But we may have gone on too long, in too many books and articles, expounding Keats's intended "meaning" in the symbolism of the nightingale, the Grecian urn's climactic utterance (*if* it is the urn who speaks the quoted lines), and the hoodwinking of Madeline. Keats's thoughts, in Woodhouse's note quoted above, came *while* he was creating – "in troops, as though soliciting to be accepted" – and he culled "what appear[ed] to him at the time the best" from a "redundancy . . . of images." It does not sound as if he made an outline before starting to write.

If denial of prior intention in Keats's spontaneous art undermines the validity of interpretation in certain theoretical schemes, perhaps there will be some compensation in the refocusing of our critical attention on Keats's subject matter, pictorial effects, music, and narrative and dramatic techniques. These were the components that interested him, not only in his own poetry but in that of Shakespeare, Spenser, Milton, and the rest of the "laurel'd peers" whom he hoped one day to join. When he wrote, in a marginal annotation in an edition of Shakespeare, "Is *Criticism* a true thing?" he was objecting to Dr Johnson's faulting Shakespeare for having "lost an opportunity of exhibiting a moral lesson" in *As You Like It*.[11] Seizing on moral lessons was all right for the eighteenth century, as it has been in literary interpretation for much of the twentieth century. But Keats was, as he would say, "righter" in his skepticism of its being a "true thing."

NOTES

1 I quote from the manuscript at Harvard, soon to be available, with all or parts of three dozen other holographs, in a facsimile edition, *John Keats: Poetry Manuscripts at Harvard* (Cambridge, Mass., 1990). For standard references to the poems I use my Harvard Press edition of 1978, *The Poems of John Keats* (hereafter cited as *Poems*).

2 The holographs and other manuscripts are listed and described in my *The Texts of Keats's Poems* (Cambridge, Mass., 1974), Chapter 2, "The Manuscripts and the Transcribers," pp. 14–62, and in *Poems*, appendix 5, "Summary Account of the Manuscripts," pp. 741–52; their variants, cancellations, revisions, and other peculiarities are discussed in the individual textual histories in *Texts*, pp. 84 ff., and are recorded in the apparatuses and textual notes of *Poems*, *passim*. Many of the manuscripts can be examined in facsimile. In addition to the Harvard facsimile edition cited in the preceding note, I have edited seven volumes of Keats facsimiles in Garland's series entitled "The Manuscripts of the Younger Romantics": 1, Richard Woodhouse's annotated copy of Keats's *Poems* (1817); 2, the holograph fair copy of *Endymion*; 3, Woodhouse's annotated copy of the printed *Endymion*; 4, Woodhouse's scrapbook of letters and poetry transcripts in the Pierpont Morgan Library; 5, holographs and transcripts in the British Library; 6, Woodhouse's poetry transcripts

at Harvard; 7, Charles Brown's transcripts, also at Harvard (New York, Vols. 1–4, 1985; Vols. 5–7, 1988). (The materials in Vols. 1, 3, and 6 are particularly relevant to the present subject; Woodhouse was centrally concerned with Keats's processes of composition and revision, and some of his variorum-like textual annotations draw on as many as three, four, and even five different sources for a single poem). For other facsimiles see Robert Gittings, *The Odes of Keats and Their Earliest Known Manuscripts* (Kent, Ohio, 1970), and the numerous references in *Texts* to individual reproductions in books, periodicals, and sale catalogues. The most useful sources for Keats's and his friends' comments about writing and revising are *The Letters of John Keats, 1814–1821*, ed. Hyder E. Rollins, 2 vols. (Cambridge, Mass., 1958, hereafter cited as *Letters*), and *The Keats Circle: Letters and Papers, 1816–1878*, ed. Rollins, 2 vols. (Cambridge, Mass., 1948). Claude Lee Finney collected and studied several hundred photocopies of manuscripts for his *The Evolution of Keats's Poetry*, 2 vols. (Cambridge, Mass., 1936), and there is of course discussion of Keats's methods of composition in the standard biographies, particularly Walter Jackson Bate's *John Keats* (Cambridge, Mass., 1963) and Gittings's *John Keats* (Boston, 1968). The fullest critical account of Keats's work in the manuscripts is M.R. Ridley's *Keats' Craftsmanship: A Study in Poetic Development* (1933; reprinted Lincoln, Nebraska, 1963).

3 For otherwise undocumented quotations and facts of this sort, see the commentary section in my 'reading' edition, *John Keats: Complete Poems* (Cambridge, Mass., 1982).

4 *The Keats Circle*, 2, p. 65. Gittings, *John Keats*, p. 311 n., reasonably suggests that Brown in his recollection has confused "Nightingale" with "Ode on Indolence." But Brown's description is useful in any case: clearly Keats wrote *some* important "fugitive" poem in such circumstances.

5 A couple of exceptions – Brown's remark that "There is a Joy in Footing Slow' was composed "with more than usual care" (*The Keats Circle*, 2, p. 64) and Keats's description of "Ode to Psyche" as "the first and the only [poem] with which I have taken even moderate pains" (*Letters*, 2, p. 105) – simply emphasize the "fugitive" character of the rest. Keats continues his comment on "Psyche": "I have for the most part dash'd of[f] my lines in a hurry."

6 *The Keats Circle*, 1, pp. 128–9. This comment (in a manuscript at Harvard) is a rough draft with numerous abbreviations and cancellations. In quoting, I have expanded the abbreviations and made some other minor changes for the sake of readability.

7 In this and the next two paragraphs I draw on Chapter 2 ('Keats and His Helpers: The Multiple Authorship of *Isabella*) in *Multiple Authorship and the Myth of Solitary Genius* (New York, 1991).

8 W.K. Wimsatt, Jr., and Monroe C. Beardsley, "The Intentional Fallacy," *Sewanee Review*, 54 (1946), pp. 468–88, republished in revised form in Wimsatt's *The Verbal Icon* (Lexington, Kentucky, 1954) and many times reprinted; E.D. Hirsch, Jr., *Validity in Interpretation* (New Haven, 1967); Steven Knapp and Walter Benn Michaels, "Against Theory," *Critical Inquiry*, 8 (1982), pp. 723–42, reprinted among other places in *Against Theory: Literary Studies and the New Pragmatism*, ed. W.J.T. Mitchell (Chicago, 1985). For background to the last decade of controversy, see the

collection *On Literary Intention: Critical Essays*, ed. David Newton-De Molina (Edinburgh, 1976).

9 R.G. Collingwood, *The Principles of Art* (1938; reprinted as a Galaxy Book, New York, 1958), p. 29; quoted by George Watson (in a section headed "Is Intention Prior to Creation?") in *The Study of Literature* (London, 1969), as excerpted in Newton-De Molina's *On Literary Intention* (Edinburgh, 1976), p. 170. More recent theorists who deny the existence of significant prior intention include John R. Searle, *Intentionality: An Essay in the Philosophy of Mind* (Cambridge, 1983), esp. pp. 92–5, and Hershel Parker, *Flawed Texts and Verbal Icons* (Evanston, Illinois, 1984), esp. pp. 21–6. Parker, however, makes an illogical leap to the position – a main point of his book – that an author's intentions are represented *only* in the first writing of a work and that every subsequent revision should therefore be thrown out as violation of the author's original intention.

10 H.W. Garrod, *Keats*, 2nd edn (Oxford, 1939), p. 61.

11 *The Poetical Works and Other Writings of John Keats*, ed. H. Buxton Forman, revised by Maurice Buxton Forman, 8 vols. (New York, 1938–9), Vol. 5, p. 276; Caroline F.E. Spurgeon, *Keats's Shakespeare: A Descriptive Study* (Oxford, 1928), p. 31 and plate 9 opposite p. 32. It is worth observing that Woodhouse, who was in some ways the best contemporary reader of Keats's poetry and who made many hundreds of biographical and critical notes about the poems, showed no interest whatsoever in the overall ideas, themes, and "meaning" of the texts that he was annotating.

16

KEATS'S TWO *HYPERIONS* AND THE
PROBLEM OF MILTON

JONATHAN BATE

ONE of the most powerful chapters in Walter Jackson Bate's magisterial biography of John Keats is the thirteenth, 'The Burden of the Mystery: The Emergence of a Modern Poet'.[1] It is there that we are presented with an image of the young Keats grappling with the problem of the inherited literary tradition. Out of Wordsworth's pregnant phrase, as quoted by Keats, 'The Burden of the Mystery', grew Jackson Bate's conception of 'The Burden of the Past'. *John Keats* was published in 1963; the following year Harold Bloom wrote his essay, 'Keats and the Embarrassments of Poetic Tradition', one of the first airings of his theory of influence.[2] In the early 1970s both Bate and Bloom, having tested their theories on Keats, developed them in more general terms in short but groundbreaking books, *The Burden of the Past* and *The Anxiety of Influence*.[3] Jackson Bate's study is centrally concerned with the decline of the major poetic genres, while Bloom advances a more personal, explicitly Oedipal, model of literary history, but in each case Milton plays a key role.

The prime symptom of 'the burden of the past' is the inability of English poets to write epic after *Paradise Lost*, that summation and transumption of all previous epic. I use the term 'transumption' in John Hollander's sense, with regard to Milton's capacity simultaneously to summon up and to subsume his predecessors: 'he . . . transcend[s] the prior allusions, even as he has alluded to them. It is like a summing up of the range of texts for him, tempting us to play with the notion of transumption as if the Latin word were a portmanteau of transcending and summing up'.[4] Dryden and Pope only managed mock-epic or the translation of Classical epic. The ground of English Romanticism is strewn with the fragments of failed undertakings in epic – one thinks of Blake's incompletion of *The Four Zoas*, Coleridge's inability to write *The Fall of Jerusalem*, and pre-eminently Wordsworth's non-publication and restless revision of his epic of the individual mind, the age's boldest attempt to overgo Milton's cosmic theme. *Endymion* is Keats's experiment in romance; from there he moved on to his endeavour in epic. *Hyperion* has a more traditional epic theme and structure than any other project by a major Romantic poet: an opening *in medias res*, a Titanic battle in heaven, the fall of a divinity, the rise of a new god. The original version has a manifestly Miltonic shape, in that its first two books dwell on fallen gods while the third begins in the realm of light. But then it breaks off. Did Keats first revise and then abandon *Hyperion* because of Milton's overbearing influence?

For Bloom, Milton is the great inhibitor, the strangler of later poetic imaginations: 'The motto to English poetry since Milton was stated by Keats: "Life to him would be Death to me"' (*Anxiety*, p. 32). Keats wrote this apropos of giving up his project to write on the subject of Hyperion;[5] *Hyperion* has thus become a crucial test-case for interpretations of the Romantic attempt to deal with – in Bloom's special sense, to 'revise' – Milton.[6] It will, however, be my argument in this essay that criticism's emphasis on Milton's inhibiting effect has led to an oversimplification, not least in that the model of a development from the more Miltonic poem (*Hyperion*) to the less Miltonic one (*The Fall of Hyperion*) ignores the complex sequence of composition from *Hyperion* (1818) to *The Fall of Hyperion* (1819) to the published *Hyperion* (1820). The problem of Milton is only one of a number of problems, most important of which is that of tragedy: Keats's revisions are bound up not only with questions of poetic diction but also with the articulation of a tragic vision in place of a vision of progress for which the most appropriate medium was epic narrative. Furthermore, that movement from epic progress-poem to meditative tragedy has significant political ramifications.

To begin, however, with Milton. Important evidence concerning Keats's reading of *Paradise Lost* may be gleaned from the underlinings and annotations in his copy of the poem, which is now held at Keats House in Hampstead.[7] Milton's centrality to the diction of the first *Hyperion* is apparent even from the famous line with which the poem begins, 'Deep in the shady sadness of a vale'. This locution evokes not only a location – what Keats in his Miltonic marginalia called a 'stationing'[8] – but also a mood, derived primarily from the word 'vale', with its simultaneous suggestion of enclosure and a veil of mourning ('sadness' activates the pun). It was Milton who showed Keats how to use this word 'vale' with resonance. In a situation analogous to that with which *Hyperion* begins – we are among the fallen, the giant forms who have been defeated in the war in heaven – Satan rouses his followers:

> or have ye chosen this place
> After the toil of battle to repose
> Your wearied virtue, for the ease you find
> To slumber here, as in the vales of Heaven?
> (*PL*, I, 318–21, final line underscored by Keats)

Beside these lines Keats wrote in his copy of *Paradise Lost*:

There is a cool pleasure in the very sound of vale. The english word is of the happiest chance. Milton has put vales in heaven and hell with the very utter affection and yearning of a great Poet. It is a sort of delphic Abstraction – a beautiful – thing made more beautiful by being reflected and put in a Mist. The next mention of Vale is one of the most pathetic in the whole range of Poetry.

> Others, more mild,
> Retreated in a silent Valley &c.
> [*PL*, II, 546–7]

How much of the charm is in the Valley! –
(Wittreich, p. 554)

While the opening of *Hyperion* is indebted to *Paradise Lost* in its poetic diction, Keats's annotations reveal that his reading of Milton's vales was revisionary. Contrary to Harold Bloom's kind of revisionism, however, what the force of Keats's rewriting indicates is dependence on a memory, not a forgetting, on a recollection of the precise words and context of the precursor text. For Milton, the point about Satan's question is that the vales of hell are not like those of heaven; the recollection of heaven's vales is used by the devil to provoke his cohorts out of slumber and back into action. Immediately before Satan speaks he is seen walking with 'uneasy steps / Over the burning marl, not like those steps / On heaven's azure' (*PL*, I, 295–7). Milton's 'not like' exposes Satan's subsequent 'as in' for what it is – a characteristic rhetorical imposture. Keats, however, implies that the sound of 'vale' cools hell down and that the vales of both heaven and hell are the product not of Milton the moralist, but of Milton the poet, the maker of beautiful images. Keats has much to say about vales, nothing to say about 'virtue', a word which from Milton's point of view is not ironic coming from Satan's mouth. So too with the next mention of vale: as Keats quotes it, in company with 'mild', 'Retreated' and 'silent', it does indeed have a 'charm'; but Keats's '&c.' conceals the context:

> Others more mild,
> Retreated in a silent valley, sing
> With notes angelical to many a harp
> Their own heroic deeds and hapless fall
> By doom of battle; and complain that fate
> Free virtue should enthral to force or chance.
> (*PL*, II, 546–51)

This is less than charming: in the infernal epic that they are composing here, the fallen angels are proudly praising their own prowess and are constructing a distorted version of their fall in which they stand for 'Free virtue' and God for 'force or chance'. In each 'vale' passage, then, the fallen angels falsely

323

appropriate 'virtue'. While Milton means the reader to notice this, Keats veils the ethical reading in a mist and concentrates on the pathos and poetic beauty. In annotating Book II, he underlined the whole of the sentence in question with the exception of 'and complain that fate / Free virtue should enthral to force or chance'; furthermore, he wrote in the margin of how 'the delicacies of passion' in the fallen angels are 'of the most softening and dissolving nature' (Wittreich, p. 557). This is in keeping with the wholesale revision of the first two books of *Paradise Lost* in the first two books of *Hyperion* whereby the reader's sympathy is enlisted for the pathetic fallen gods while the admonitory Miltonic voice is silenced.

Keats made his *Paradise Lost* annotations in 1818, the year of the first *Hyperion*. Before considering the revisionary process in detail, it is worth recollecting the chronology of composition. The poem was begun in autumn 1818 and the first attempt abandoned in April 1819. Soon after Tom's death in December 1818, we find Keats writing 'Just now I took out my poem to go on with it – but . . . I could not get on'; in March 1819, he is 'in a sort of qui bono temper, not exactly on the road to an epic poem'; and the following month his friend Richard Woodhouse notes, 'K. lent me the fragment . . . abt 900 lines in all . . . He said he was dissatisfied . . . and should not complete it.'[9] A few months later, in July 1819, he began a reconstruction, but on 21 September 1819 he wrote to J. H. Reynolds, 'I have given up Hyperion' (i.e. the second version, *The Fall of Hyperion*). It is here that he blames Milton. The previous month he had twice written of the wonders of *Paradise Lost*,[10] but now he suggests that he is stultified by it:

I have given up Hyperion – there were too many Miltonic inversions in it – Miltonic verse cannot be written but in artful or rather artist's humour. I wish to give myself up to other sensations. English ought to be kept up. It may be interesting to you to pick out some lines from Hyperion and put a mark X to the false beauty proceeding from art, and one // to the true voice of feeling. Upon my soul 'twas imagination I cannot make the distinction – Every now and then there is a Miltonic intonation – But I cannot make the division properly. The fact is I must take a walk[.]   (*Letters*, 2, p. 167)

'I have given up' sounds decisive, yet Keats asks Reynolds to go through the first version looking for Miltonisms, presumably with the intention of cutting or altering in the second version such lines as his friend marked with a cross. The need to clear his head with a walk shows that revision is a struggle. On the same day he wrote in his journal-letter to the George Keatses, 'I have but lately stood on my guard against Milton. Life to him would be death to me. Miltonic verse cannot be written but i[n] the vein of art – I wish to devote myself to another sensation' (*Letters*, 2, p. 212). 'The vein of art' suggests that Keats has come to the conclusion that writing Miltonically is not only a struggle but also a questionable departure from life, from immediate sensation. Keats always loved a pun and it is not implausibie to hear the several senses of 'vain' in 'vein'.

Whether or not Keats undertook any further work on *The Fall* after 21 September 1819 is unclear. According to Charles Brown, he was 'remodelling' contemporaneously with the writing of *The Jealousies*, which he may have been working on later that autumn.[11] What is certain is that in the following year the first version was prepared for publication. It appeared under the title 'Hyperion. A Fragment' in *Lamia, Isabella, The Eve of St Agnes, and Other Poems* (published July 1820). In a number of places the published text restored readings of Keats's original holograph manuscript that had been altered in Woodhouse's transcript, which became the printer's copy. Since it is highly probable that Keats made these corrections himself, it is also likely that he was responsible for a number of new readings introduced in the 1820 text.[12] The second unfinished version was not published until 1857, long after Keats's death. His friends preferred the first version, which is probably one reason why he chose it for the 1820 volume. The latter carried a publisher's advertisement:

If any apology be thought necessary for the appearance of the unfinished poem of HYPERION, the publishers beg to state that they alone are responsible, as it was printed at their particular request, and contrary to the wishes of the author. The poem was intended to have been of equal length with ENDYMION but the reception of that work discouraged the author proceeding.

But in a presentation copy Keats crossed this out, saying that it was inserted without his knowledge when he was ill, and that it was 'a lie' to say that he failed to finish the first *Hyperion* because of the poor critical reception accorded to *Endymion*. Clearly, then, there were other reasons for this first discontinuation.

The Miltonic influence is usually taken to be the major one.[13] The epic tone and structure of the first version is manifest in its division into *books*; the revised title, *The Fall of Hyperion. A Dream*, and the new opening section in which the poet has his vision, denote a shift to a structure that bears more resemblance to romance or 'dream-poem'. Internalization and subjectification separate *The Fall* off from Milton. Furthermore, it has 'cantos' instead of books: Keats had been reading in the Italian classics, especially Dante and Ariosto, over the summer of 1819 and this is the likeliest source of the change in form. Revision to cantos – which Keats had in fact been contemplating even when writing the first *Hyperion*[14] – also suggests a reversion to Spenser, Keats's earliest master, and in particular to the 'Mutabilitie Cantos', which were such a rich source for the maturing poet who in 1819 was becoming less of an Endymion yearning for transcendence and more of an Oceanus recognizing the necessity of transience.[15]

The revised structure was also bound up with the state of contemporary English poetry, where 'visions' and 'dreams' seemed to be having more success than epics. Most significantly, there was 'Kubla Khan: or, A Vision in a Dream. A Fragment'. The new substance of *The Fall*, the poet's meeting with Moneta, revises the climax of the first *Hyperion*, Apollo's assumption of godhead through his reading of Mnemosyne's face. It was with regard to this passage that Keats told his friend Woodhouse: 'It seemed to come by chance or magic – to be as it were something given to him' (*Keats Circle*, 1, p. 129). He is following Coleridge's famous prefatory note to 'Kubla Khan': 'Yet from the still surviving recollections in his mind, the Author has frequently purposed to finish for himself what had been originally, as it were, given to him.'[16] Both 'Kubla Khan' and *The Fall of Hyperion* are poems centrally concerned with the activity of imagination; each exemplifies what it means by poetry through metaphors of inspiration. The poem is said to be given, not made; instead of being apostrophized or summoned in epic fashion, the Muse is conjured from within by means of 'a vision in a dream'.

There are, then, numerous indications that whereas in *Hyperion* Keats is manifestly imitating Milton, in *The Fall* he is absorbing other models. Yet he nowhere talks about the oppressive Miltonic influence as the reason for his first abandonment. The chronology is as follows: Keats gives up the first version, starts the second, then re-reads *Paradise Lost* and is struck by its beauties, and finally gives up the second version because of its persistent Miltonics. If Keats did give up the first version because he was unhappy with its poetic diction, the problem perhaps was not so much the Miltonics as a certain return to Endymionese, to luxuriant imagery at the expense of narrative focus, in the third book. In fact, it seems to me that Keats did not know why *Hyperion* was going wrong the first time. His reasons for stopping work on it were more extrinsic – his health, the difficulty of sustaining a long poem, and, more positively, the discovery of the form that suited him best, the ode. But soon after he took the poem up again in summer 1819, he re-read Milton and then realized how excessively Miltonic it was. In late August he wrote to Reynolds to the effect that 'the Paradise Lost becomes a greater wonder – The more I know what my diligence may in time probably effect; the more does my heart distend with Pride and Obstinacy' (*Letters*, 2, p. 146). The pride here – which evinces a characteristic Romantic identification with Milton's Satan, whose 'heart / Distends with pride' (*PL* I, 571–2) – stems from the hope of creating a poem that is a true successor to *Paradise Lost*; the obstinacy, from refusal to give up on it. But within a month Keats does give up precisely because of the feeling that he is writing as a successor to Milton and is accordingly trapped in a style incompatible with the naturalness and fluidity of diction he had perfected in the odes. All this, however, takes place in the second half of 1819: critics have attached too much weight to the letters of 21 September, assuming that what

Keats perceived as the problem then must have been the problem back in April. It is not surprising that Bloom values this late correspondence so highly, given the identification with Satan and the dramatic cry that 'Life to him would be death to me', but the processes of composition and revision are never as simple or as single-minded as an *ex post facto* explanation in a letter might make them appear to be. In comparing the two *Hyperions* and testing the hypothesis about Miltonic influence, one needs to consider both the broad revisions (changes in structure, cuts, additions) and the particular ones (verbal alterations in lines that are taken over from the first version). Local changes provide the most tangible form of evidence; they also offer fascinating instances of the poetic craftsman at work.

In the published text of 1820, Hyperion's minions stand amazed and full of fear 'like anxious men / Who on wide plains gather in panting troops, / When earthquakes jar their battlements and towers' (*H* I, 198–200), but in *The Fall* they are 'like anxious men / Who on a wide plain gather in sad troops' (*FH* II, 42–3). 'Sad' is a wonderful choice, almost Shakespearean in its tragic foreboding (one recalls Cleopatra's gathering of her 'sad captains'). What is interesting about this 'revision' is that it is actually a return to Keats's original text, for the holograph manuscript of *Hyperion* shows that 'panting' was Keats's third attempt, the second being 'sad eyed' and the first 'sad' (in the second and third versions the 'a' before 'plain' is cut to make room for the extra syllable later in the line). Keats famously remarked that 'things which [I] do half at Random are afterwards confirmed by my judgment in a dozen features of Propriety' (*Letters*, I, p. 142): in exercising his judgment as he revised *Hyperion* into *The Fall*, Keats discovered that his half random first thought was his best.

At several points Keats actually improved the text of *Hyperion* as a result of working on *The Fall*. Saturn's shady vale gave him trouble in the original manuscript. The second sentence of the poem originally read

> No stir of air was there,
> Not so much Life as what an eagle's wing
> Would spread upon a field of green-ear'd corn
> But where the dead leaf fell, there did it rest.

Unhappy (and rightly so) with 'as what', Keats erased 'what an eagle's' and replaced it with 'a young vultur[e]'s'. Still unhappy – the ornithological uncertainty is symptomatic – he cancelled the whole two lines and replaced them with the following, written vertically in the right hand margin: 'Not so much life as on a summer's day / Robs not at all the dandelion's fleece.' The next time Keats worked on his manuscript, it was to use it as a source for *The Fall*. And it was at this point that the image came good:

> No stir of life
> Was in this shrouded vale, not so much air
> As in the zoning of a summer's day
> Robs not one light seed from the feather'd grass,
> But where the dead leaf fell there did it rest[.]
>
> (*FH* I, 310–14)

The *Hyperion* manuscript and the Woodhouse transcripts of it retained the dandelion version, but when the 1820 volume was in proof Keats altered the lines in accordance with the revision for *The Fall*, to produce the published text:

> No stir of air was there,
> Not so much life as on a summer's day
> Robs not one light seed from the feather'd grass,
> But where the dead leaf fell, there did it rest.
>
> (*H* I, 7–10)

Two things are striking about this revision. First, there is Keats's capacity to recognize when an image does *not* need changing – from first version to last, the final line of the sentence remains perfect in its stasis. And secondly, the fact that his concern with local poetic texture is not confined to 'Miltonic' passages, for none of the several versions here is perceptibly embroiled with the language of *Paradise Lost*.

Again, in his original manuscript Keats struggled in an attempt to convey the sickly sweet smell of incense. 'A nausea', he begins. 'A nauseous feel', he then tries, but 'feel' is heavily crossed out, perhaps because it smacked of Leigh Huntism. 'Poison' then replaces 'nauseous' and 'feel' has to be reinstated: the line thus becomes 'A poison feel of brass and metal sick' (manuscript draft of *H* I, 189). But when the manuscript is adapted for *The Fall*, Keats again rejects 'feel', so that in the new poem the line becomes 'Savour of poisonous brass and metals sick' (*FH* II, 33). The next year, the published text of *Hyperion* follows this, though with 'metal' back in the singular to avoid the clashing 's'.

In these cases, there is an equivalence between *The Fall* and the published text of *Hyperion*. Sometimes, however, the two manuscript versions share details that the published text lacks. Thea addresses Saturn in the published *Hyperion*: 'to the level of his ear / Leaning with parted lips, some words she spake' (*H* I, 46–7). In *The Fall of Hyperion* this reads: 'to the level of his *hollow* ear / Leaning, with parted lips, some words she spake' (*FH* I, 348–9, my italics). Thanks to the epithet 'hollow', the reader may visualize the ear more vividly, while also gaining a fuller sense of loss and emptiness. Saturn has been dispossessed of his kingdom and his body has correspondingly been emptied out. His unsceptred hand is listless and his realmless eyes are closed; so too his kingly ear, which his subjects must often have tried to bend and whisper in for favour, is now hollow.

This turns out to be another of Keats's fine first thoughts afterwards confirmed by his judgment: the holograph manuscript of *Hyperion* shares 'hollow' with *The Fall*. The word has been sacrificed in the published text because of a more technical concern about 'propriety': the problem with 'hollow' is that it makes the line hypermetric by a full foot. For this reason it was cut, almost certainly by Woodhouse.[17] Here, then, revision belongs not to the poet but to his 'editor' – Woodhouse has undertaken in a modest way the kind of tidying up that Keats's publisher, John Taylor, performed so extensively and damagingly upon the works of John Clare. 'Revision' occurs in the process of transforming the text from script to print. The manuscript belongs to the poet and is not subject to the strictures of critics, but Woodhouse recognizes that the reviewers who had savaged *Endymion* would have been quite capable of pouncing on a hypermetric line in *Hyperion* and condemning it as an inept Cockneyism. He revises accordingly.

These four examples show that the revision of *Hyperion* is complex and various. It involves two versions of the original poem with *The Fall* standing between them; it involves Woodhouse as well as Keats. And it does not always involve the question of Miltonic language. Even where there is a 'Miltonic inversion', the process is not always the straightforward one of 'de-Miltonizing and de-latinizing'[18] that critical orthodoxy takes it to be. Here are the two versions of some lines towards the end of Thea's address to Saturn:

> Saturn, sleep on: – Me thoughtless, why should I
> Thus violate thy slumbrous solitude?

and

> Saturn, sleep on: – O thoughtless, why did I
> Thus violate thy slumbrous solitude?

If we are to believe that Keats is going through his poem de-Miltonizing it, we would expect 'Me thoughtless' to be the original version – for that is a highly Miltonic locution – and 'O thoughtless' to be the revised one. But in fact it is the other way round: 'Me thoughtless' is from *The Fall* (*FH* I, 368–9; *H* I, 68–9). Keats has introduced a Miltonism, contaminated the innocuous 'O thoughtless' of *Hyperion*.

This is not a unique instance. A wholly new line, 'Ponderous upon my senses a whole moon' (*FH* I, 392), has a Miltonic word order, yet it occurs a few lines after what is obviously a cut aimed at de-Miltonization, the removal of the circumlocutory description of oak trees as 'Those green-rob'd senators of mighty woods' (*H* I, 73). It is also shortly after the substitution of 'bending' (*FH* I, 386) for the Miltonic, latinate 'couchant' (*H* I, 87). There is a similar pattern of de-Miltonizing cheek by jowl with re-Miltonizing in Keats's treatment of the lines that became the opening of canto two of *The Fall*. 'Mortal omens drear' (*H* I, 169), with its Miltonic postponed adjective, becomes the uninverted 'dire prodigies' (*FH* II, 18), and the idiosyncratic Miltonic verbal form of 'Came slope upon the threshold of the west' (*H* I, 204) is simplified to 'Is sloping to the threshold of the west' (*FH* II, 48). Yet in the same sequence the plain English of 'And so, when harbour'd in the sleepy west' (*H* I, 190) is polysyllabized into 'Wherefore when harbour'd in the sleepy west' (*FH* II, 34).[19] And if Keats had been attempting extensive de-Miltonization he would surely have removed the whole of the epic simile concerning Hyperion's minions and the anxious men gathering on the plain, rather than merely changed 'panting' back to 'sad'.

This apparent confusion of strategies suggests that the pattern of revision was less coherent than Keats made out in his letters of September 1819. At the local level of vocabulary he is simply following his instincts, proving his imagery upon his pulses. Sometimes those instincts lead him to de-Miltonize, while on other occasions his mind continues to move in a Miltonic way. Only when he rationalizes afterwards does he single out the issue of Miltonic diction.

Nor can the new introductory section be described as single-mindedly anti-Miltonic. One moment Keats writes new and highly Miltonic lines:

> a feast of summer fruits,
> Which, nearer seen, seem'd refuse of a meal
> By angel tasted, or our mother Eve[.]
> (*FH* I, 29–31)

This makes the garden in which the poet finds himself specifically Edenic; he is a belated Miltonist picking up the refuse left after the meal in book five of *Paradise Lost*. Just six lines later, however, Keats introduces in a distinctly un-Miltonic way a mythological figure who had become associated with Milton. Romantic figurations of Proserpina, especially Keats's, almost invariably allude to Milton's fair field of Enna where Proserpine gathered flowers,[20] but here in *The Fall* Keats writes of a banquet for 'Proserpine return'd to her own fields, / Where the white heifers low' (*FH* I, 37–8). Those white heifers are unlike anything in Milton – they come from the Elgin marbles and the 'Ode on a Grecian Urn', while Proserpine's return to 'her own fields' anticipates the homecoming of 'To Autumn'.

Some of the finest touches in the second *Hyperion* are the products of the distinctively post-Odes Keats. Shortly after the heifer image, the idiom of the Grecian urn recurs in conjunction with 'Nightingale'-like intoxication and slumber:

> Among the fragrant husks and berries crush'd,
> Upon the grass I struggled hard against
> The domineering potion; but in vain:
> The cloudy swoon came on, and down I sunk
> Like a Silenus on an antique vase.
>
> (FH I, 52–6)

In the very thorough footnotes of Miriam Allott's edition of the poems, the phrasing of this passage is said to recall some lines in Henry Cary's translation of Dante: 'When I, who had so much of Adam with me, / Sank down upon the grass, o'ercome with sleep'.[21] This echo is bound up with a major complexity in Keats's revisionary procedure. It is undoubtedly true that, although there are certain marks of the *Inferno* in the first *Hyperion*, both the structure and the vocabulary of *The Fall* are a great deal more Dantesque. In particular, the earthly paradise cantos at the end of the *Purgatorio* are a vital source for what is new in the second poem.[22] It is attractive to suppose that Milton gives way to Dante as a model. Dante might be seen as a less oppressive influence: since he did not write in the same language as the ephebe, he does not strangle him. To become the English Dante is a nice solution to the problem of the impossibility of being a second Milton.

But in a sense the English Dante already existed, and Keats was close to him: he knew both Henry Cary and his translation (it had been one of the few books he had taken on the Scottish walking tour immediately after which he began the first *Hyperion*). And Cary's translation, far from being in Dantesque terza rima, was in Miltonic blank verse, replete with inversions and latinate vocabulary. Cary started Miltonizing Dante as soon as he started translating him, as may be seen from the very beginning of his *Hell*:

> Nel mezzo del cammin di nostra vita
>   mi ritrovai per una selva oscura
>   che la diritta via era smarrita.
> Ah quanto a dir qual era è cosa dura
>   esta selva selvaggia e aspra e forte
>   che nel pensier rinova la paura!
>
> (*Inferno* I, 1–6)

is rendered

> In the midway of this our mortal life,
> I found me in a gloomy wood, astray
> Gone from the path direct: and e'en to tell,
> It were no easy task, how savage wild
> That forest, how robust and rough its growth,
> Which to remember only, my dismay
> Renews[.]   (*Hell* I, 1–7)

'Gloomy' will do for 'oscura', but the long vowel sounds are gloomily Miltonic; 'astray' hangs and 'Renews' is run on in the manner of *Paradise Lost*'s blank verse; 'diritta via' is inverted to 'path direct'; 'task' is not so much licensed by 'cosa' as generated by Milton's 'sad task' in the invocation to book nine (*PL* IX, 13). Because of Cary, Milton and Dante were not really alternative models for Keats. He tried reading Dante in the original before revising *Hyperion*, as if to distance himself from the Miltonic Cary, but in reading a poem in a language not well known to him he could not get away from the idiom of the translation that he knew.

There is a further reason why the hypothesis of Dante replacing Milton will not do, and this brings us to the broader aspect of Keats's revision. The first *Hyperion* breaks off with Apollo about to become a god. His achievement of godhead depends on his initiation into suffering. He looks into the face of Mnemosyne and seems to achieve knowledge:

> Mute thou remainest – mute! yet I can read
> A wondrous lesson in thy silent face:
> Knowledge enormous makes a God of me.
> Names, deeds, gray legends, dire events, rebellions,
> Majesties, sovran voices, agonies,
> Creations and destroyings, all at once
> Pour into the wide hollows of my brain,
> And deify me[.]
>
> (*H* III, 111–18)

The germ of the second *Hyperion* resides in these lines. In the revised poem Keats develops this idea of Mnemosyne teaching how it is necessary to embrace suffering; he applies it, however, to the poet instead of the emergent god. Mnemosyne, now called Moneta, says that the poet, the first-person narrator, cannot achieve vision until for him 'the miseries of the world / Are misery' and he 'will not let them rest' (*FH* I, 148–9). In famous lines, she distinguishes between the poet and the dreamer – they are 'Diverse, sheer opposite, antipodes' (*FH* I, 200); the true poet's vision is agonizingly tragic, not dreamily romantic. Moneta's lesson is that of the sonnet 'On Sitting Down to Read *King Lear* Once Again': the book of romance must be closed and that of tragedy burned through instead. It is also the lesson of Keats's letter to Reynolds about the mind as a mansion of many apartments – the poet must pass through the light intoxicating chamber into the dark passages beyond (*Letters*, 1, p. 281). Significantly, it was while he was working on *The Fall* that Keats wrote his tragedy *Otho the Great* – not by any stretch of imagination his greatest work, but one that reveals the direction in which he was developing. A letter to Bailey of 14 August 1819 juxtaposes the two works: 'I [hav]e a[l]so been writing parts of my Hyperion [i.e. *Fall*] and [c]ompleted 4 Acts of a Tragedy' (*Letters*, 2, p. 139). In *The Fall*'s dialogue between narrator and Moneta, Keats dramatizes the concerns he had previously explored monologically in the letters; it is here if it is anywhere that he takes his 'first Step towards the chief Attempt in the Drama' (*Letters*, 1, p. 218). The move towards tragedy is central to the revision of both the content and the form of *Hyperion*.

In the revised version the fall of the Titans becomes not the substance of the poem but a narrative which Moneta tells the poet in order to initiate him into tragedy. Keats is specific about this in lines, influenced by those of Apollo, that occur shortly before the vision begins and we hear the familiar 'Deep in the shady sadness of a vale, / Far sunken from the healthy breath of morn':

> So at the view of sad Moneta's brow,
> I ached to see what things the hollow brain
> Behind enwombed: what high tragedy
> In the dark secret chambers of her skull
> Was acting, that could give so dread a stress
> To her cold lips, and fill with such a light
> Her planetary eyes; and touch her voice
> With such a sorrow.
>
> (*FH* I, 275–82)

Apollo in *Hyperion* finds knowledge of dire events pouring 'into the wide hollows' of his brain. The dream structure of *The Fall* means that the whole poem takes place in the wide hollows of the poet's brain; now, in a further layer of vision, the poet looks into the hollows of Moneta's brain and sees a drama enacted there. Moneta, a figuration of Memory, carries within the dark secret chambers of her skull the dark memory of the primal tragedy, that of Fall. The Fall is the same event as in the first version of the poem but its function is changing: it now serves as an admonition. The revision of the name Mnemosyne (memory) into *Moneta* signals the darkening. Paradoxically, however, the darkened vision also provides comfort: Moneta's eyes beam 'like the mild moon, / Who comforts those she sees not, who knows not / What eyes are upward cast' (*FH* I, 269–71). Christopher Ricks says finely of this, 'The blank splendour of the moon is a type of the blank (not empty) splendour of art . . . The consolation which Keats here imagines, he at the same time provides; he comforts those he sees not, and this is of the essence of art.'[23] For Keats, as is made clear by both the *Lear* sonnet and Moneta's claim that only those poets to whom the miseries of the world are misery can pour out a balm upon the world, this capacity to give comfort is the preserve of tragedy.

It is in this idea of Fall as tragedy that Keats departs radically from both Milton and Dante. Milton originally intended to write the story of the Fall of man as a tragedy called *Adam Unparadised*, but he changed his mind and incorporated it into a larger pattern which embraced redemption and made the Fall fortunate, *felix culpa*. So too with the structure of Dante's epic: the *Inferno* contains many tragedies within it, but it is followed by the experience of *Purgatorio* and ultimately the redemption of *Paradiso* – it is a divine *comedy*. There are strong purgatorial elements in *The Fall of Hyperion*, as in the *Lear* sonnet, but there is no sense of an emergence into a New Jerusalem.

The first *Hyperion*, like *Paradise Lost* and the *Divine Comedy*, has a progressive pattern, a sense of acceptance, summed up in Oceanus' magnificent lines on the movement towards 'ripeness' and his belief that the older gods 'fall by course of Nature's law' (*H* II, 181), that

> on our heels a fresh perfection treads
> A power more strong in beauty, born of us
> And fated to excel us, as we pass
> In glory that old Darkness . . .
>
> (*H* II, 212–15)

All this must go if the Fall of the Titans is to be rewritten as a tragedy rather than a necessary, if pathos-filled, process in the progress of history. The new gods like Apollo must be excluded, as must Oceanus' speech and other consolations. As part of the revision into tragedy, Keats inserts into the story of Saturn lines like the following, in which the poet makes himself into a tragic artist, taking on the burden of suffering, even assuming the aura of a tragic character who longs for death:

> Without stay or prop
> But by my own weak mortality, I bore
> The load of this eternal quietude,
> The unchanging gloom . . .
> Oftentimes I pray'd
> Intense, that death would take me from the vale
> And all its burthens. Gasping with despair
> Of change, hour after hour I curs'd myself[.]
>
> (*FH* I, 388–91, 396–9)

Contrast this 'Despair / Of change' with Oceanus' language of progress. The tone of Saturn's own speech is transformed from questioning ('search, Thea, search!' – *H* I, 116, 121) to lamentation ('Moan, brethren, moan' – *FH* I, 412, 427). *Hyperion* does not use the word 'moan' in Saturn's speech; *The Fall* uses it thirteen times, transforming what Saturn says into something like a Greek tragic lament, a 'dolorous accent from a tragic harp' (*FH* I, 444). In *Hyperion* Saturn is one of Milton's bold fallen angels plotting recovery; in *The Fall* he is enfeebled, lost, tragic (his plan to form and rule a new world, reminiscent of

Satan's proposal to make mischief on earth, has been cut). In *Hyperion*, passion makes Saturn stand at the end of the speech – he has roused himself, if no other. In *The Fall* he remains seated, forlorn (*H* I, 135; *FH* I, 446).

The obvious pattern for a tragedy on the fall of the Titans was Aeschylus' *Prometheus Bound*, but, as Shelley was demonstrating at this time, that play always implies a *Prometheus Unbound* – a release, a happy ending, an overall comic structure. While the obvious pattern for writing tragedy in English was Shakespeare, the lameness of *Otho the Great* had shown Keats that Shakespearean drama was inimitable. Tragedy, as much as Milton, could be an impasse. It was, furthermore, an impasse that was not merely formal.

Keats interpreted *Paradise Lost* as a politically progressive, republican poem. One of his marginal notes reads:

How noble and collected an indignation against Kings . . . His [Milton's] very wishing should have the power to pull that feeble animal Charles from his bloody throne. 'The evil days' had come to him – he hit the new System of things a mighty mental blow – the exertion must have had or is yet to have some sequences –   (Wittreich, p. 556)

Here Keats hints at an analogy between Milton during the Restoration and himself in post-1815 Europe, confronted with the Bourbon Restoration in France, the Holy Alliance of monarchs, and what Hazlitt scathingly called 'Legitimacy' all around. Like Shelley, Keats hoped that Milton could exert a positive political influence. The Miltonic first *Hyperion* is a progressive poem; it concerns a revolution, and Oceanus' lines make clear that the new regime is superior to the old.[24] Leigh Hunt spoke of the poem's 'transcendental cosmopolitics',[25] and contemporary readers would have recognized the 'progress poem' as a liberal genre, concerned with the development of enlightened political institutions. Apollo is a progressive figure, associated by Keats with 'the march of passion and endeavour' (*Letters*, 1, p. 207) – a kind of superior Napoleon. Like Hazlitt, Keats viewed Napoleon as the sword-arm of revolutionary values, but when it came to *The Fall*, his artistic interest was focused on those defeated by revolution; his sympathies were with the fallen gods, the old regime. In *Hyperion* Saturn is 'quiet as a stone' (*H* I, 4), whereas in *The Fall* he *is* a stone, a sculptural representation rather than a realized character: *The Fall* looks to the past not the future, to the statues of the old gods, not the progress of the new ones; it is about the recovery of memory, not the birth of a bright new regime.

Keats's poetry and his politics are at odds here. At precisely the time he gave up the second *Hyperion*, the third week of September 1819, he wrote his most sustained and progressive political letters: 'All civil[iz]ed countries become gradually more enlighten'd and there should be a continual change for the better . . .' (*Letters*, 2, p. 193). Keats gives examples of how the tyranny of monarchy has been overthrown; he posits a model of historical development: 'Three great changes have been in progress – First for the better, next for the worse, and a third time for the better once more.' It is a pattern of revolution, reaction, and new struggle – a pattern which is being acted out in 'The present struggle in England of the people' (*ibid.*). Keats was writing the month after the Peterloo massacre; indeed on 13 September he witnessed the throng, which he estimated at thirty thousand people, that had taken to the streets to greet the radical orator Henry Hunt as he entered London. Within three days he resolved to abandon *The Fall of Hyperion*. His tragic vision and his progressive politics proved incompatible; he had learnt the lesson of Hazlitt's essay on *Coriolanus*, with its claim that poetry is an aristocratic, not a levelling, principle: tragedy sympathizes with the fallen rulers. Perhaps with this lesson in mind, and out of a desire to resist it, he chose to publish the more progressive work, *Hyperion* rather than *The Fall*, in 1820.

Keats's concern with the possibility that salvation will be political should not, however, be overemphasized. At his most characteristic he enables us to live with loss, not to glimpse some future salvation. Keats did not trumpet prophecies in the manner of Shelley. He believed, with Moneta, that it was not the business of poets to 'Labour for mortal good' (*FH* I, 159) in the same manner as political activists like Henry Hunt. Perhaps because of his personal and familial circumstances, he always engaged most deeply with the mystery of suffering. His remarks about giving up on the Hyperion project because of its Miltonic diction are a screen for the deeper sense in which he wanted to detach himself from Milton, namely his agnostic need to get away from a structure of *felix culpa* stemming from belief in some ultimate spiritual redemption. Keats said in his letter on life as a mansion of many apartments that Wordsworth had gone further than Milton in seeing into the pain of the human heart. The problem with Milton was his imposition of a divine pattern upon human suffering, his faith in a Christian solution to the mystery of life. Keats rejected this irritable reaching after a conclusion. No longer striving for the moon with Endymion, he had become a profoundly uneschatological poet. In the second *Hyperion* he reached a similar state to that of Wordsworth in the darker passages of 'Tintern Abbey' and *The Excursion*. As King Lear takes upon himself 'the mystery of things' and as Wordsworth feels 'the burthen of the mystery', so Keats, when he looks into the face of Moneta, takes on 'the depth / Of things' (*FH* I, 304–5). This revision of 'the life of things' takes the Wordsworthian in the tragic direction that Keats imagined as his own, away from the 'chearful faith' which Wordsworth had inherited from Milton and the lightening of the burden in which 'Tintern Abbey' invests its hopes. The state which Lear and the personae of Wordsworth and Keats enter is the one which Keats called negative capability, the willingness to live with uncertainties and doubts. From this state follows a refusal to come to conclusions. 'The only means of strengthening one's intellect is to make up one[']s mind about nothing', Keats wrote during that same momentous week in September 1819 (*Letters*, 2, p. 213). He could not therefore conclude *The Fall*; it had to remain a fragment like the poem it was revising. In its lack of closure *Hyperion* had found its true form.

NOTES

1 *John Keats* (Cambridge, Mass., 1963), pp. 316–38.
2 Published in *From Sensibility to Romanticism: Essays Presented to Frederick A. Pottle*, ed. F. W. Hilles and H. Bloom (New York, 1965), repr. with the date 1964 in Bloom's *The Ringers in the Tower: Studies in Romantic Tradition* (Chicago, 1971).
3 Bate, *The Burden of the Past and the English Poet* (Cambridge, Mass., 1970); Bloom, *The Anxiety of Influence: A Theory of Poetry* (New York, 1973). In the case of Bloom, the key intermediary text was his study of Yeats, published in 1970.
4 Hollander, *The Figure of Echo: A Mode of Allusion in Milton and After* (Berkeley, Los Angeles, and London, 1981), p. 120.
5 Letter to George and Georgiana Keats, 24 September 1819, in *The Letters of John Keats 1814–1821*, ed. Hyder E. Rollins, 2 vols. (Cambridge, Mass., 1958), Vol. 2, p. 212. Subsequent quotations from Keats's letters are followed in my text by volume and page reference to this edition.
6 For Bloom's reading of *The Fall of Hyperion* as a 'revision' of Milton and Wordsworth, see Chapter 5 of his *Poetry and Repression: Revisionism from Blake to Stevens* (New Haven, 1976).
7 The annotations are reproduced in *The Romantics on Milton: Formal Essays and Critical Asides*, ed. J. A. Wittreich Jr (Cleveland, Ohio, 1970), cited hereafter as Wittreich.
8 'Milton in every instance pursues his imagination to the utmost – he is "sagacious of his Quarry" [*PL* X, 281], he sees Beauty on the wing, pounces upon it and gorges it to the producing his essential verse ... in no instance is this sort of perseverance more exemplified than in what may be called his *stationing or statu[a]ry*. He is not content with simple description, he must station' – annotation to *Paradise Lost* VI, 422–3, Wittreich, p. 559. The description of Saturn and Thea early in *Hyperion* is a fine piece of Miltonic statuary: 'these two were postured motionless, / Like natural sculpture in cathedral cavern' (I, 85–6).
9 *Letters*, 2, pp. 14–15, 42; Woodhouse, note in his copy of *Endymion*, cited in *The Poems of John Keats*, ed. Miriam Allott (London, 1970), p. 394.
10 'Shakspeare and the paradise Lost every day become greater wonders to me' (to Bailey, 14 August 1819, *Letters*, 2, p. 139); 'the Paradise Lost becomes a greater wonder' (to Reynolds, 24 August 1819, *Letters*, 2, p. 146).
11 See *The Keats Circle*, ed. H. E. Rollins, 2 vols. (2nd ed., Cambridge, Mass., 1965), Vol. 2, p. 72. According to Stillinger, Brown's reference cannot be dated more precisely than 'toward the end of 1819' (*Poems of John Keats*, p. 676).
12 Here I paraphrase Jack Stillinger, in his edition of *The Poems of John Keats* (Cambridge, Mass., 1978), p. 640. All my quotations (save those from the holograph manuscript) are taken from this edition. The poet's holograph manuscript of the first *Hyperion* is extant and now held by the British Library. There is a fine facsimile edited

by Ernest de Selincourt: *Hyperion: A Facsimile of Keats's Autograph Manuscript with a Transliteration of the MS of The Fall of Hyperion. A Dream* (Oxford, 1905). Keats's holograph of *The Fall* is not extant; there are two complete transcripts, one by Woodhouse and one by two of his clerks, and a transcript of the first 326 lines only by Charlotte Reynolds.

13 See John D. Rosenberg, 'Keats and Milton: The Paradox of Rejection', *Keats–Shelley Journal*, 6 (1957), pp. 87–95; Stuart M. Sperry Jr, 'Keats, Milton and *The Fall of Hyperion*', *PMLA*, 77 (1962), pp. 77–84; Paul Sherwin, 'Dying into Life: Keats's Struggle with Milton in *Hyperion*', *PMLA*, 93 (1978), pp. 383–95; Nancy Moore Goslee, *Uriel's Eye: Miltonic Stationing and Statuary in Blake, Keats, and Shelley* (Alabama, 1985). Verbal details are charted in M. R. Ridley, *Keats' Craftsmanship* (Oxford, 1933, repr. London, 1964), and the notes to Miriam Allott's edition.

14 It is not often noted that the holograph manuscript of *Hyperion* runs 'Book 1st', 'Canto 2nd', 'Canto 3'. 'Book II' and 'Book III' in the 1820 printed text derive from the transcript by Woodhouse, which was in turn transcribed by two of his clerks and then used as the printer's copy.

15 For the influence of the 'Mutabilitie Cantos' on *The Fall* and the 1819 odes, see Helen Vendler, *The Odes of John Keats* (Cambridge, Mass., 1983), pp. 205–8, 242–3.

16 *The Complete Poetical Works of Samuel Taylor Coleridge*, ed. E. H. Coleridge, 2 vols. (Oxford, 1912), Vol. 1, pp. 296–7. Marjorie Levinson notes the connection between the two passages in *The Romantic Fragment Poem* (Chapel Hill, 1986), p. 169.

17 See Stillinger's textual notes, *The Poems of John Keats*, p. 640.

18 Sidney Colvin's phrase, *John Keats* (London, 1917), p. 447.

19 Woodhouse noticed this emendation: in the transcript that was used as printer's copy in 1820, he underscored 'And so' and wrote 'Wherefore' on the opposite verso (Stillinger, *The Poems of John Keats*, p. 641).

20 *PL* IV, 268–72, praised by Keats as one of two extraordinary Miltonic beauties 'unexampled elsewhere' (Wittreich, p. 559).

21 *Purgatory* IX, 9–10, in Dante, *The Divine Comedy*, trans. Cary (1814, repr. London, 1908).

22 See John Livingston Lowes, '*Hyperion* and the *Purgatorio*', *TLS* (11 January 1936), p. 35; John Saly, 'Keats's Answer to Dante: *The Fall of Hyperion*', *Keats–Shelley Journal*, 14 (1965), pp. 65–78; and Ralph Pite, 'Dante's Influence on Coleridge and Keats: "The Circle of our Vision"' (unpubl. Cambridge Ph.D. diss., 1989). For Keats's markings in his copy of Cary's 1814 Dante, see Robert Gittings, *The Mask of Keats* (London, 1956).

23 *Keats and Embarrassment* (Oxford, 1974), p. 191.

24 For the politics of the first *Hyperion*, see Marilyn Butler, *Romantics, Rebels and Reactionaries* (Oxford, 1981), p. 151, and Alan J. Bewell, 'The Political Implication of Keats's Classicist Aesthetics', *Studies in Romanticism*, 25 (1986), pp. 220–9.

25 Hunt's *Autobiography*, in *Keats: The Critical Heritage*, ed. G. M. Matthews (London, 1971), p. 255.

17

REVISING CLARE

JOHN LUCAS

IN 1869 a memorial to John Clare was erected on the village green at Helpston. It was paid for by the Fitzwilliam family and by public subscription, and commemorates, *John Clare, The Northamptonshire Peasant Poet*. The epithet, which had been attached to Clare from the time of his first published volume, *Poems Descriptive of Rural Life and Scenery*, has permanently affected the presentation of his work. Clare was aware of the soubriquet – how could he not be – and there were occasions when he introduced himself to others as 'the pheasant poet' (*sic*). More often however, he did his best to struggle free of the containments and condescension which the term implies. In a late poem he speaks of himself as

> A silent man in lifes affairs
> A thinker from a Boy
> A Peasant in his daily cares –
> The Poet in his joy[1]

The poem, which was written in Northampton Asylum, is one of a number in which Clare asserts his autonomy as 'The Poet'; and it may well be that the horror of his predicament urged him to claim that his identity as *The* Poet was as unassailable as it was essential. It didn't do him much good. Whoever transcribed the poem gave it the one title that Clare could not have intended. 'The Peasant Poet' it was, and still is, called.

This brings me to the subject of my essay. Clare ran up against a number of ultimately insoluble problems in wanting to distinguish between being *a* peasant and *The* poet. In the first place, many of his greatest poems are about daily cares. In the second, 'The poet' is a received image with which he often enough – and rightly – feels ill at ease, especially since it means that he has to align himself with a particular kind of metropolitan culture to which he knows he doesn't really belong and which tolerates him only as it can condenscend to him. In 'The Flitting' he says:

Give me no highflown fangled things
No haughty pomp in marching time
Where muses play on golden strings
& splendour passes for sublime

The sardonic pun on 'golden strings' shows how readily Clare understood that poetry as an artifact was typically linked to money and class-bound assumptions of 'natural' superiority. From this standpoint, these assumptions, what else could he be but a peasant? The question was bound to press in on him with an especially disturbing force because of what was done to his poetry. It is not simply that from the moment of publication he was promoted as a peasant poet. More important is the fact that his poems were adapted so as to reinforce the image. I am therefore concerned not with revisions made *by* Clare but with revisions made *to* him. He may have hoped to shelter under a received image of 'The Poet', but his publishers wanted him to appear in the guise of a very different image: He was their 'Peasant Poet,' and in order to secure this image they were prepared to interfere decisively with his work.

The image of the Peasant Poet has a specific if complex history and it would take a long monograph to disentangle the various threads that went into its composition. They include the 'Unlettered Bard', the 'Uneducated Poet', the 'Natural Genius'. It should, however, be said that while these terms indicate a succession of struggles for liberation from cultural orthodoxy – the giving of a voice to those who are not part of official 'poetic utterance', as it were – the struggles are repeatedly brought under control by forms of cultural containment. 'Unlettered bards' need not be taken seriously. They are at best 'quaint'. The *OED* dates the first modern use of this word to 1795. Before then it had meant 'clever' or 'ingenious' or even 'elegant'. Now, a new meaning is added which will eventually become the dominant one. 'Quaint: Unusual or uncommon in character or appearance, but agreeable or attractive, esp. having an old-fashioned prettiness or daintiness.' Quaintness becomes a marketable commodity. As evidence of this we could cite those many late-eighteenth-century painters – Morland, Opie, the Norwich School – who specialized in 'quaint' landscapes, as well as poets of the picturesque who, as Crabbe contemptuously remarked, 'paint the cot' very much from the outside. 'Go look within,' he commanded, 'and ask if peace be there.' But looking within doesn't form part of the genre's tactic, in either painting, poetry, or prose. And on those rare occasions when we do see 'within' we find unsurprising images of tranquil contentment. What is quaint is peaceable, contented. It is also an engaging freak of nature. The 'quaint' natural genius is therefore a harmless curiosity.

Of course, rare spirits could exploit this, as Burns brilliantly did. Hence, the tongue-in-cheek Preface to his famous *Poems Chiefly in the Scottish Dialect*, which begins

The following trifles are not the production of the Poet, who, with all the advantages of learned art, and perhaps amid the elegancies and idlenesses of upper life, looks down for a rural theme . . . Unacquainted with the necessary requisites for commencing Poet by rule, he sings the sentiments and manners, he felt and saw himself and his rustic compeers around him, in his and their native language.'[2]

Burns freely admitted to his friend, Robert Anderson, that it was 'a part of the machinery, as he called it, of his poetical character to pass for an illiterate ploughman who wrote from pure inspiration . . . [but] in company he would not suffer his pretensions to pure inspiration to be challenged, and it was seldom done where it might be supposed to affect the success of the subscription for his *Poems*'.[3]

Where Burns led others were quick to follow. Among them were Robert Anderson. 'The Cumberland Bard', Robert Bloomfield, and James Hogg, 'The Ettrick Shepherd', whose poetry, as Louis Simpson points out, suffers from the problem that Hogg can never make up his mind for whom he is writing: Tory Edinburgh or his own 'common people'.[4] Anderson's *Cumberland Ballads* appeared for the first time in 1798, Bloomfield's *Farmer's Boy* in 1800 and *Rural Tales* in 1802; and Hogg's *The Mountain Bard* followed in 1807. At which point, one might think, the cult for peasant poetry should have died a natural death. It was kept alive, however, by the fact that poetry as a whole was becoming both fashionable and marketable (each acting as cause and effect and as such strengthening the other).

> Within a costly case of varnish'd wood
> In level rows her polished volumes stood;
> Shown as a favour to a chosen few
> To prove what beauty for a book could do.

In these lines from 'Procrastination', one of the *Tales in Verse* (1812), Crabbe deftly unpicks the language of taste. 'Polished' and 'beauty'; these are the cliches of literary approbation. But such polish, such beauty, are also literally skin deep, a matter of leather binding. And binding is a form of packaging, a way of making books acceptable as the possessions of gentlemen and ladies and of those who aspire to their ranks. Since poetry and literature were virtually inter-changeable terms — as the novel and literature assuredly were not — it is hardly surprising that Crabbe should identify the purpose of books which are used to furnish a room in a manner reminiscent of Wordsworth's attack on the world of taste, in the Preface to *Lyrical Ballads*. There, Wordsworth speaks contemptu-ously of those who 'furnish food for fickle tastes and fickle appetites'. By implication he rightly traces to its root meaning the newly-fashionable word, 'aesthetic': 'received by the senses' – which definition the *OED* dates to 1798. And he sees the vendors of 'tasteful' literature as supplying 'gross and violent stimulants' to readers who then 'talk of Poetry as a matter of amusement and idle pleasure; who will converse with us as gravely about a *taste* for Poetry as they express it, as if it were a thing as indifferent as a taste for Rope-dancing or Frontiniac, or Sherry'.[5]

It is noteworthy that large sums of money were at this time paid to poets for their work: £2000 in 1812 to Scott, for *Rokeby*; £3000 in 1817 to Moore for *Lallah Rooke*; the same amount to Crabbe in 1819 for *Tales of the Hall*. And after the publication of *Childe Harold* Byron woke to find himself not only famous but rich. Poetry was fashionable and fashion meant business. According to Lee Erickson, much of the explanation for this had to do with printing costs. During the Napoleonic wars, the importation of rags, from which paper was then made, became inevitably curtailed; accordingly the cost of paper rose steeply. 'The greater cost of books generally encouraged poetry at the expense of prose and made poetry a more important part of the publishing market.'[6]

With this in mind, it is possible to recognize that by the time Clare's first volume appeared fashions were already changing. 'Peasant poets' had had their day. Not only that. Poetry itself was no longer as fashionable as it had been during the war period. It was perhaps inevitable that Clare's publishers should have decided that to market his book at all required them to go for the hard sell. Hence Taylor's Introduction:

The following poems will probably attract some notice by their intrinsic merit; but they are also entitled to attention from the circumstances under which they were written. They are the genuine productions of a young Peasant, a day-labourer in husbandry, who has had no advantages of education beyond others of his class; and though poets of this country have seldom been fortunate men, yet he is, perhaps, the least favoured by circumstances, and the most destitute of friends, of any that ever existed.[7]

There then follows an account of Clare's birth and early years.

Taylor means to be sympathetic. Yet that placing term 'Peasant' clearly reveals the publishers' shaping intentions, and these are underpinned by the design of the title page, which identifies Clare as 'A NORTHAMPTONSHIRE PEASANT'. Below is affixed as epigraph

> The Summer's Flower is to the Summer sweet.
> Though to itself it only live and die.
>
> *Shakspeare*

Clare, the summer flower, the child of nature, is thus produced in a manner that inevitably calls to mind Gray's plangent description of the flowers, born to bloom and die, which waste their sweetness on the desert air.

The placing runs through the entire volume, and is so complete that it is doubtful whether Taylor and Hessey have the right to speak of the book as housing Clare's 'genuine productions'. For they alter his spelling and his punctuation, lay out the poems according to the dictates of acceptable literary conventions; and lines, stanzas and, on occasions, entire poems are dropped. *Poems Descriptive* is ruthlessly editorialized in order to market Clare as a 'peasant poet'. The upshot is that he is denied his own voice. Moreover, Taylor and Hessey not only interfere with the poems to bring them more into line with what was expected of peasant poets, they also bow to the wishes of Clare's self-appointed patron, Lord Radstock, who had a very strong dislike of Clare's unsentimental writing about the society he knew intimately, and an even stronger dislike of Clare's politics.

Clare was therefore not likely to be mollified by the fact that *Poems Descriptive* was a publishing success. On the occasion of the third edition of *Poems Descriptive* he wrote to Hessey:

I am cursed mad about it the judgement of T. is a button hole lower in my opinion – it is good – but too subject to be tainted by *false delicacy* damn it I hate it beyond everything[8]

Clare is referring to Taylor's decision to drop 'My Mary' and 'Ways of the Wake', as altogether too strong for fashionable taste to swallow. That taste is typified by a writer to the *Morning Post* of 11 February 1820. This 'Well-Wisher to Merit' calls Clare a '*heaven born Poet*' and a 'wonderful child of Nature', and then goes on to propose a second edition of his volume from which

some two or three poems in the present edition might be expunged, in order to make room for others of riper and purer growth . . . much allowance must be made for a seeming want of refinement, which it must be confessed appears in one or two instances, in this otherwise most admirable little work . . .'[9]

And a substantial and rhapsodically enthusiastic review of the volume in the *Eclectic Review* nevertheless complains of 'inaccuracies and provincialisms'. The reviewer then remarks that 'as the permanent interest of the volume will depend on the intrinsic merits of the composition, we cannot imagine that a few corrections from the hand of Clare himself, at the suggestion of his Editor, would render a new edition less valuable'. Moreover, certain poems ought to be replaced, in particular 'My Mary', 'Dolly's Mistake', and 'The Country Girl'.[10] And so, of course, they were.

Worse was to come. In the fourth edition Taylor cut the following lines from 'Helpstone', which detail the effects of enclosure.

> Oh who could see my dear green willows fall
> What feeling heart but dropped a tear for all
> Accursed wealth o'er bounding human laws

Of every evil thou remainst the cause
Victims of want those wretches such as me
Too truly lay their wretchedness to thee
Thou art the bar that keeps from being fed
And thine our loss of labour and of bread
Thou art the cause that levels every tree
And woods bow down to clear a way for thee[11]

The first couplet seems initially to speak for that regret at the principle of change which is at the heart of the picturesque aesthetic. This is often enough voiced through the 'fall' of trees, as in Cowper's 'Poplar Field'. 'The poplars are fell'd; farewell to the shade, / And the whispering sound of the cool colonnade.' But lovely though the aural effects of this poem are, they collaborate with Cowper's musings on 'the perishing pleasures of man', where the loss of such pleasure is taken to be inevitable. (The poplars 'are felled', and this passive construction implies that nobody and nothing need be identified as the agent of their felling.)

The drive of Clare's lines is very different. The cursed wealth 'o'er bounding human laws' is an echo of Milton's Satan who, on arriving at the heavily wooded entrance to paradise, 'Due entrance . . . disdained, and in contempt, / At one slight bound high over leaped all bound' (*Paradise Lost* IV, 180–1). Human laws – natural rights – are helpless to oppose those thousands of acts which in the latter half of the eighteenth century and the early part of the nineteenth legalized enclosures and then dropped the bar on labourers, not necessarily in the sense that those men immediately lost employment (new improvements in arable farming led in some instances to an increased work force), but because particular kinds of labour became obsolete and more importantly because the already poor relationships between landowners and labourers now deteriorated still further. But after 1815 rural depopulation grew. The Corn Laws meant that farmers inevitably did deny labourers their bread. In addition, 'improving' landlords are from Clare's vantage point a malign power. There is a bitter wit in his identifying the trees as a crowd of near-fawning supplicants who conspire in their own degradation as they 'bow down to clear a way for thee'.

Those who o'er bound human laws have state laws on their side. True, since 1722 it had been a capital offence to 'cut down or otherwise destroy any trees planted in any avenue, or growing in any garden, orchard or plantation, for ornament, shelter or profit'. But this law was directed towards the protection of private woodland. Where open woods began to come under law it again worked against the common people. From 1766 wood-gathering became an criminal offence. According to Robert Bushaway, 'where records survive, it would seem that wood theft was the most common form of crime in the countryside, possibly the most common way in which the laws and rights of landed property were infringed'. During the period of the Napoleonic wars timber for ships was obviously in great demand. Nevertheless, in the shadow of the law

forest communities . . . continued to affirm their customary rights, gleaning faggots and offal wood, cutting young trees for maypole and green oak for Maytime processions and, on occasion, mutilating or destroying trees in plantations to signify their disaffection with the encroaching gentry.[12]

The woods which Clare is writing about are clearly those of customary rights. Hence his bitterness that they should 'bow down', should lose their rights.

This brings us to a further point. Clare's woods provide a kind of sweet, equal republic, they are wild woods, whereas from the point of view of authority 'The most agreeable woodland was tidily planted or securely partitioned in great estates. Here trees confirmed power of property.'[13] That Clare's woods now 'bow down' means therefore that they confess subservience to a greater, o'er bounding, power. It follows that Radstock was quite right to recognize the 'radical slang' of Clare's lines, for the account of woods as non-subservient implies a vision of society as essentially republican, egalitarian, and the lines' sadness comes from his recognition of the defeat of this vision. Such a defeat is made the more complete by Radstock's having the lines removed. They, too, bow down. Clare is revised in the interest of producing him as a safe, 'peasant poet'.

Poems Descriptive of Rural Life and Scenery was a critical and commercial success. It was favourably reviewed and inside a year was into its fourth edition. Given this, it might seem reasonable to assume that Clare's publishers would have wanted to rush out another volume, especially as Clare had one ready. *Ways in a Village* he called it, and from such letters of his as survive it appears that Taylor had given him cause to hope that it would be published early in 1821. In the end, it did not come out until late that year. Taylor was busy with other projects. He may well have suspected that fashionable taste would be moving on. (What else is fashion for?) Then again, he was having trouble keeping Clare to his role as peasant poet. He insisted that Clare's projected title for the volume be changed to *The Village Minstrel*. This gave off the necessary aroma. The echo of Beattie's *The Minstrel*, that sentimental tale of the inspired bard, reinforced Clare's place in the tradition of the native genius to which reviewers and admiring readers had, with the help of Taylor's revisions, assigned him.

But the vocabulary remained a problem. Taylor made many 'corrections' to Clare's work, most of which he seems to have communicated to the poet, at least if we are to judge from the number of letters in which Clare speaks of his gratitude to his publisher and at the same time voices his doubts.

I am very fearful your turning your mind to take the original readings as you hinted in your last letter will be no improvement they cannot read better than they do in your alterations sent to me & had I been informed sooner I should certainly raised my little voice to dissuade you from it but take your opinion & you cannot do wrong – you cross'd '*gulsh'd*' I think the word expressive but doubt its a provincialism it means tearing or thrusting up with great force take it or leave it . . .[14]

Taylor took it, just as he took many other words which Clare doubted – feared – were 'provincialisms', a word to which I suspect Taylor had introduced him.

We touch here on a vast subject, and one which cannot be adequately discussed in this essay. Yet it requires some comment, for without it we will not fully understand what lies behind Taylor's revisions. Much can be attributed to Clare's reviewers. They did most to sell his work and Taylor clearly felt it necessary to attend to what they had to say. A key document is the essay that appeared in two parts in *The Gentleman's Magazine* for January and April 1821, called 'Remarks on the Spontaneous Display of Native Genius'. The writer took Clare as his example: 'nursed in the lap of poverty of the most chilling description', and therefore unable to acquire 'even the commonest rudiments of education'. This then is the explanation for

his occasional unpleasing collocation of words – which indeed he, doubtless, it may be presumed, found most intelligibly expressive of his ideas, but, from the scanty limits of his vocabulary, he was unable, in his phraseology, to make those selections of copiousness which would have imparted a more modulated form of harmony to his periods.[15]

This is of a piece with the frequent complaints of Clare's lack of 'refinement'. Without a 'proper' education, he must be without a 'proper' vocabulary. Hence his colloqualisms, his 'provincialisms', his 'unpleasing collocation of words'. He hasn't a vast storehouse from which to select the choicest elements of language. Moreover, his vocabulary, just *because* it it local or provincial, lacks permanence or universal appeal. When Clare gives birds and plants their local names he falls guiltlessly into the error from which Linnaean classification had come to free naturalists. (Crabbe, it will be remembered, burnt a botanical study because he was told by a Fellow of Trinity that he should have given the plants their Latin names.) The names Clare gives to birds, beasts and flowers aren't to be found in any dictionary, and dictionaries are there to fix the language, to give it propriety.

In announcing the principles on which he had chosen words for inclusion in his *Dictionary*, Samuel Johnson remarked that he had refused to countenance

the diction of the laborious and mercanile part of the people [because it] is in great measure casual and mutable: many of their terms [being] formed to some temporary or local convenience, and though current at certain times and places, are in others utterly unknown. This fugitive cant, which is always in a state of increase or decay, cannot be regarded as any part of the durables of a language, and therefore must be suffered to perish with other things unworthy of preservation.

By the time Clare came to write, his 'casual and mutable' language could be seen as a form of un-English, in the sense that since it was not the language of an educated person it was not fully civilized, was not part of what England and English should be. This point is well made by Raymond Williams:

> To be able to read and write is a major advance in the possibility of sharing in the general culture of a literate society, but there are still typically determinate conditions in which the exercise of these faculties is differently directed. Thus in late eighteenth-century England it was argued that the poor should be taught to read, but not to write. Reading would enable them to read the Bible, and learn its morality, or later to read instructions and notices. Having anything to write on their account was seen as a crazy or mischievous idea.[16]

To write as one of the uneducated was, in other words, a contradiction in terms. Alternatively, to write was to submit oneself to terms that homogenized 'English', that provided an orthodoxy in matters of vocabulary and grammar. The hundred years between 1750 and 1850 is the century of dictionaries, of grammatical rules, and of the standardizing of pronunciation. As I have elsewhere remarked this is, in short, the period when the language is being enclosed.[17] Small wonder, then, that Taylor should have wished to revise Clare in order to try to bring him within the enclosed areas of official or orthodox English. In his introduction to *The Village Minstrel* Taylor anxiously recommends Clare's 'refinement'.[18] But it is clear that such refinement was bought at a cost, and Clare's letters vividly testify to his unease, impatience, and, sometimes, downright fury at what his publisher required of him.[19] As he says, he will never get the 'polish' Taylor wants.[20]

Nor did he. There were reviews aplenty ready to point out Clare's failings. And such reviews were more severe on *The Village Minstrel* than they had been on *Poems Descriptive*. Take, for example, the one that appeared in *The Monthly Review*. The writer insists that Clare's language is not good enough. 'We do not conceive that occasional sweetness of expression, or accurate delineations of mere exterior objects, can atone for a general deficiency of poetical language, or the indulging in a style devoid of uniformity and consistency.' Clare, that is, lapses into and out of the provincial (much as Burns may be said to lapse into and out of Lallans). Well, it is true, he does, although Taylor's editorial procedures made the inconsistencies more rather than less marked. But then greater consistency would not have mollified the reviewer. It would simply have led away from 'poetical language' in the direction of the uncouth. The critic comments of the title poem that

To himself this topic is no doubt peculiarly interesting; and his descriptions may very probably be productive of amusement to those who are familiar with the originals. To us, however, the writer's mention of himself appears, in general, too egotistical and querulous, and the local subjects and rural amusements . . . have not, we think, been very judiciously selected for the purpose of inspiring general interest.[21]

Like it or not, this makes a particularly sharp point. For whom *is* Clare writing? His 'provincialisms' imply readers 'who are familiar with the originals'. But of course there were no such readers. As Williams notes, the kinds of 'originals' Clare writes about, read, if they read at all, Bibles and notices. Even if we regard that as something of an exaggeration, it is clear that Clare's fellow labourers didn't read *him*. We have it on his own authority that being a published poet did nothing to endear him to his neighbours. They thought he was getting above himself. And in a sense, he was. In some of his poems, especially *The Parish*, he is plainly 'looking down' on the people he had grown up with. The poem is a satire on village pretension. But what greater pretension can there be for a day-labourer than wanting to be a poet?

We can gauge just how keenly Clare felt his predicament from a passage in his projected autobiography. It describes 'My Visit to London', by the Stamford coach.

I felt very awkward in my dress . . . seeing people at my old occupation of ploughboy and ditching in the fields by the roadside while I was lolling in a coach the novelty created such strange feelings that I could almost fancy that my identity as well as my occupation had changed that I was not the same John Clare but that some stranger soul had jumped into my skin.[22]

This memorably captures the condition of lapsing into and out of the 'provincial' which reviewers noted as belonging to the poems and which is undoubtedly the case with the man who wrote them, the more especially as the poems were then revised in a manner that still further split Clare's sense of himself. Taylor knew better than to aim for a readership among those who were familiar with or who *were* Clare's originals. Instead, the poet has to appeal to a 'general interest'.

How far Clare fell short of achieving this is made plain by *The Monthly Review*. The reviewer prints lines that offend against 'poetical language' and 'uniformity and consistency' of style. (The italicized words and phrases are those which he singles out as being especially defective.)

But soldiers, *they're the boys to make a rout.*
The *bumptious* serjeant struts before his men.
And *don't* despise your betters *'cause* they're old.
Up he'd *chuck sacks* as one would hurl a stone.

Of these lines the writer notes: 'If it be urged that such language is appropriate to the subjects treated of, we reply, that subjects to which such language is best adapted, are not those which a poet should have chosen . . .'[23] I imagine that most readers would now think the lines energized by precisely the words and phrases to which the reviewer objects. But his objections at least make clear what Clare – and Taylor – were up against. Such 'unrefined', vitalizing, colloquial handling of the language is not appropriate to poetry, may not indeed be appropriated by it.

Nor may radical sentiment. This is not to say that at that time poets were politically conformist. It is, however, to say that *peasant* poets had to be. If an uneducated writer was a contradiction in terms so, too, was a discontented peasant. Hence, no doubt, the absence of one of Clare's finest poems from *The Village Minstrel*. 'To a Fallen Elm' was written some time in 1821 and must have been ready for inclusion in the volume. In his long Introduction to Clare's second book, Taylor deals with the poet's anguish at the prospect of the cutting down of the elms that had stood over the cottage where he had grown up and where he still lived. I say 'deals with' deliberately, for how else are we to account for this?

If an old post had such attractions for Pope, surrounded as he was with comfort and luxury, what allowance ought not to be made for the passionate regard of poor CLARE for things which were the landmarks of his life, the depositories of almost all his joys? But the poet can be as much a philosopher as another man when the fit is off: in a letter to the writer of these lines he laments the purposed destruction of two elm trees which overhang his little cottage, in language which would surprise a man whose blood is never above temperate; but the reflection of a wiser head instantly follows: –
My two favourite elm trees at the back of the hut are condemned to die – it shocks me to relate it, but 'tis true. The savage who owns them thinks they have done their best, and now wants to make use of the benefits he can get from selling them. O was this country Egypt, and was I but Caliph, the owner should lose his ears for his arrogant presumption . . . yet this mourning over trees is all foolishness – they feel no pains – they are but wood, cut up or not. A second thought tells me I am a fool: were people all to feel as I do, the world could not be carried on, – a green would not be ploughed . . . This is my indisposition, and you will laugh at it . . .[24]

The original of this letter does not appear to survive, although we do have one dated March 1821 in which Clare thanks Taylor 'for your honest liberallity in wishing to purchase the Elms for me & shall certainly never forget it – but you shall not buy them – let them dye like the rest of us'.[25] But there is no reason to suppose that Taylor tampered with Clare's letter. More likely, Clare remembered to whom he was writing and tried to control his anger. And Taylor's offer to buy the elms *was* one of 'honest liberallity'. (In the event it turned out to be unnecessary because the owner changed his mind.) But to call Clare's anger a 'fit' is to make it clear why the poem couldn't be published. For 'To a Fallen Elm' very precisely directs anger against those who claim the right to trample on the rights of others. Clare imagines the elm felled by the man who 'barked of freedom'. 'O I hate that sound', he explodes:

> It grows the cant terms of enslaving tools
> To wrong another by the name of right
> It grows a liscence with oer bearing fools
> To cheat plain honesty by force of might
> Thus came enclosure – ruin was her guide
> But freedoms clapping hands enjoyed the sight
> Tho comforts cottage soon was thrust aside
> And workhouse prisons raised upon the scite
> Een natures dwelling far away from men
> The common health became the spoilers prey
> The rabbit had not where to make his den
> And labours only cow was drove away
> No matter – wrong was right and right was wrong
> And freedoms bawl was sanction to the song
>
> Such was thy ruin music making Elm
> The rights of freedom was to injure thine
> As thou wert served so would they overwhelm
> In freedoms name the little that is mine
> And these are knaves that brawl for better laws
> And cant of tyranny in stronger powers
> Who glut their vile unsatiated maws
> And freedoms birthright from the weak devours[26]

If there is better poetry of voiced, radical anger than this then I don't know it. Small wonder that the poem was never published in Clare's lifetime.

But that is true of other such poems. It is also true of the volume called *The Shepherd's Calendar*. For when that finally appeared in 1827 it was so massively editorialized that to call it Clare's own work is to mock the facts. Taylor claimed that because of its excessive length he had been forced 'to cut out a vast many lines', but as Robinson and Summerfield remark, that tells only half the story.

Every month of [the Poem] was lopped with greater or lesser brutality . . . Most of Taylor's excisions are frankly unintelligible to us, unless on the supposition that he found many passages too 'unphilosophical', and too concerned with everyday events . . . On other occasions Taylor seems to have cut out lines because they did not agree with his sense of poetical fitness, as when Clare describes fairies crowding in cupboards 'As thick as mites in rotting cheese' . . . In Taylor's version, too, the labourer, 'stript in his shirt', is not allowed to sit beside the maiden 'in her unpined gown'; no criticism of enclosing farmers or 'tyrant justice' appears; and labourers are not even allowed, in an age of industriousness, to be:

> Glad that the harvests end in nigh
> And weary labour nearly bye

It goes without saying that Taylor 'mended' grammar and punctuation throughout; and he removed dialect words. 'Similarly the names of country games are omitted because they are not familiar to the editor.'[27]

The unkindest cuts of all were aimed at the last volume published in Clare's lifetime. In the preparation of this, Taylor had been joined by Eliza Emmerson, that other 'improving' friend of Clare's. She and her husband offered to edit and arrange the poems for the press. Clare's proposed title for the volume had been *The Midsummer Cushion*. Mrs Emmerson was no more ready to accept that than she was ready to publish many of the poems. Edward Storey remarks that at a late stage Clare discovered 'that less than half of the poems he had submitted were to be included and most of those had been selected by Mrs Emmerson'. Storey exaggerates when he says that 'All the best poems were excluded', but he is right to point out that Clare's chosen title 'was discarded to make way for the more prosaic, unimaginative and trite title given by Mrs Emmerson, *The Rural Muse*. It is ironic', Storey concludes, 'that the lady who had helped him so much should fail to appreciate his true quality.'[28] Ironic wouldn't be my word for it, and anyway I am not so sure that Mrs Emmerson failed to appreciate Clare's true quality. For when the volume appeared, it included (*pace* Storey) one of Clare's greatest poems but with an altered title. He had called it 'The Flitting'. She calls it 'On Leaving The Cottage of My Birth', which has the effect of pointing towards a sugary pathos which is utterly foreign to the poem's astringent anger, its passion.[29] Her title aims to denature the poem. Given that it ends by imagining the vengeance of the people over their masters, this is not to be wondered at.

> Time looks on pomp with careless moods
> Or killing apathys disdain
> – So where old marble citys stood
> Poor persecuted weeds remain
> She feels a love for little things
> That very few can feel beside
> And still the grass eternal springs
> Where castles stood and grandeur died

In the last lines grass replaces the 'poor persecuted weeds', and it 'springs' to avenge all the wrongs visited on those weeds. As I have argued elsewhere, the well-tended fields of enclosure weeded out tenant-smallholders as surely as they weeded out groundsel and shepherd's purse. By the time Clare wrote those lines it was by no means uncommon to think of grass as 'plebians': 'the more they are taxed and trod upon, the more they multiply'.[30] Clare's grass is an invading army, intent on reclaiming rights from the castles and grandeur which 'stood' and 'died'. I do not find it surprising that Mrs Emmerson should have wished to cover over the power of this, although I *am* surprised that she allowed the poem into the volume. Perhaps she felt that in retitling it she had safely defused it.

In a way, she had. The volume was tepidly reviewed, sold badly; and Clare disappeared from view as a published poet. Soon, he would be institutionalized. For a long time after his death in 1864 he became more or less invisible. And when twentieth-century poets and editors began again to take an interest in him they relied for the most part on the editions that had appeared in his lifetime. Now, at last, we are getting the proper texts.

Or are we? When I recently looked at the manuscripts held in the Peterborough Museum I was startled to see that in the margins of some were small sketches. Edward Storey refers to two of these.

One is of a group of people pushing a cart, presumably the Clare family on its way to Northborough, and another is the head and shoulders of a fair-haired young woman on a pedestal. Could it be anyone but Mary Joyce – or at least Clare's conscious longing for her, as he wrote his poem within a mile of where she lived?[31]

It could, indeed, be Mary Joyce. Yet that is not the point. What matters is that Clare seems to have intended the sketches to be part of a total statement of which the relevant poem is a part. And if this is so, it has to be said that the vastly expensive Oxford Edition of Clare's poems is incomplete. Revising Clare goes on.[32]

NOTES

1 Eric Robinson and David Powell (eds.), *John Clare* (Oxford, 1984), p. 408. All future references to Clare's poems are to this edition.
2 Robert Burns, *Poems 1786 and 1787* (Menston, 1971).
3 Thomas Crawford, *Robert Burns: A Study of the Poems and Songs* (Edinburgh, 1960), p. 199.
4 Louis Simpson, *James Hogg: A Critical Study* (Edinburgh, 1962), p. 57.
5 R.L. Brett and A.R. Jones (eds.), *Wordsworth and Coleridge's Lyrical Ballads* (London, 1963), p. 250.
6 Lee Erickson, 'The Poets Corner: The Impact of Technological Changes in Printing on English Poetry, 1800–1850', *ELH*, 52 (1985), p. 894.
7 John Clare, *Poems Descriptive of Rural Life and Scenery* (London, 1820). The Introduction is unsigned.
8 J.W. and Anne Tibble (eds.), *The Letters of John Clare* (London, 1951), p. 50.
9 *Critical Heritage* (London, 1973), p. 81.
10 *Critical Heritage*, p. 91.
11 *John Clare*, p. 4.

12 Stephen Daniels, 'The Political Iconography of Woodland', in D. Cosgrove and S. Daniels (eds.), *The Iconography of Landscape* (Cambridge, 1988), pp. 44–50.
13 'The Political Iconography of Woodland', p. 44.
14 *The Letters of John Clare*, p. 107.
15 *Critical Heritage*, pp. 115–16.
16 Raymond Williams, 'Culture', in David McLellan (ed.), *Marx: The First Hundred Years* (Oxford, 1983), pp. 37–8.
17 'The Idea of the Provincial', in J. Lucas, *Romantic to Modern* (Sussex, 1982), pp. 15–17.
18 Storey, *Critical Heritage*, p. 137.
19 See especially *The Letters of John Clare*, pp. 91 and 98.
20 *Ibid.*, p. 41.
21 *Critical Heritage*, p. 152.
22 J. W. and Anne Tibble (eds.), *The Prose of John Clare* (London, 1951), p. 79.
23 *Critical Heritage*, p. 152.
24 *Ibid.*, p. 138.
25 *The Letters of John Clare*, p. 101.
26 *John Clare*, p. 98.
27 E. Robinson and G. Summerfield (eds.), *John Clare: The Shepherd's Calendar* (Oxford, 1973), pp. ix–xii.
28 Edward Storey, *A Right to Song: The Life of John Clare* (London, 1982), pp. 242–3.
29 *Ibid.*, p. 236.
30 There is a full account of the poem in my *Modern English Poetry: From Hardy to Hughes* (London, 1986), pp. 14–19. See also Keith Thomas, *Man and the Natural World* (London, 1983), p. 66.
31 *A Right to Song*, p. 236.
32 We have also to note that the Oxford Authors *John Clare*, in many ways the most comprehensive and fully edited selection of the poems on the market, disastrously abandons chronology after the opening poems of the 'Helpston Period'. Suddenly, we are confronted with a section called 'Bird Poems', with no indication as to when or where they were composed. Given that many of them are political poems in the fullest sense this is inexcusable.

INDEX

The following abbreviations have been used;
STC – Coleridge; PBS – Shelley; WW – Wordsworth